R E Q U I E M
OF THE
ROSE KING

VOLUME 6
VIZ Media Edition

STORY AND ART BY
AYA KANNO

TRANSLATION	JOCELYNE ALLEN
LETTERING	SABRINA HEEP
DESIGN	IZUMI EVERS
EDITOR	JOEL ENOS

BARAOU NO SOURETSU Volume 6
© 2016 AYA KANNO
First published in Japan in 2016 by AKITA PUBLISHING CO., LTD., Tokyo
English translation rights arranged with AKITA PUBLISHING CO., LTD.
through Tuttle-Mori Agency, Inc., Tokyo

The stories, characters and incidents mentioned in this
publication are entirely fictional.

Additionally, the author has no intention to discriminate
with any of the depictions within this work.

Printed in the U.S.A.

Published by VIZ Media, LLC
P.O. Box 77010
San Francisco, CA 94107

10 9 8 7 6 5 4 3 2 1
First printing, May 2017

www.viz.com

Fate approaches from behind with a knife in its hand, smiling all the while.

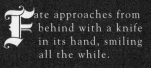

was born in Tokyo, Japan.
She is the creator of
Soul Rescue, *Blank Slate* and the
New York Times best-selling
series *Otomen*.

Story Thus Far

White Rose

House of York

RICHARD

The third son of York, he has been shunned by his mother since childhood.

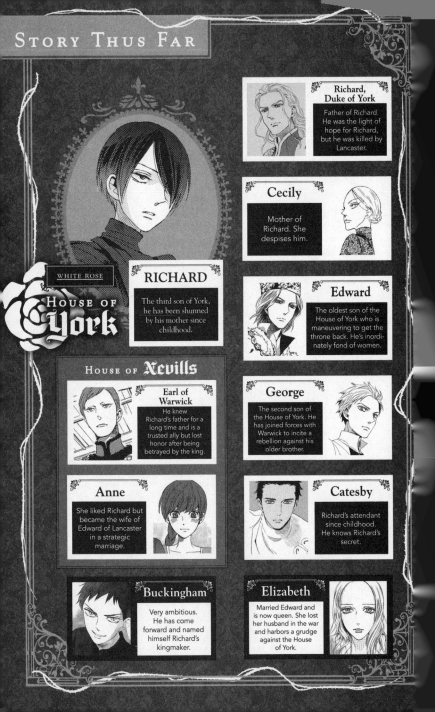

Richard, Duke of York

Father of Richard. He was the light of hope for Richard, but he was killed by Lancaster.

Cecily

Mother of Richard. She despises him.

Edward

The oldest son of the House of York who is maneuvering to get the throne back. He's inordinately fond of women.

George

The second son of the House of York. He has joined forces with Warwick to incite a rebellion against his older brother.

Catesby

Richard's attendant since childhood. He knows Richard's secret.

House of Nevills

Earl of Warwick

He knew Richard's father for a long time and is a trusted ally but lost honor after being betrayed by the king.

Anne

She liked Richard but became the wife of Edward of Lancaster in a strategic marriage.

Buckingham

Very ambitious. He has come forward and named himself Richard's kingmaker.

Elizabeth

Married Edward and is now queen. She lost her husband in the war and harbors a grudge against the House of York.

Requiem
of the
Rose King

6

AYA KANNO

Based on *Henry VI* and *Richard III*
by William Shakespeare

Characters &

RED ROSE

House of Lancaster

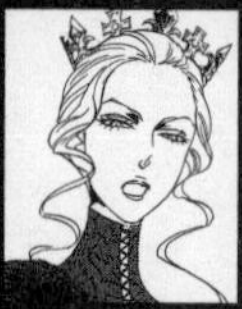

Margaret

She is Henry's wife, but she feels little love for him. She has currently fled to France.

Edward

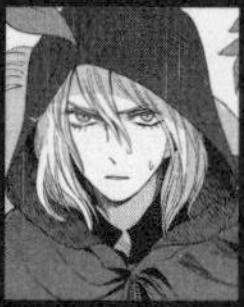

Son of Henry. Strong willed. He has taken an interest in Richard.

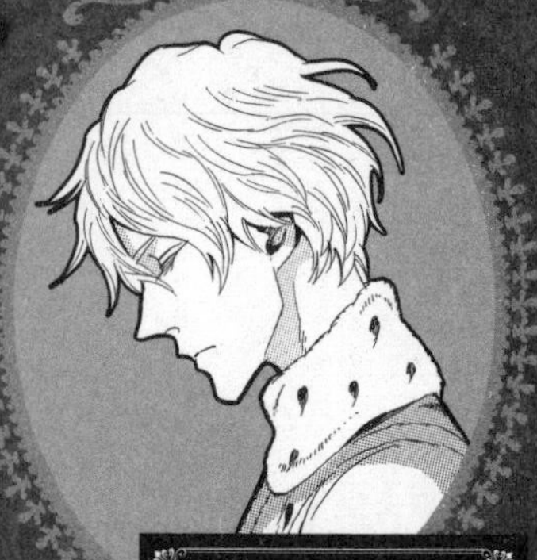

HENRY THE SIXTH

King once more. He's very pious and hates fighting. Occasionally, he disguises himself as a shepherd and meets up incognito with Richard.

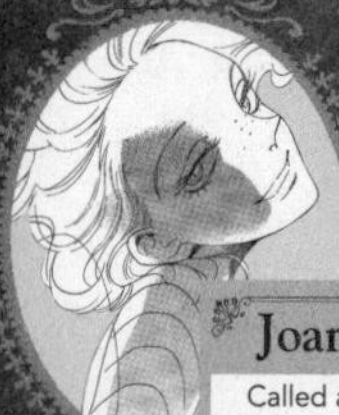

Joan of Arc

Called a French witch and burned at the stake. She appears to Richard as a ghost.

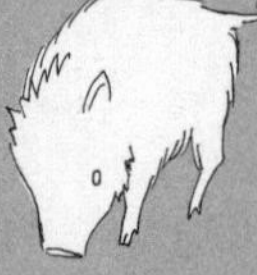

White boar

Saved by Richard when it was injured. The boar is very close to Richard.

Story thus far...

England, the Middle Ages.

The two houses of York and Lancaster are caught in repeated royal contest, the age of the War of the Roses.

King Edward welcomes Elizabeth as his queen, without discussing it with his retainers. Furious at the king's selfish behavior, Warwick incites a rebellion in collusion with George and captures the king.

Richard sets out to save the king in order to prevent Warwick from taking the reins of power. He disguises himself as a woman to hide his true identity, and when he happens upon Prince Edward of Lancaster, also in disguise, he decides to make use of this guest of Warwick's. Richard sneaks into the castle as a prostitute and manages to safely rescue the king.

Warwick is forced to join hands with Margaret. When he has his daughter Anne marry Prince Edward and then restores Henry the Sixth to the throne, Warwick becomes regent, gaining power equivalent to that of the king.

Meanwhile, on his brother Edward's orders, Richard sets off to win back George. After he is attacked and injured along the way by Lancaster soldiers, he runs into Henry again. During the several nights they spend together, Richard realizes that he is in love with Henry.

Requiem
of the
Rose
King

Contents

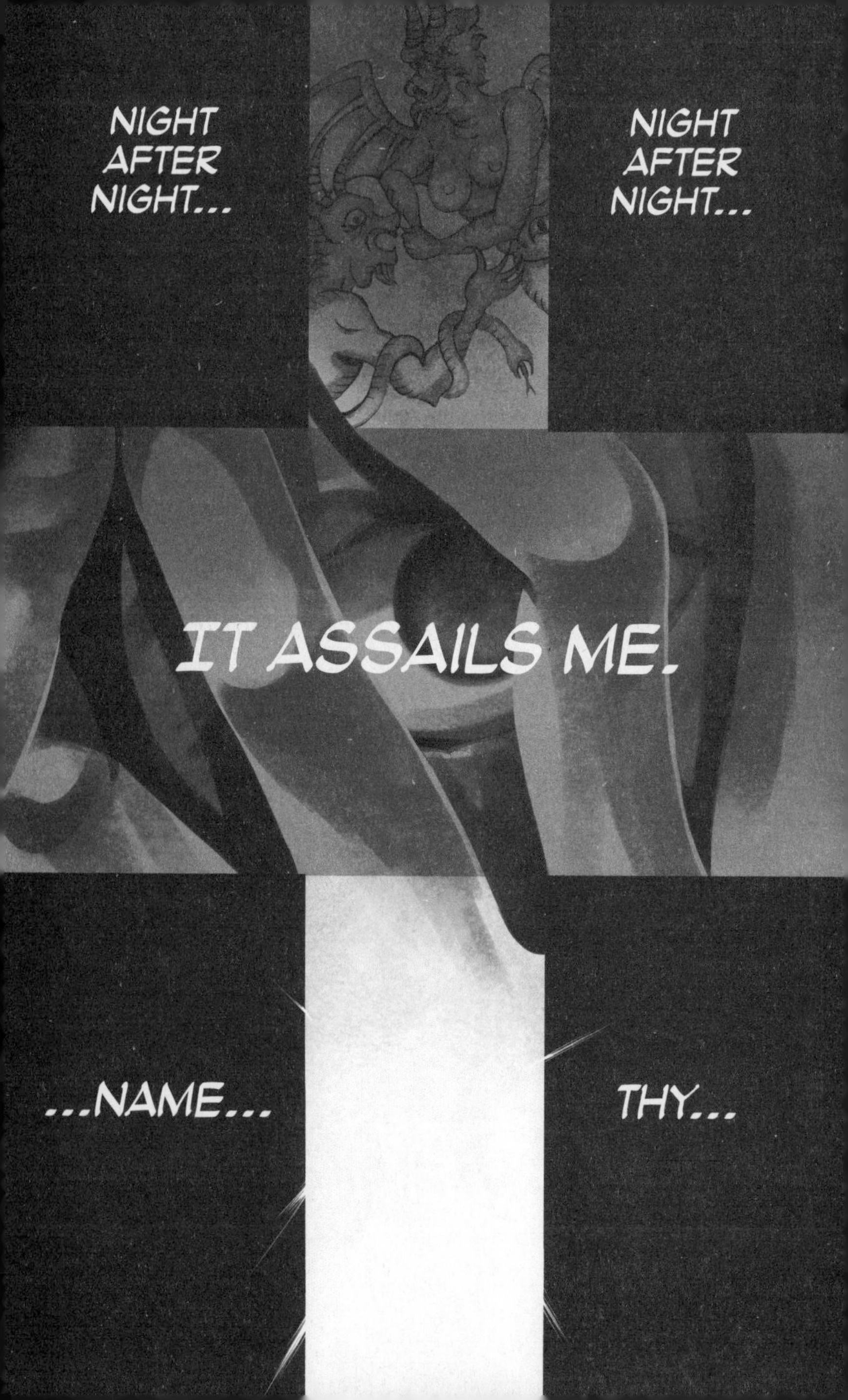
NIGHT AFTER NIGHT...
NIGHT AFTER NIGHT...
IT ASSAILS ME.
THY...
...NAME...

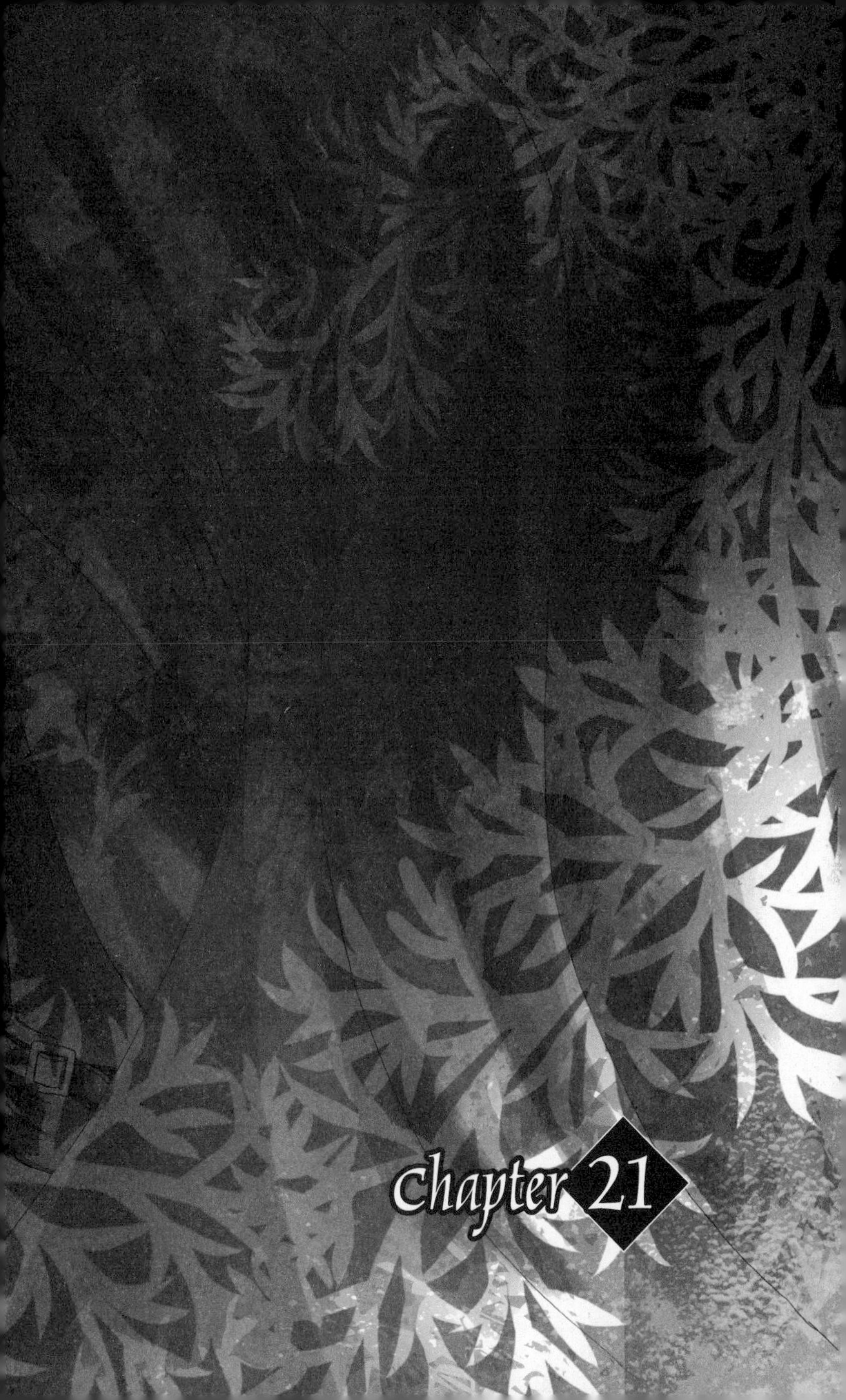
Chapter 21

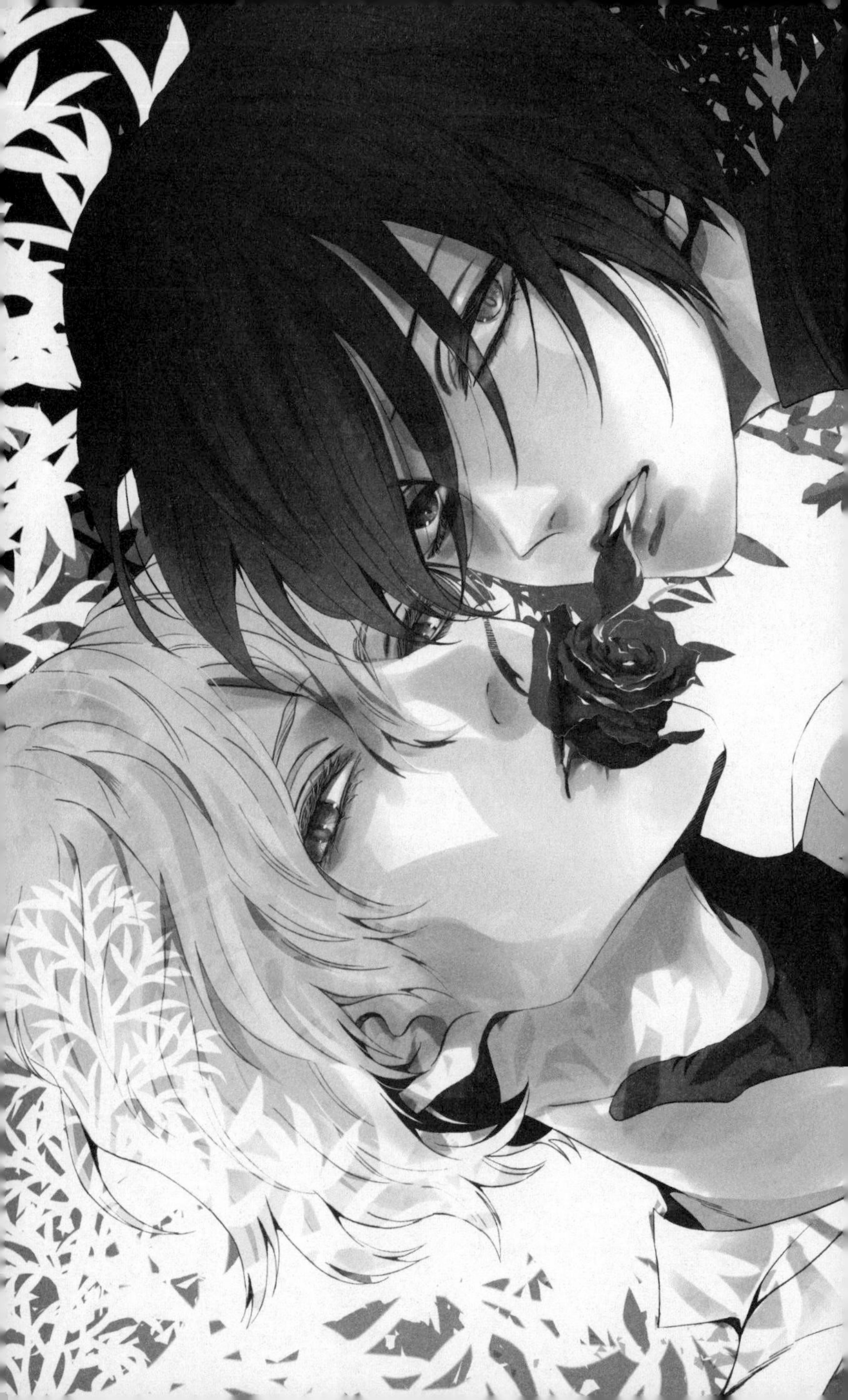

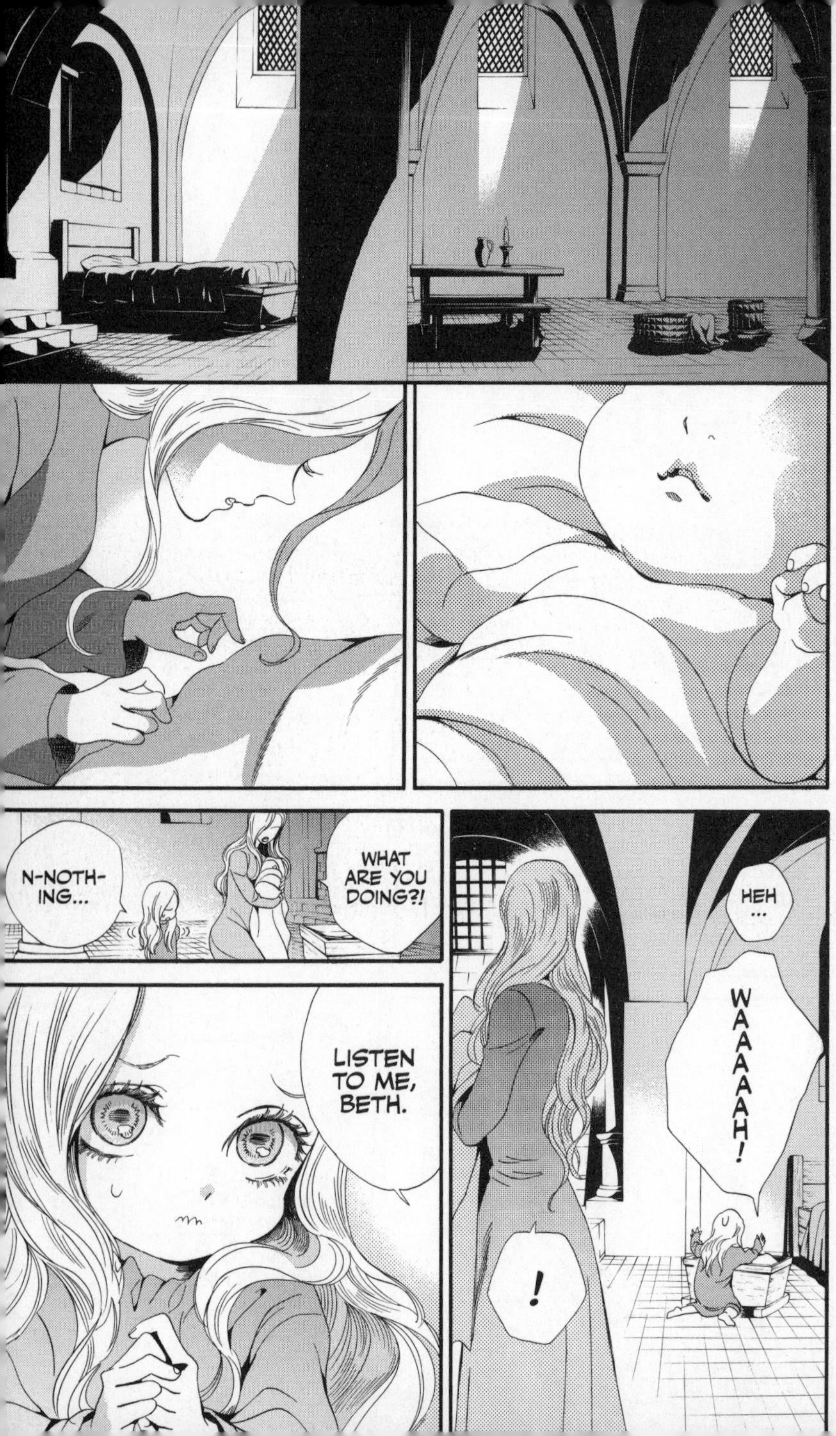
HEH...
WAAAAAH!
!
WHAT ARE YOU DOING?!
N-NOTHING...
LISTEN TO ME, BETH.

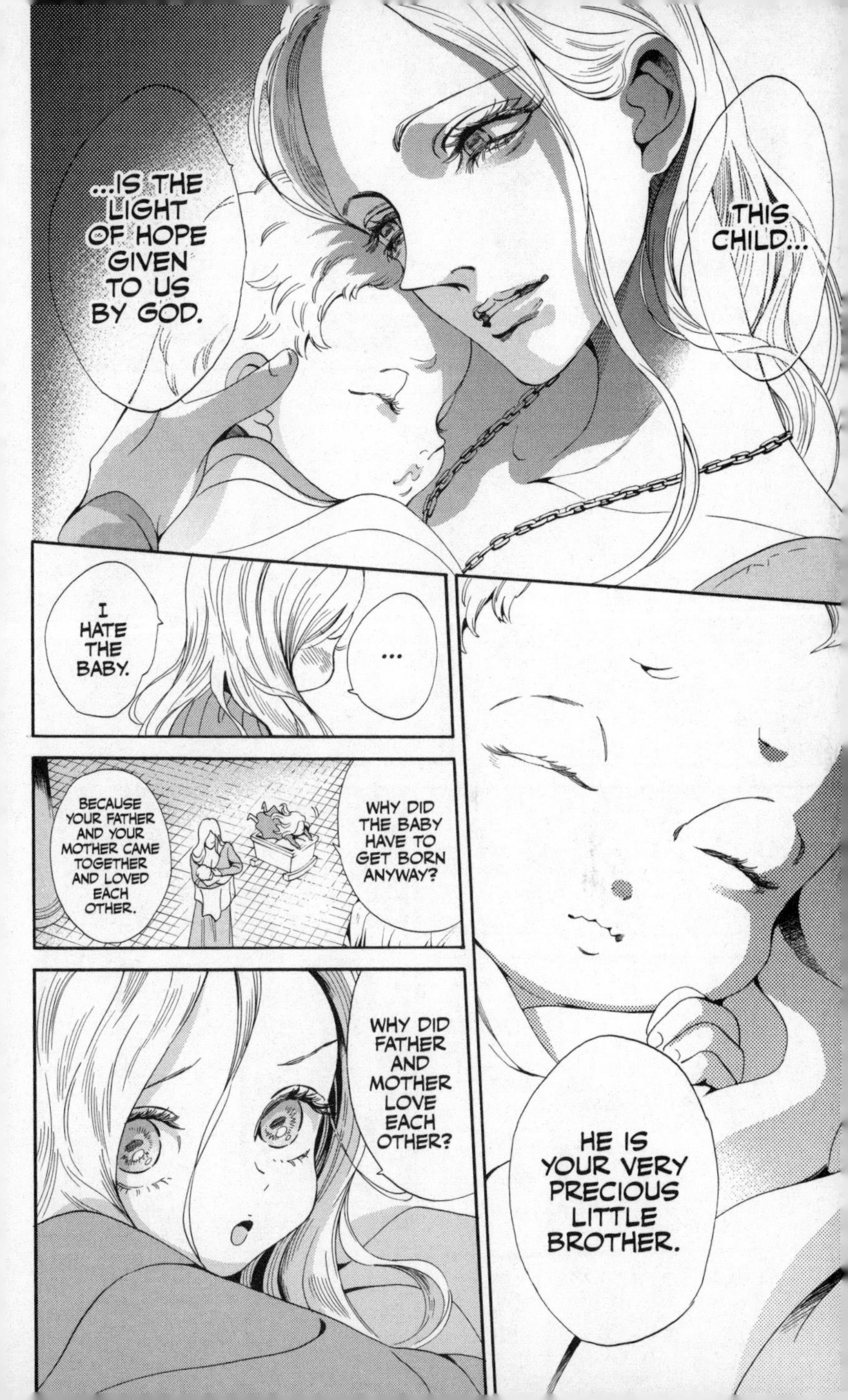
THIS CHILD...
...IS THE LIGHT OF HOPE GIVEN TO US BY GOD.
HE IS YOUR VERY PRECIOUS LITTLE BROTHER.
...
I HATE THE BABY.
WHY DID THE BABY HAVE TO GET BORN ANYWAY?
BECAUSE YOUR FATHER AND YOUR MOTHER CAME TOGETHER AND LOVED EACH OTHER.
WHY DID FATHER AND MOTHER LOVE EACH OTHER?

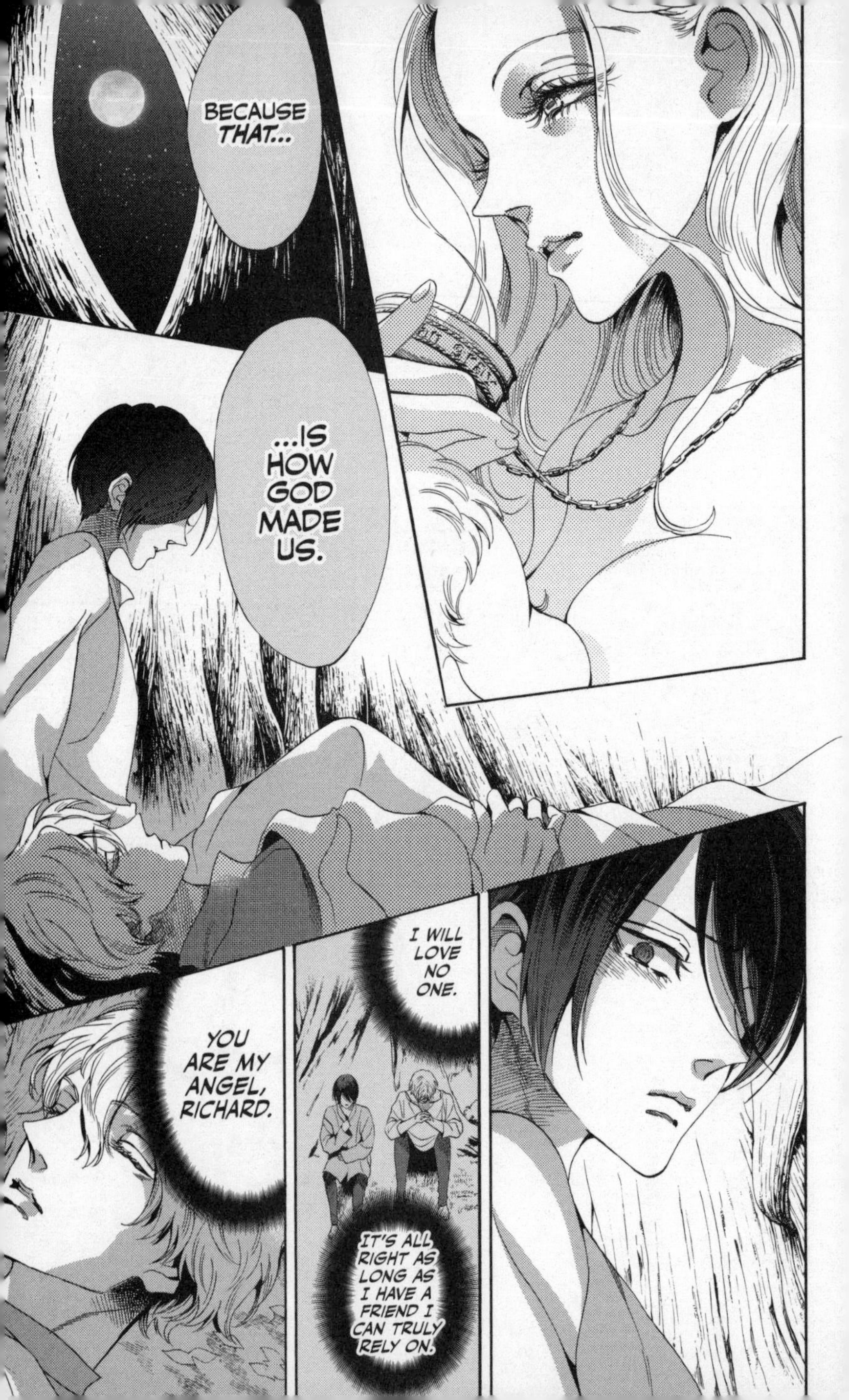
BECAUSE THAT...
...IS HOW GOD MADE US.
I WILL LOVE NO ONE.
IT'S ALL RIGHT AS LONG AS I HAVE A FRIEND I CAN TRULY RELY ON.
YOU ARE MY ANGEL, RICHARD.

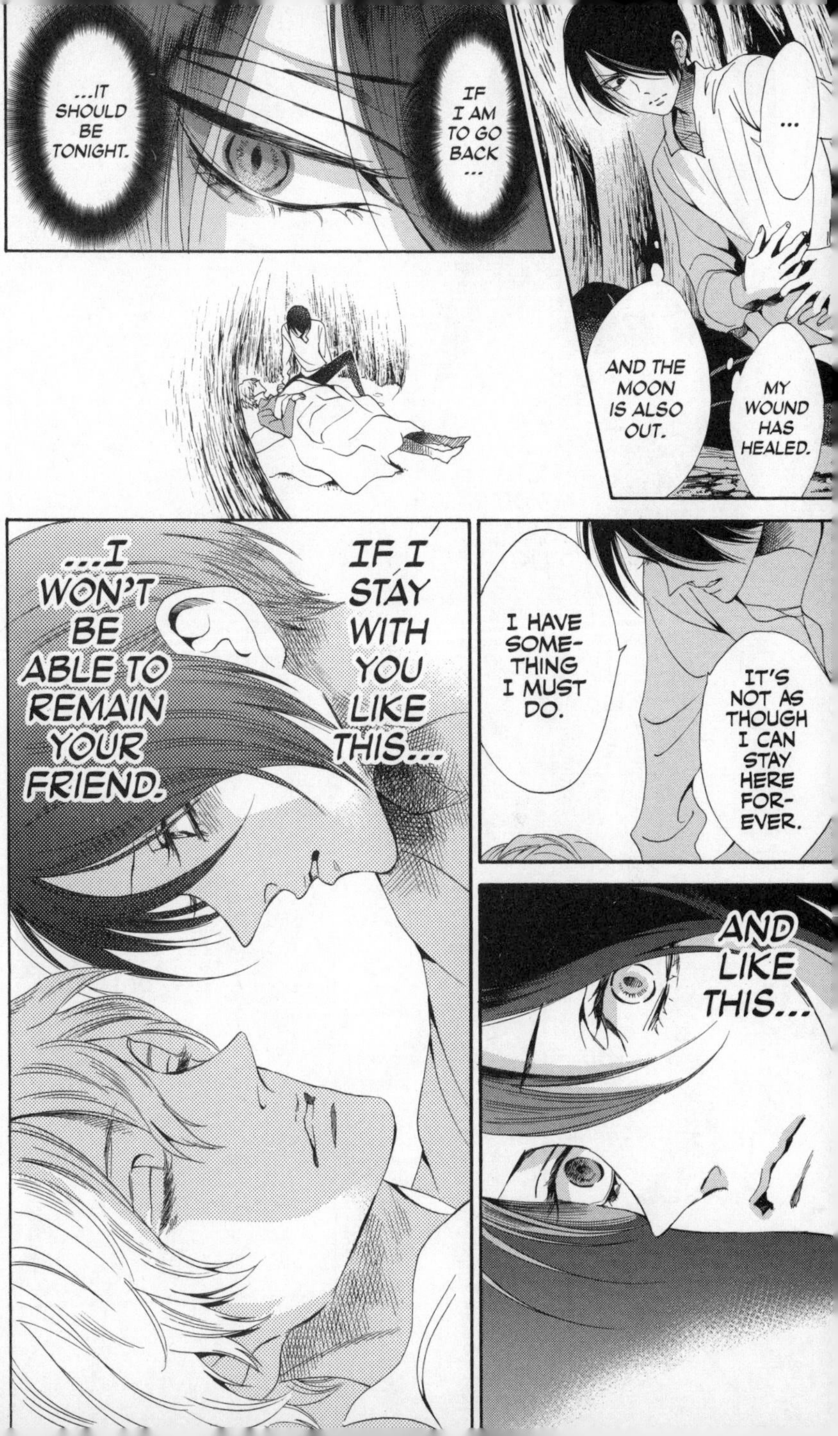
...
MY WOUND HAS HEALED.
AND THE MOON IS ALSO OUT.
IF I AM TO GO BACK...
...IT SHOULD BE TONIGHT.
IT'S NOT AS THOUGH I CAN STAY HERE FOREVER.
I HAVE SOMETHING I MUST DO.
AND LIKE THIS...
IF I STAY WITH YOU LIKE THIS...
...I WON'T BE ABLE TO REMAIN YOUR FRIEND.

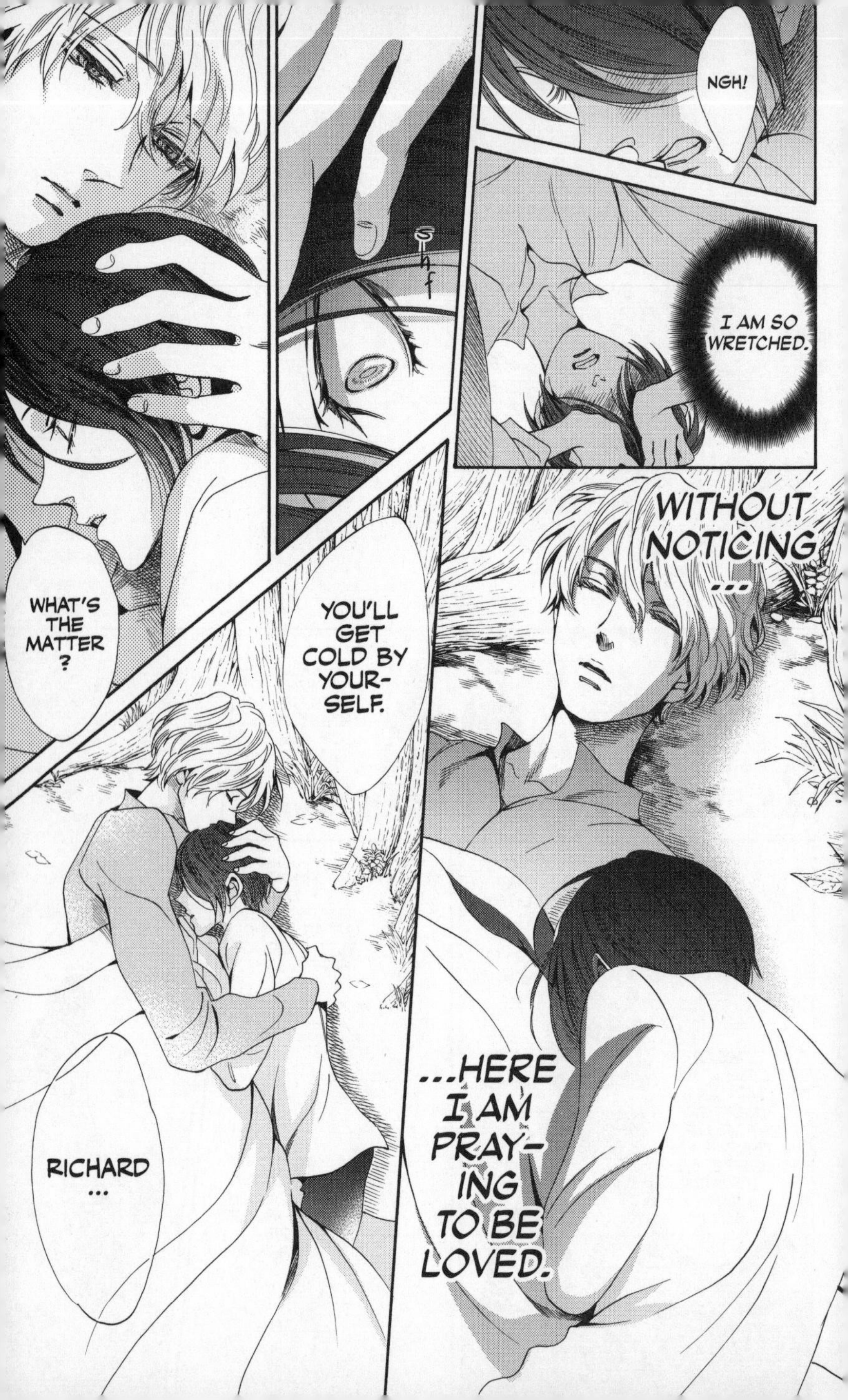
NGH!
I AM SO WRETCHED.
shf
WHAT'S THE MATTER?
WITHOUT NOTICING...
...HERE I AM PRAYING TO BE LOVED.
YOU'LL GET COLD BY YOURSELF.
RICHARD...

IT'S NO USE.
PERHAPS HE HAS ALREADY MADE IT OUT OF THE WOODS.
ANY OTHER INFORMATION?
THIS ISN'T ABOUT LORD RICHARD, BUT...
...HENRY OF THE LANCASTERS APPARENTLY FLED DURING HIS PILGRIMAGE.
WEARING A ROUGH CLOAK, IN THE GUISE OF A PEASANT.
LORD CATESBY, YOU KNOW HENRY'S FACE, YES?
THERE COULD BE NOTHING BETTER FOR US THAN IF WE WERE TO CAPTURE HENRY.

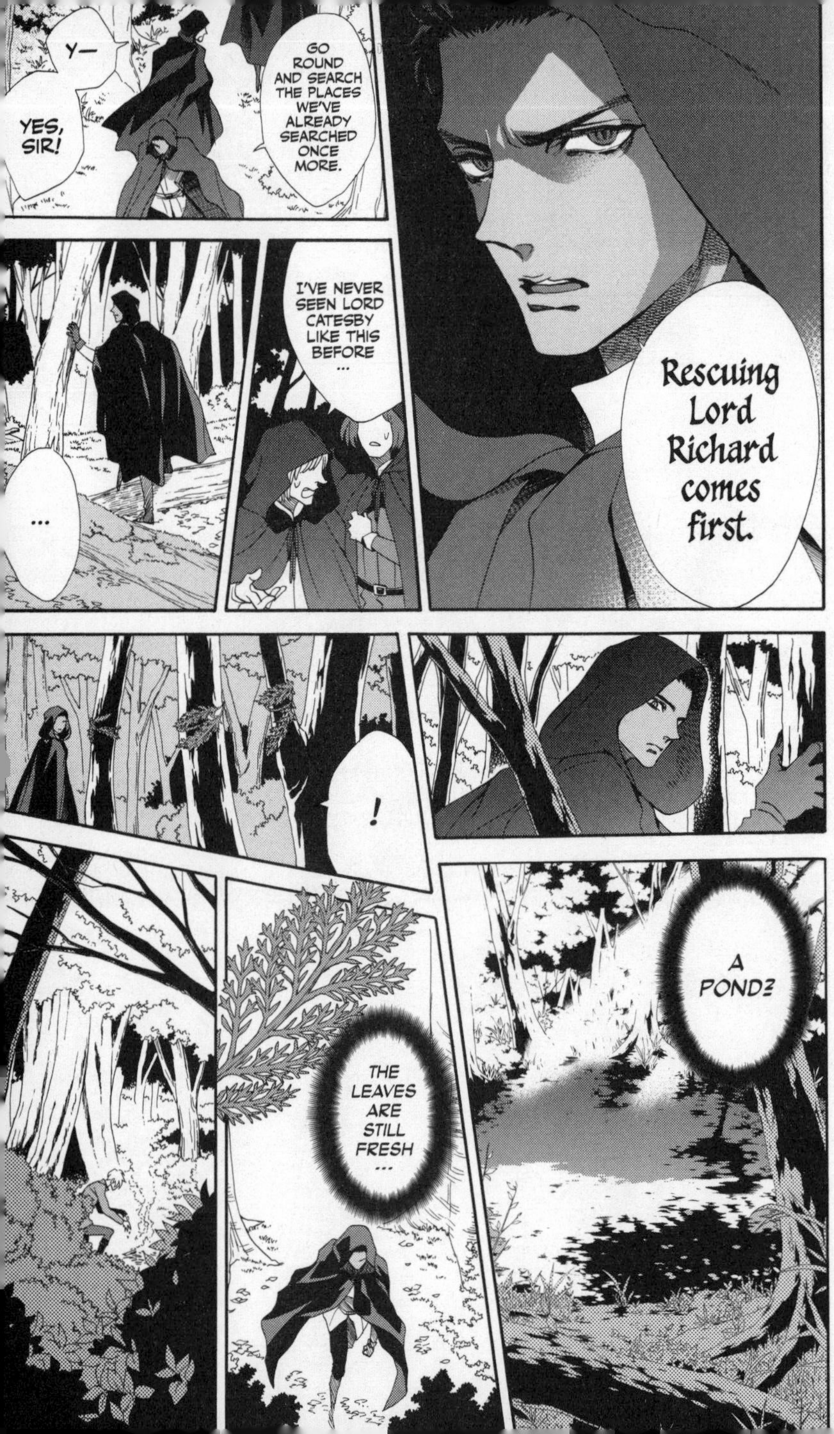
Rescuing Lord Richard comes first.
GO ROUND AND SEARCH THE PLACES WE'VE ALREADY SEARCHED ONCE MORE.
Y—
YES, SIR!
I'VE NEVER SEEN LORD CATESBY LIKE THIS BEFORE ...
...
!
A POND?
THE LEAVES ARE STILL FRESH ...

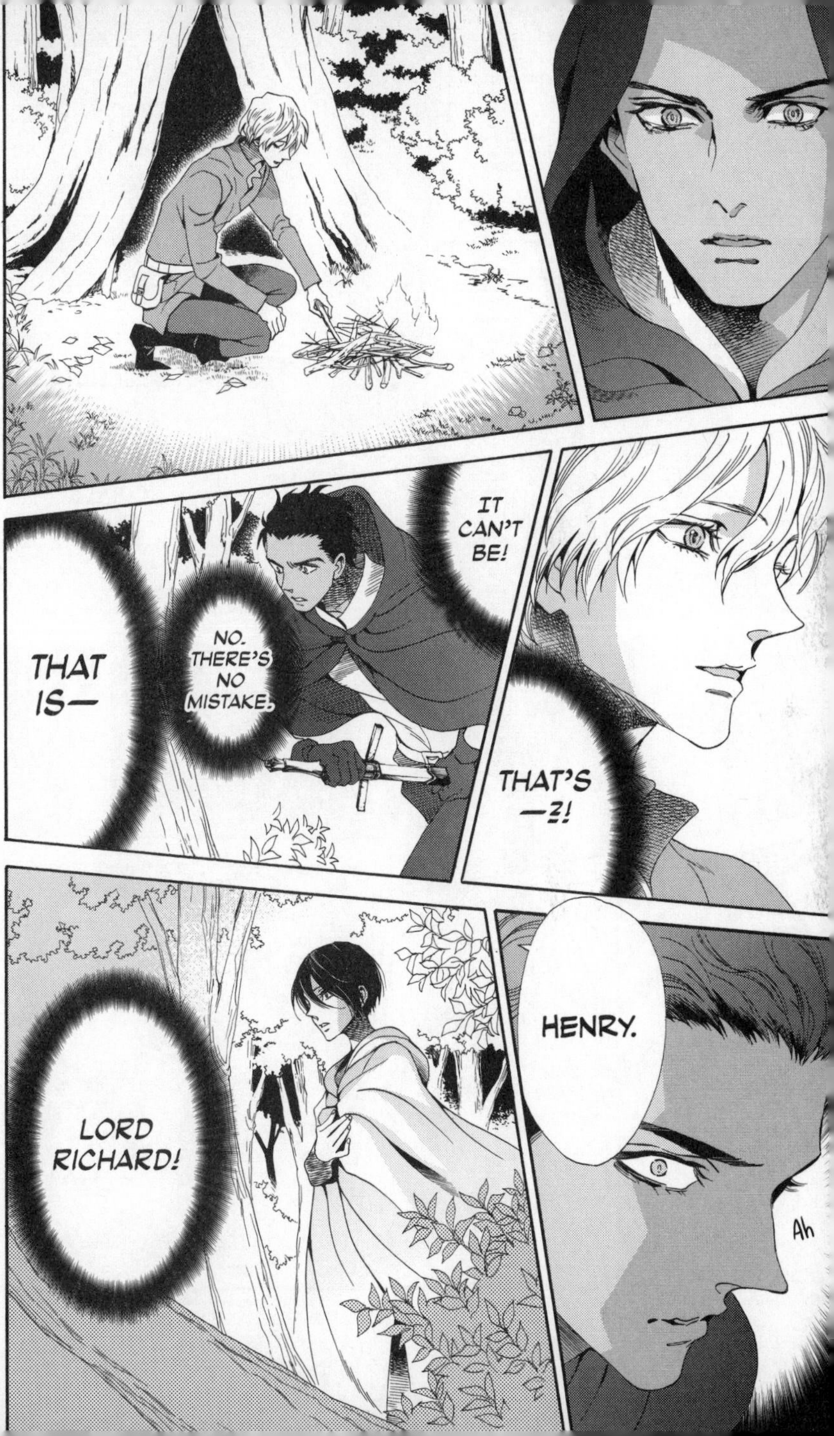
THAT'S —?!
IT CAN'T BE!
NO. THERE'S NO MISTAKE.
THAT IS—
HENRY.
Ah
LORD RICHARD!

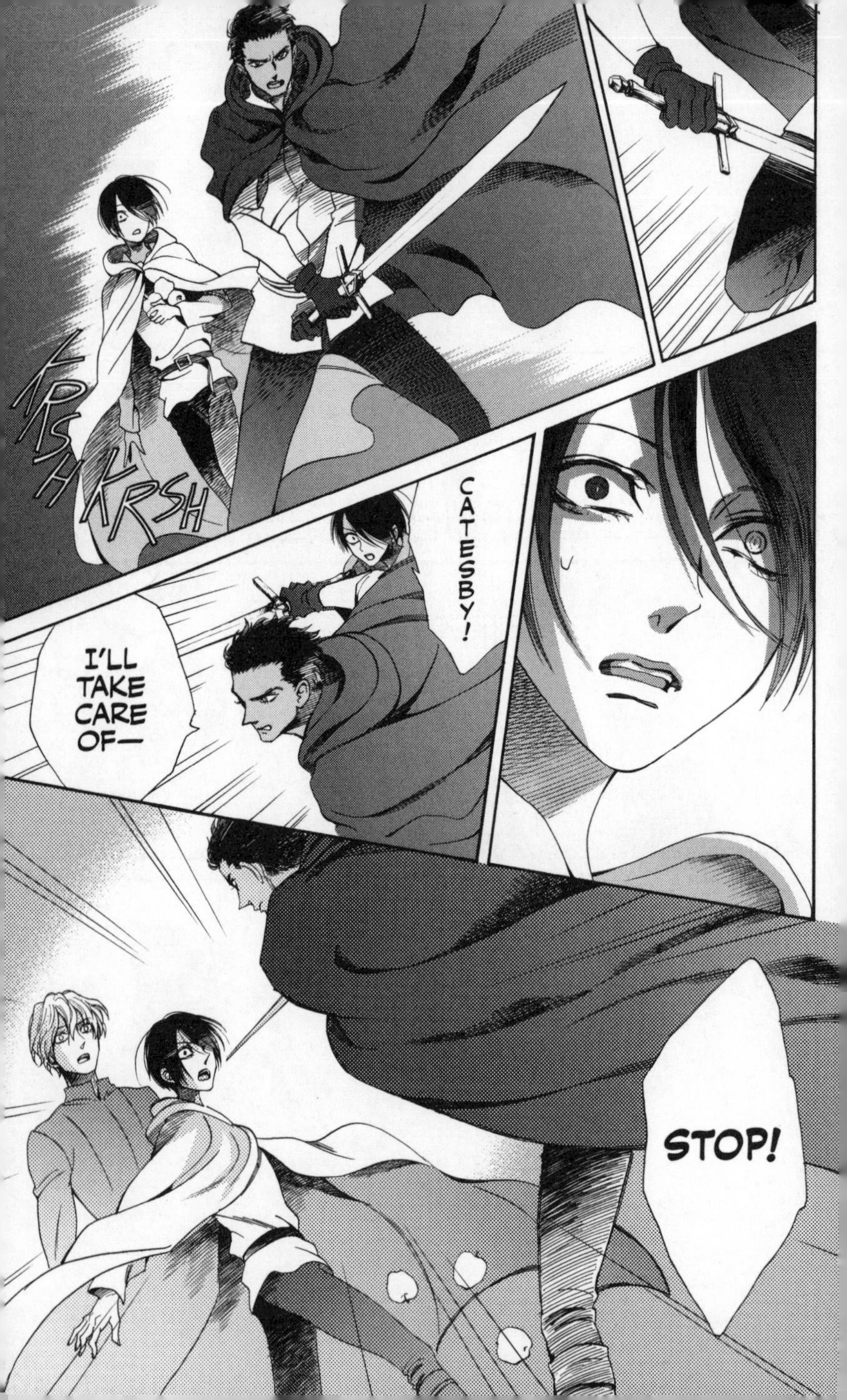
KRSH KRSH
CATESBY!
I'LL TAKE CARE OF—
STOP!

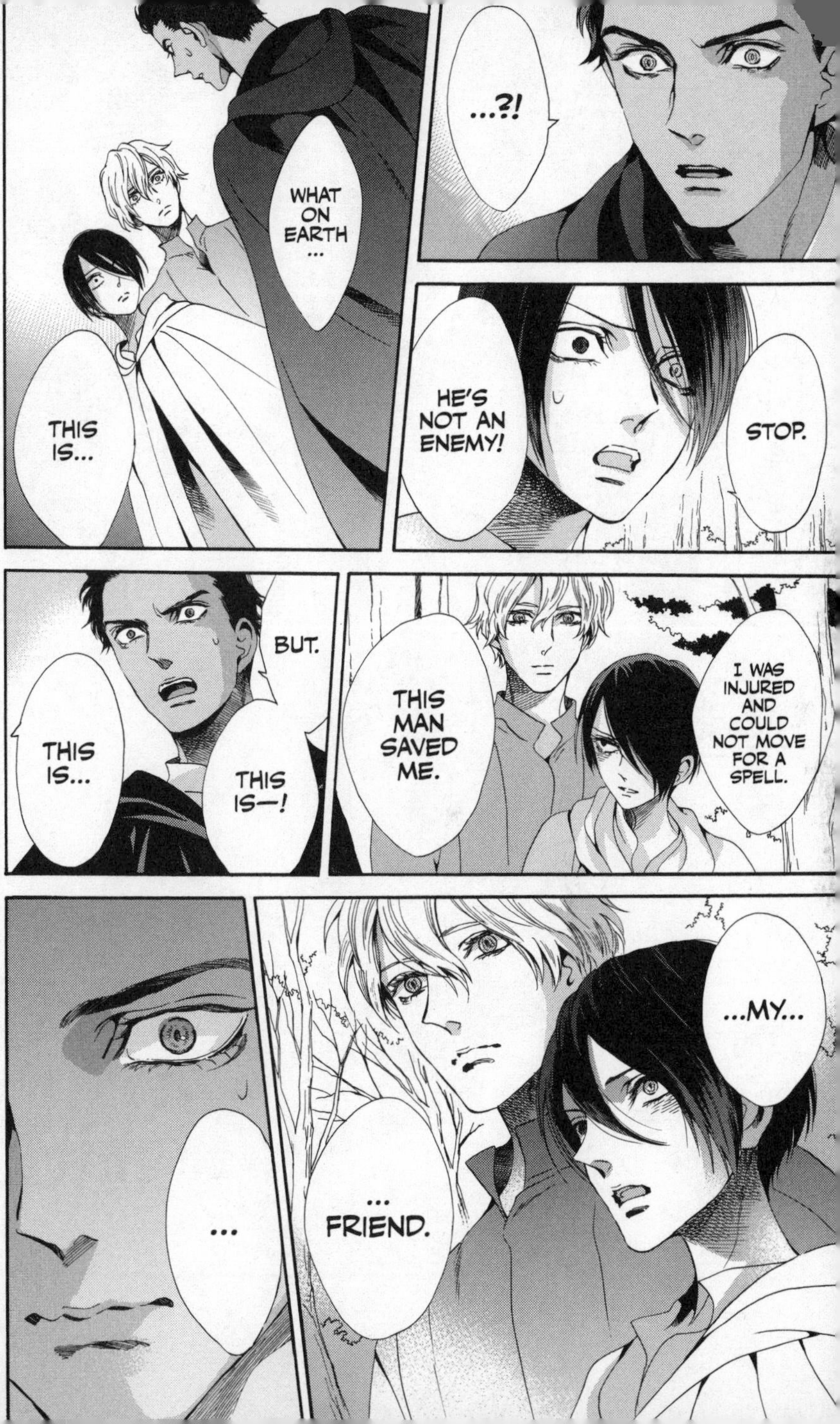
...?!
STOP.
HE'S NOT AN ENEMY!
WHAT ON EARTH...
THIS IS...
I WAS INJURED AND COULD NOT MOVE FOR A SPELL.
THIS MAN SAVED ME.
BUT.
THIS IS—!
THIS IS...
...MY...
...FRIEND.
...

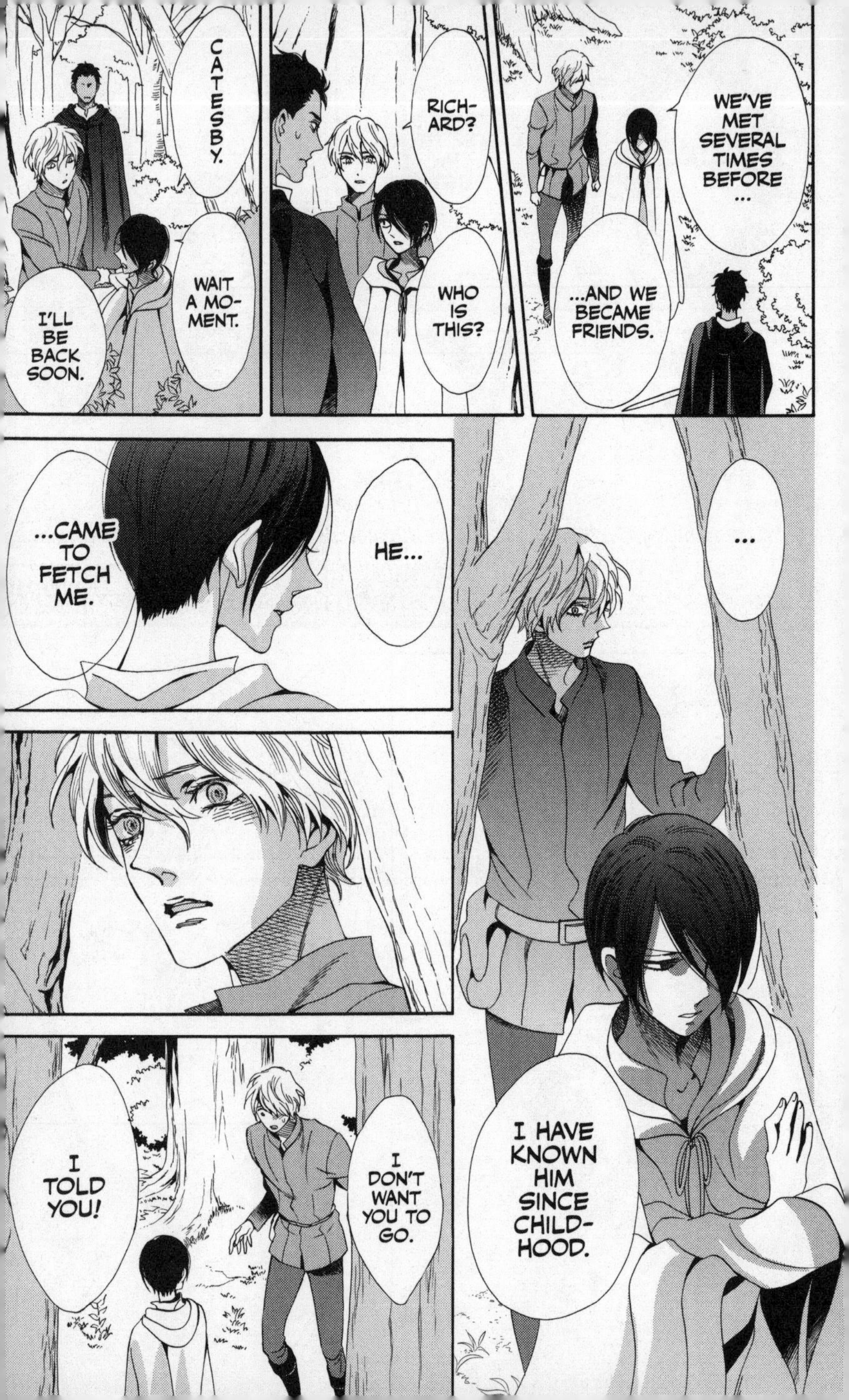
WE'VE MET SEVERAL TIMES BEFORE...
...AND WE BECAME FRIENDS.
RICH-ARD?
WHO IS THIS?
CATESBY.
WAIT A MO-MENT.
I'LL BE BACK SOON.
...
I HAVE KNOWN HIM SINCE CHILD-HOOD.
HE...
...CAME TO FETCH ME.
I DON'T WANT YOU TO GO.
I TOLD YOU!

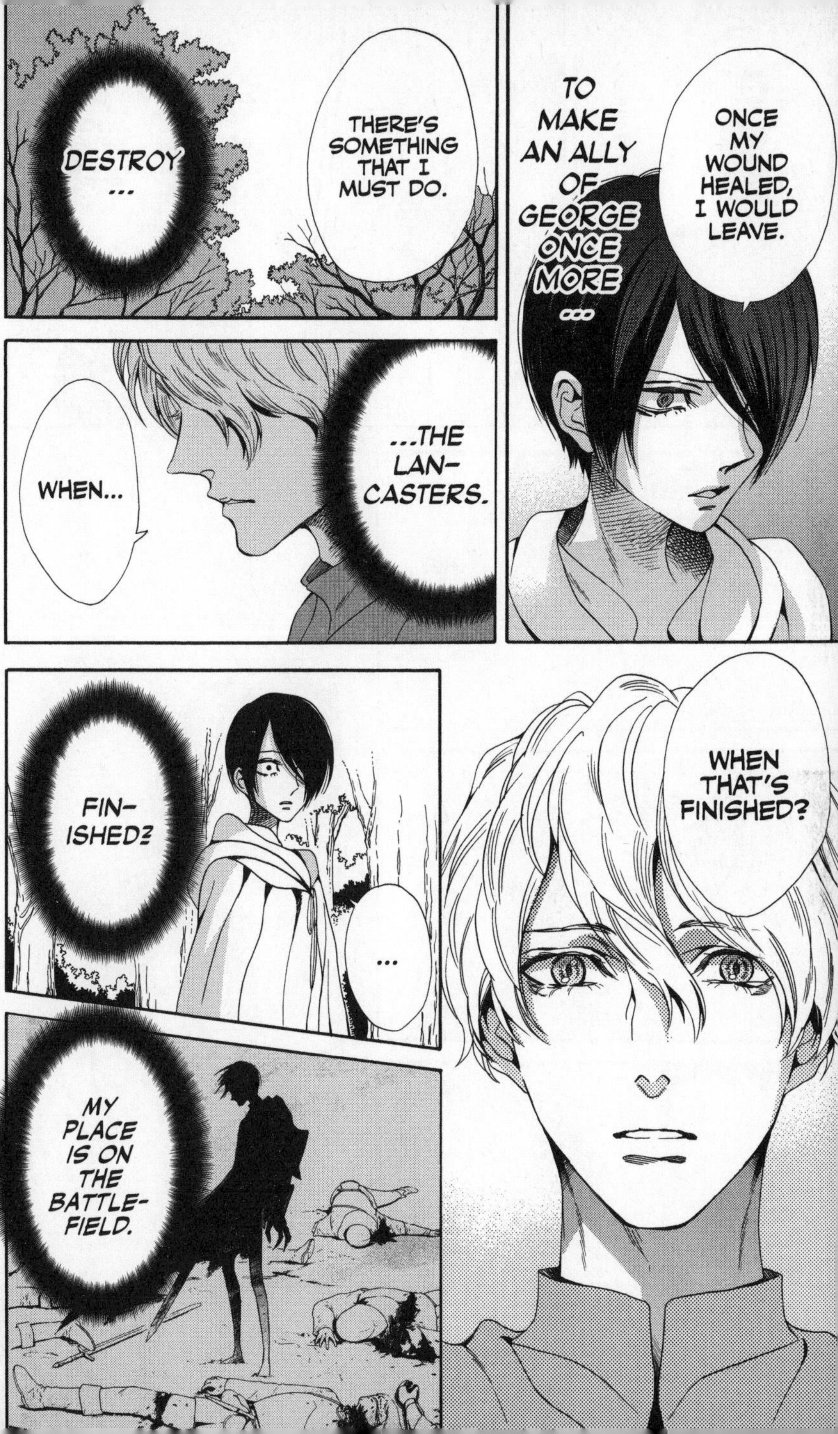
ONCE MY WOUND HEALED, I WOULD LEAVE.
TO MAKE AN ALLY OF GEORGE ONCE MORE...
THERE'S SOMETHING THAT I MUST DO.
DESTROY...
...THE LAN-CASTERS.
WHEN...
WHEN THAT'S FINISHED?
...
FIN-ISHED?
MY PLACE IS ON THE BATTLE-FIELD.

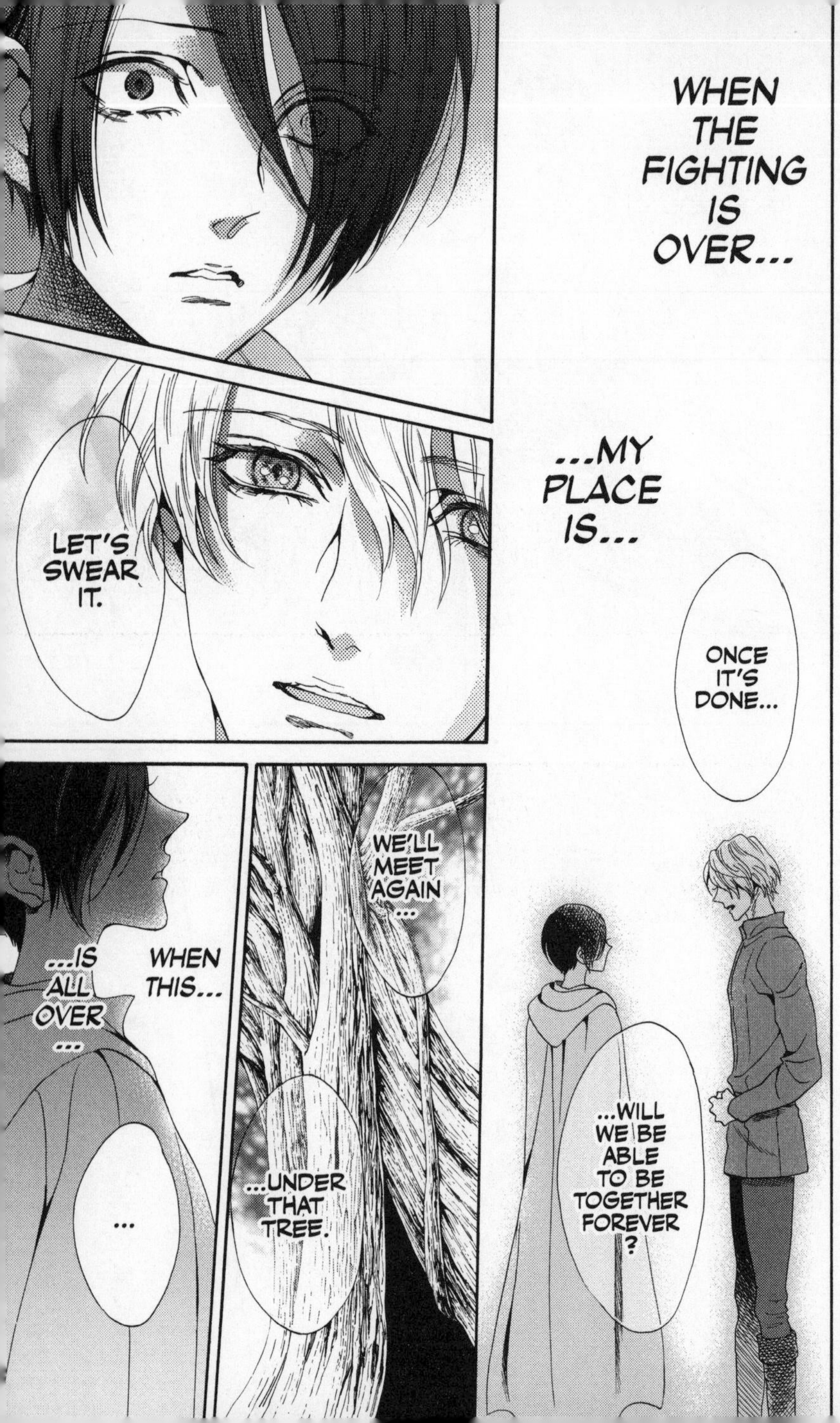
WHEN THE FIGHTING IS OVER...
...MY PLACE IS...
ONCE IT'S DONE...
...WILL WE BE ABLE TO BE TOGETHER FOREVER?
LET'S SWEAR IT.
WE'LL MEET AGAIN...
...UNDER THAT TREE.
WHEN THIS...
...IS ALL OVER...
...

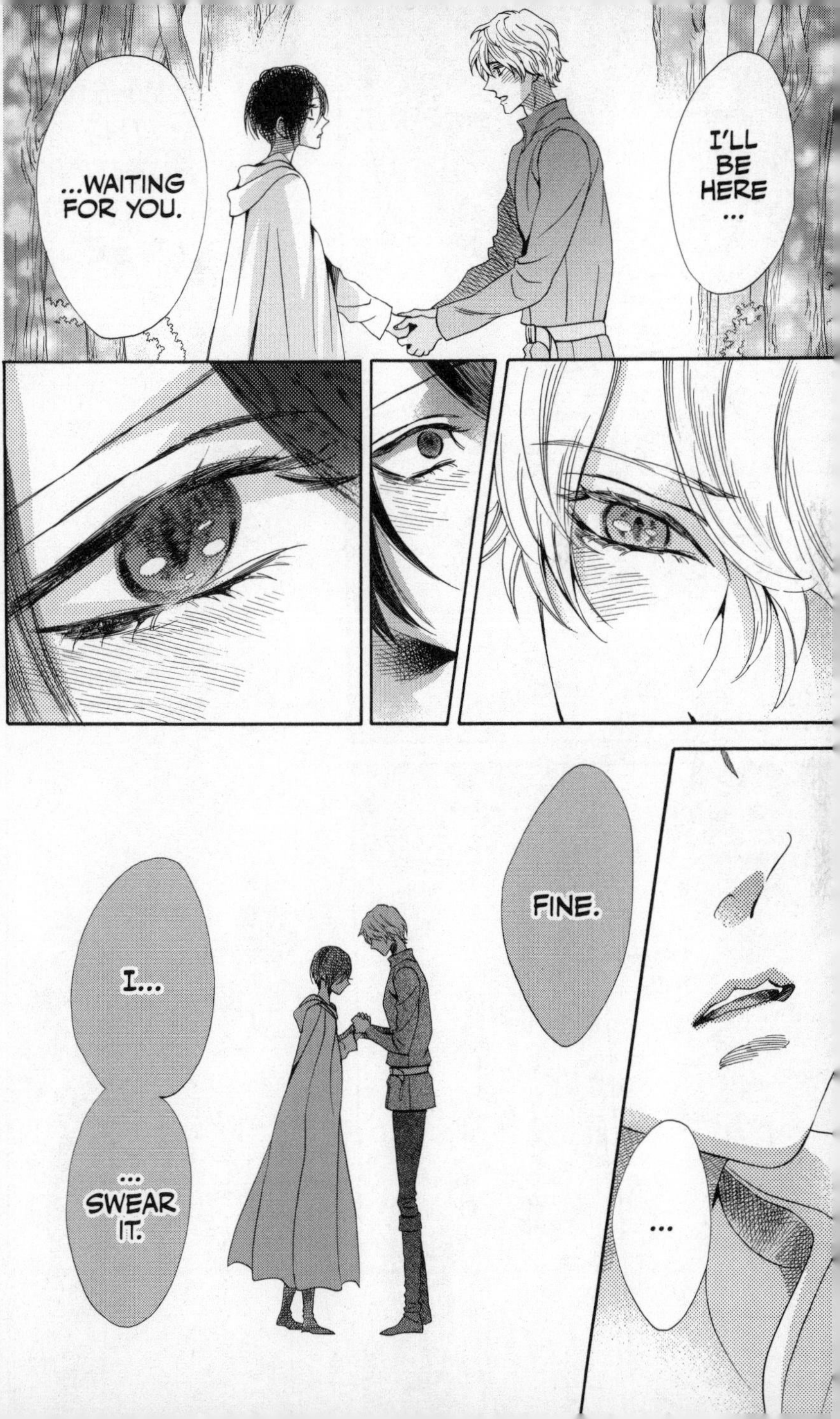
I'LL BE HERE ...
...WAITING FOR YOU.
...
FINE.
I...
... SWEAR IT.

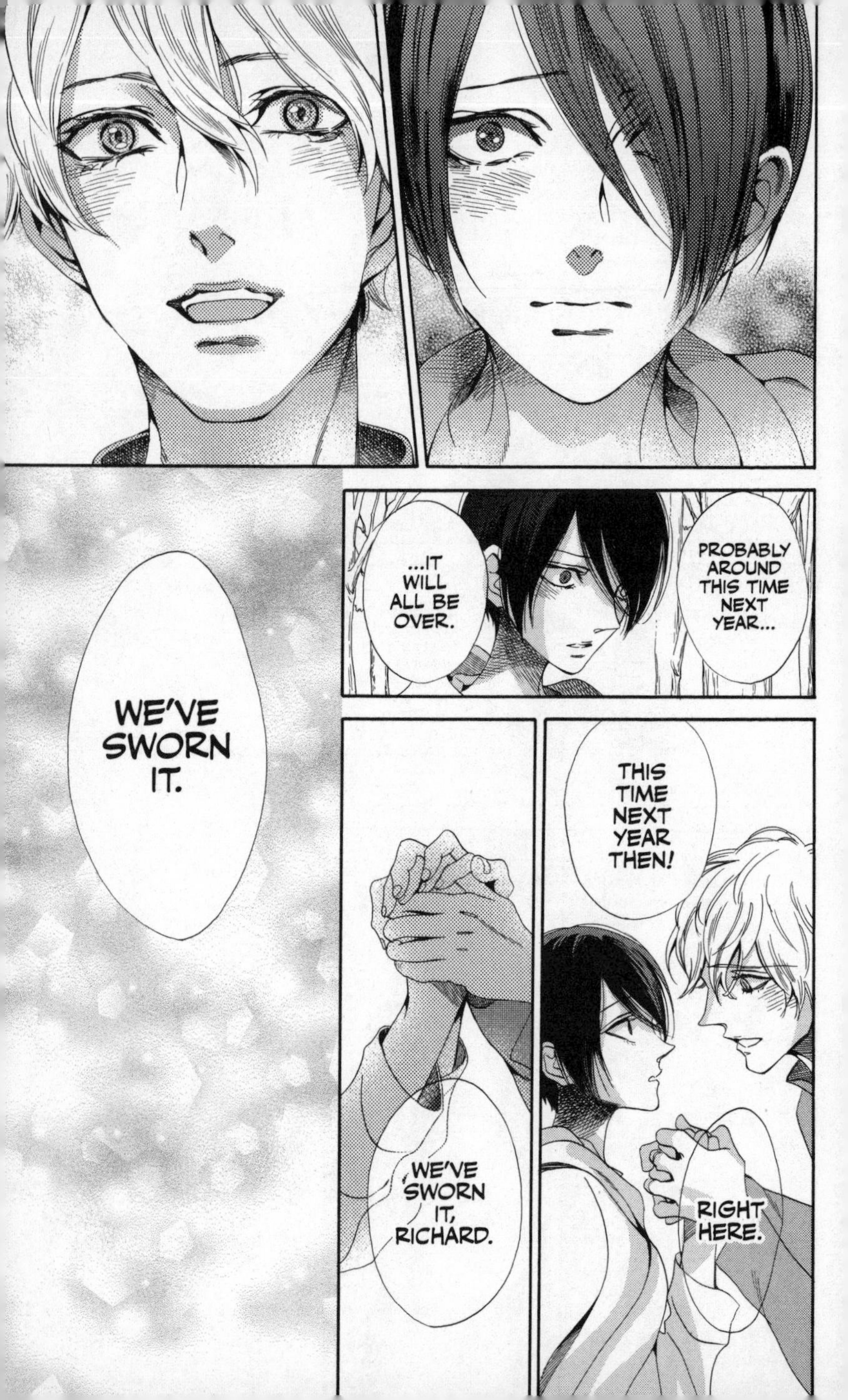
PROBABLY AROUND THIS TIME NEXT YEAR...
...IT WILL ALL BE OVER.
THIS TIME NEXT YEAR THEN!
RIGHT HERE.
WE'VE SWORN IT, RICHARD.
WE'VE SWORN IT.

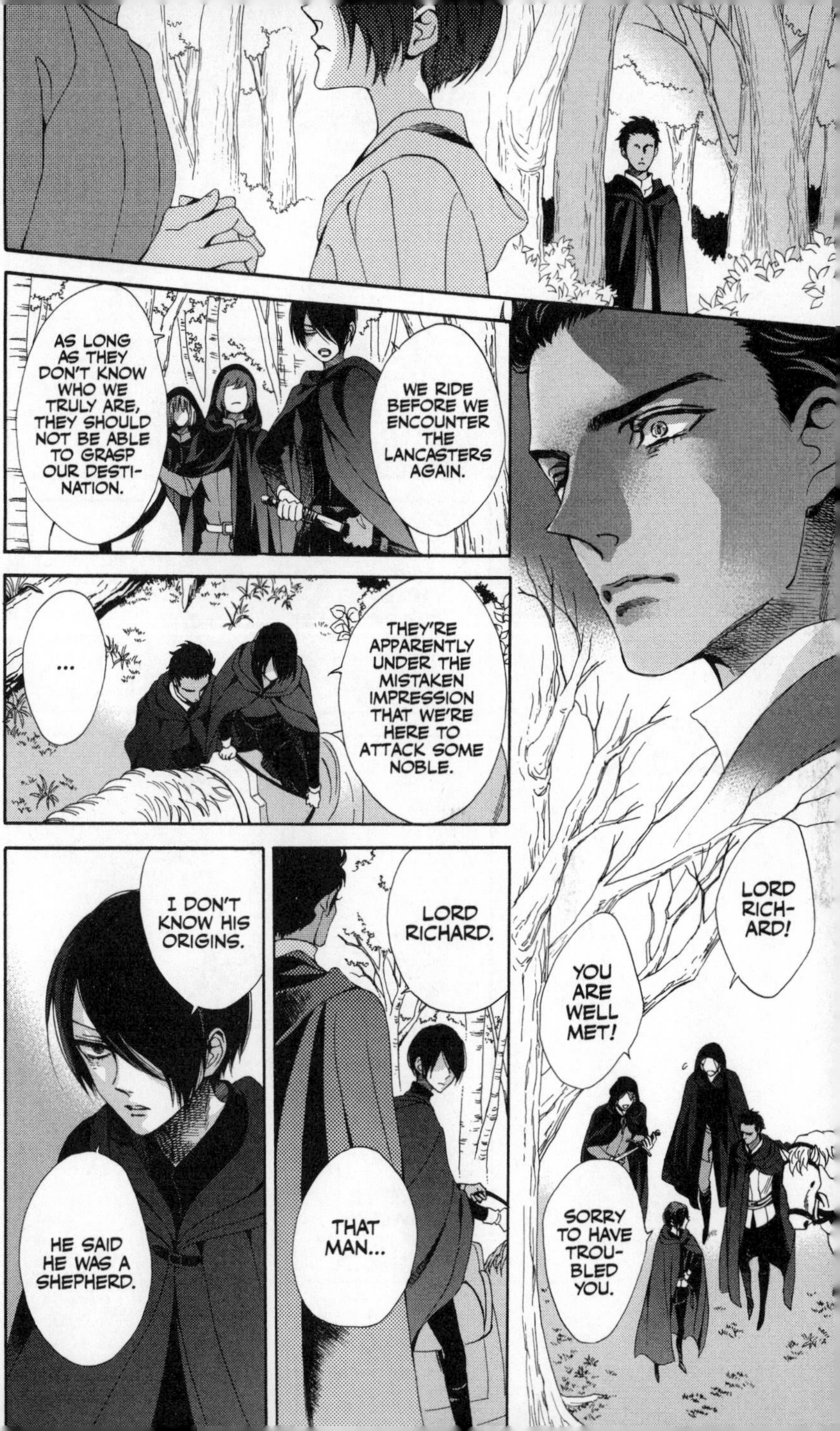
LORD RICHARD!
YOU ARE WELL MET!
SORRY TO HAVE TROUBLED YOU.
WE RIDE BEFORE WE ENCOUNTER THE LANCASTERS AGAIN.
AS LONG AS THEY DON'T KNOW WHO WE TRULY ARE, THEY SHOULD NOT BE ABLE TO GRASP OUR DESTINATION.
THEY'RE APPARENTLY UNDER THE MISTAKEN IMPRESSION THAT WE'RE HERE TO ATTACK SOME NOBLE.
...
LORD RICHARD.
THAT MAN...
I DON'T KNOW HIS ORIGINS.
HE SAID HE WAS A SHEPHERD.

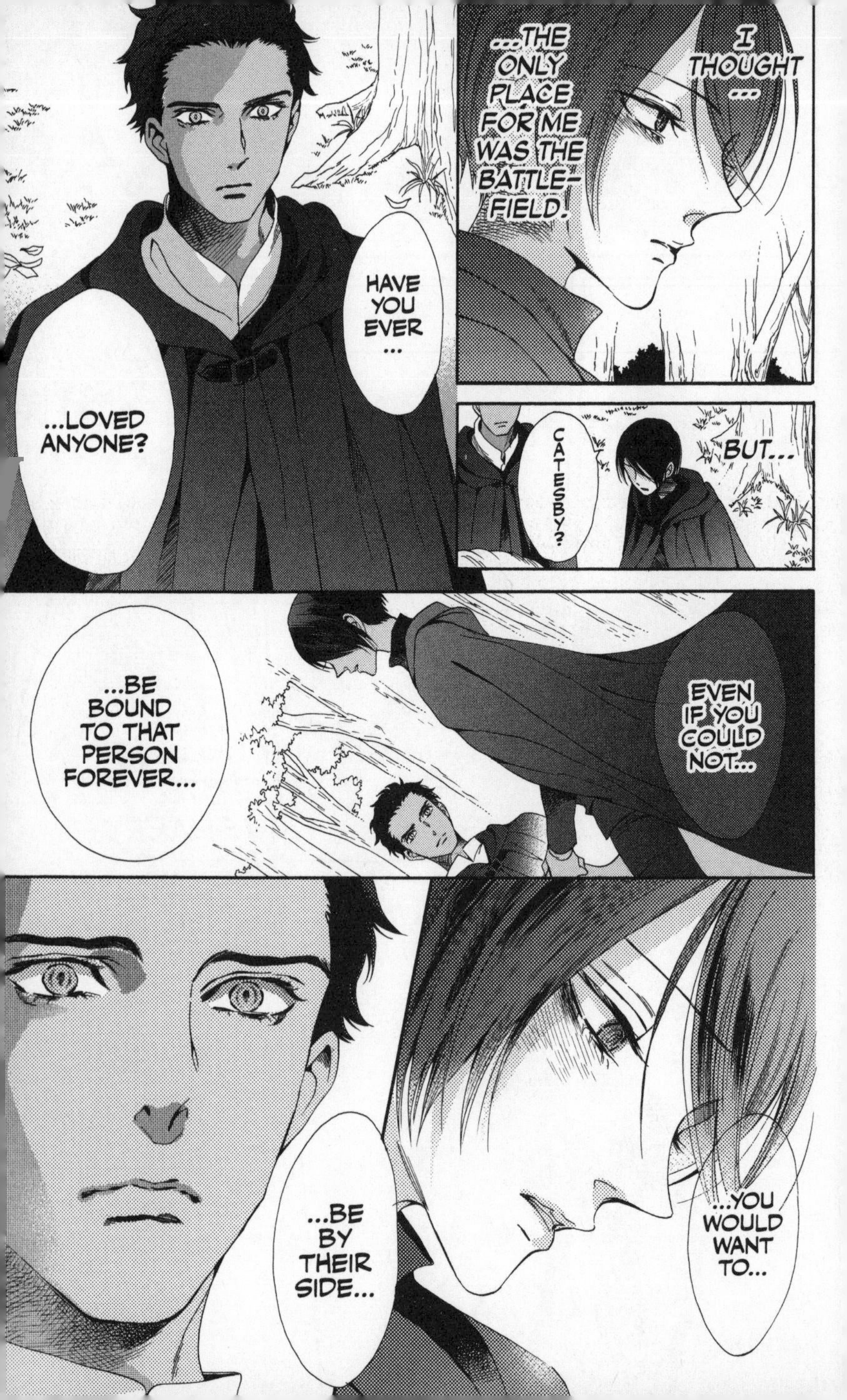
I THOUGHT...
...THE ONLY PLACE FOR ME WAS THE BATTLE-FIELD.
BUT...
CATESBY?
HAVE YOU EVER...
...LOVED ANYONE?
EVEN IF YOU COULD NOT...
...BE BOUND TO THAT PERSON FOREVER...
...YOU WOULD WANT TO...
...BE BY THEIR SIDE...

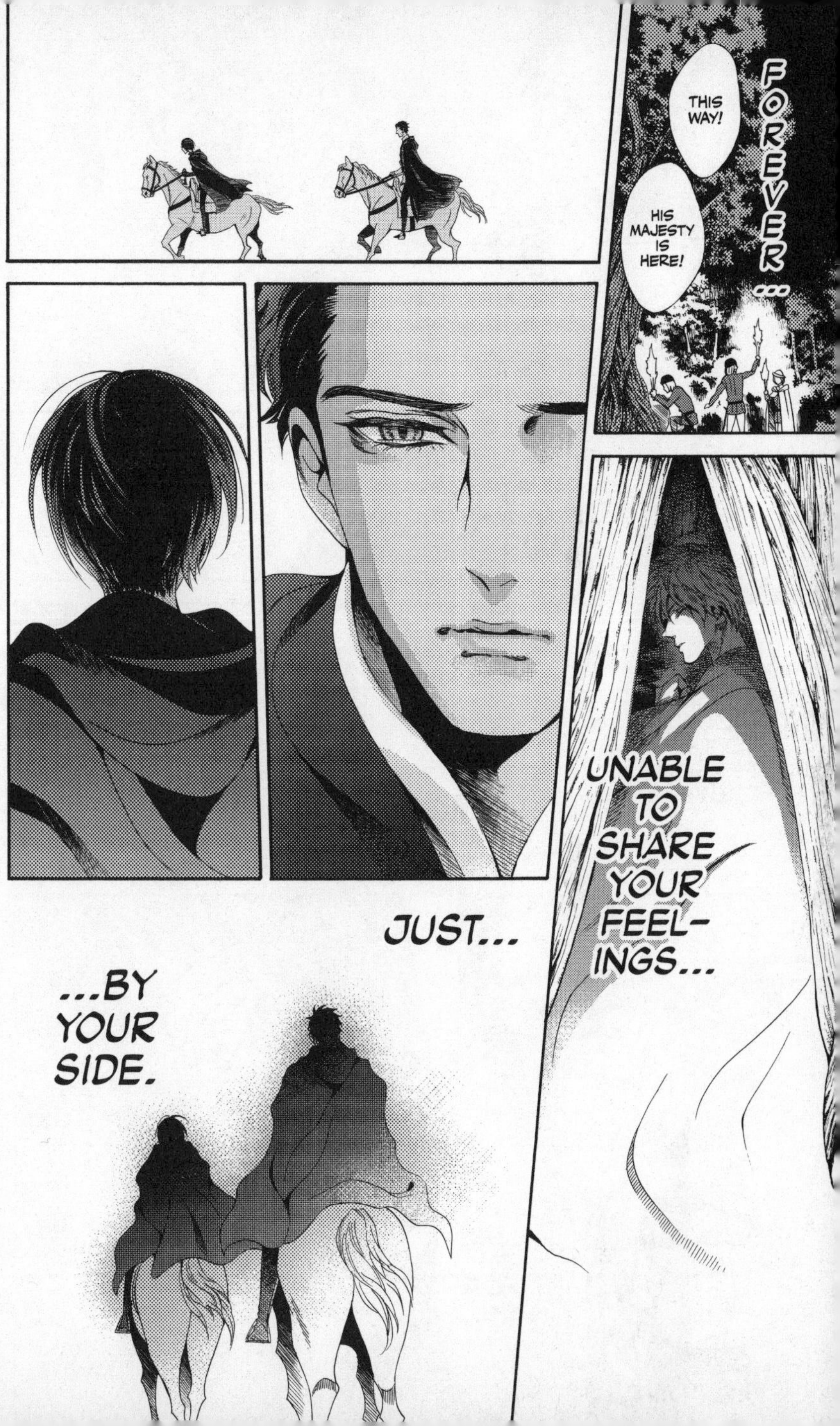
FOREVER...
THIS WAY!
HIS MAJESTY IS HERE!
UNABLE TO SHARE YOUR FEEL-INGS...
JUST...
...BY YOUR SIDE.

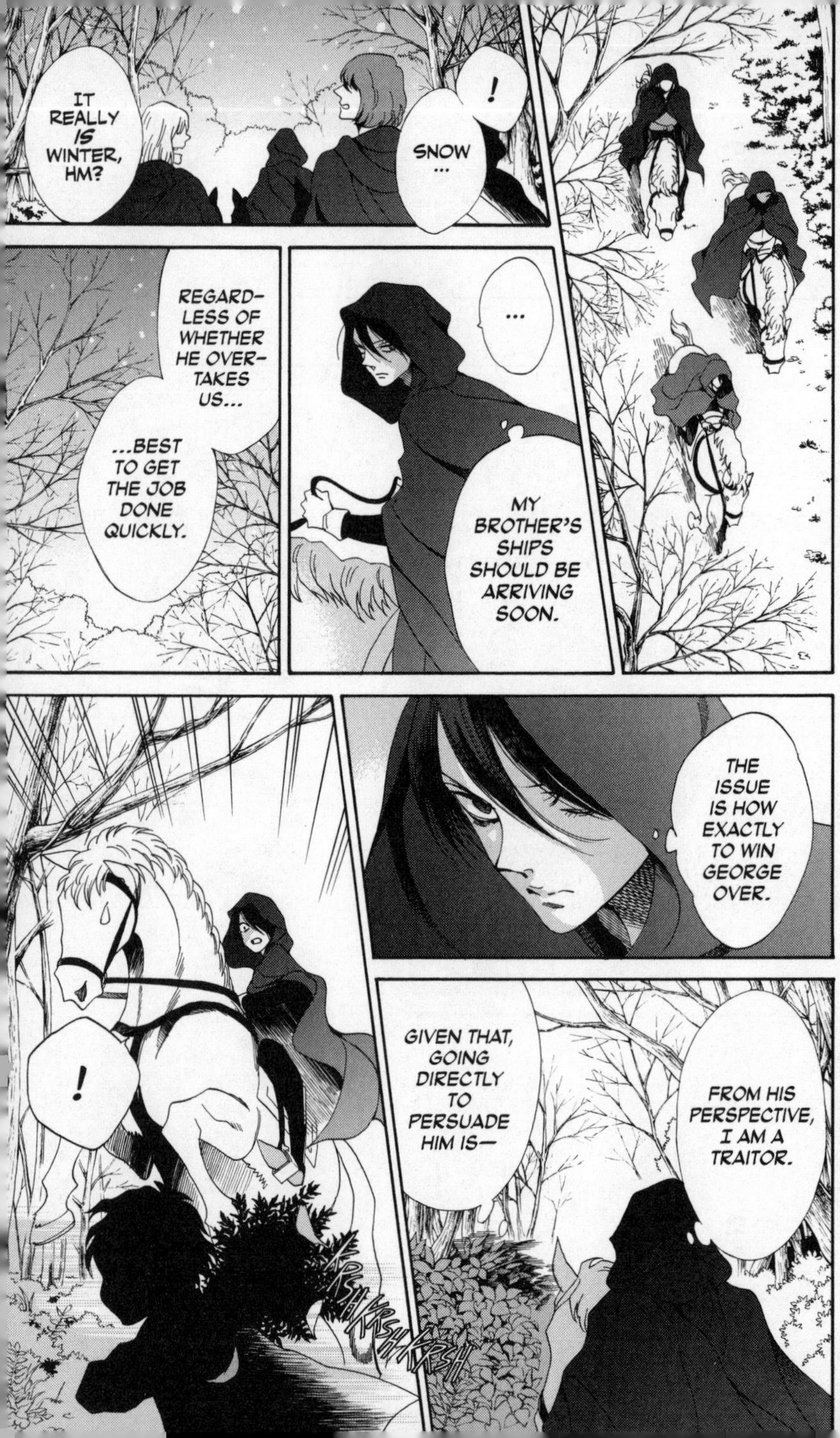
!
SNOW ...
IT REALLY IS WINTER, HM?
...
MY BROTHER'S SHIPS SHOULD BE ARRIVING SOON.
REGARDLESS OF WHETHER HE OVERTAKES US...
...BEST TO GET THE JOB DONE QUICKLY.
THE ISSUE IS HOW EXACTLY TO WIN GEORGE OVER.
FROM HIS PERSPECTIVE, I AM A TRAITOR.
GIVEN THAT, GOING DIRECTLY TO PERSUADE HIM IS—
!
KRSH KRSH KRSH KRSH

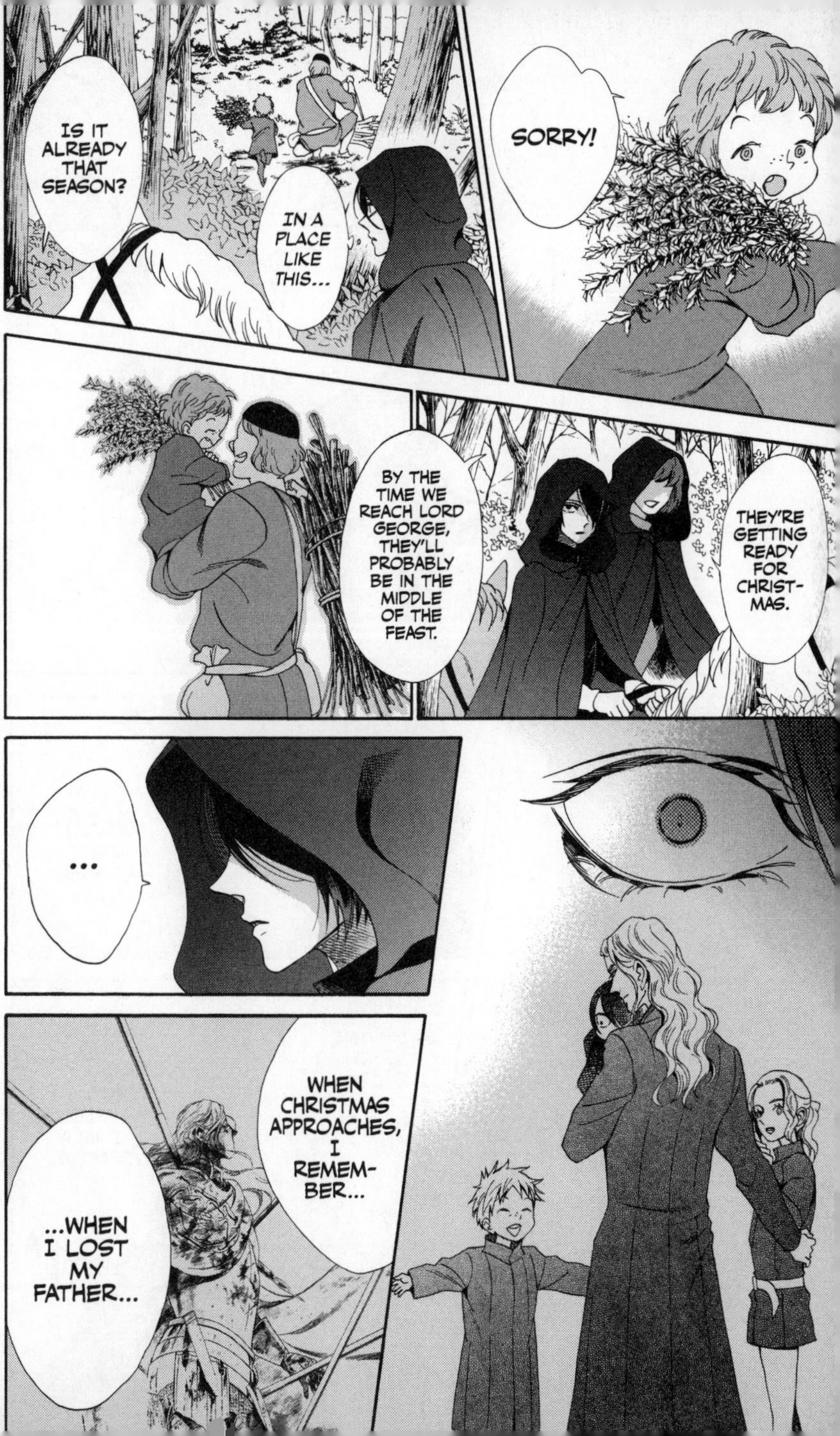
SORRY!
IS IT ALREADY THAT SEASON?
IN A PLACE LIKE THIS...
THEY'RE GETTING READY FOR CHRIST-MAS.
BY THE TIME WE REACH LORD GEORGE, THEY'LL PROBABLY BE IN THE MIDDLE OF THE FEAST.
...
WHEN CHRISTMAS APPROACHES, I REMEM-BER...
...WHEN I LOST MY FATHER...

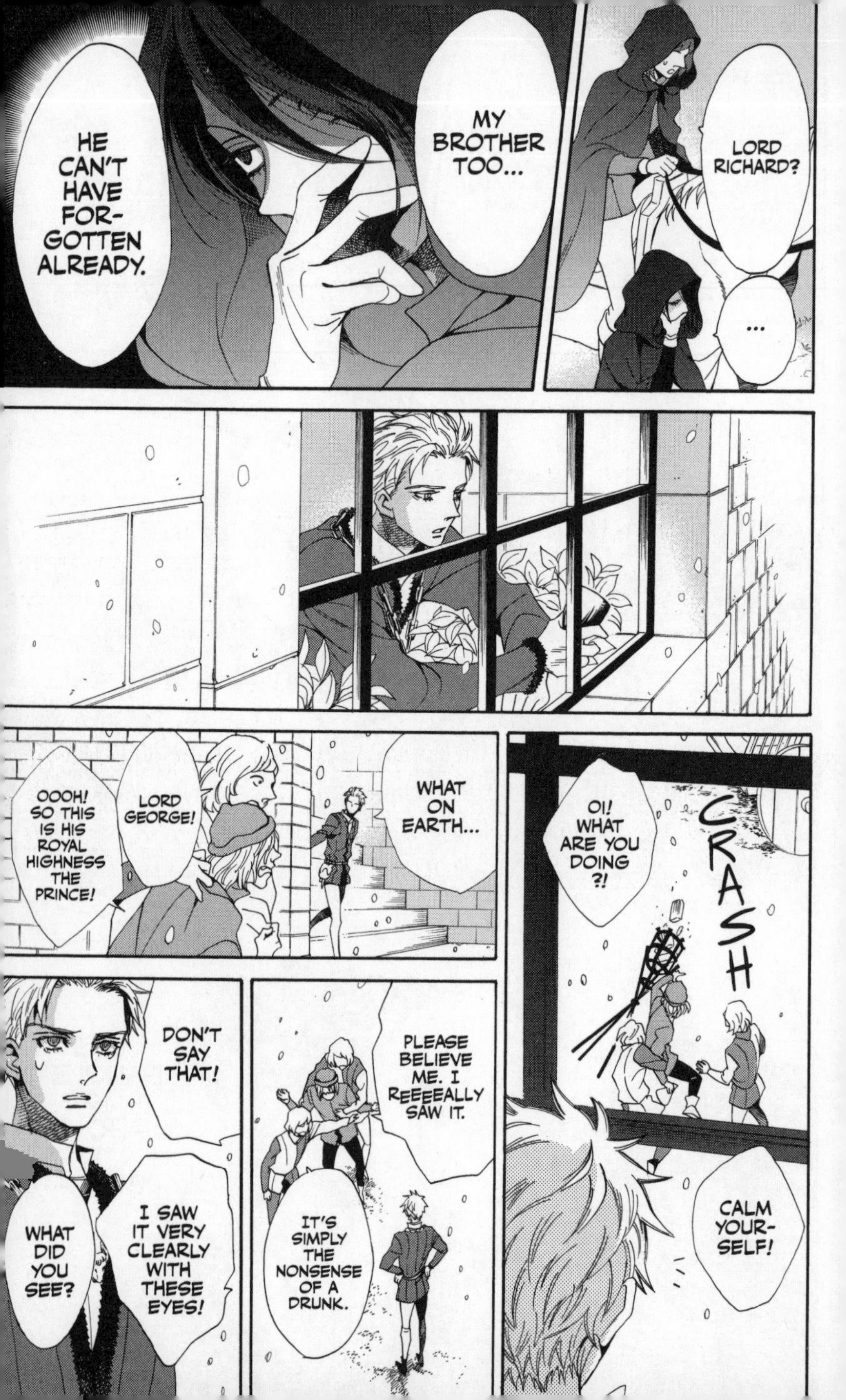
LORD RICHARD?
...
MY BROTHER TOO...
HE CAN'T HAVE FOR-GOTTEN ALREADY.
CRASH
OI! WHAT ARE YOU DOING?!
CALM YOUR-SELF!
WHAT ON EARTH...
LORD GEORGE!
OOOH! SO THIS IS HIS ROYAL HIGHNESS THE PRINCE!
PLEASE BELIEVE ME. I REEEEALLY SAW IT.
IT'S SIMPLY THE NONSENSE OF A DRUNK.
DON'T SAY THAT!
I SAW IT VERY CLEARLY WITH THESE EYES!
WHAT DID YOU SEE?

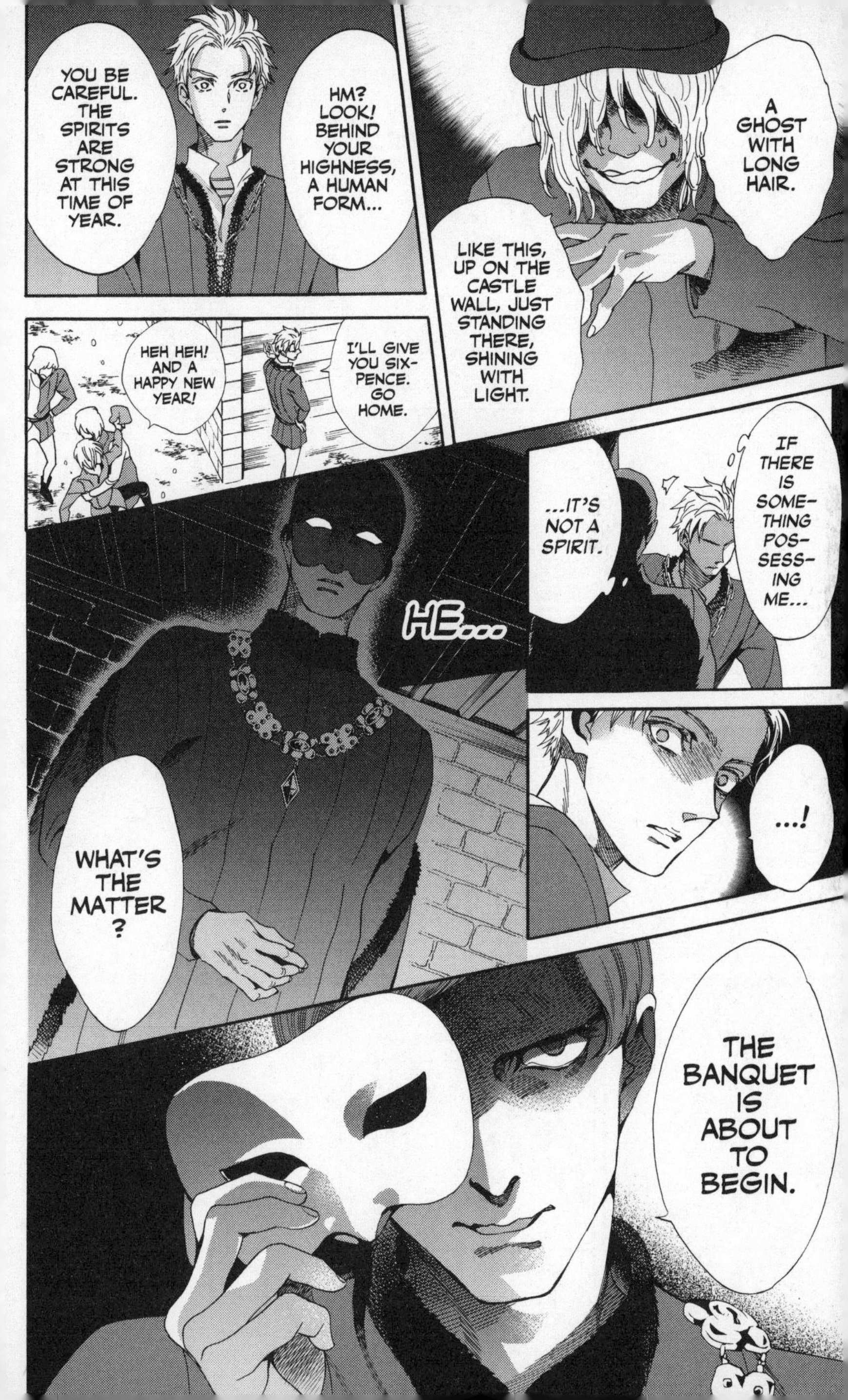
A GHOST WITH LONG HAIR.
LIKE THIS, UP ON THE CASTLE WALL, JUST STANDING THERE, SHINING WITH LIGHT.
HM? LOOK! BEHIND YOUR HIGHNESS, A HUMAN FORM...
YOU BE CAREFUL. THE SPIRITS ARE STRONG AT THIS TIME OF YEAR.
I'LL GIVE YOU SIX-PENCE. GO HOME.
HEH HEH! AND A HAPPY NEW YEAR!
IF THERE IS SOME-THING POS-SESS-ING ME...
...IT'S NOT A SPIRIT.
...!
HE...
WHAT'S THE MATTER?
THE BANQUET IS ABOUT TO BEGIN.

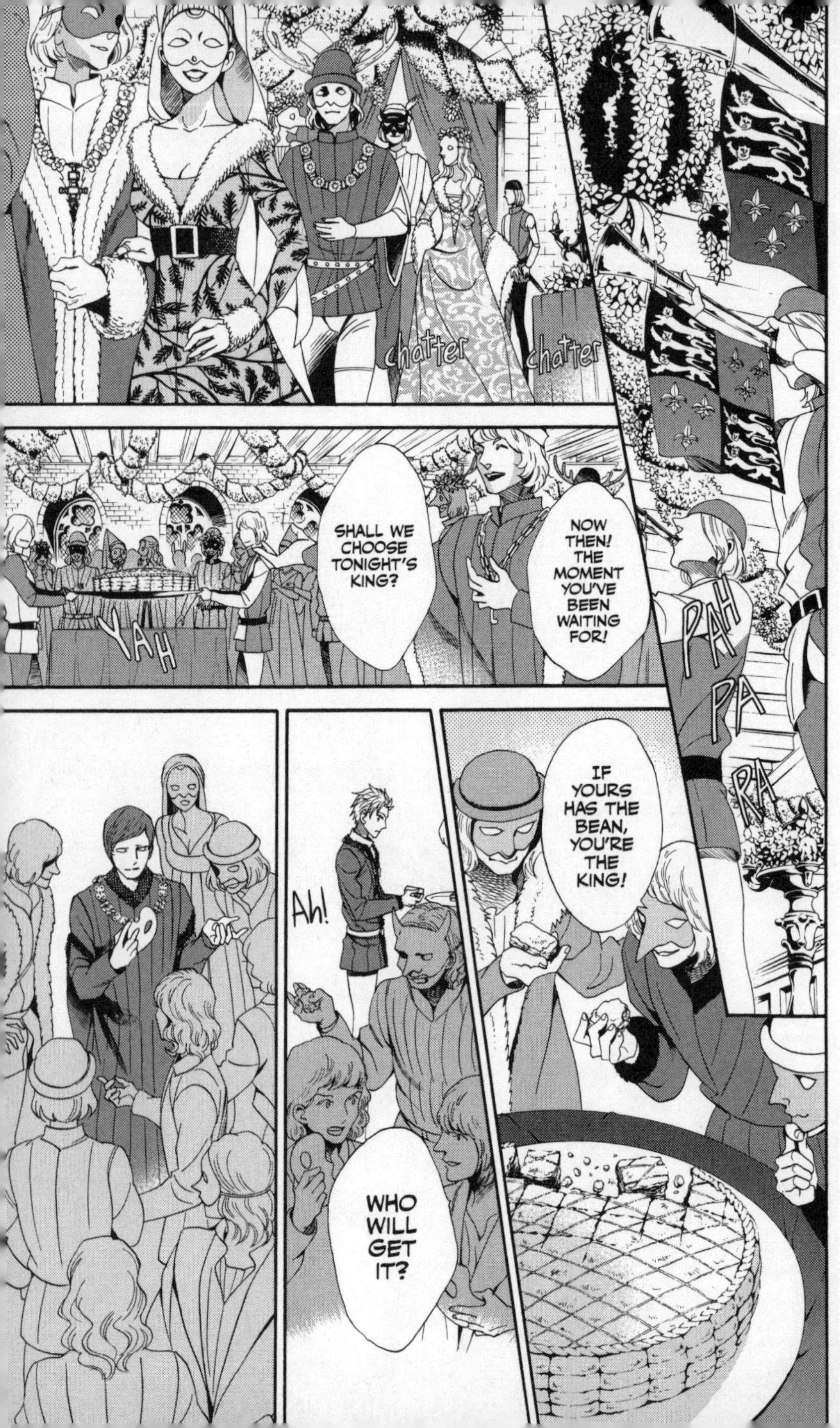
PAH
PA
RA
chatter
chatter
NOW THEN! THE MOMENT YOU'VE BEEN WAITING FOR!
SHALL WE CHOOSE TONIGHT'S KING?
YAH
IF YOURS HAS THE BEAN, YOU'RE THE KING!
Ah!
WHO WILL GET IT?

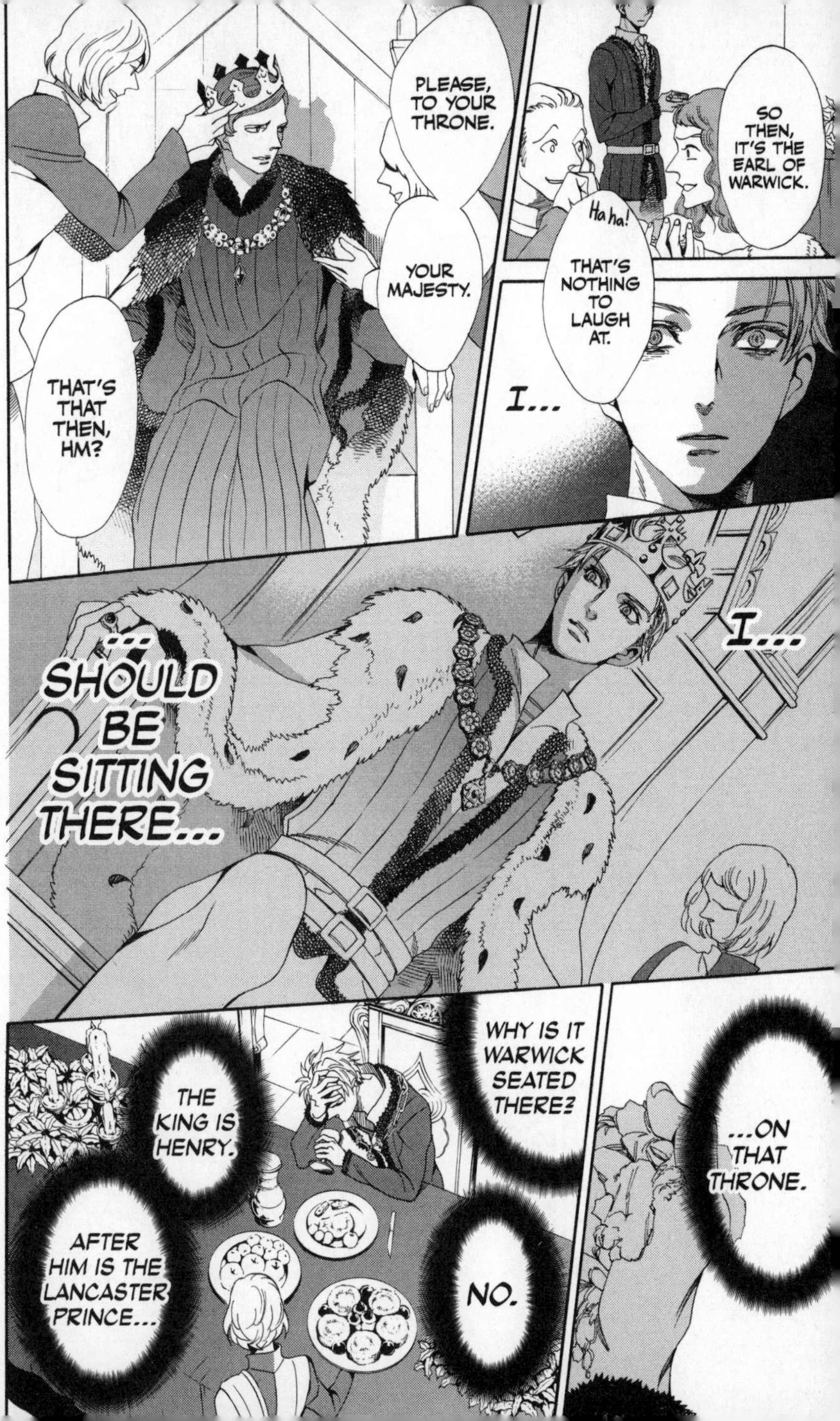
SO THEN, IT'S THE EARL OF WARWICK.
Ha ha!
THAT'S NOTHING TO LAUGH AT.
I...
PLEASE, TO YOUR THRONE.
YOUR MAJESTY.
THAT'S THAT THEN, HM?
I...
...SHOULD BE SITTING THERE...
THE KING IS HENRY.
AFTER HIM IS THE LANCASTER PRINCE...
NO.
WHY IS IT WARWICK SEATED THERE?
...ON THAT THRONE.

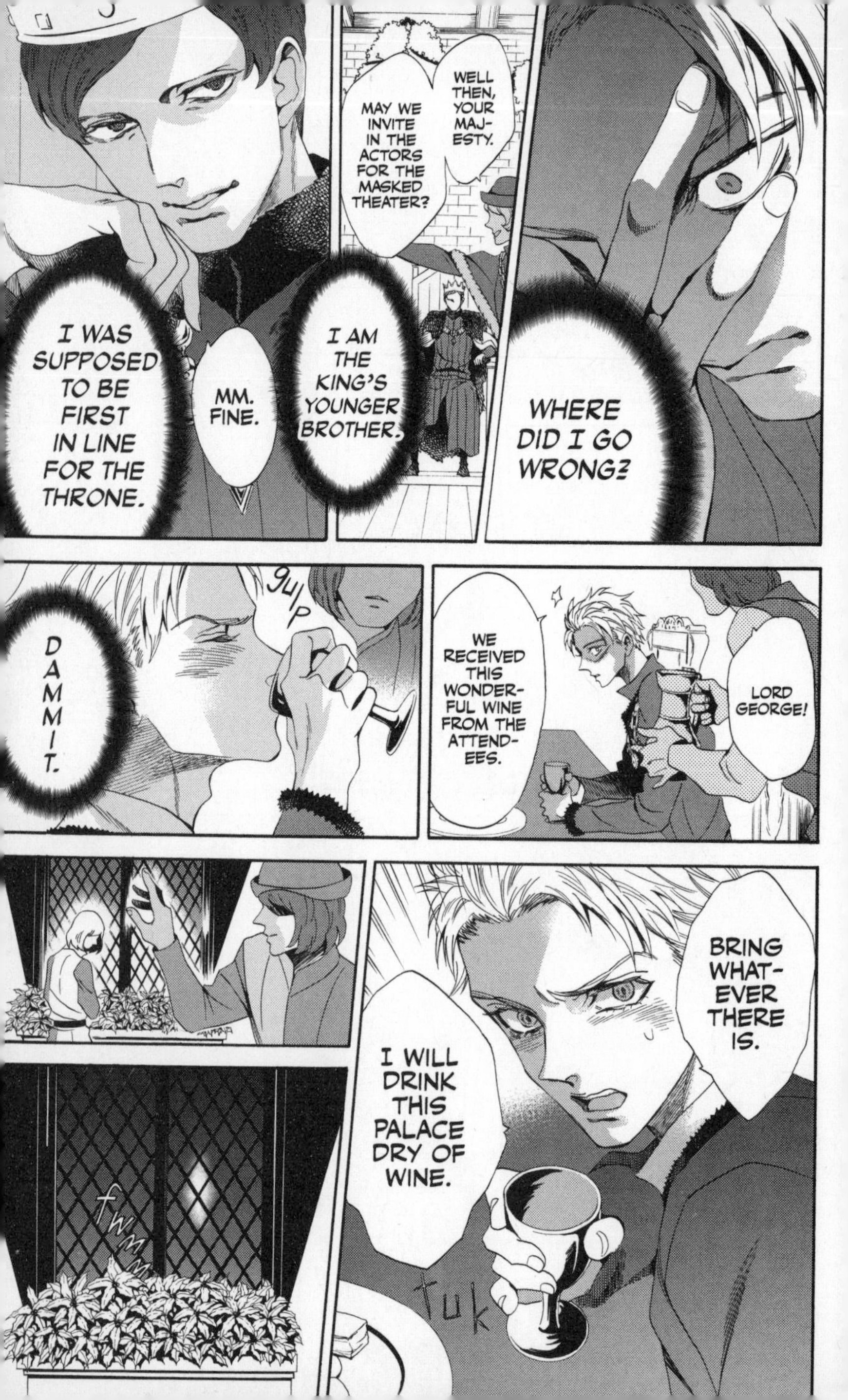
WHERE DID I GO WRONG?
WELL THEN, YOUR MAJESTY.
MAY WE INVITE IN THE ACTORS FOR THE MASKED THEATER?
I AM THE KING'S YOUNGER BROTHER.
MM. FINE.
I WAS SUPPOSED TO BE FIRST IN LINE FOR THE THRONE.
LORD GEORGE!
WE RECEIVED THIS WONDERFUL WINE FROM THE ATTENDEES.
gulp
DAMMIT.
BRING WHATEVER THERE IS.
I WILL DRINK THIS PALACE DRY OF WINE.
tuk
fwmm

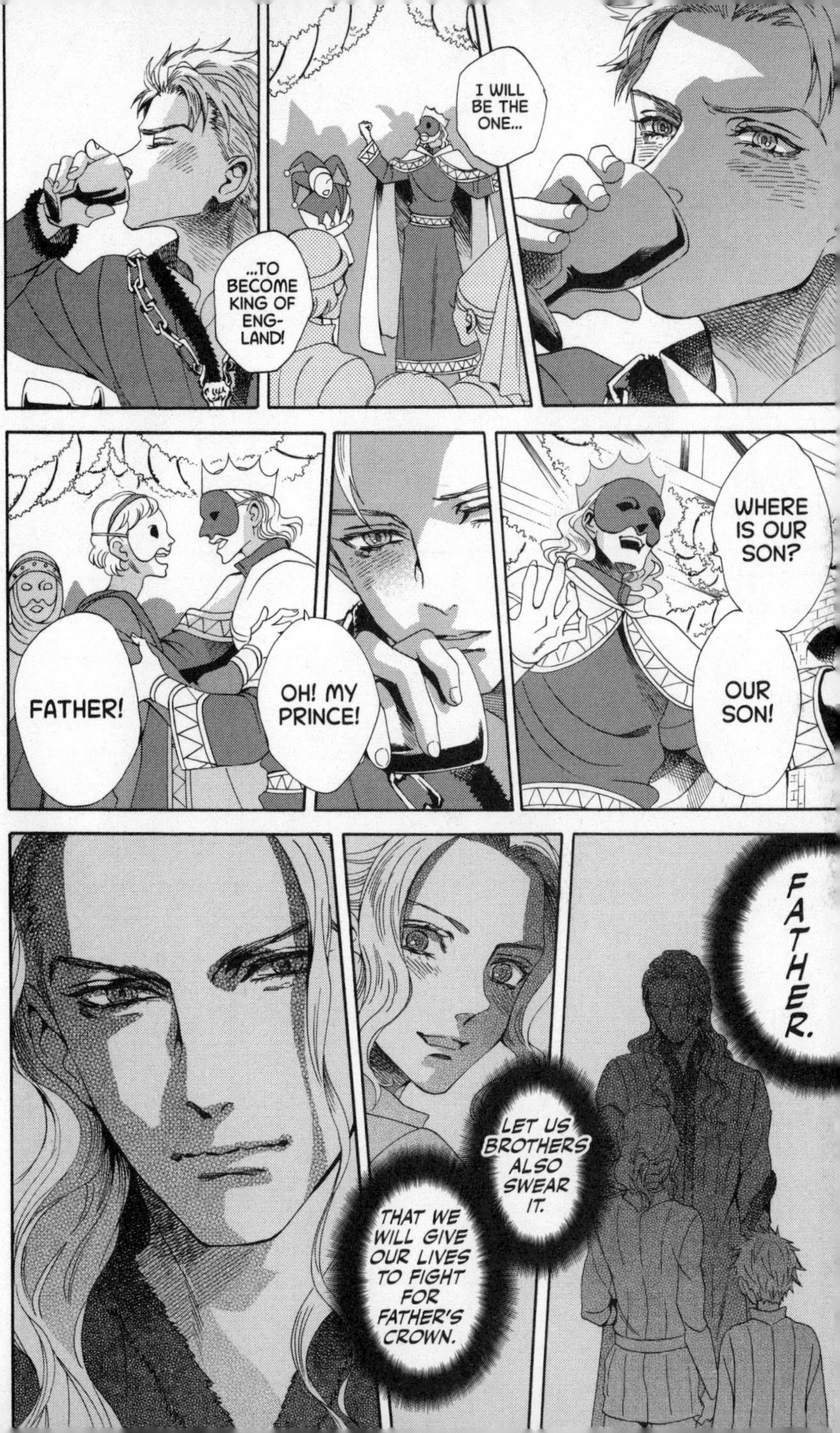
I WILL BE THE ONE...
...TO BECOME KING OF ENG-LAND!
WHERE IS OUR SON?
OUR SON!
OH! MY PRINCE!
FATHER!
FATHER.
LET US BROTHERS ALSO SWEAR IT.
THAT WE WILL GIVE OUR LIVES TO FIGHT FOR FATHER'S CROWN.

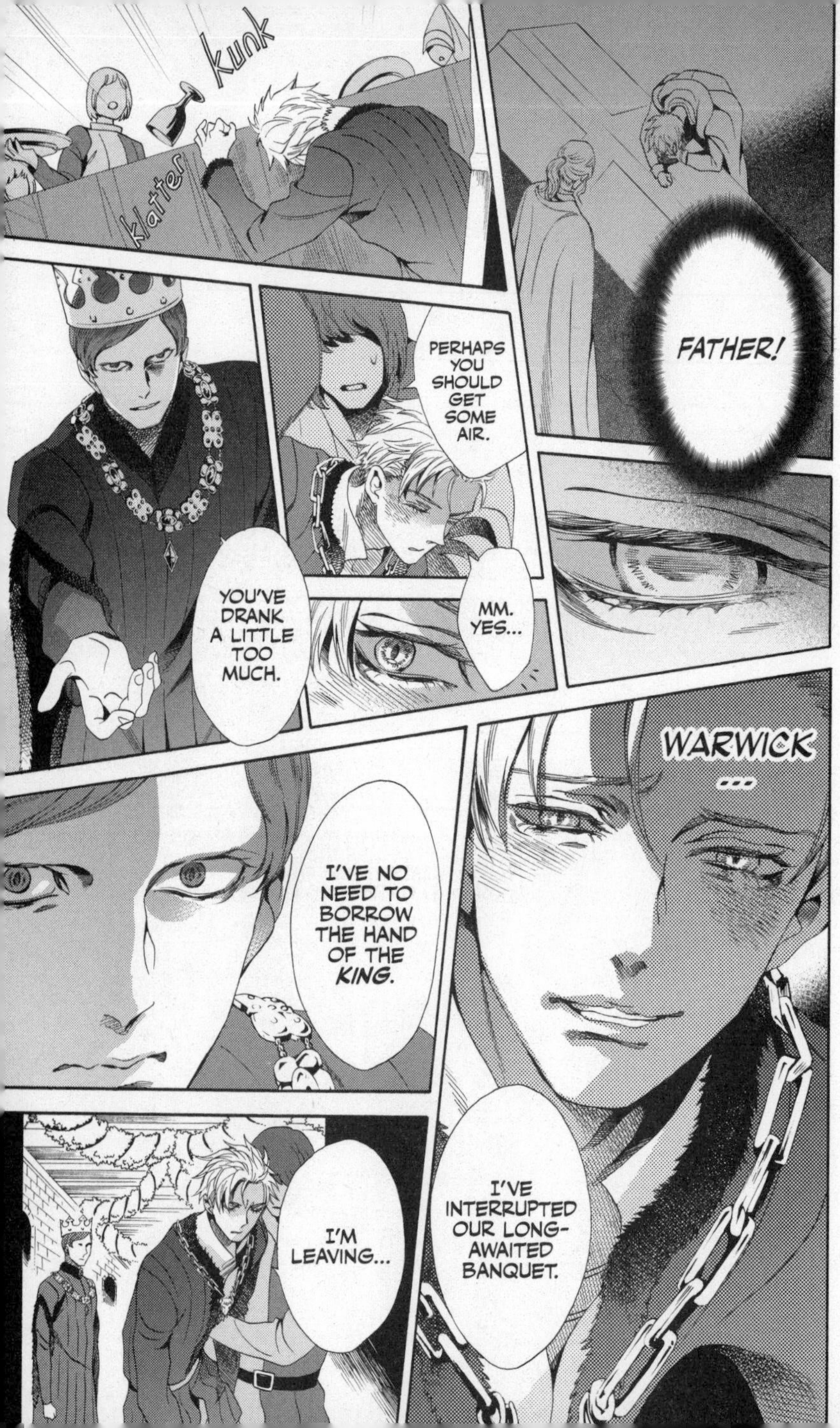
FATHER!
kunk
klatter
PERHAPS YOU SHOULD GET SOME AIR.
MM. YES...
YOU'VE DRANK A LITTLE TOO MUCH.
WARWICK ...
I'VE INTERRUPTED OUR LONG-AWAITED BANQUET.
I'VE NO NEED TO BORROW THE HAND OF THE *KING*.
I'M LEAVING...

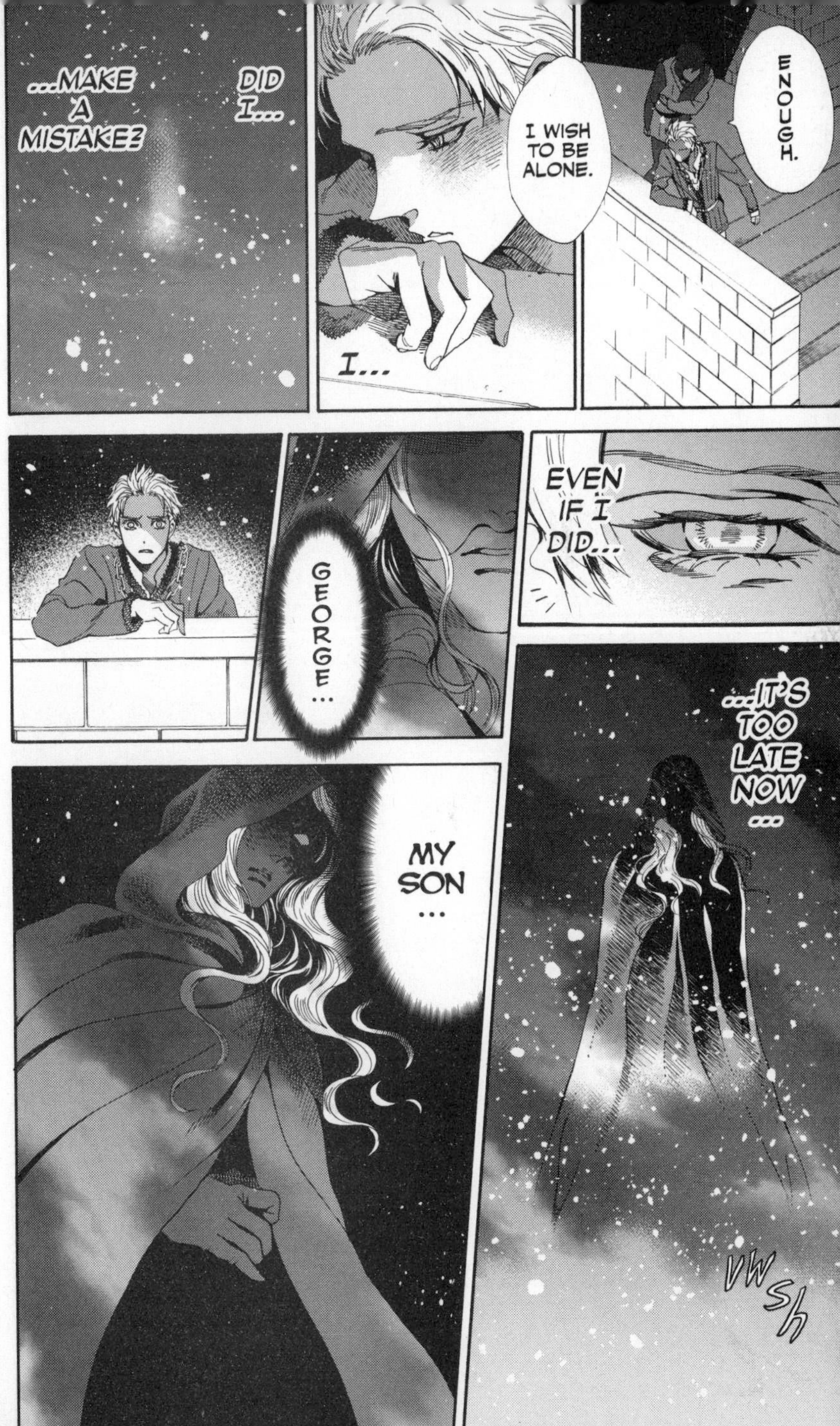
ENOUGH.
I WISH TO BE ALONE.
I...
DID I...
...MAKE A MISTAKE?
EVEN IF I DID...
GEORGE...
...IT'S TOO LATE NOW ...
VWSH
MY SON ...

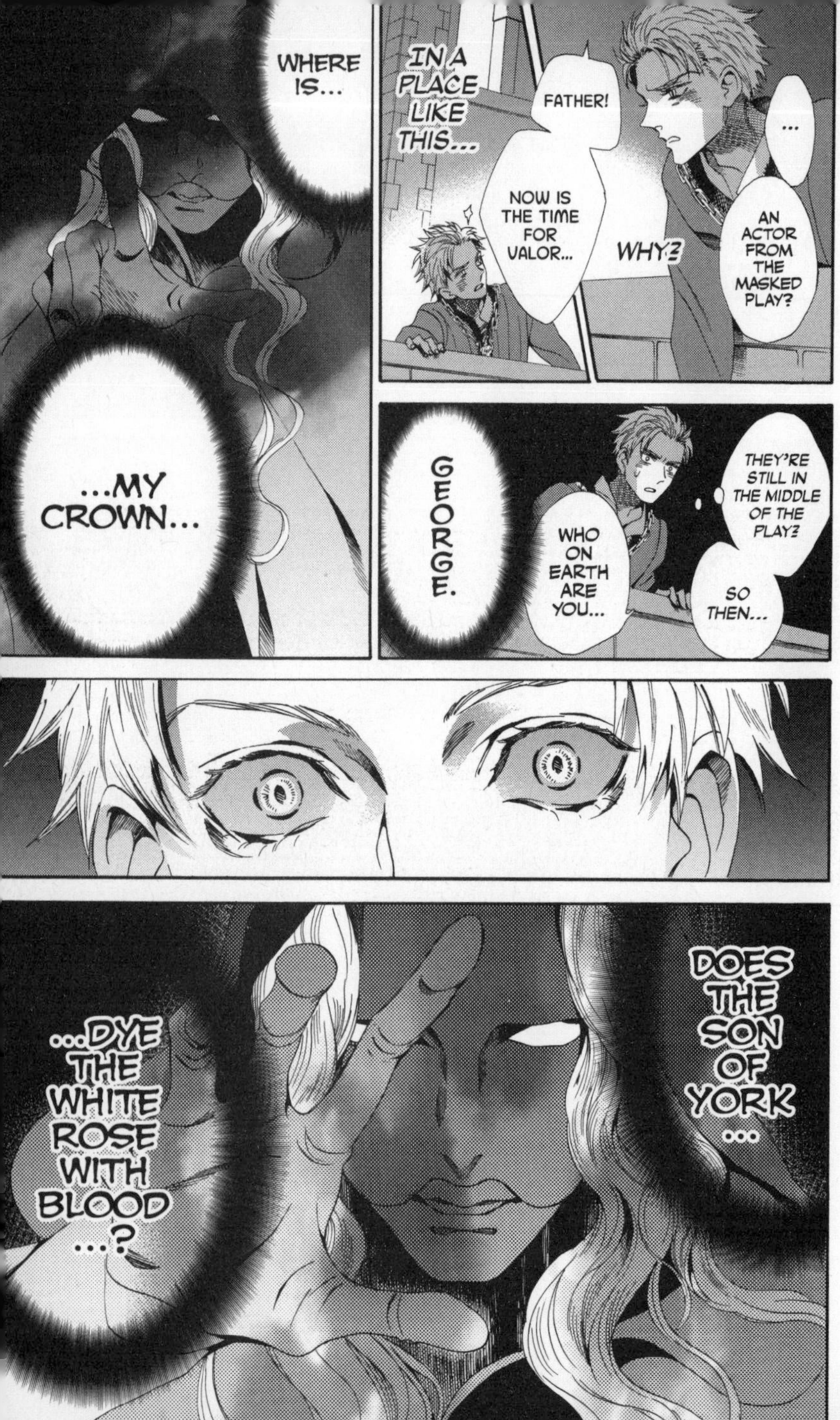
...
FATHER!
NOW IS THE TIME FOR VALOR...
IN A PLACE LIKE THIS...
AN ACTOR FROM THE MASKED PLAY?
WHY?
THEY'RE STILL IN THE MIDDLE OF THE PLAY?
SO THEN...
WHO ON EARTH ARE YOU...
GEORGE.
WHERE IS...
...MY CROWN...
DOES THE SON OF YORK...
...DYE THE WHITE ROSE WITH BLOOD...?

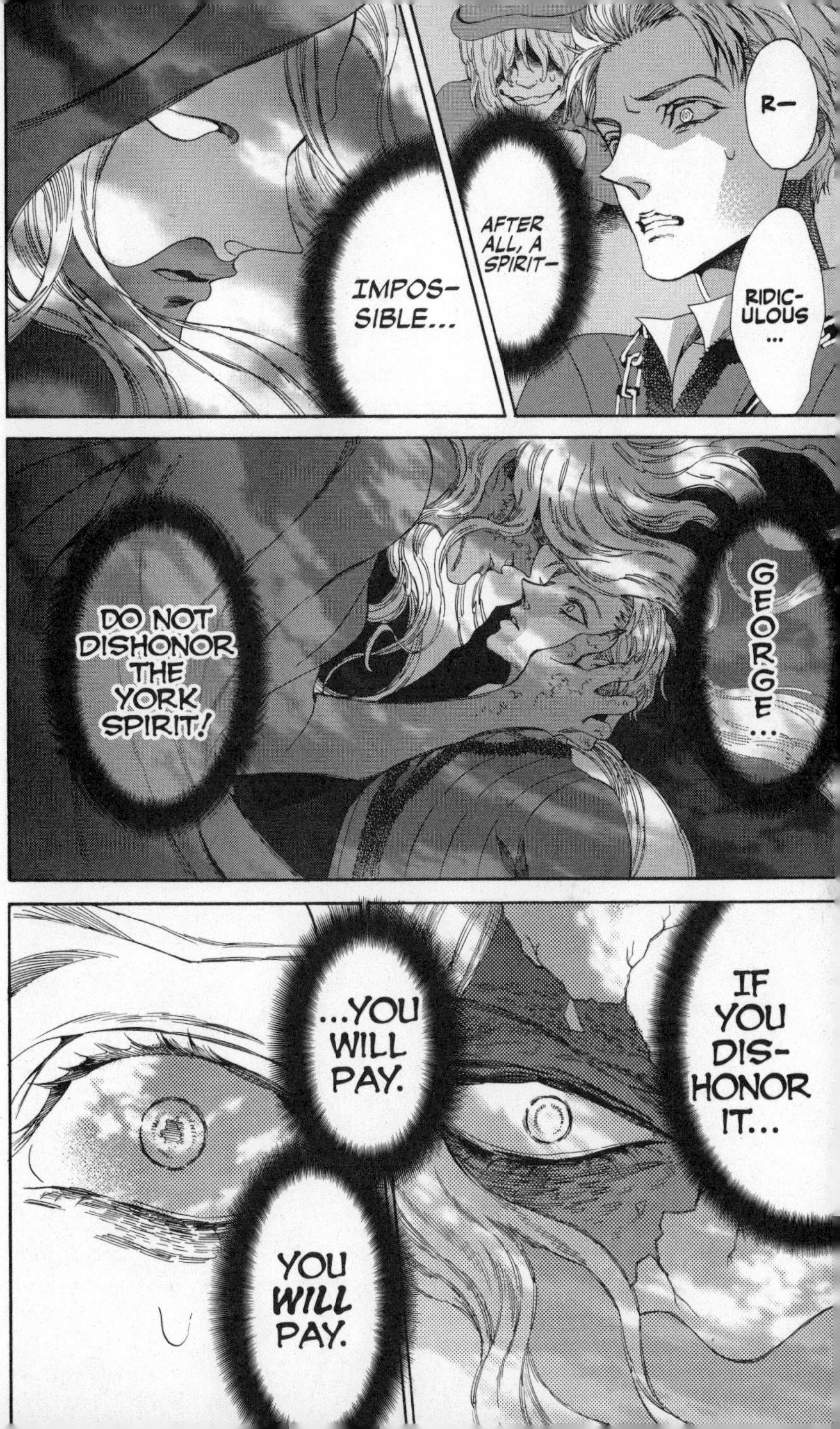
R—
RIDIC-ULOUS ...
AFTER ALL, A SPIRIT—
IMPOS-SIBLE...
GEORGE...
DO NOT DISHONOR THE YORK SPIRIT!
IF YOU DIS-HONOR IT...
...YOU WILL PAY.
YOU ***WILL*** PAY.

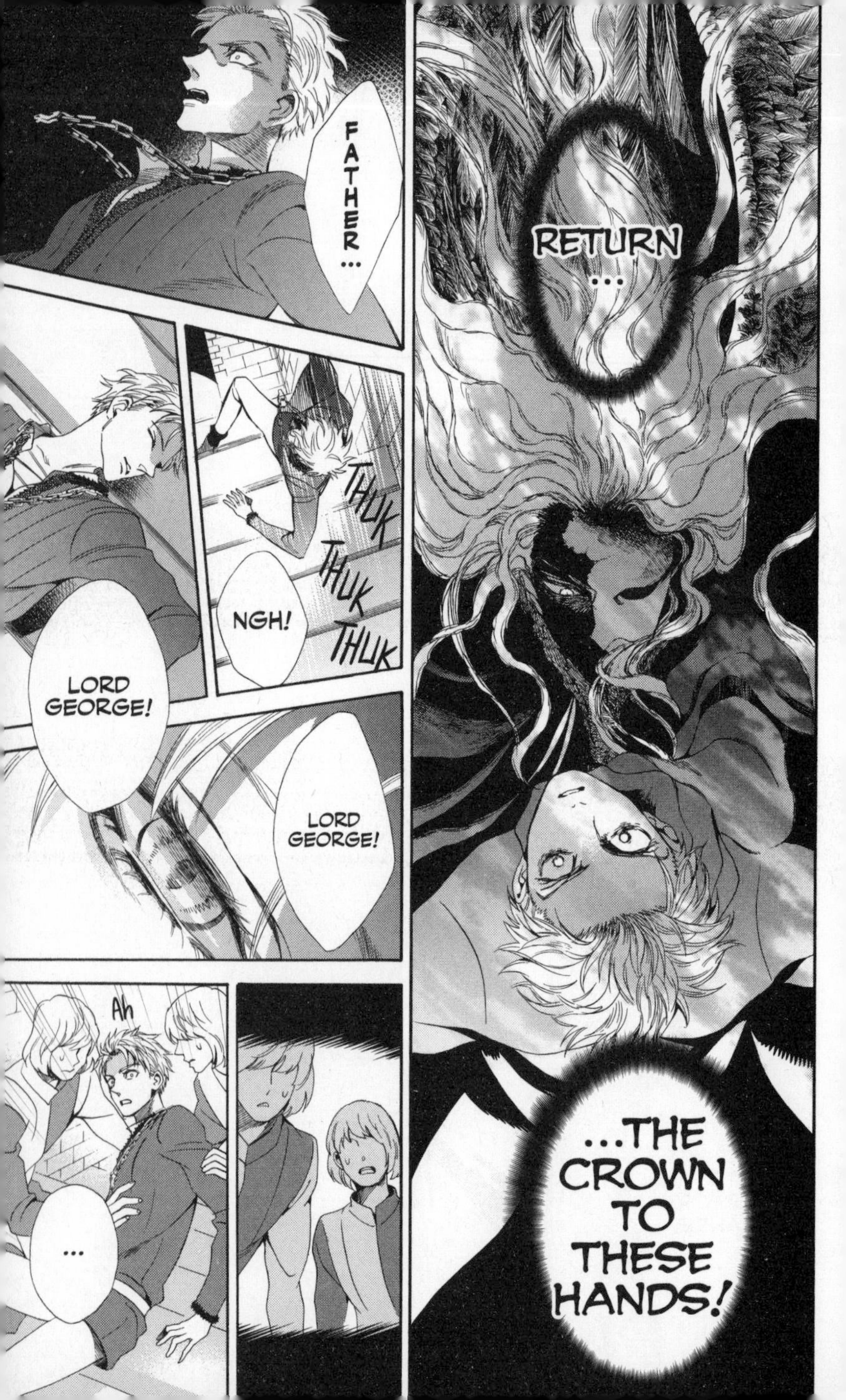
RETURN...
...THE CROWN TO THESE HANDS!
FATHER...
THUK THUK THUK
NGH!
LORD GEORGE!
LORD GEORGE!
Ah
...

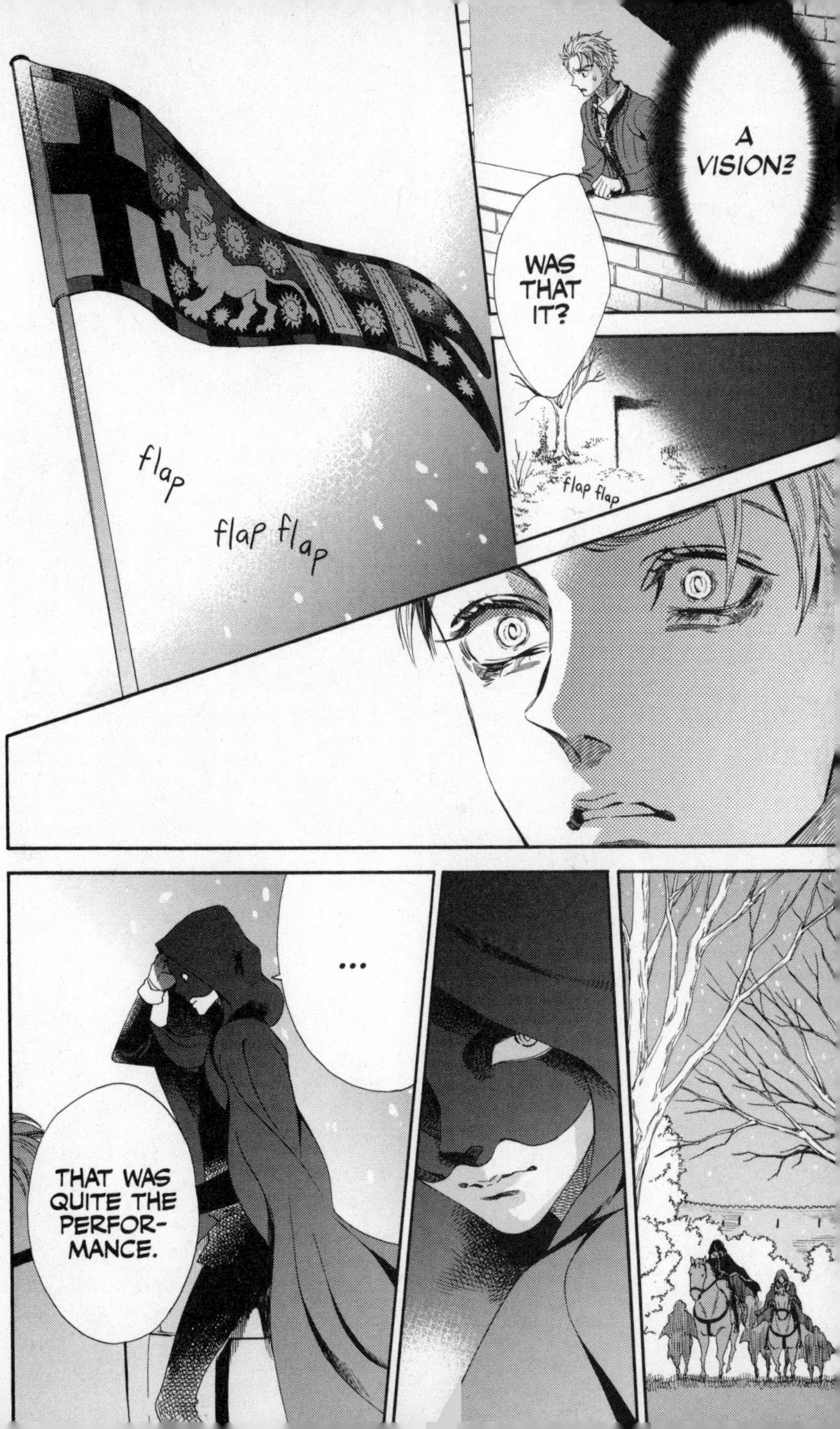
A VISION?
WAS THAT IT?
flap flap
flap
flap flap
...
THAT WAS QUITE THE PERFOR-MANCE.

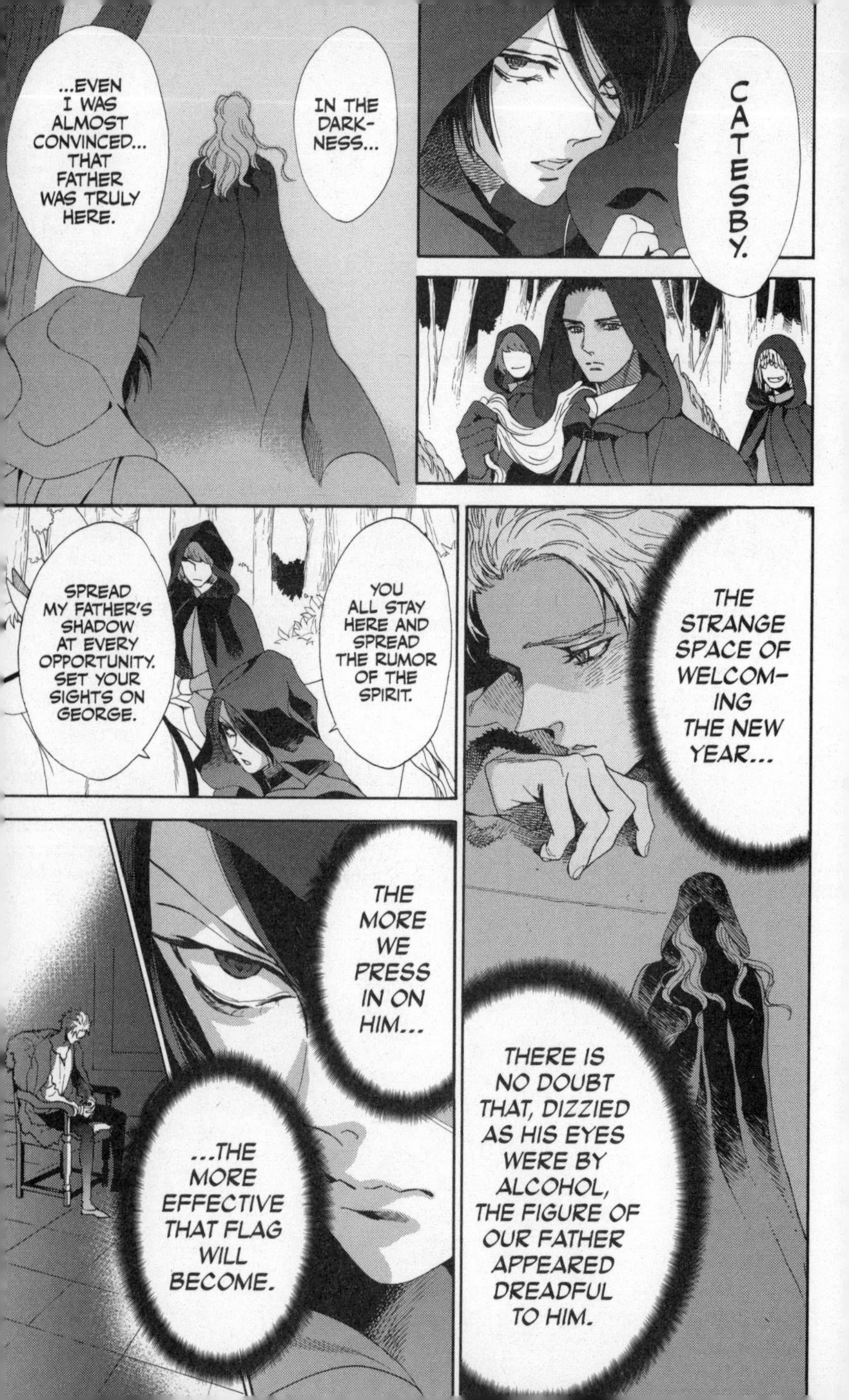
CATESBY.
IN THE DARK-NESS...
...EVEN I WAS ALMOST CONVINCED... THAT FATHER WAS TRULY HERE.
THE STRANGE SPACE OF WELCOM-ING THE NEW YEAR...
THERE IS NO DOUBT THAT, DIZZIED AS HIS EYES WERE BY ALCOHOL, THE FIGURE OF OUR FATHER APPEARED DREADFUL TO HIM.
YOU ALL STAY HERE AND SPREAD THE RUMOR OF THE SPIRIT.
SPREAD MY FATHER'S SHADOW AT EVERY OPPORTUNITY. SET YOUR SIGHTS ON GEORGE.
THE MORE WE PRESS IN ON HIM...
...THE MORE EFFECTIVE THAT FLAG WILL BECOME.

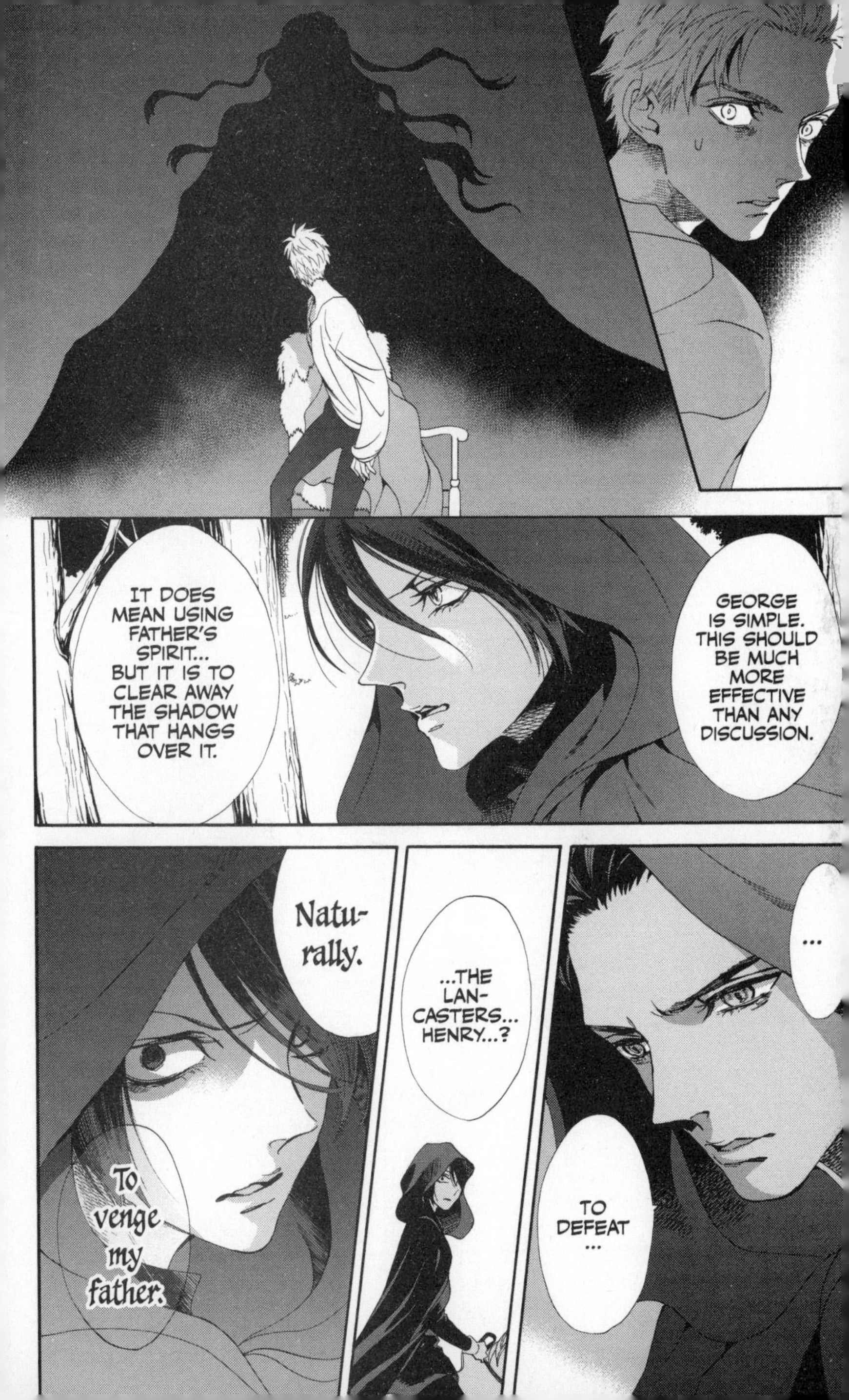
GEORGE IS SIMPLE. THIS SHOULD BE MUCH MORE EFFECTIVE THAN ANY DISCUSSION.
IT DOES MEAN USING FATHER'S SPIRIT... BUT IT IS TO CLEAR AWAY THE SHADOW THAT HANGS OVER IT.
...
TO DEFEAT ...
...THE LAN-CASTERS... HENRY...?
Natu-rally.
To venge my father.

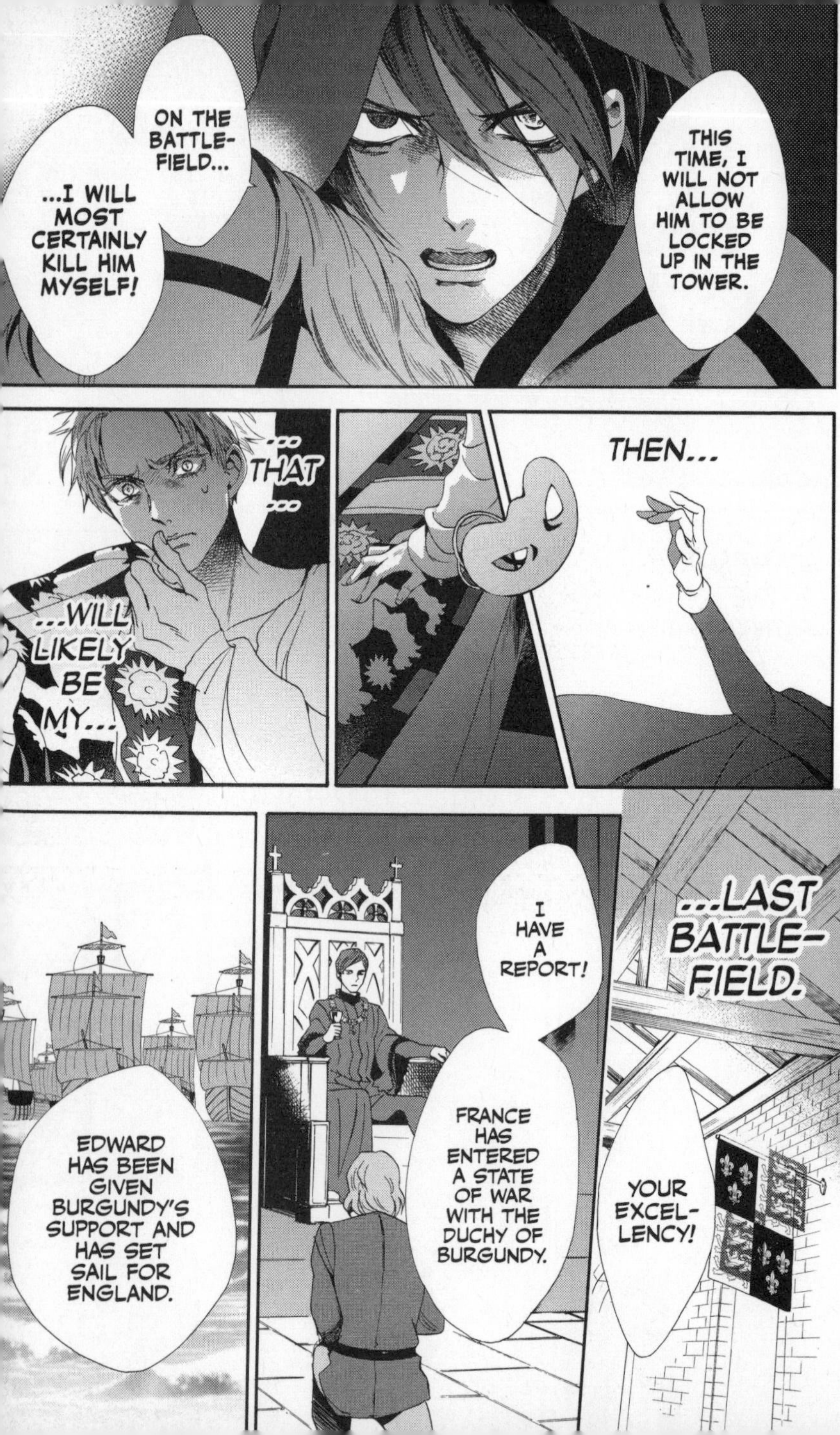
THIS TIME, I WILL NOT ALLOW HIM TO BE LOCKED UP IN THE TOWER.
ON THE BATTLE-FIELD...
...I WILL MOST CERTAINLY KILL HIM MYSELF!
THEN...
...THAT...
...WILL LIKELY BE MY...
...LAST BATTLE-FIELD.
YOUR EXCEL-LENCY!
I HAVE A REPORT!
FRANCE HAS ENTERED A STATE OF WAR WITH THE DUCHY OF BURGUNDY.
EDWARD HAS BEEN GIVEN BURGUNDY'S SUPPORT AND HAS SET SAIL FOR ENGLAND.

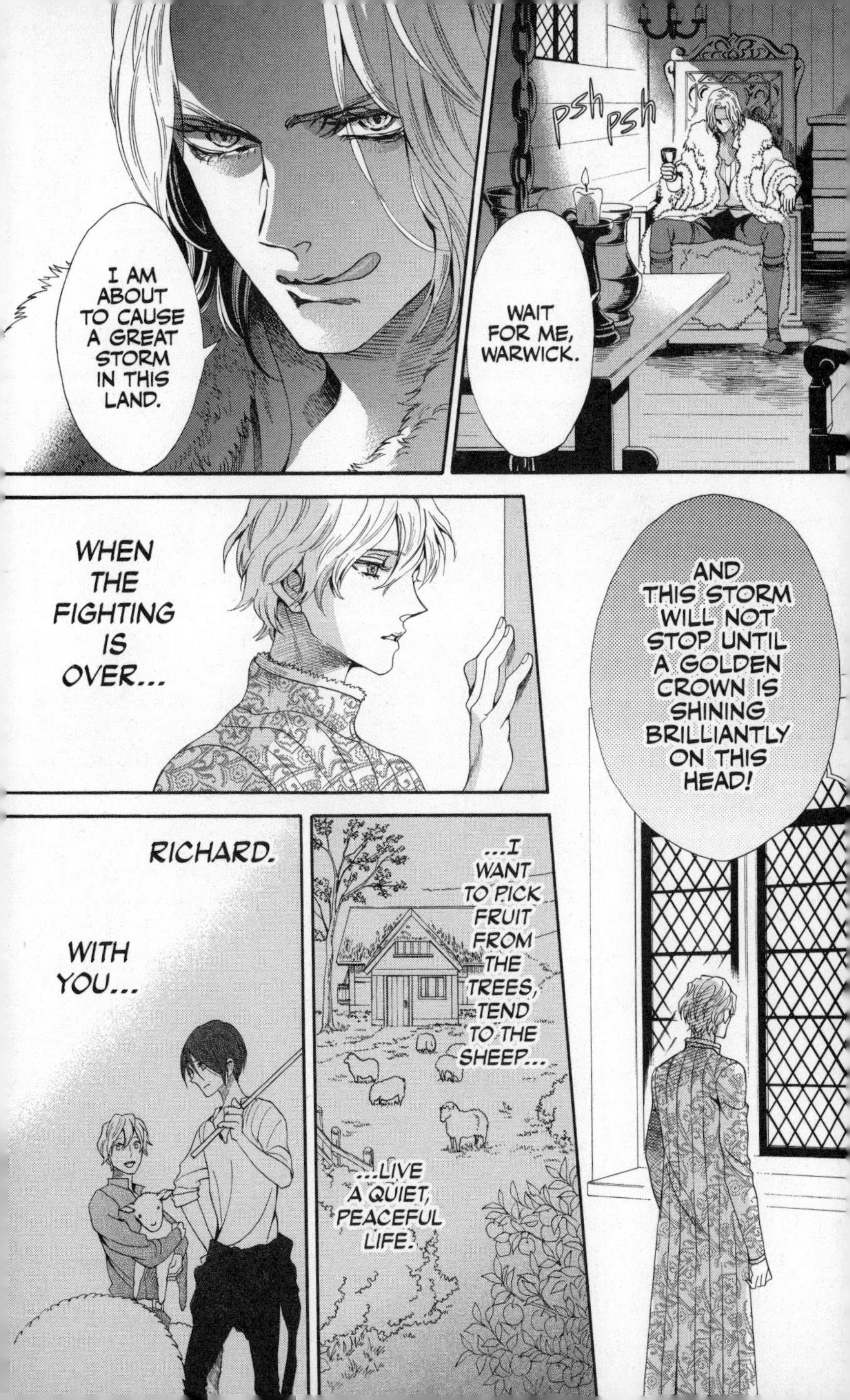
psh psh
WAIT FOR ME, WARWICK.
I AM ABOUT TO CAUSE A GREAT STORM IN THIS LAND.
AND THIS STORM WILL NOT STOP UNTIL A GOLDEN CROWN IS SHINING BRILLIANTLY ON THIS HEAD!
WHEN THE FIGHTING IS OVER...
...I WANT TO PICK FRUIT FROM THE TREES, TEND TO THE SHEEP...
...LIVE A QUIET, PEACEFUL LIFE.
RICHARD.
WITH YOU...

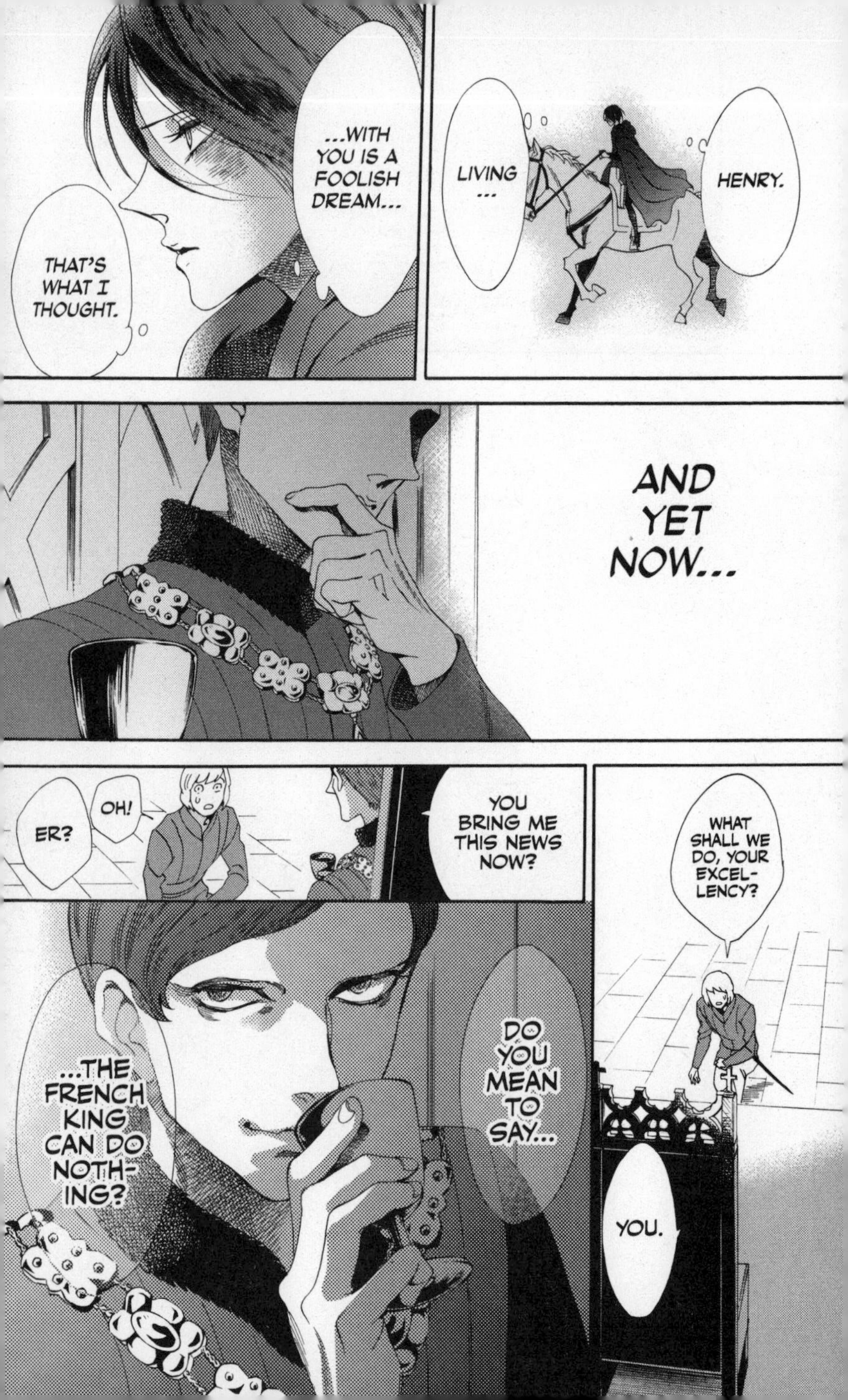
HENRY.
LIVING ...
...WITH YOU IS A FOOLISH DREAM...
THAT'S WHAT I THOUGHT.
AND YET NOW...
WHAT SHALL WE DO, YOUR EXCEL-LENCY?
YOU.
YOU BRING ME THIS NEWS NOW?
OH!
ER?
DO YOU MEAN TO SAY...
...THE FRENCH KING CAN DO NOTH-ING?

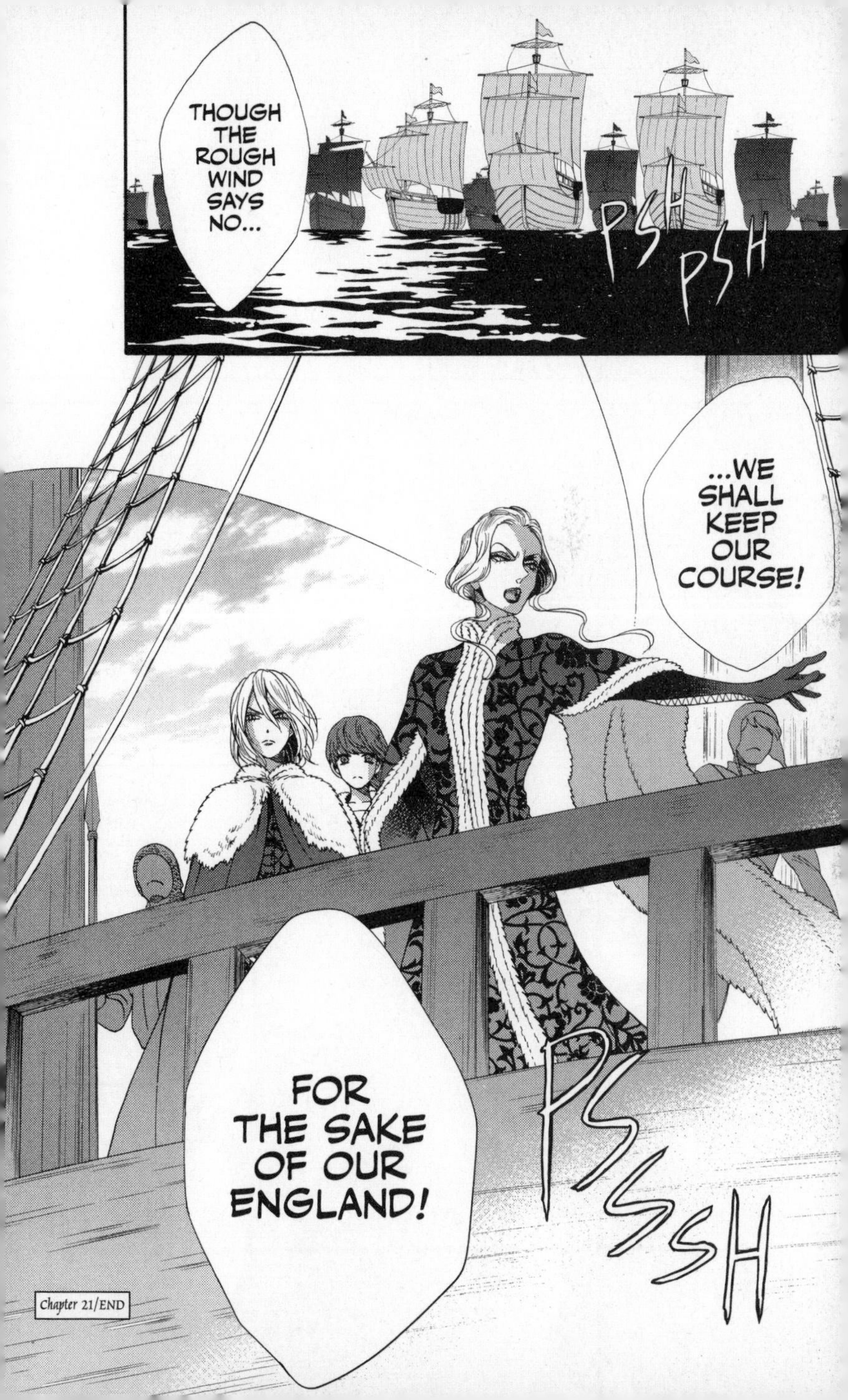
THOUGH THE ROUGH WIND SAYS NO...
PSH PSH
...WE SHALL KEEP OUR COURSE!
FOR THE SAKE OF OUR ENGLAND!
PSSSH
Chapter 21/END

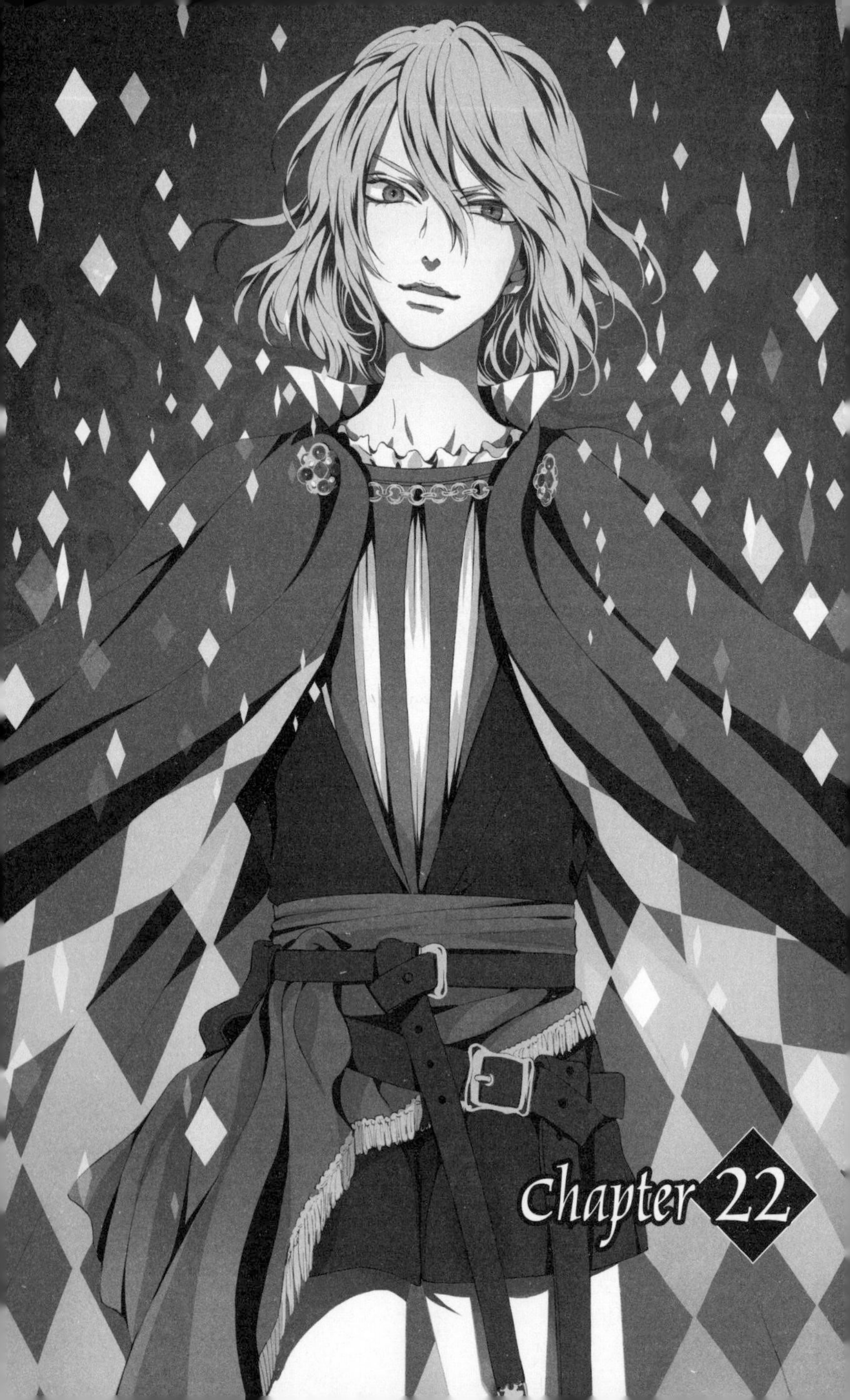
Chapter 22

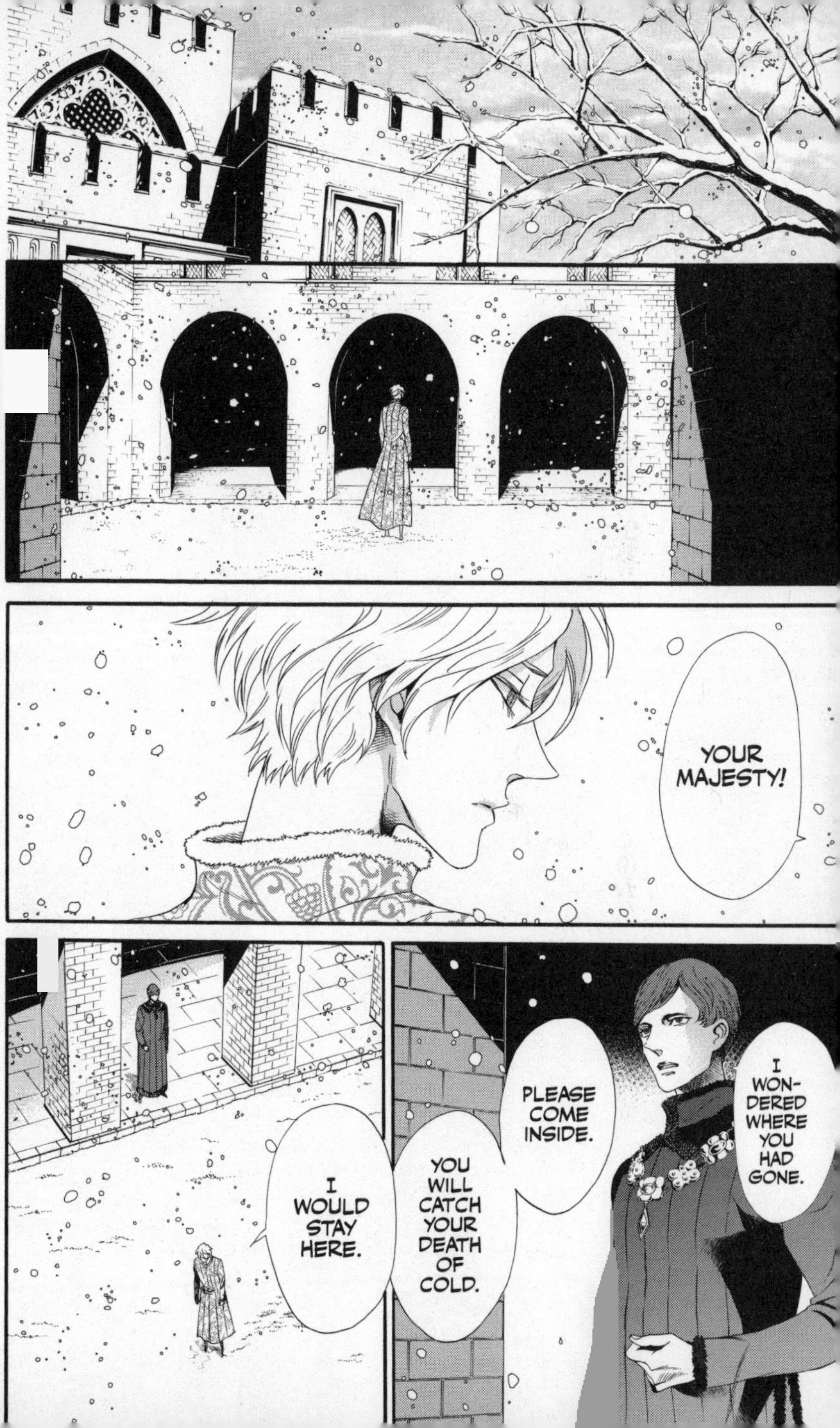
YOUR MAJESTY!
I WONDERED WHERE YOU HAD GONE.
PLEASE COME INSIDE.
YOU WILL CATCH YOUR DEATH OF COLD.
I WOULD STAY HERE.

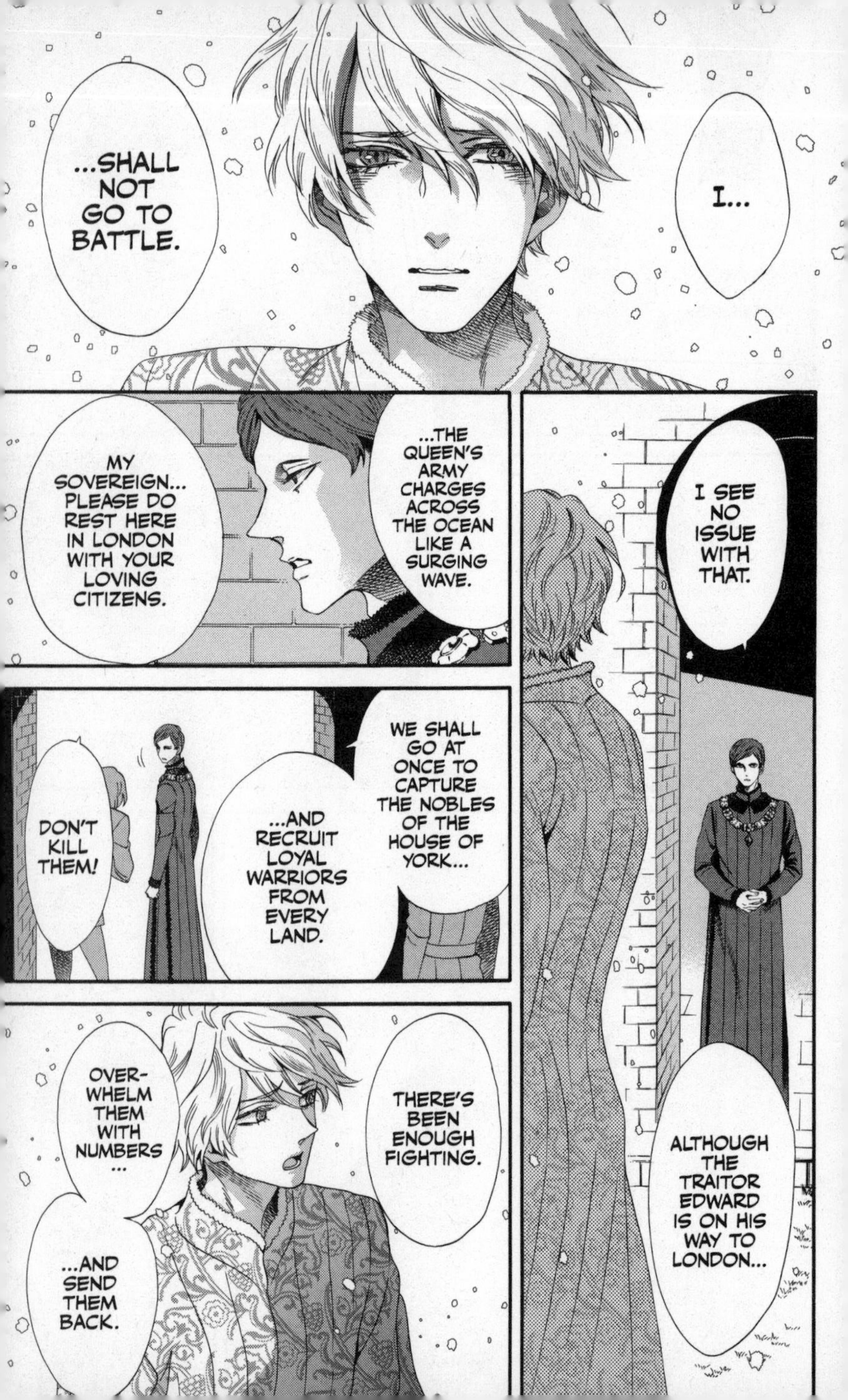
I...
...SHALL NOT GO TO BATTLE.
I SEE NO ISSUE WITH THAT.
ALTHOUGH THE TRAITOR EDWARD IS ON HIS WAY TO LONDON...
...THE QUEEN'S ARMY CHARGES ACROSS THE OCEAN LIKE A SURGING WAVE.
MY SOVEREIGN... PLEASE DO REST HERE IN LONDON WITH YOUR LOVING CITIZENS.
WE SHALL GO AT ONCE TO CAPTURE THE NOBLES OF THE HOUSE OF YORK...
...AND RECRUIT LOYAL WARRIORS FROM EVERY LAND.
DON'T KILL THEM!
THERE'S BEEN ENOUGH FIGHTING.
OVER-WHELM THEM WITH NUMBERS ...
...AND SEND THEM BACK.

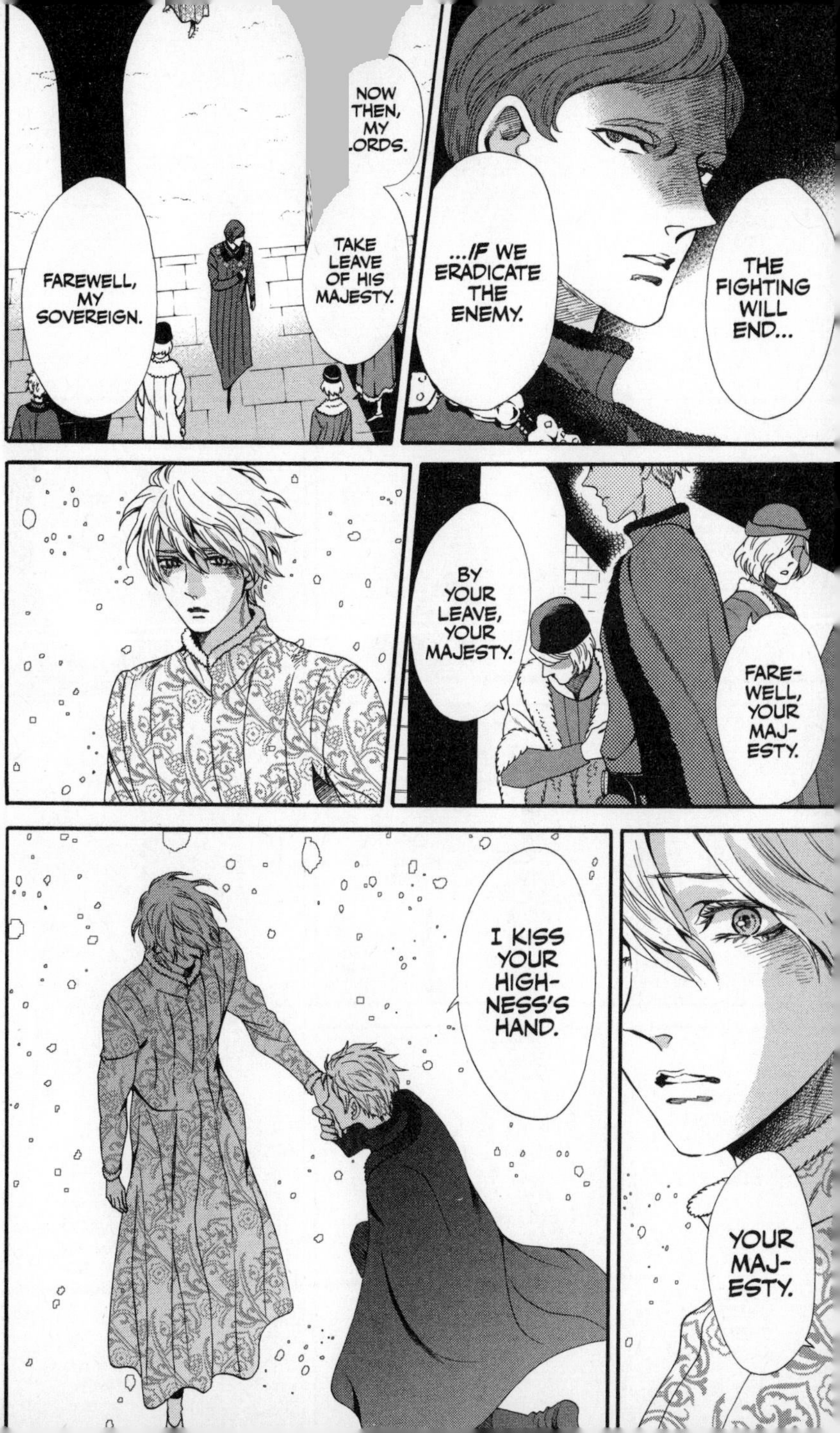
THE FIGHTING WILL END...
...IF WE ERADICATE THE ENEMY.
NOW THEN, MY .ORDS.
TAKE LEAVE OF HIS MAJESTY.
FAREWELL, MY SOVEREIGN.
FARE-WELL, YOUR MAJ-ESTY.
BY YOUR LEAVE, YOUR MAJESTY.
YOUR MAJ-ESTY.
I KISS YOUR HIGH-NESS'S HAND.

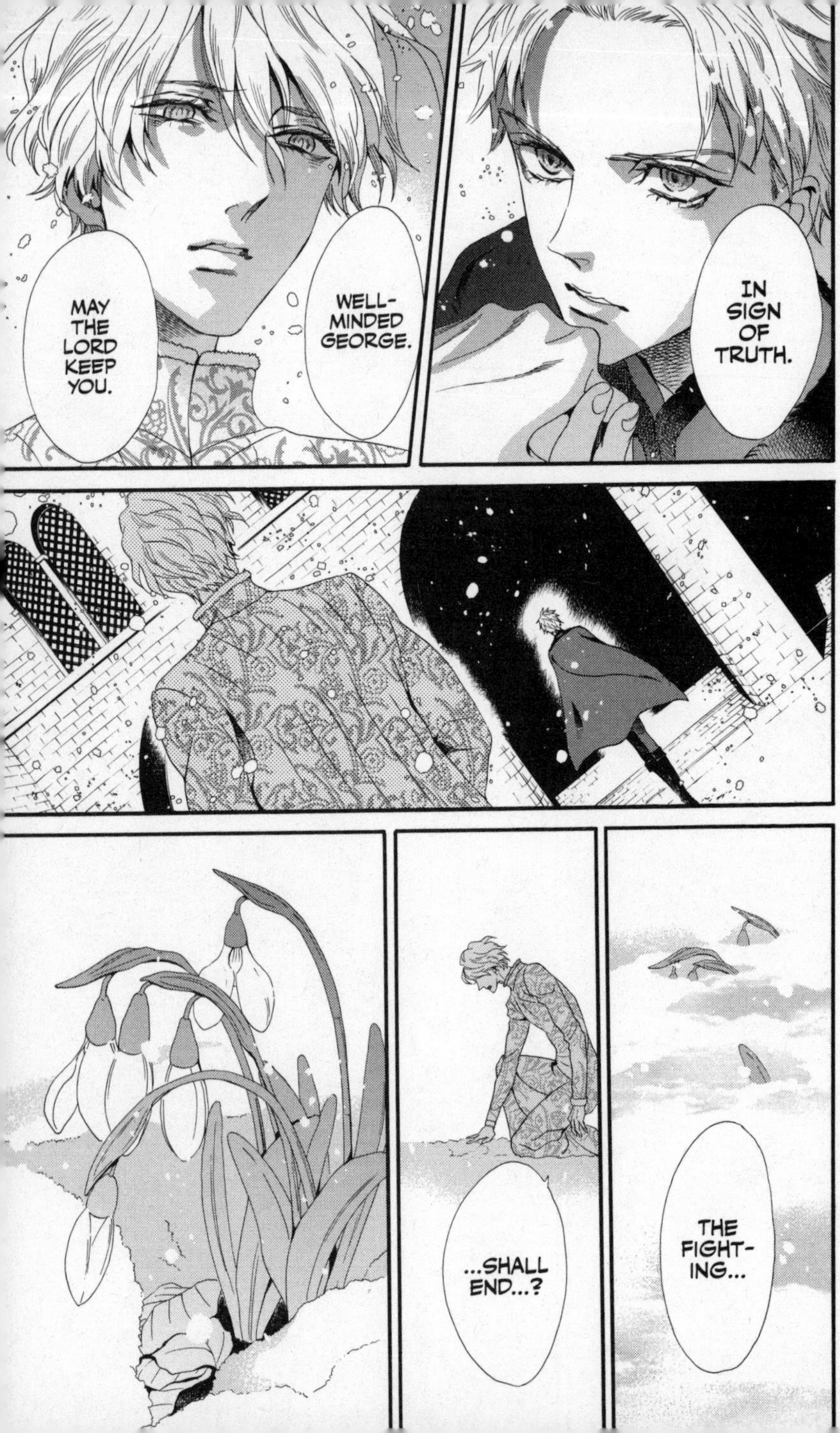
IN SIGN OF TRUTH.
WELL-MINDED GEORGE.
MAY THE LORD KEEP YOU.
THE FIGHT-ING...
...SHALL END...?

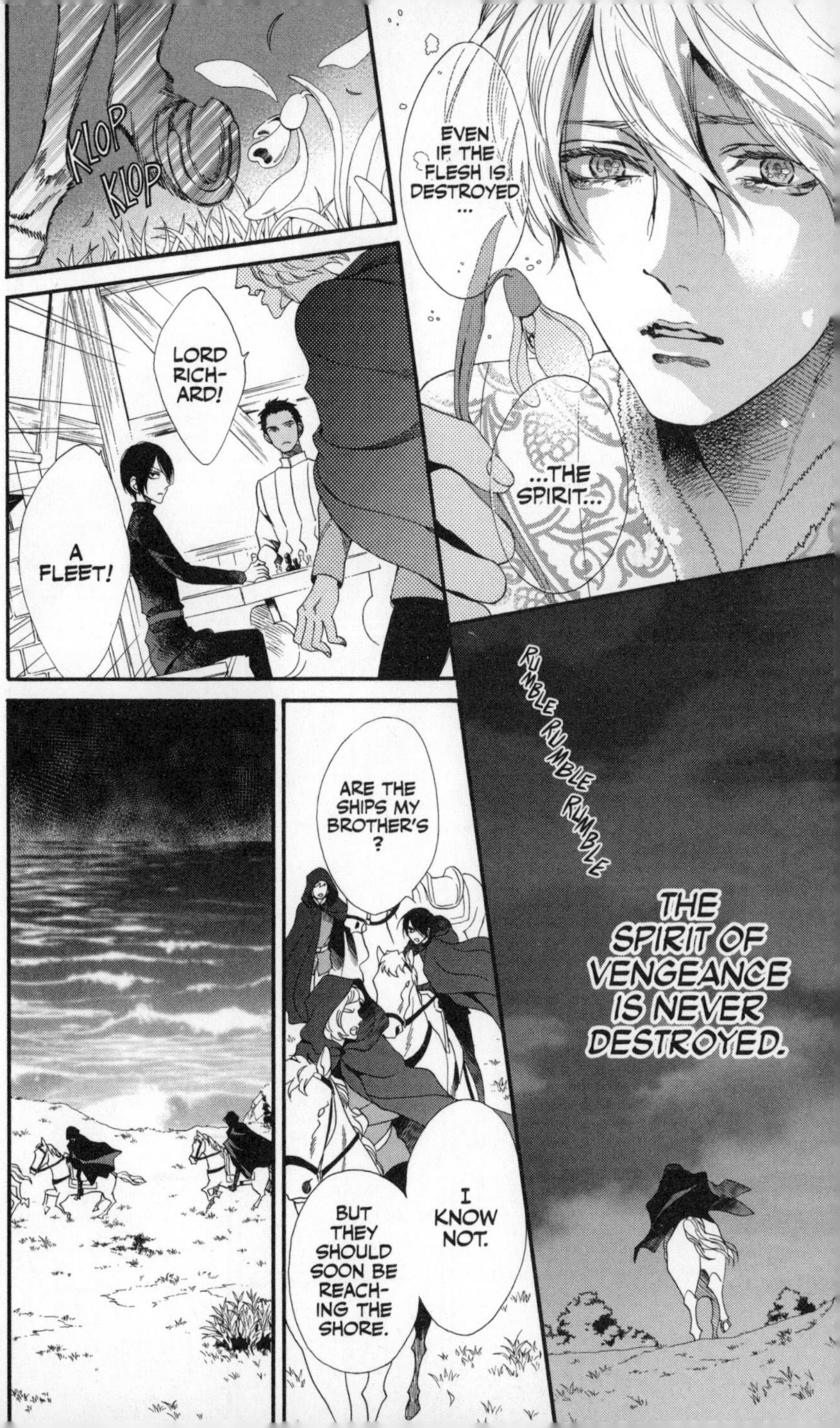
EVEN IF THE FLESH IS DESTROYED ...
...THE SPIRIT...
KLOP KLOP
LORD RICHARD!
A FLEET!
RUMBLE RUMBLE RUMBLE
THE SPIRIT OF VENGEANCE IS NEVER DESTROYED.
ARE THE SHIPS MY BROTHER'S?
I KNOW NOT.
BUT THEY SHOULD SOON BE REACHING THE SHORE.

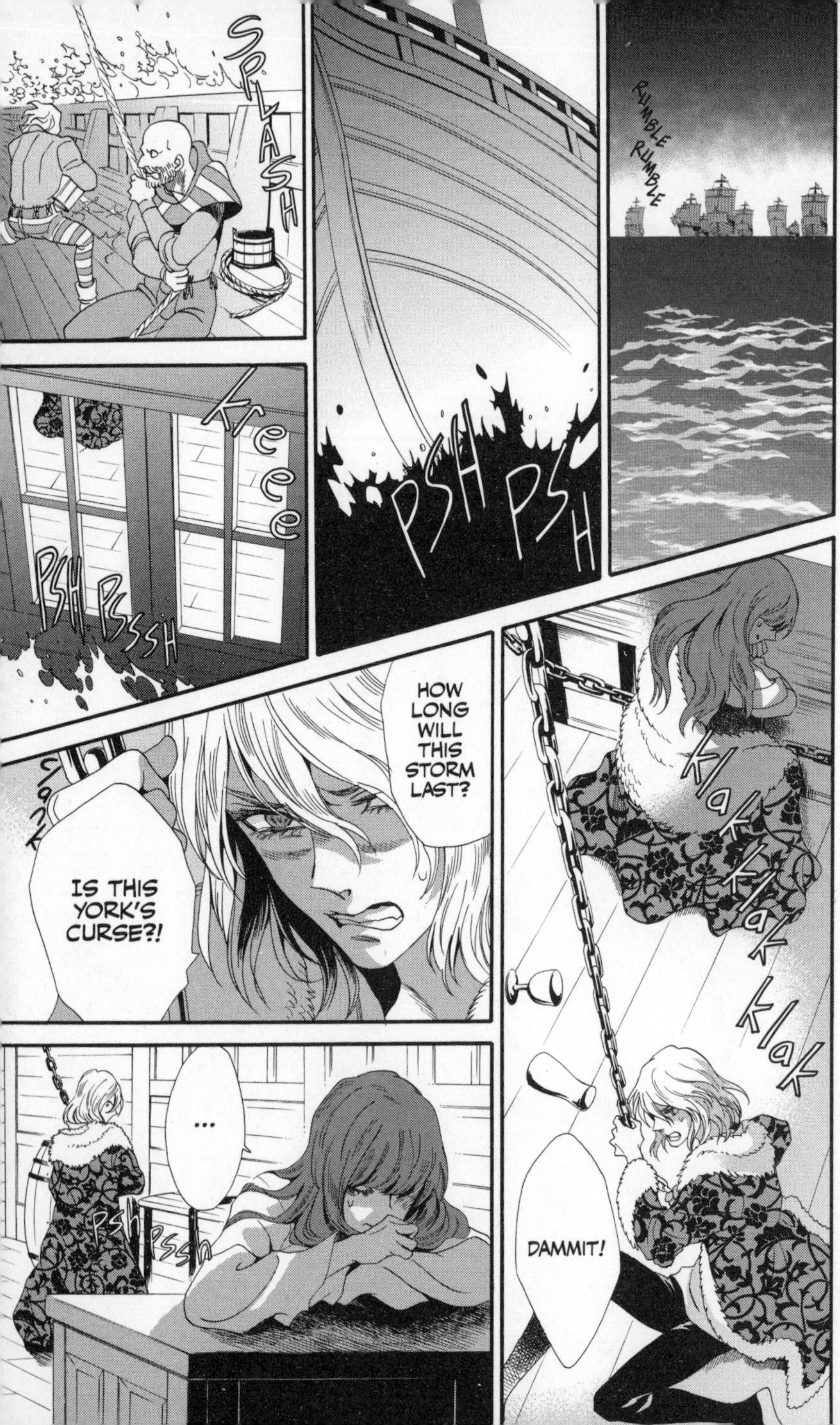
RUMBLE RUMBLE
PSH PSH
SPLASH
kreee
PSH PSSSH
klak klak klak klak
DAMMIT!
HOW LONG WILL THIS STORM LAST?
IS THIS YORK'S CURSE?!
clank
...
pshpsssh

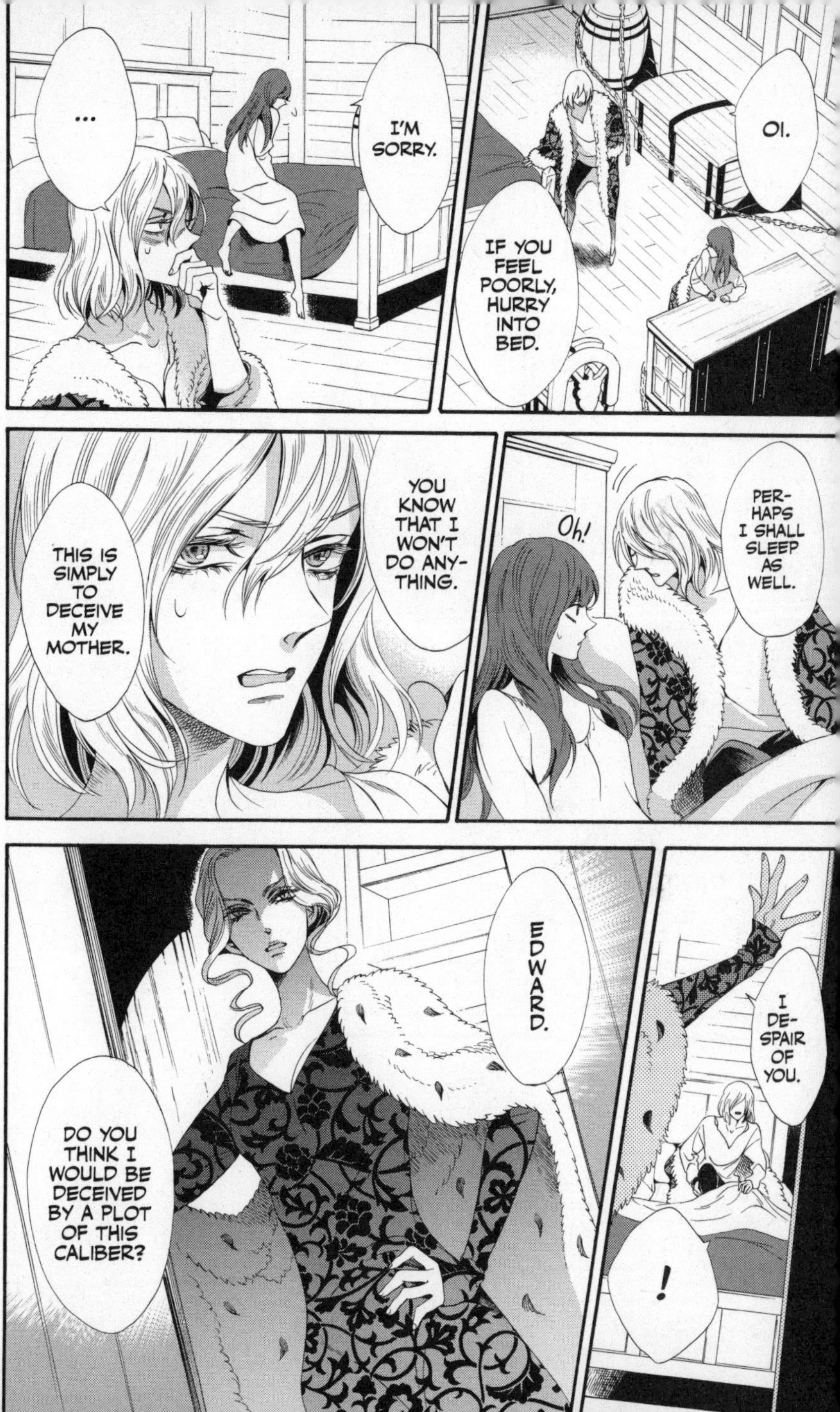
OI.
IF YOU FEEL POORLY, HURRY INTO BED.
I'M SORRY.
...
PERHAPS I SHALL SLEEP AS WELL.
Oh!
YOU KNOW THAT I WON'T DO ANYTHING.
THIS IS SIMPLY TO DECEIVE MY MOTHER.
I DESPAIR OF YOU.
!
EDWARD.
DO YOU THINK I WOULD BE DECEIVED BY A PLOT OF THIS CALIBER?

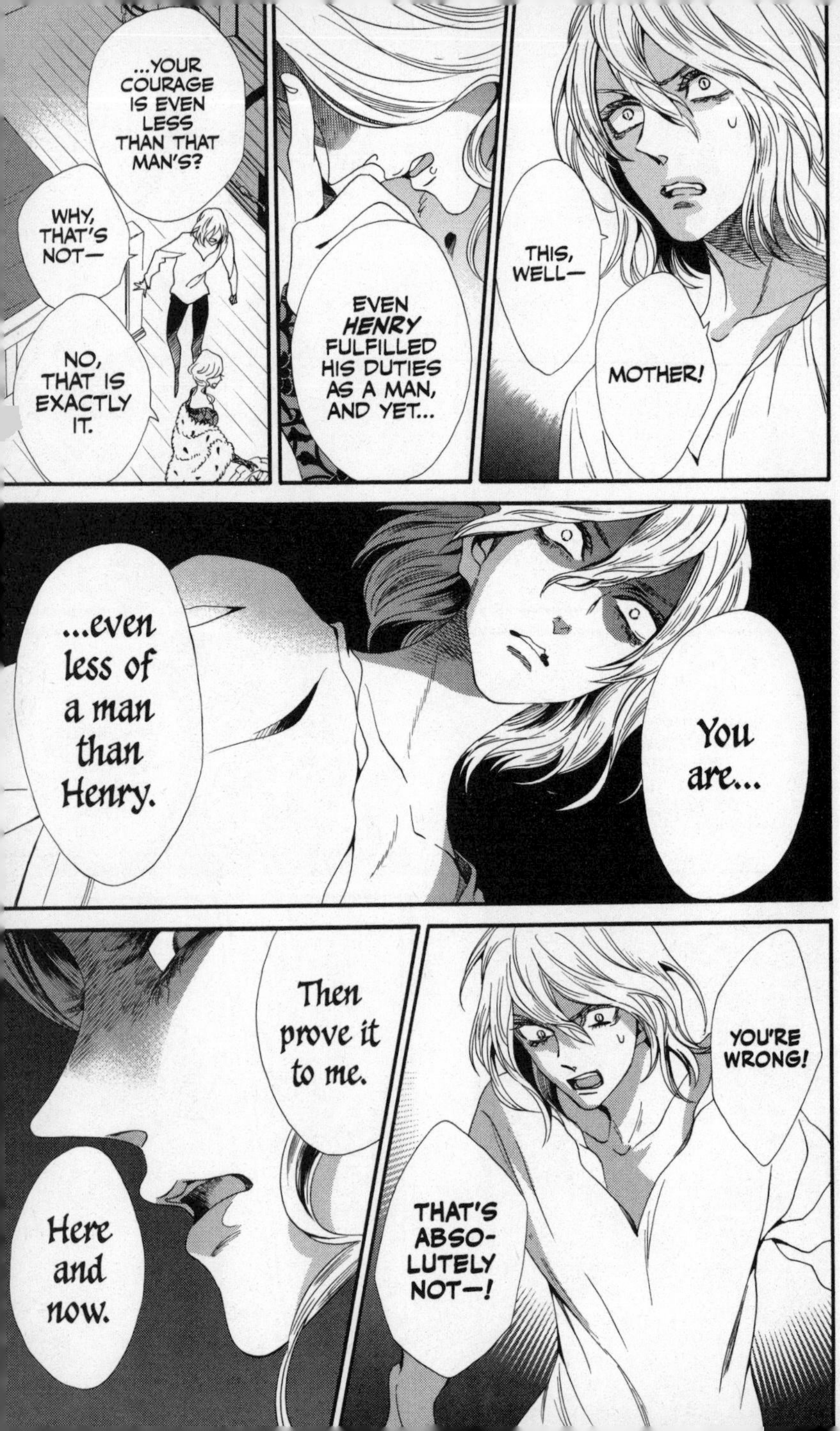
THIS, WELL—
MOTHER!
EVEN *HENRY* FULFILLED HIS DUTIES AS A MAN, AND YET...
...YOUR COURAGE IS EVEN LESS THAN THAT MAN'S?
WHY, THAT'S NOT—
NO, THAT IS EXACTLY IT.
You are...
...even less of a man than Henry.
YOU'RE WRONG!
THAT'S ABSO-LUTELY NOT—!
Then prove it to me.
Here and now.

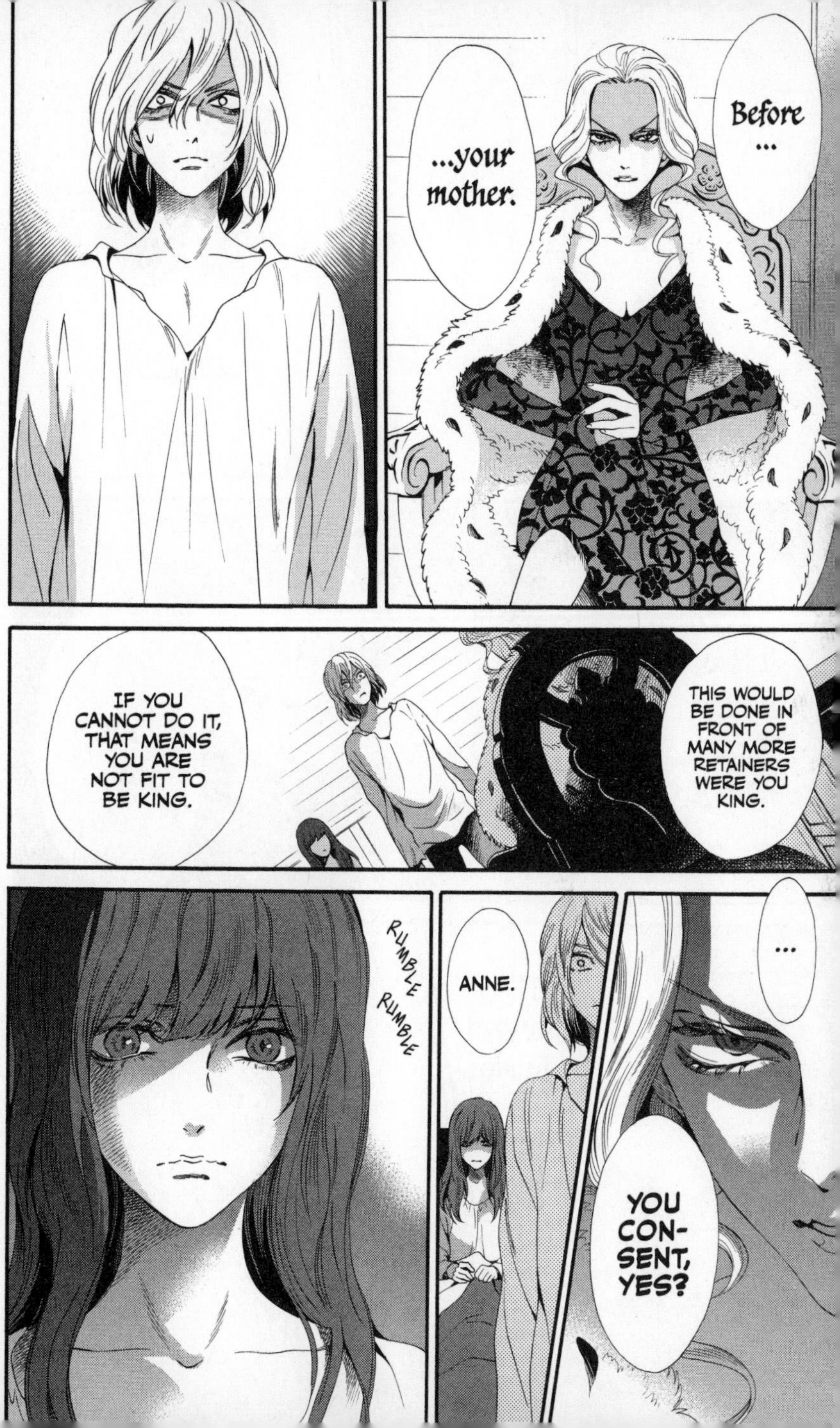
Before ...
...your mother.
THIS WOULD BE DONE IN FRONT OF MANY MORE RETAINERS WERE YOU KING.
IF YOU CANNOT DO IT, THAT MEANS YOU ARE NOT FIT TO BE KING.
...
YOU CON-SENT, YES?
ANNE.
RUMBLE RUMBLE

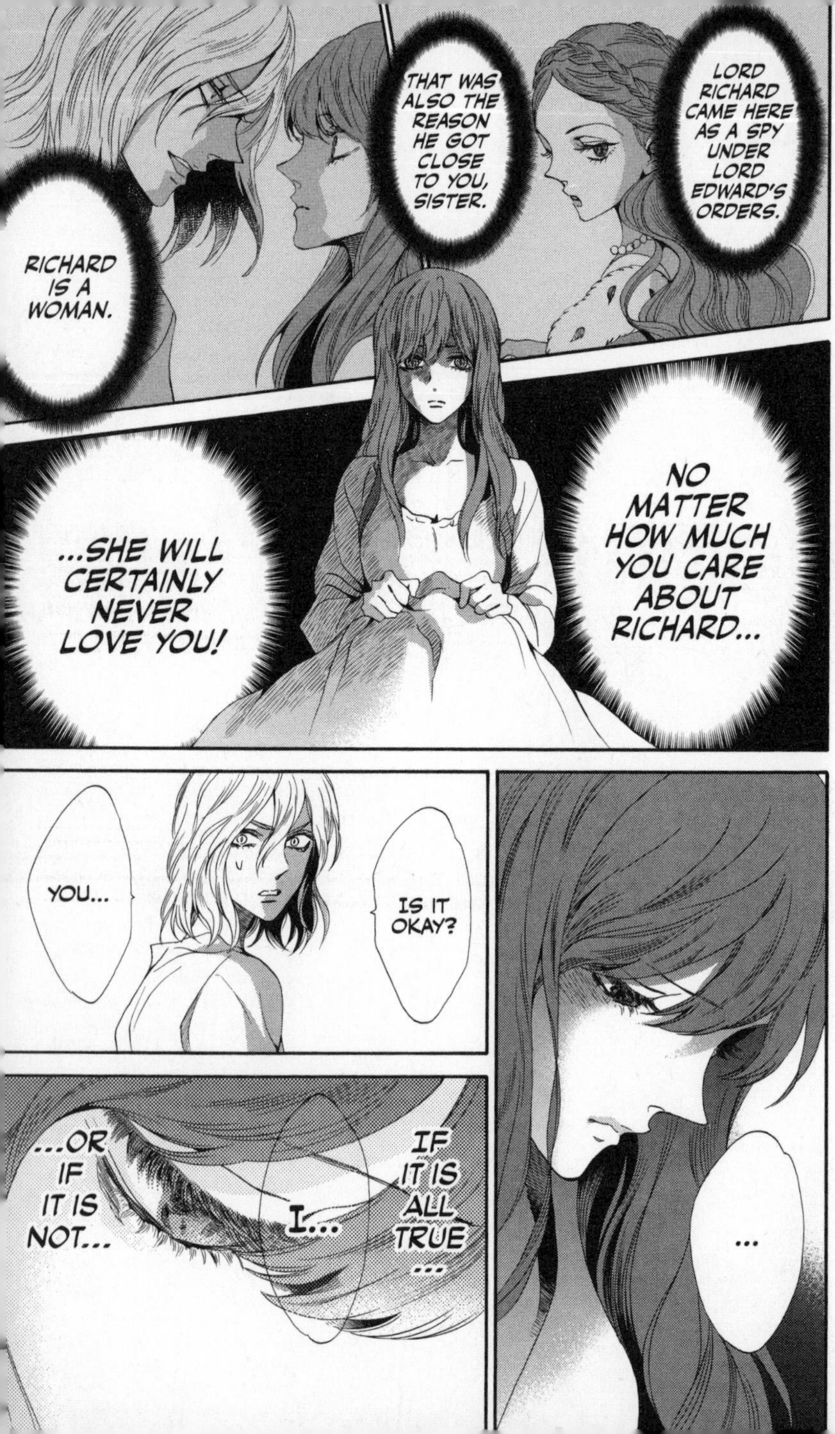
LORD RICHARD CAME HERE AS A SPY UNDER LORD EDWARD'S ORDERS.
THAT WAS ALSO THE REASON HE GOT CLOSE TO YOU, SISTER.
RICHARD IS A WOMAN.
NO MATTER HOW MUCH YOU CARE ABOUT RICHARD...
...SHE WILL CERTAINLY NEVER LOVE YOU!
...
IS IT OKAY?
YOU...
IF IT IS ALL TRUE ...
I...
...OR IF IT IS NOT...

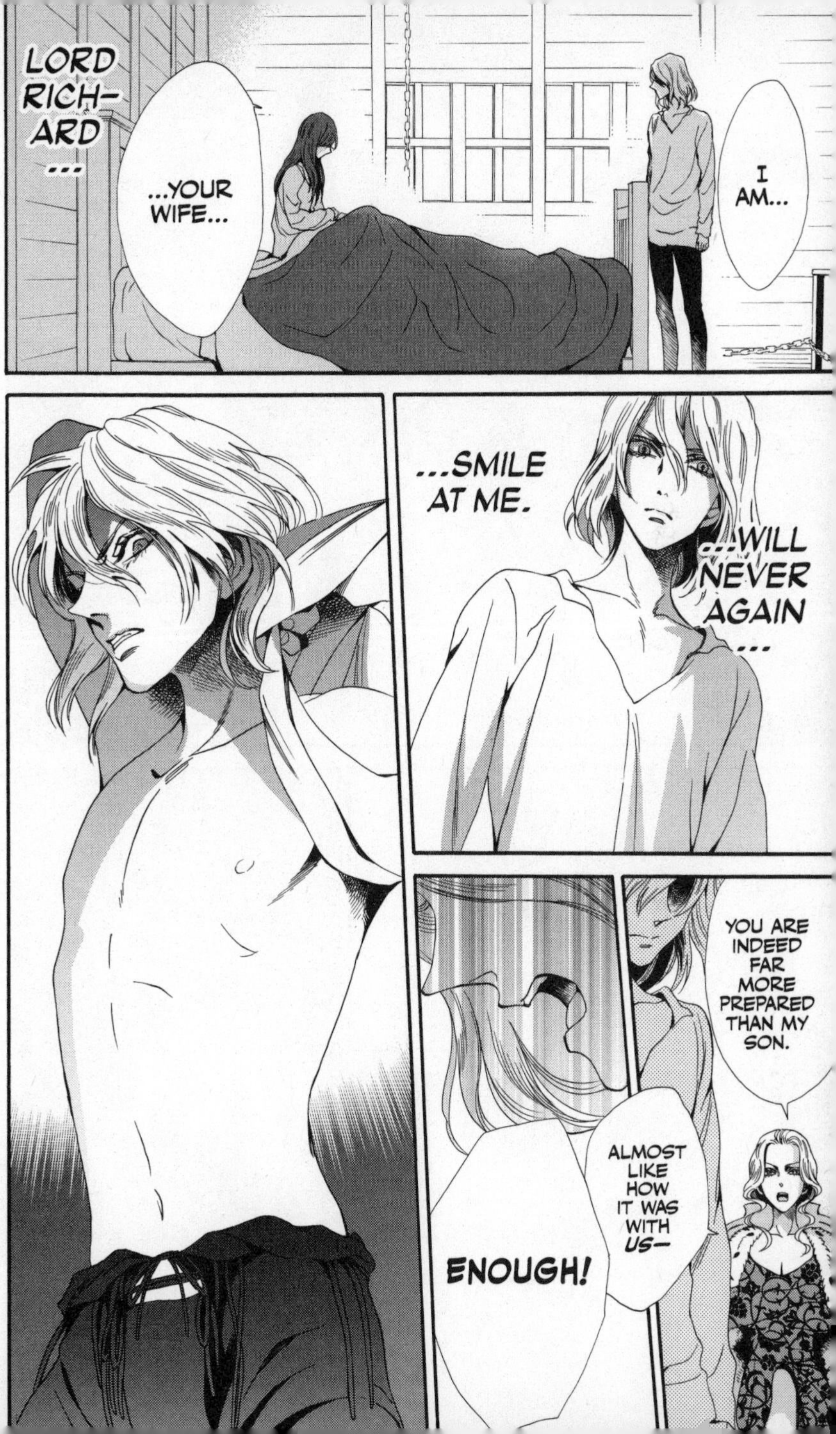
I AM...
...YOUR WIFE...
LORD RICH-ARD ...
...WILL NEVER AGAIN ...
...SMILE AT ME.
YOU ARE INDEED FAR MORE PREPARED THAN MY SON.
ALMOST LIKE HOW IT WAS WITH *US*—
ENOUGH!

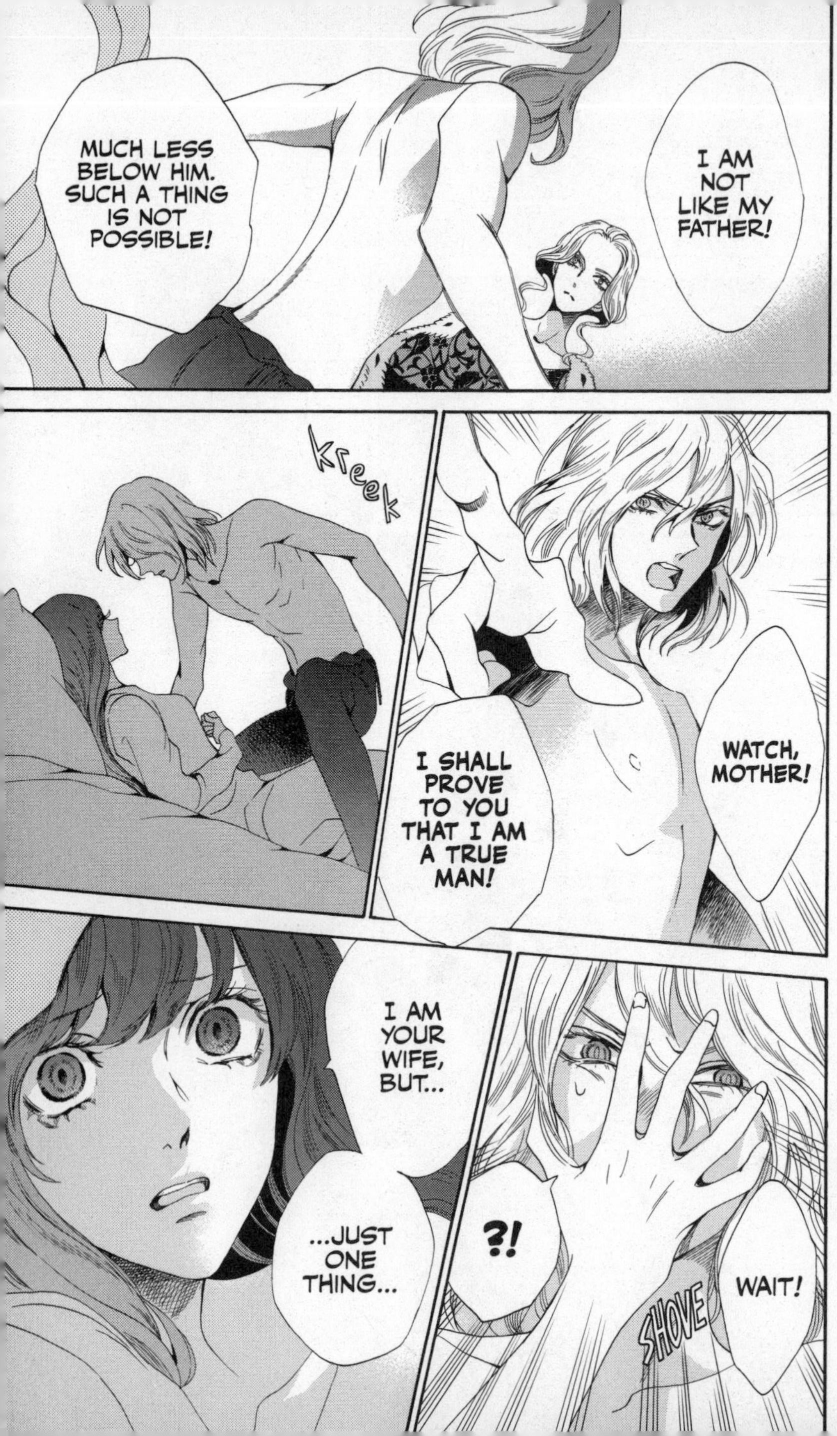
I AM NOT LIKE MY FATHER!
MUCH LESS BELOW HIM. SUCH A THING IS NOT POSSIBLE!
WATCH, MOTHER!
I SHALL PROVE TO YOU THAT I AM A TRUE MAN!
kreeek
WAIT!
?!
SHOVE
I AM YOUR WIFE, BUT...
...JUST ONE THING...

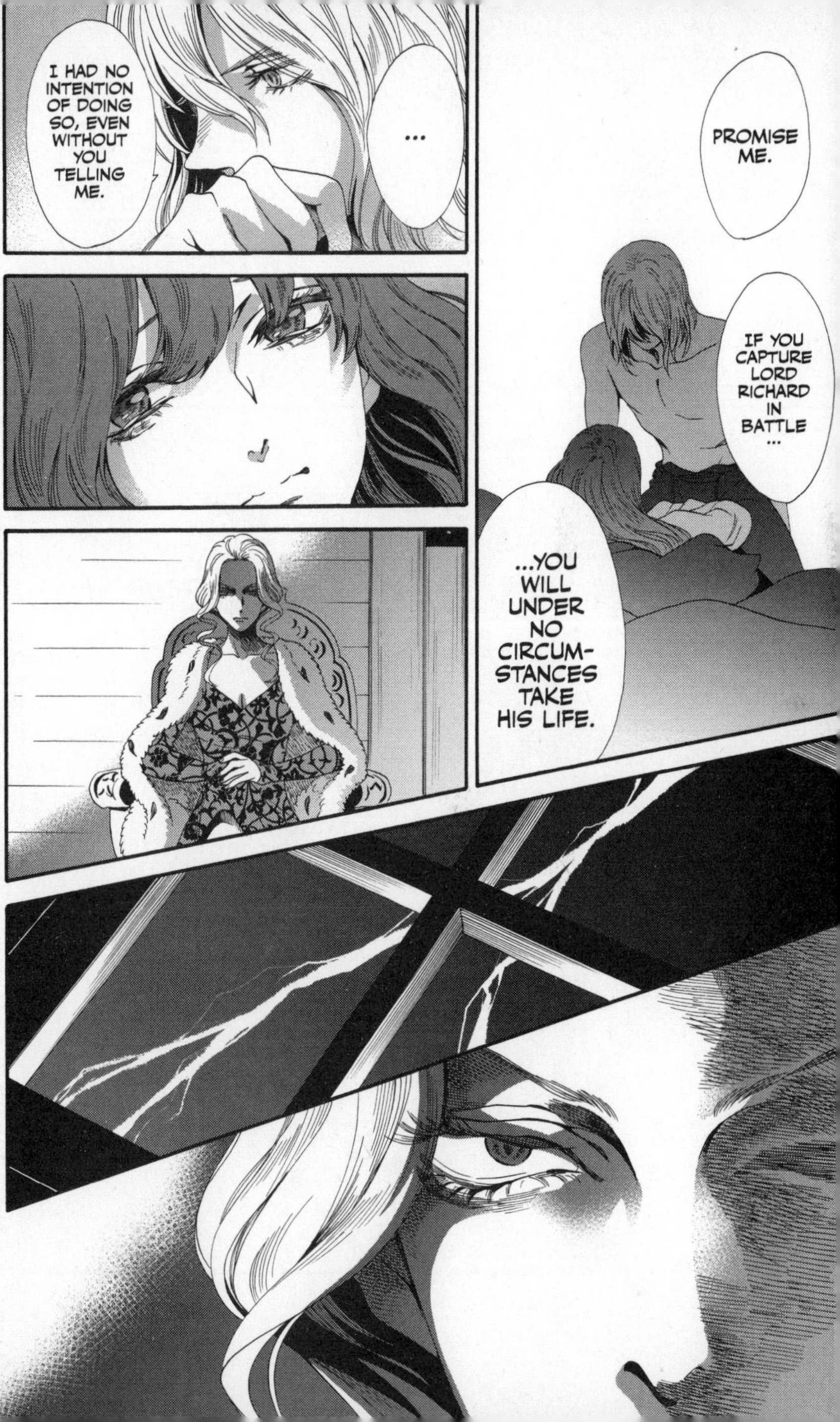

PROMISE ME.
IF YOU CAPTURE LORD RICHARD IN BATTLE ...
...YOU WILL UNDER NO CIRCUM-STANCES TAKE HIS LIFE.
...
I HAD NO INTENTION OF DOING SO, EVEN WITHOUT YOU TELLING ME.

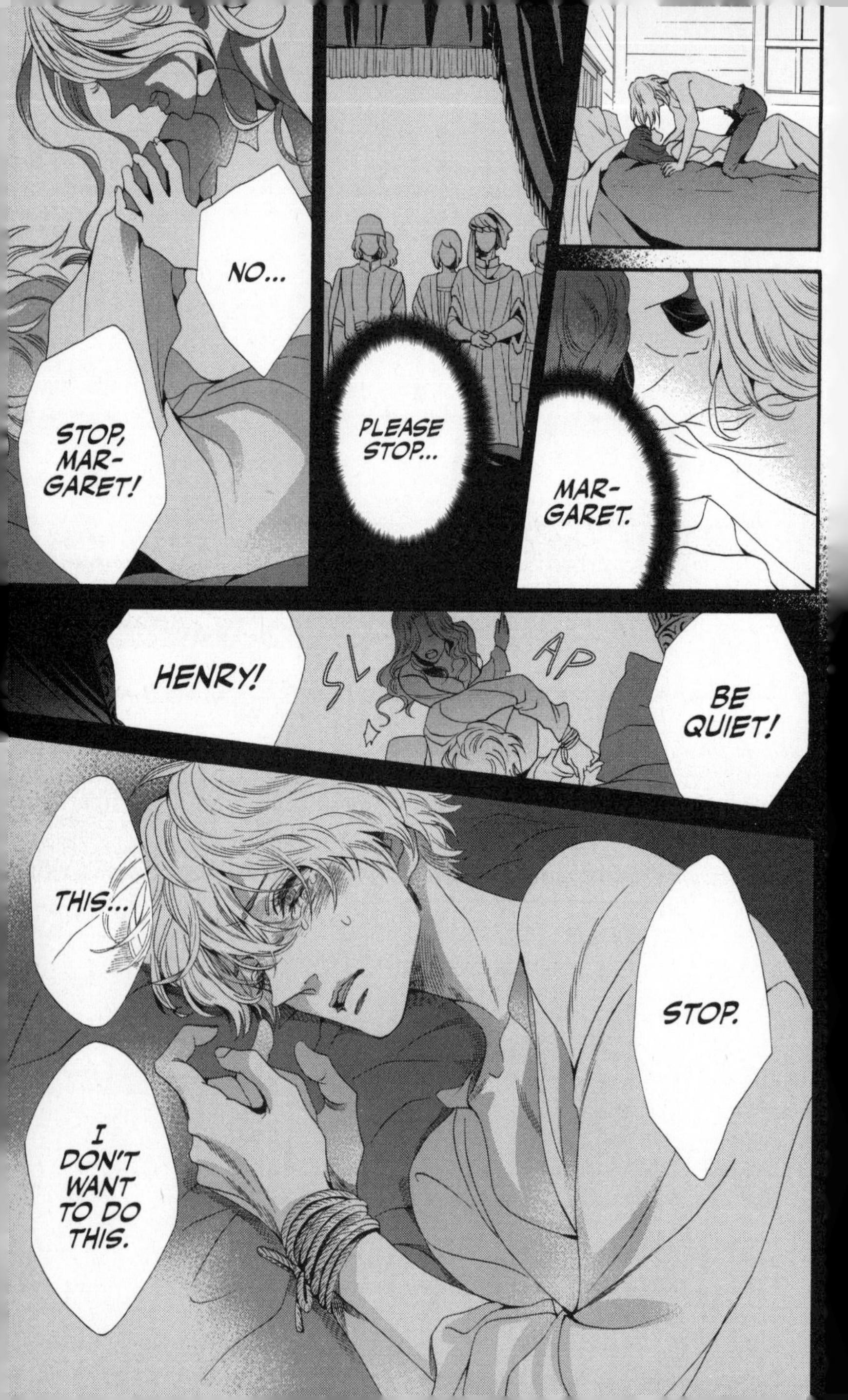
MAR-GARET.
PLEASE STOP...
NO...
STOP, MAR-GARET!
BE QUIET!
SLAP
HENRY!
STOP.
THIS...
I DON'T WANT TO DO THIS.

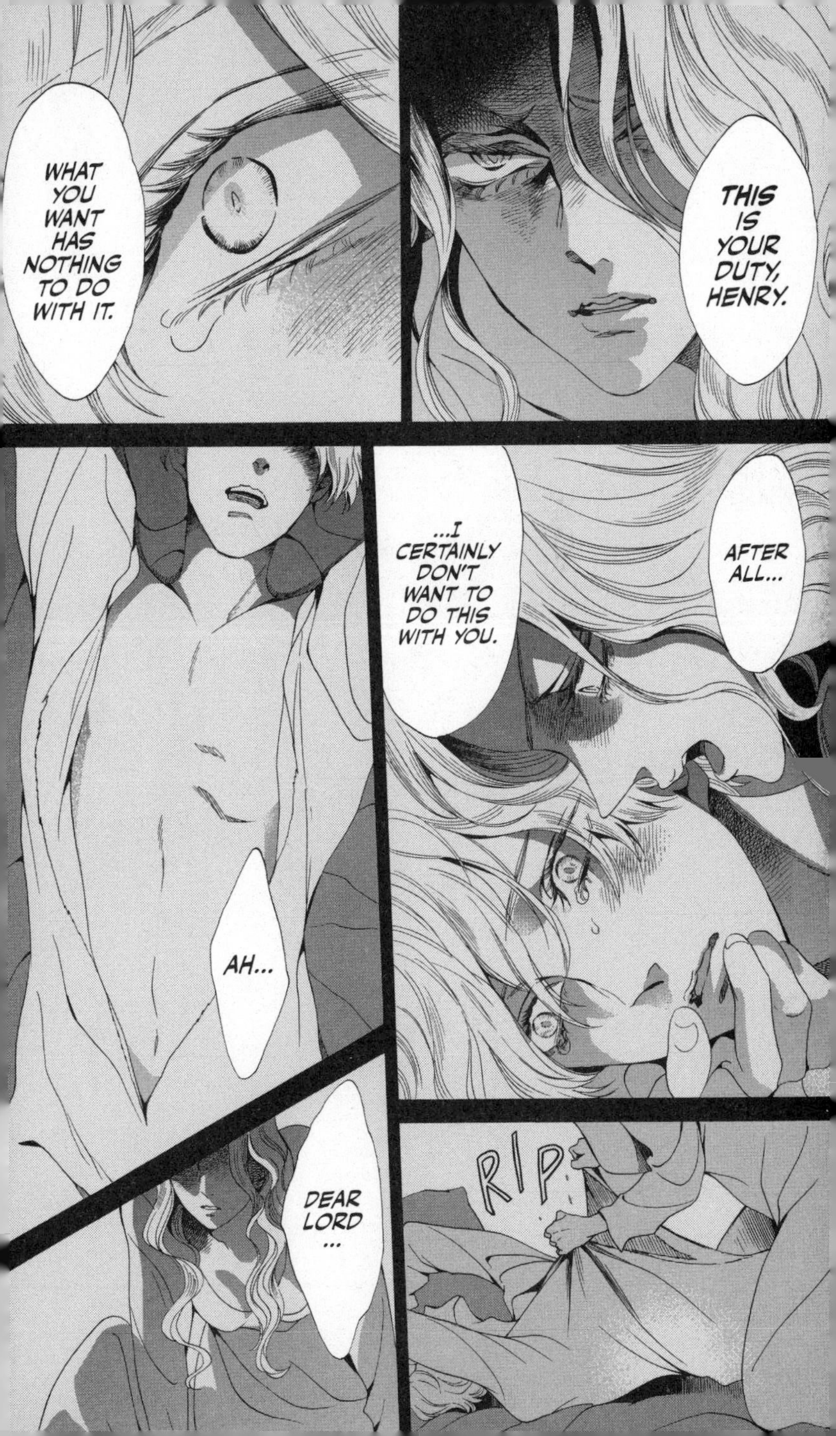
THIS IS YOUR DUTY, HENRY.
WHAT YOU WANT HAS NOTHING TO DO WITH IT.
AFTER ALL...
...I CERTAINLY DON'T WANT TO DO THIS WITH YOU.
RIP
AH...
DEAR LORD ...

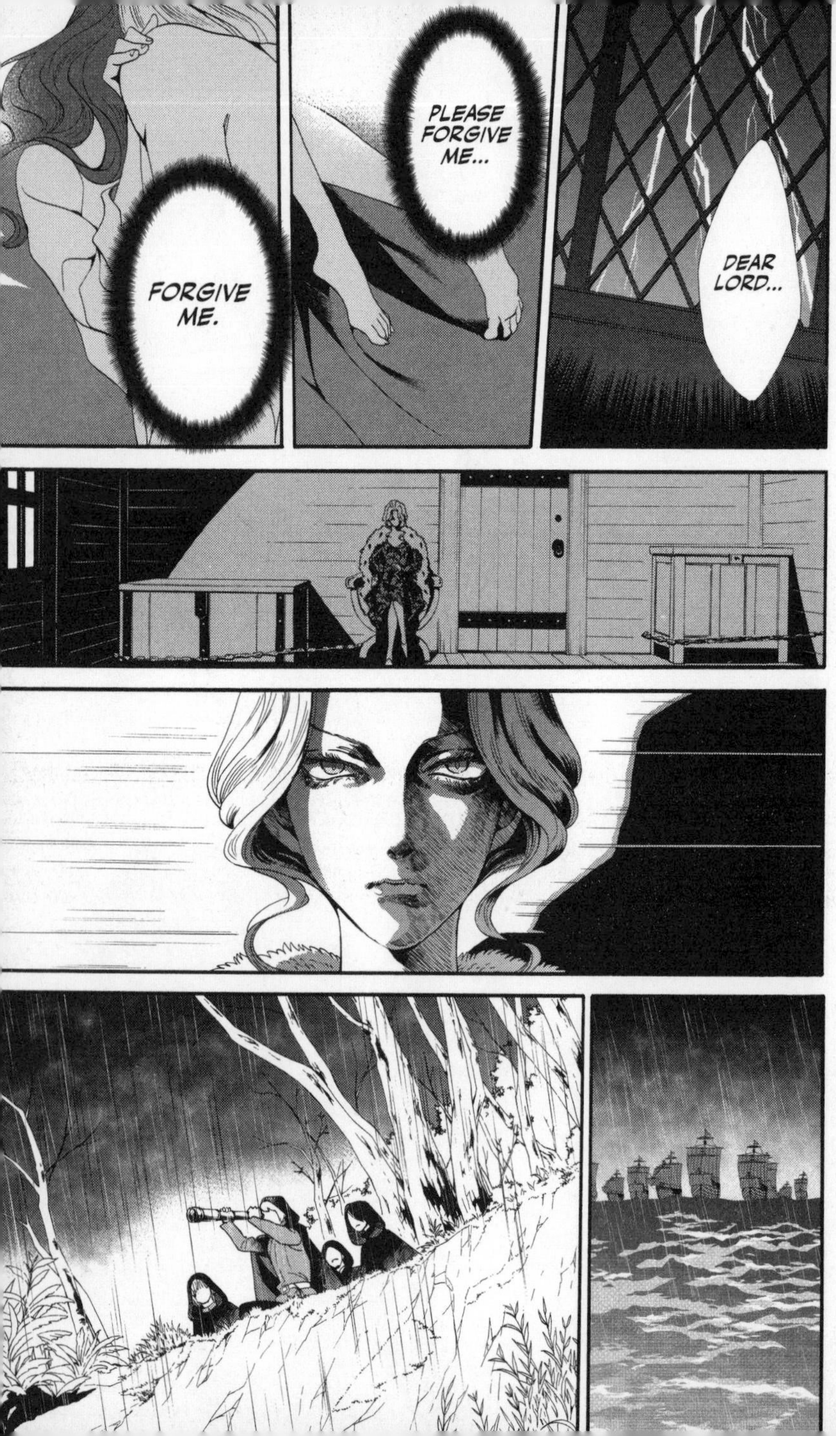
DEAR LORD...
PLEASE FORGIVE ME...
FORGIVE ME.

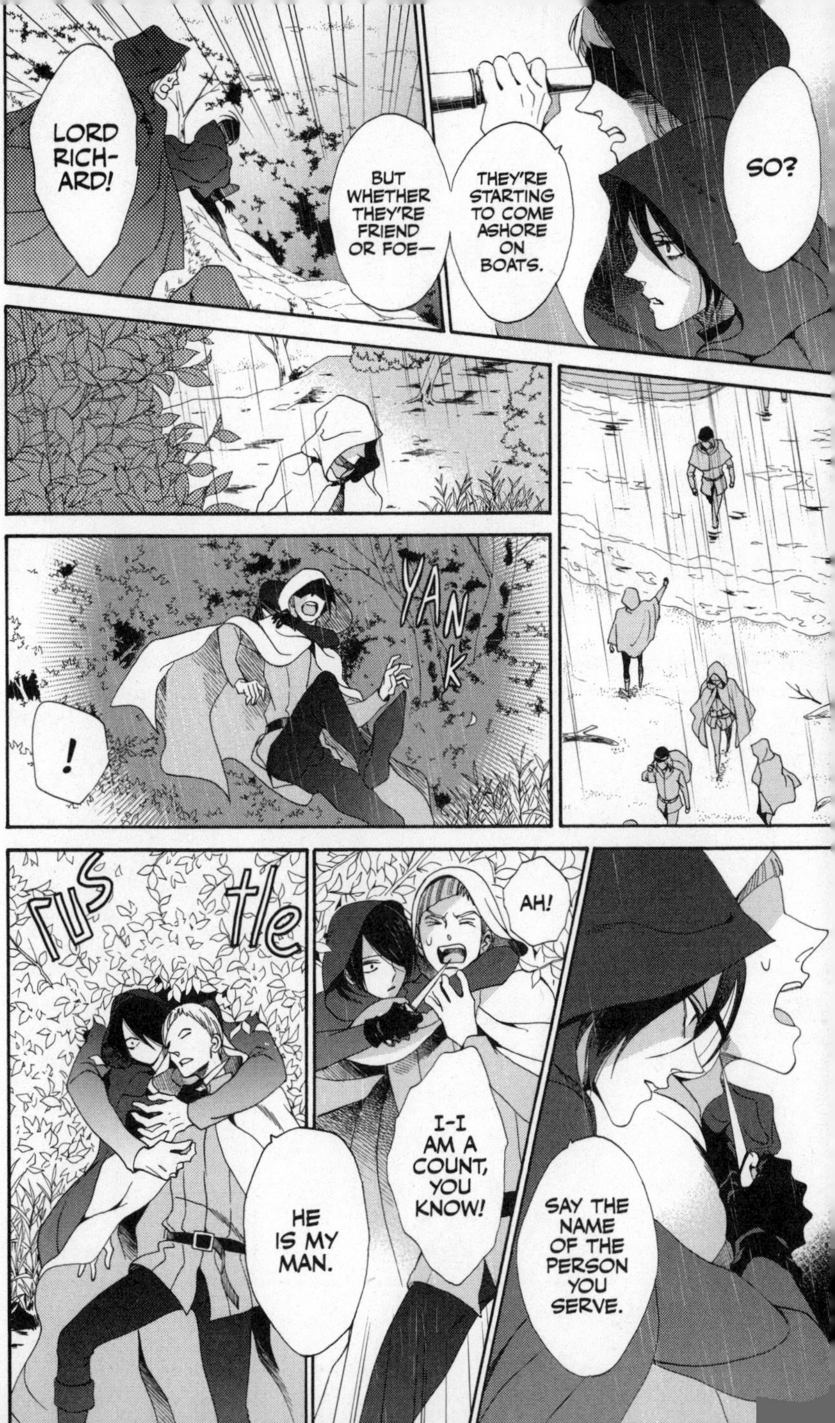
SO?
THEY'RE STARTING TO COME ASHORE ON BOATS.
BUT WHETHER THEY'RE FRIEND OR FOE—
LORD RICHARD!
YANK
!
SAY THE NAME OF THE PERSON YOU SERVE.
AH!
I-I AM A COUNT, YOU KNOW!
HE IS MY MAN.
rustle

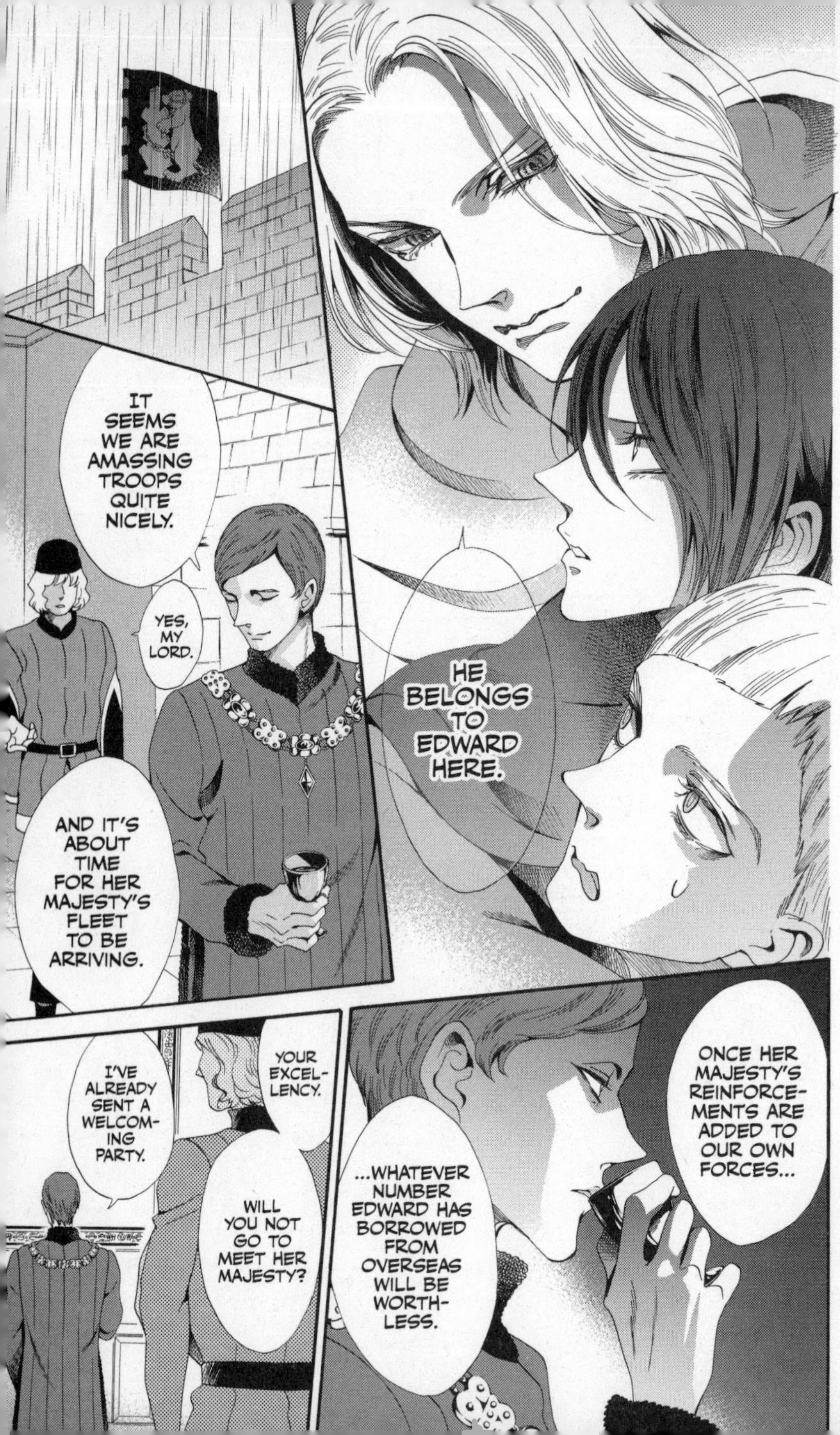
HE BELONGS TO EDWARD HERE.
IT SEEMS WE ARE AMASSING TROOPS QUITE NICELY.
YES, MY LORD.
AND IT'S ABOUT TIME FOR HER MAJESTY'S FLEET TO BE ARRIVING.
ONCE HER MAJESTY'S REINFORCEMENTS ARE ADDED TO OUR OWN FORCES...
...WHATEVER NUMBER EDWARD HAS BORROWED FROM OVERSEAS WILL BE WORTHLESS.
YOUR EXCELLENCY.
WILL YOU NOT GO TO MEET HER MAJESTY?
I'VE ALREADY SENT A WELCOMING PARTY.

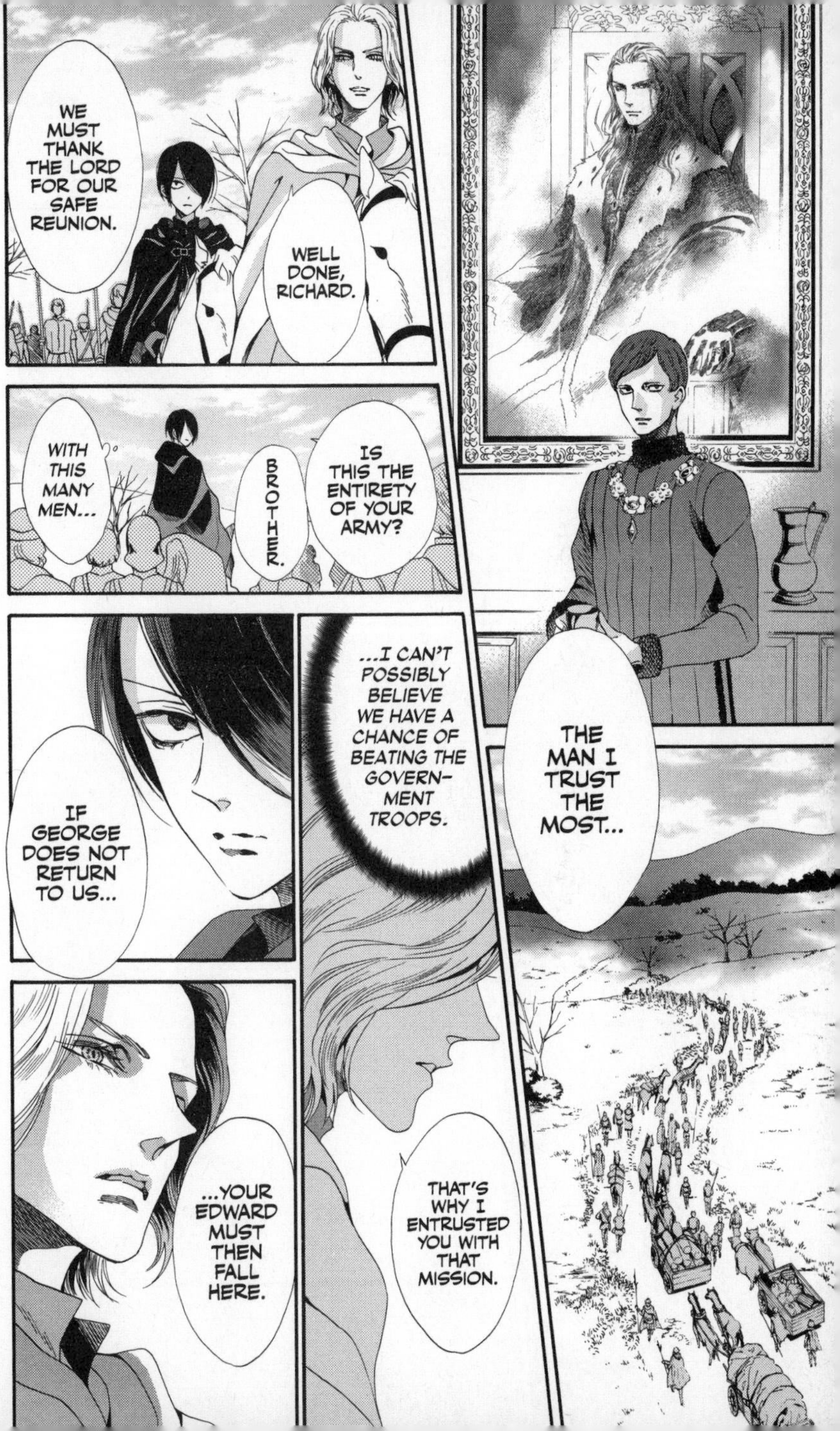
THE MAN I TRUST THE MOST...
WELL DONE, RICHARD.
WE MUST THANK THE LORD FOR OUR SAFE REUNION.
IS THIS THE ENTIRETY OF YOUR ARMY?
BROTHER.
WITH THIS MANY MEN...
...I CAN'T POSSIBLY BELIEVE WE HAVE A CHANCE OF BEATING THE GOVERN-MENT TROOPS.
IF GEORGE DOES NOT RETURN TO US...
THAT'S WHY I ENTRUSTED YOU WITH THAT MISSION.
...YOUR EDWARD MUST THEN FALL HERE.

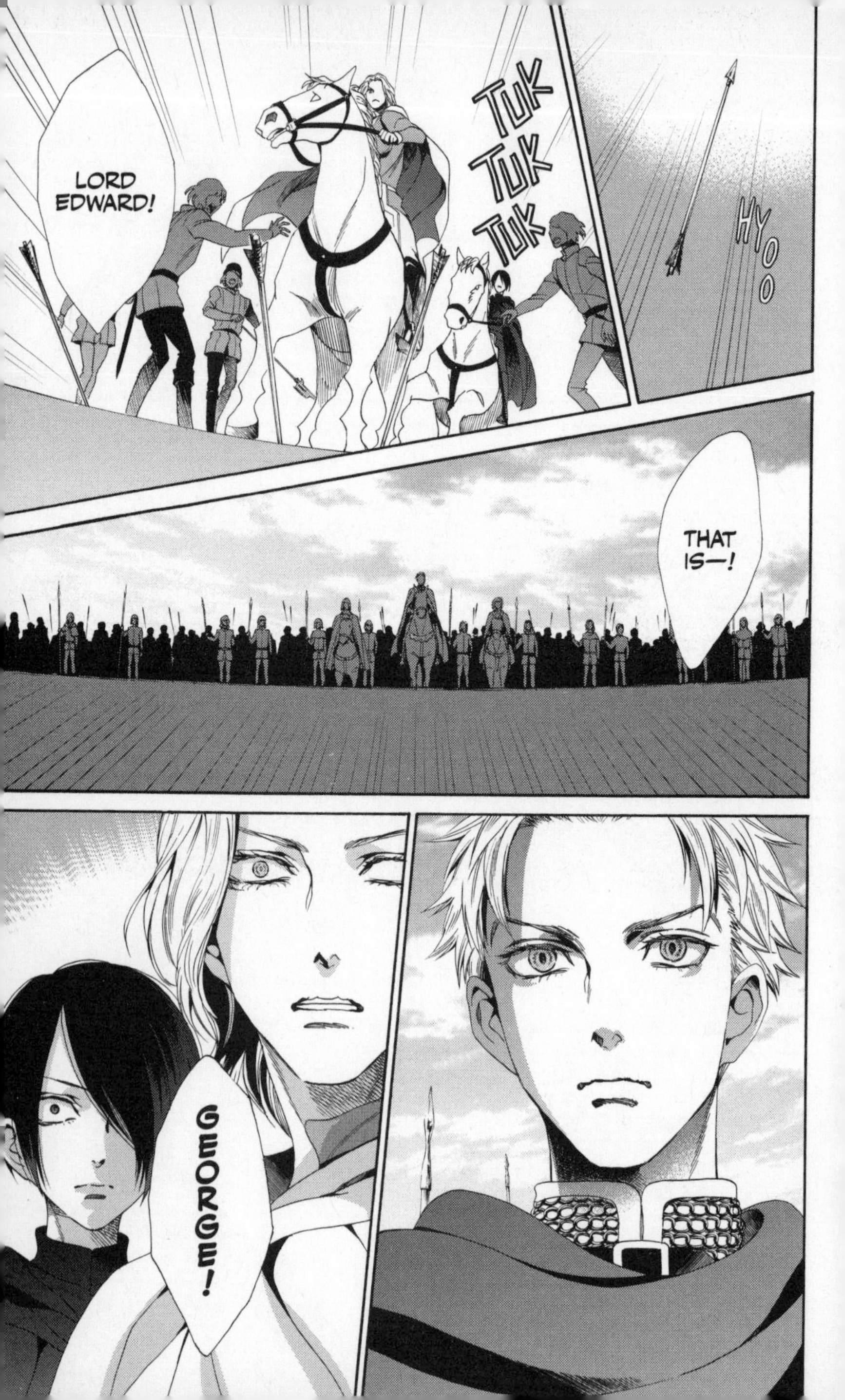
HYOO
TUK TUK TUK
LORD EDWARD!
THAT IS—!
GEORGE!

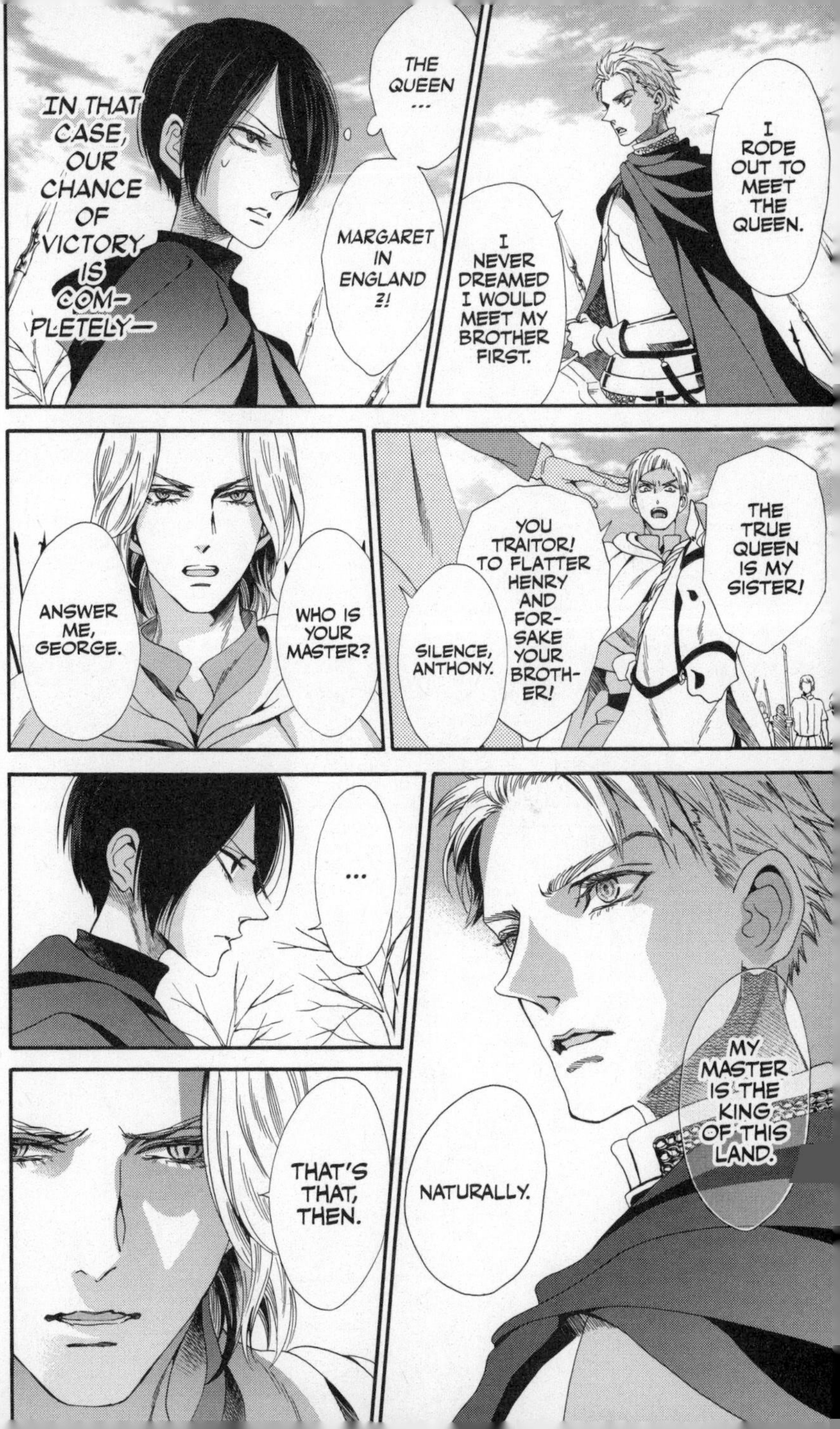
I RODE OUT TO MEET THE QUEEN.
I NEVER DREAMED I WOULD MEET MY BROTHER FIRST.
THE QUEEN...
MARGARET IN ENGLAND?!
IN THAT CASE, OUR CHANCE OF VICTORY IS COMPLETELY—
THE TRUE QUEEN IS MY SISTER!
YOU TRAITOR! TO FLATTER HENRY AND FORSAKE YOUR BROTHER!
SILENCE, ANTHONY.
WHO IS YOUR MASTER?
ANSWER ME, GEORGE.
MY MASTER IS THE KING OF THIS LAND.
NATURALLY.
...
THAT'S THAT, THEN.

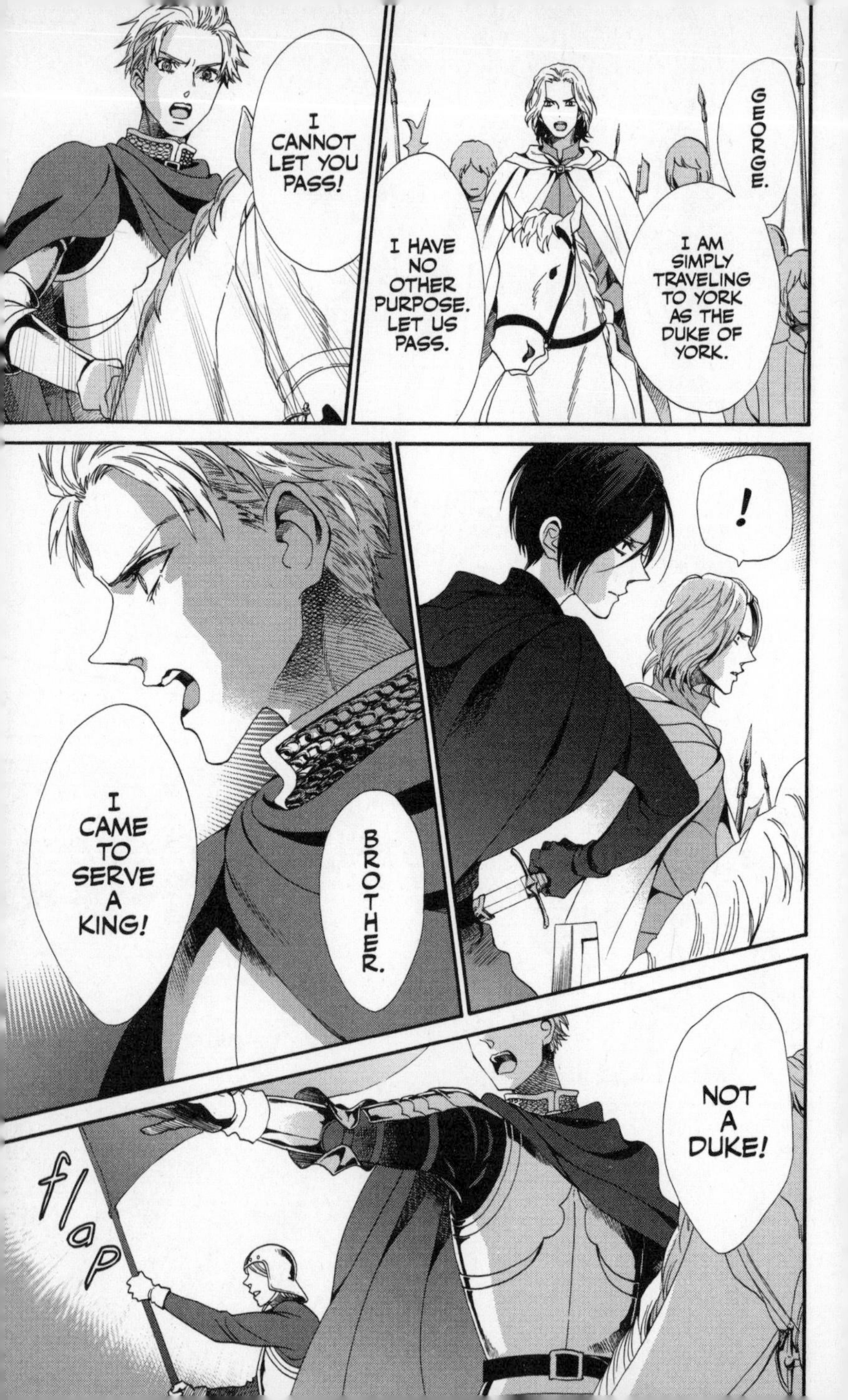
GEORGE.
I AM SIMPLY TRAVELING TO YORK AS THE DUKE OF YORK.
I HAVE NO OTHER PURPOSE. LET US PASS.
I CANNOT LET YOU PASS!
!
BROTHER.
I CAME TO SERVE A KING!
NOT A DUKE!
flap

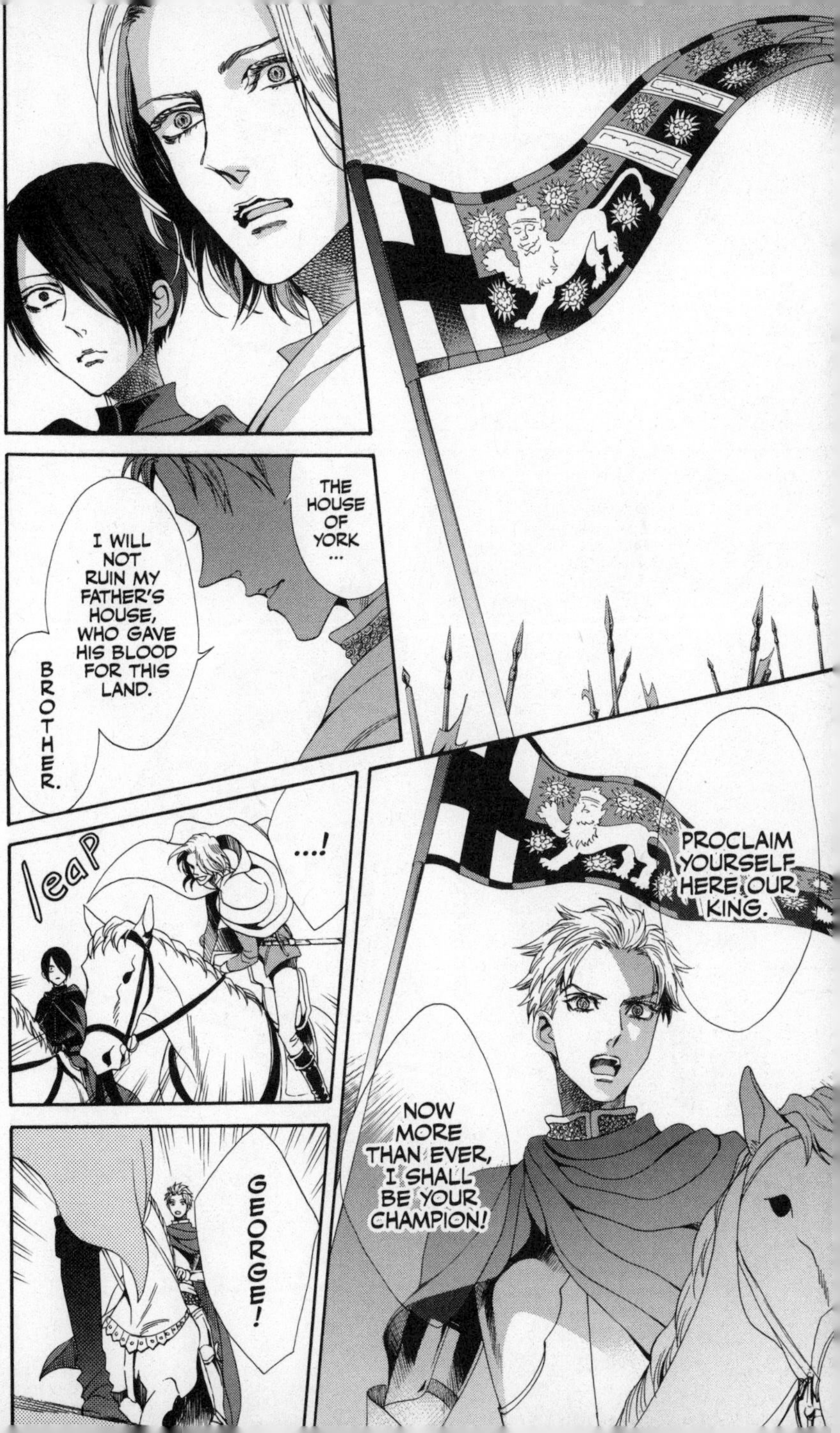
THE HOUSE OF YORK...
I WILL NOT RUIN MY FATHER'S HOUSE, WHO GAVE HIS BLOOD FOR THIS LAND.
BROTHER.
PROCLAIM YOURSELF HERE OUR KING.
NOW MORE THAN EVER, I SHALL BE YOUR CHAMPION!
leap
...!
GEORGE!

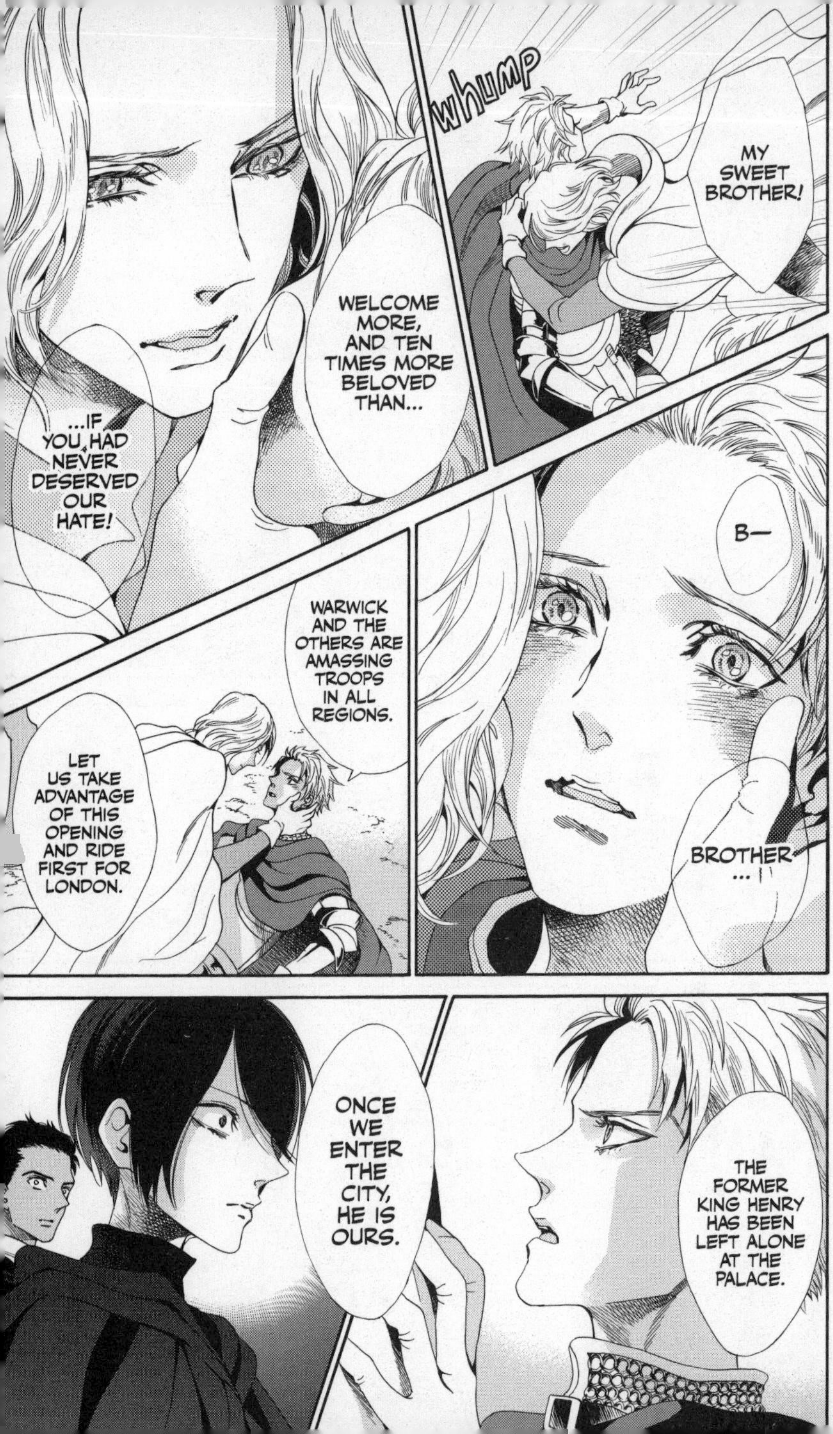
WHUMP
MY SWEET BROTHER!
WELCOME MORE, AND TEN TIMES MORE BELOVED THAN...
...IF YOU HAD NEVER DESERVED OUR HATE!
B—
BROTHER...
WARWICK AND THE OTHERS ARE AMASSING TROOPS IN ALL REGIONS.
LET US TAKE ADVANTAGE OF THIS OPENING AND RIDE FIRST FOR LONDON.
THE FORMER KING HENRY HAS BEEN LEFT ALONE AT THE PALACE.
ONCE WE ENTER THE CITY, HE IS OURS.

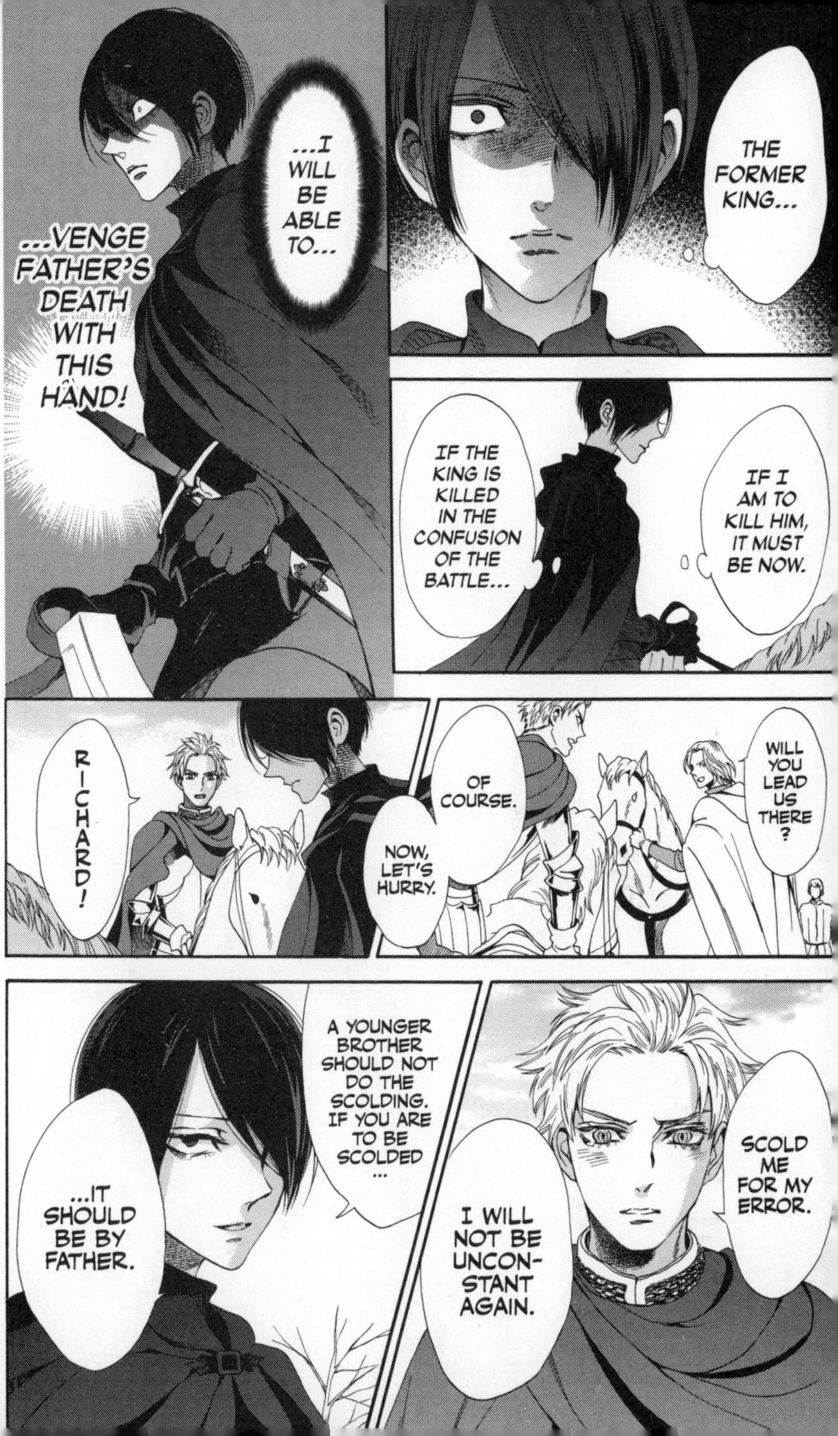
THE FORMER KING...
IF I AM TO KILL HIM, IT MUST BE NOW.
IF THE KING IS KILLED IN THE CONFUSION OF THE BATTLE...
...I WILL BE ABLE TO...
...VENGE FATHER'S DEATH WITH THIS HAND!
WILL YOU LEAD US THERE?
OF COURSE.
NOW, LET'S HURRY.
RICHARD!
SCOLD ME FOR MY ERROR.
I WILL NOT BE UNCON-STANT AGAIN.
A YOUNGER BROTHER SHOULD NOT DO THE SCOLDING. IF YOU ARE TO BE SCOLDED...
...IT SHOULD BE BY FATHER.

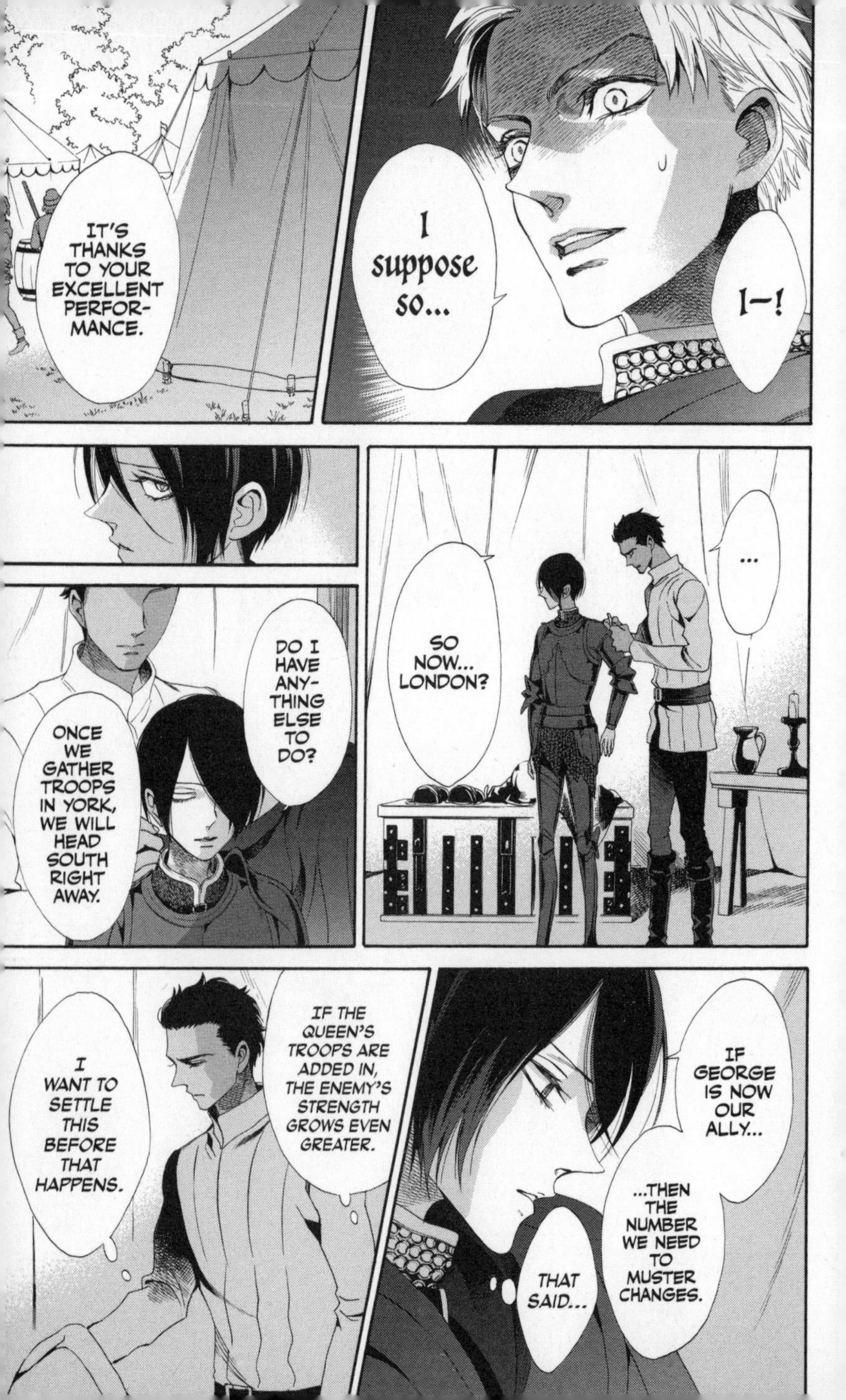
I—!
I suppose so...
IT'S THANKS TO YOUR EXCELLENT PERFORMANCE.
...
SO NOW... LONDON?
DO I HAVE ANYTHING ELSE TO DO?
ONCE WE GATHER TROOPS IN YORK, WE WILL HEAD SOUTH RIGHT AWAY.
IF GEORGE IS NOW OUR ALLY...
...THEN THE NUMBER WE NEED TO MUSTER CHANGES.
THAT SAID...
IF THE QUEEN'S TROOPS ARE ADDED IN, THE ENEMY'S STRENGTH GROWS EVEN GREATER.
I WANT TO SETTLE THIS BEFORE THAT HAPPENS.

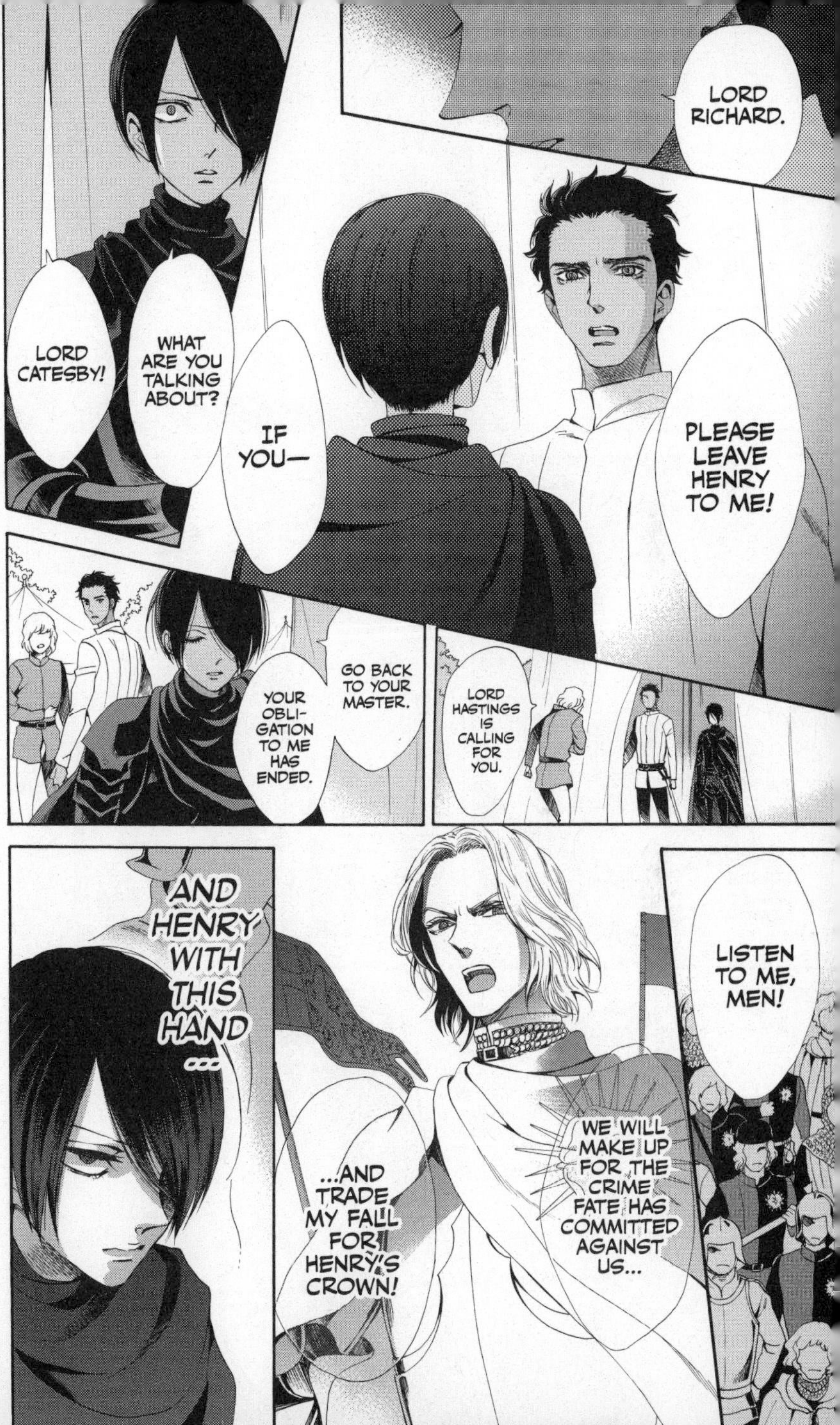
LORD RICHARD.
PLEASE LEAVE HENRY TO ME!
IF YOU—
WHAT ARE YOU TALKING ABOUT?
LORD CATESBY!
LORD HASTINGS IS CALLING FOR YOU.
GO BACK TO YOUR MASTER.
YOUR OBLIGATION TO ME HAS ENDED.
LISTEN TO ME, MEN!
WE WILL MAKE UP FOR THE CRIME FATE HAS COMMITTED AGAINST US...
...AND TRADE MY FALL FOR HENRY'S CROWN!
AND HENRY WITH THIS HAND...

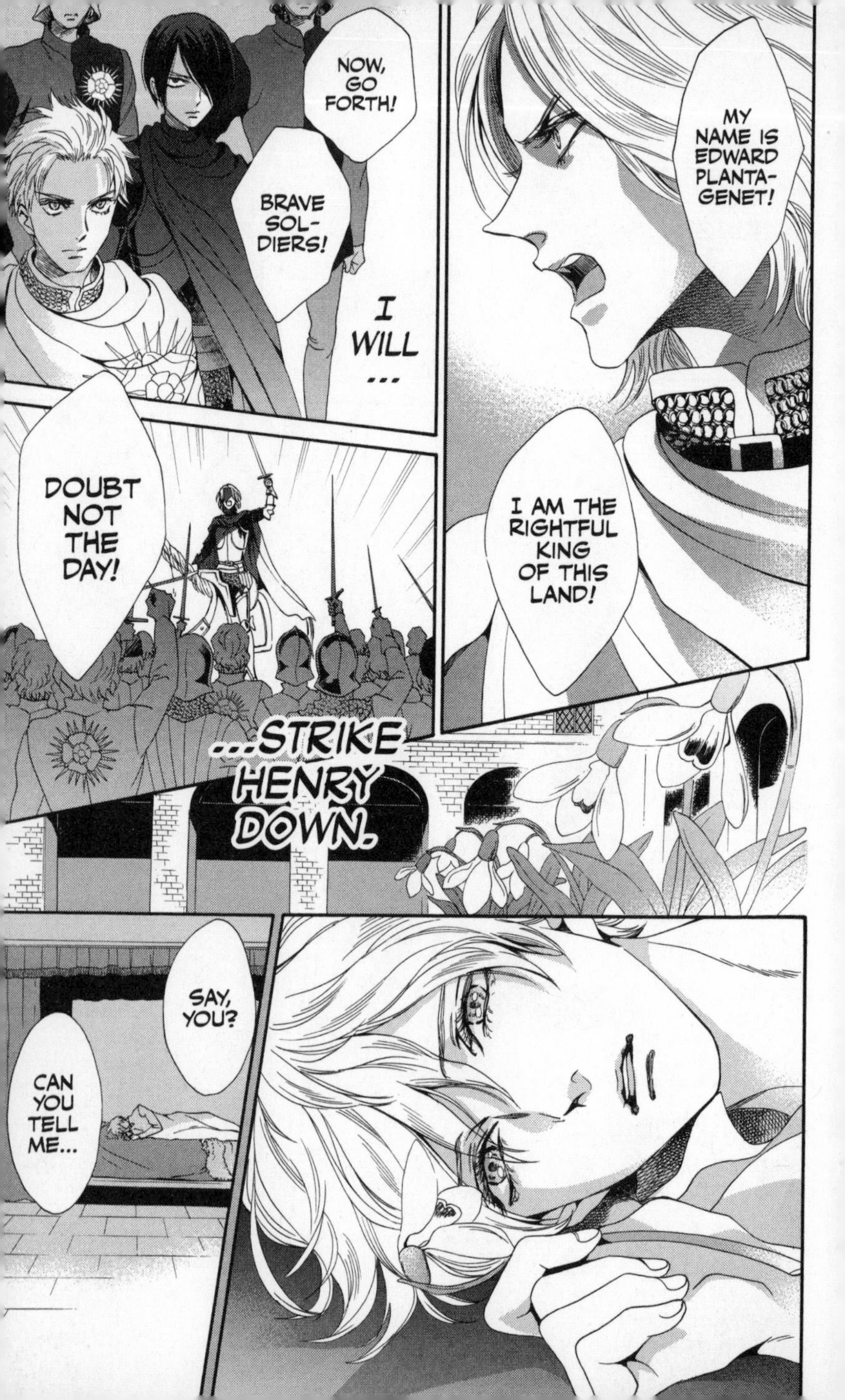
MY NAME IS EDWARD PLANTA-GENET!
I AM THE RIGHTFUL KING OF THIS LAND!
NOW, GO FORTH!
BRAVE SOL-DIERS!
I WILL ...
DOUBT NOT THE DAY!
...STRIKE HENRY DOWN.
SAY, YOU?
CAN YOU TELL ME...

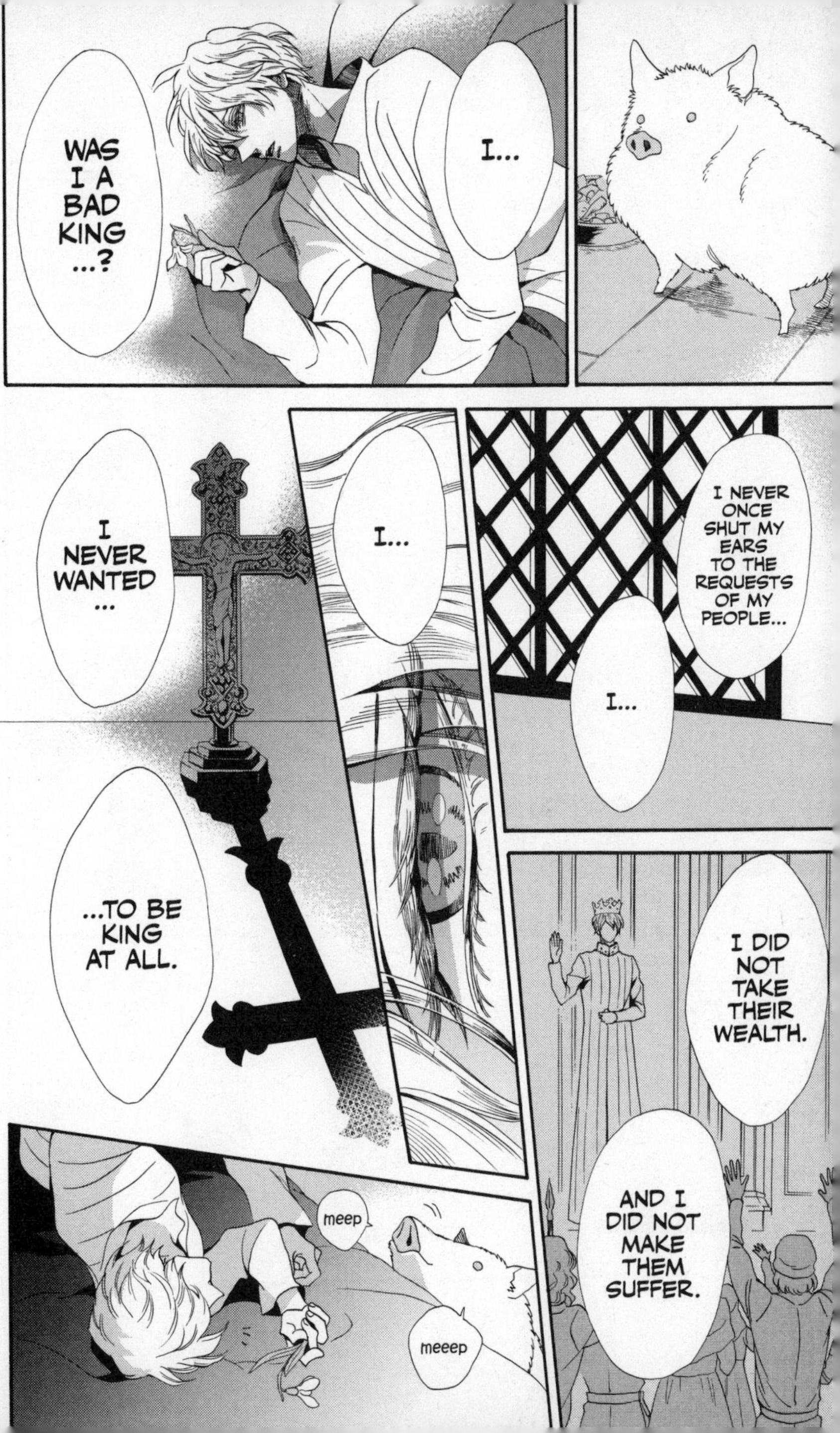
I...
WAS I A BAD KING...?
I NEVER ONCE SHUT MY EARS TO THE REQUESTS OF MY PEOPLE...
I...
I DID NOT TAKE THEIR WEALTH.
AND I DID NOT MAKE THEM SUFFER.
I...
I NEVER WANTED...
...TO BE KING AT ALL.
meep
meeep

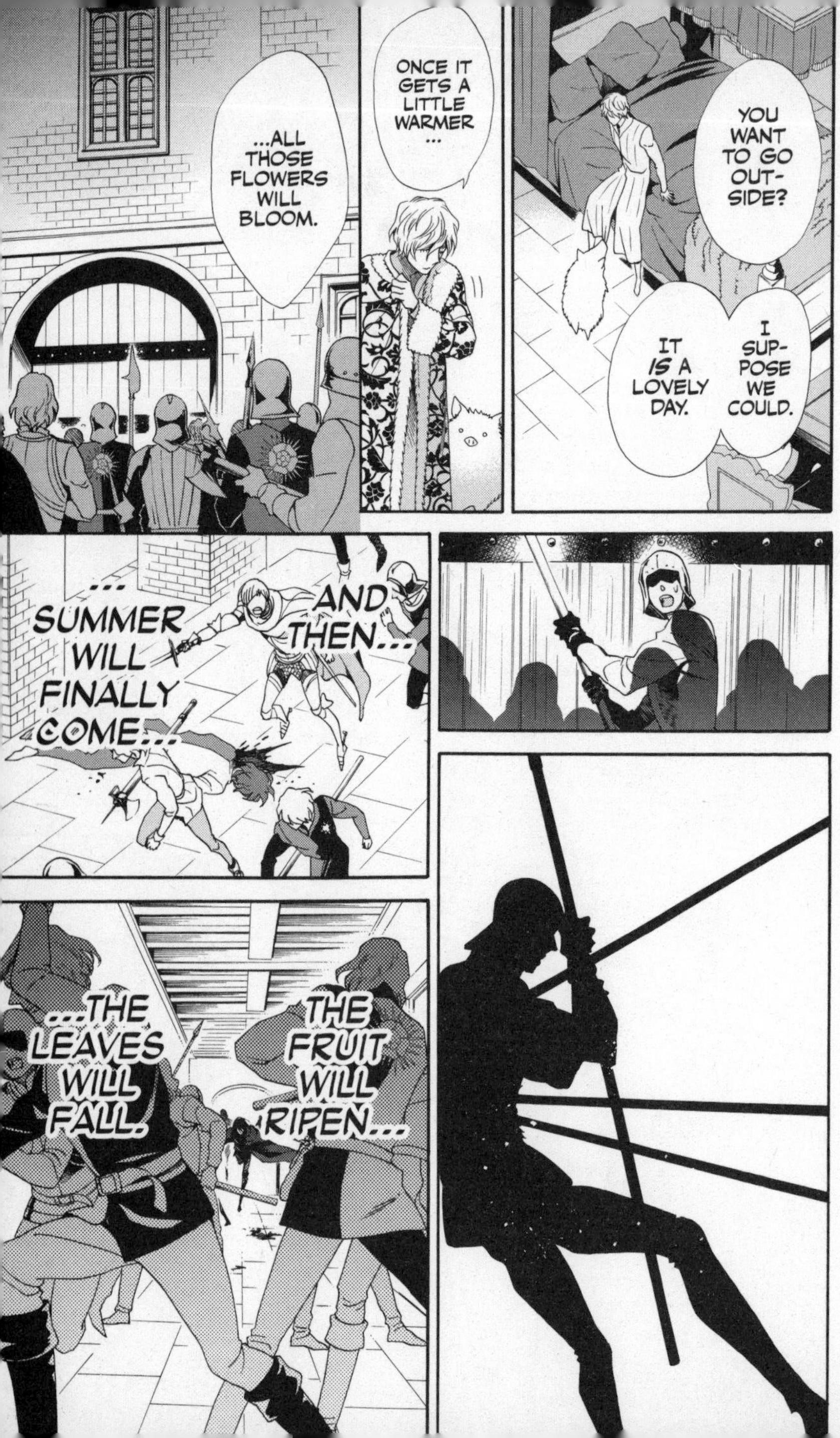
YOU WANT TO GO OUT-SIDE?
I SUP-POSE WE COULD.
IT IS A LOVELY DAY.
ONCE IT GETS A LITTLE WARMER...
...ALL THOSE FLOWERS WILL BLOOM.
AND THEN...
...SUMMER WILL FINALLY COME...
THE FRUIT WILL RIPEN...
...THE LEAVES WILL FALL.

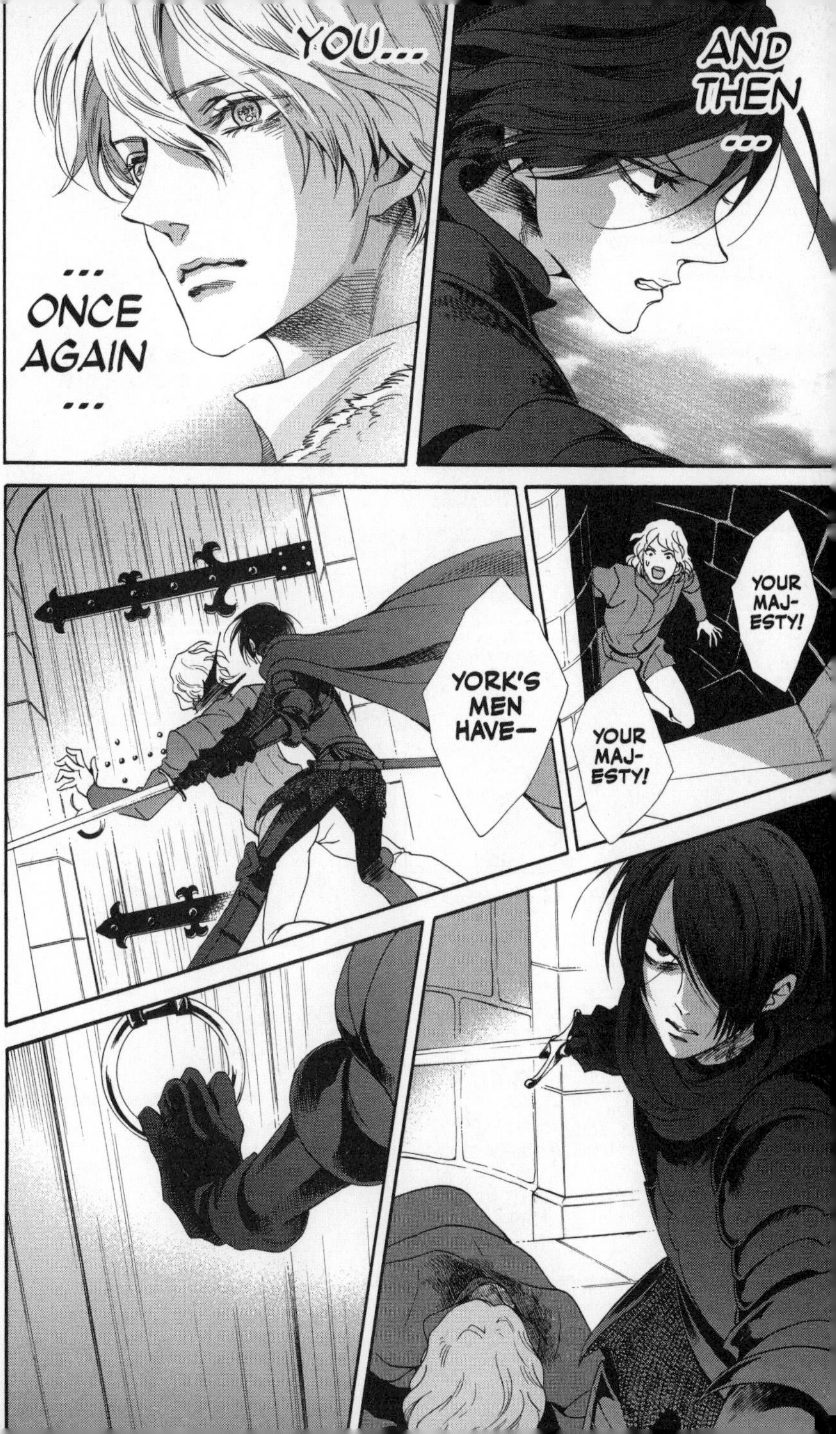
AND THEN ...
YOU...
... ONCE AGAIN ...
YOUR MAJ-ESTY!
YOUR MAJ-ESTY!
YORK'S MEN HAVE—

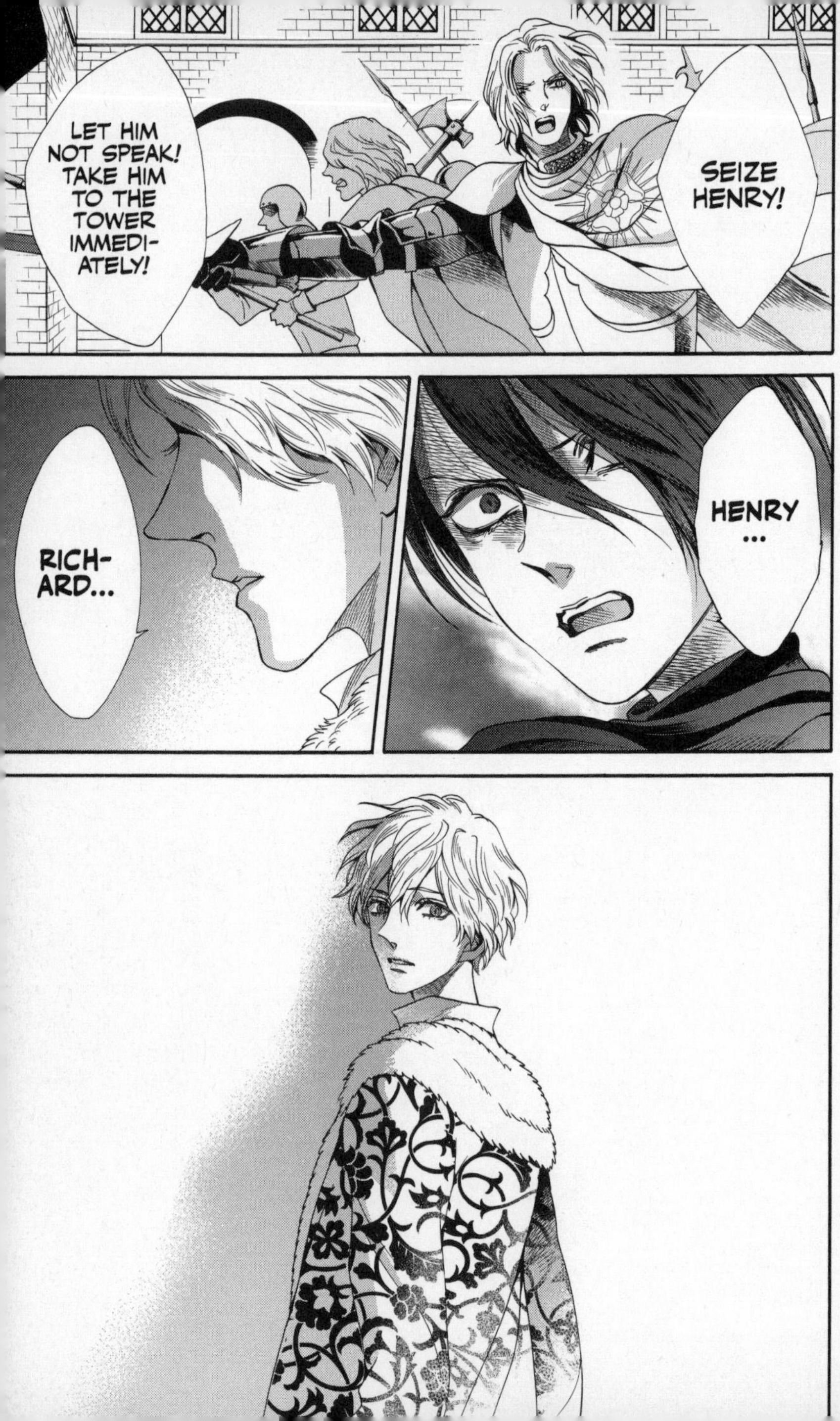
SEIZE HENRY!
LET HIM NOT SPEAK! TAKE HIM TO THE TOWER IMMEDI-ATELY!
HENRY ...
RICH-ARD...

I
WILL
BE
ABLE
TO
SEE
YOU.

Chapter 22/END

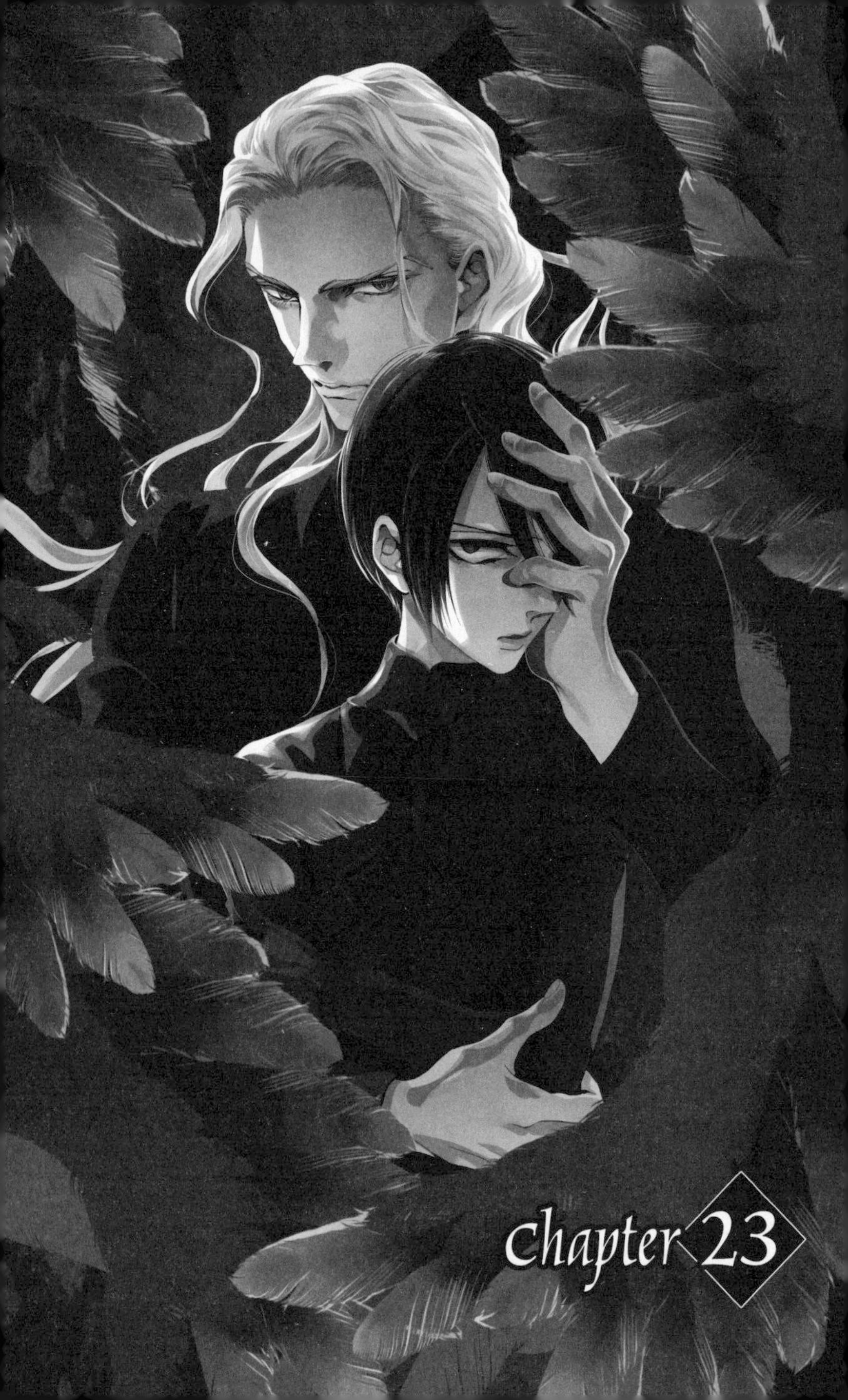
Chapter 23

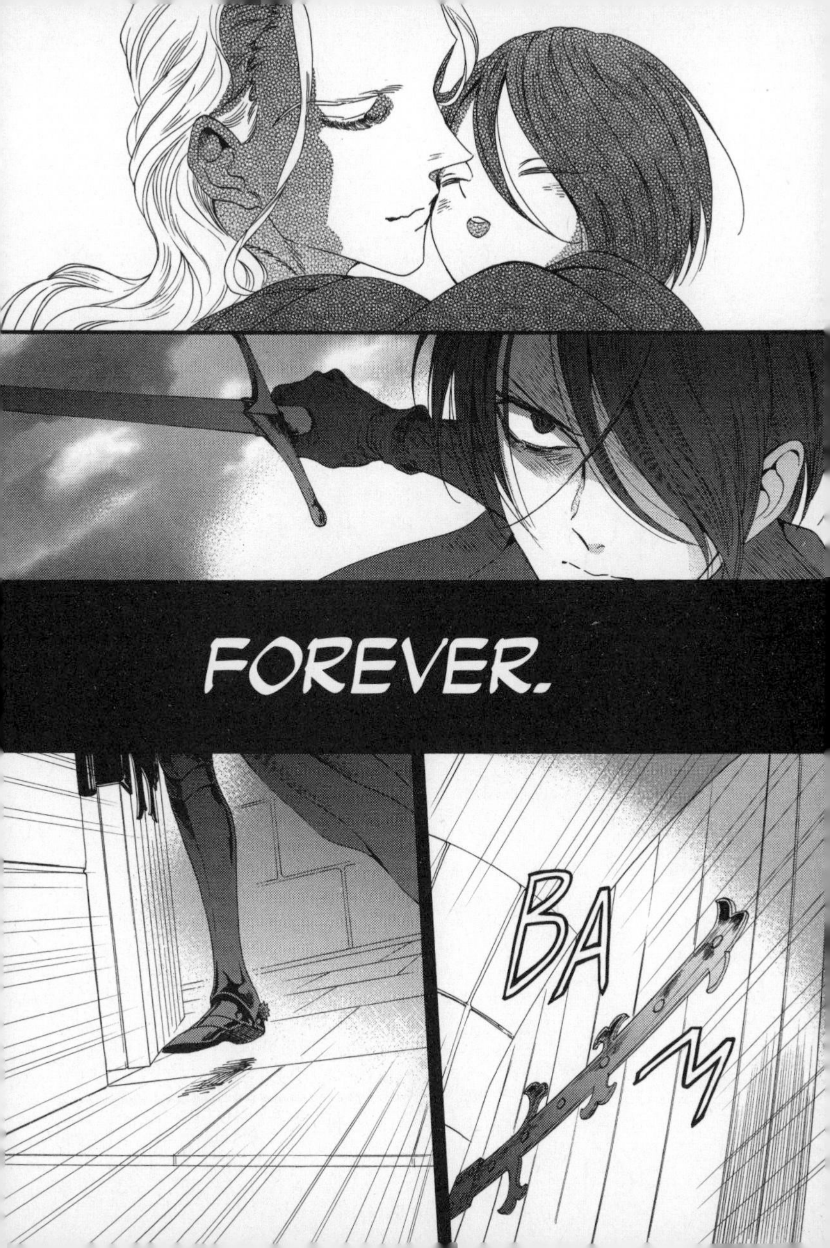
FOREVER.
BAM

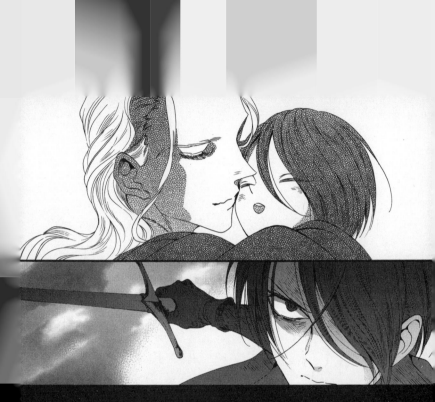

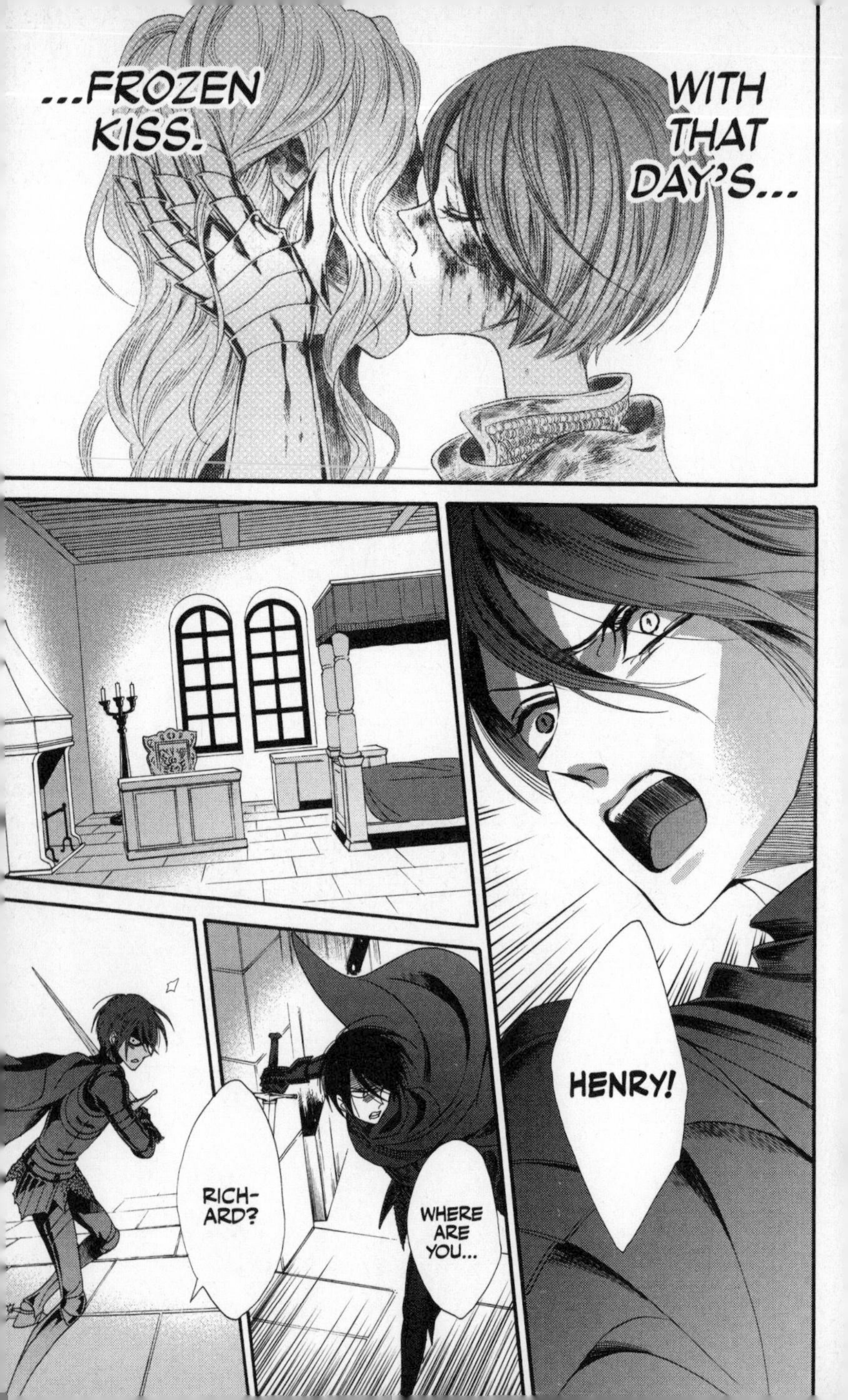
WITH THAT DAY'S...
...FROZEN KISS.
HENRY!
WHERE ARE YOU...
RICH-ARD?

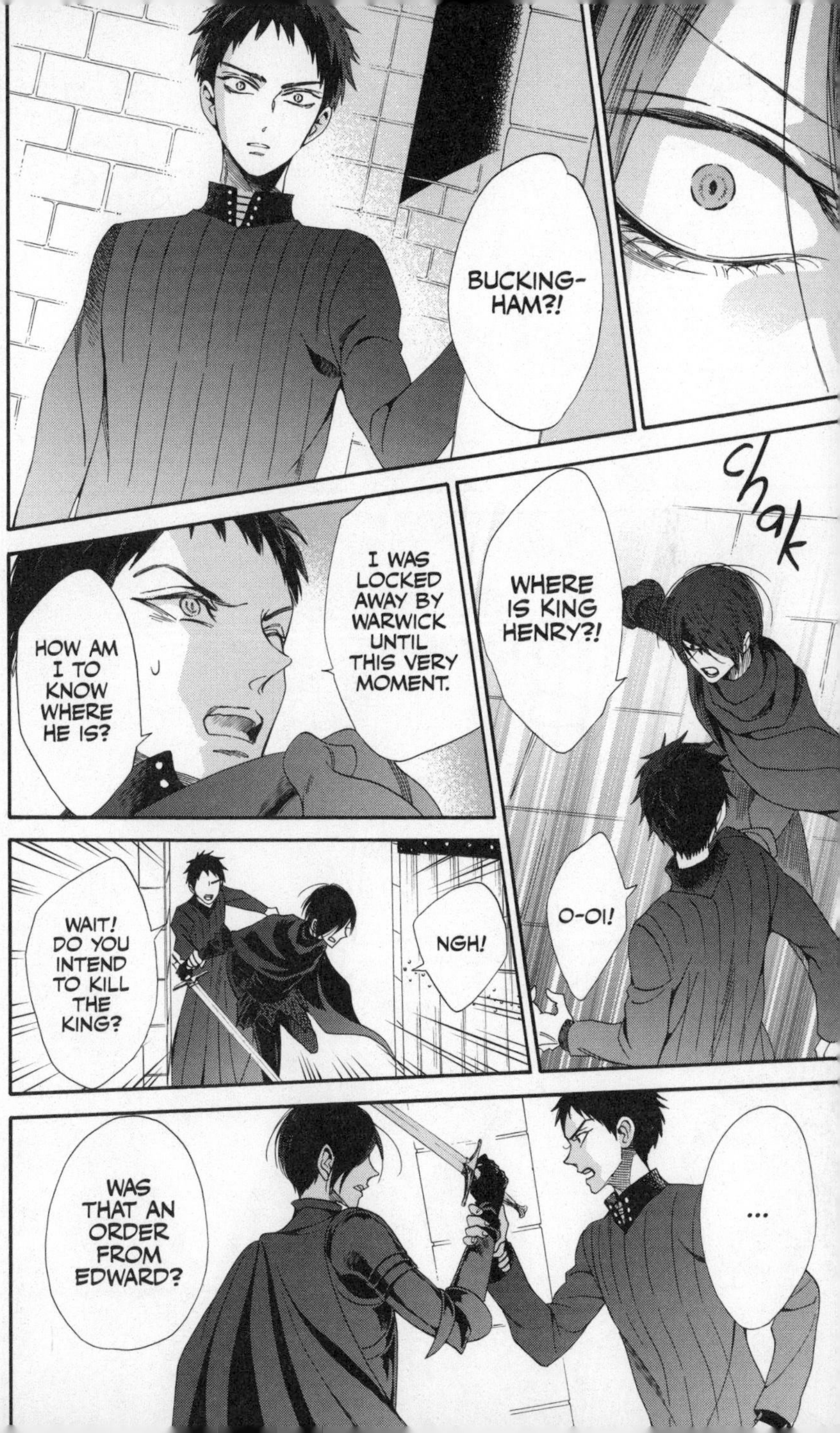
BUCKING-HAM?!
chak
WHERE IS KING HENRY?!
O-OI!
I WAS LOCKED AWAY BY WARWICK UNTIL THIS VERY MOMENT.
HOW AM I TO KNOW WHERE HE IS?
NGH!
WAIT! DO YOU INTEND TO KILL THE KING?
...
WAS THAT AN ORDER FROM EDWARD?

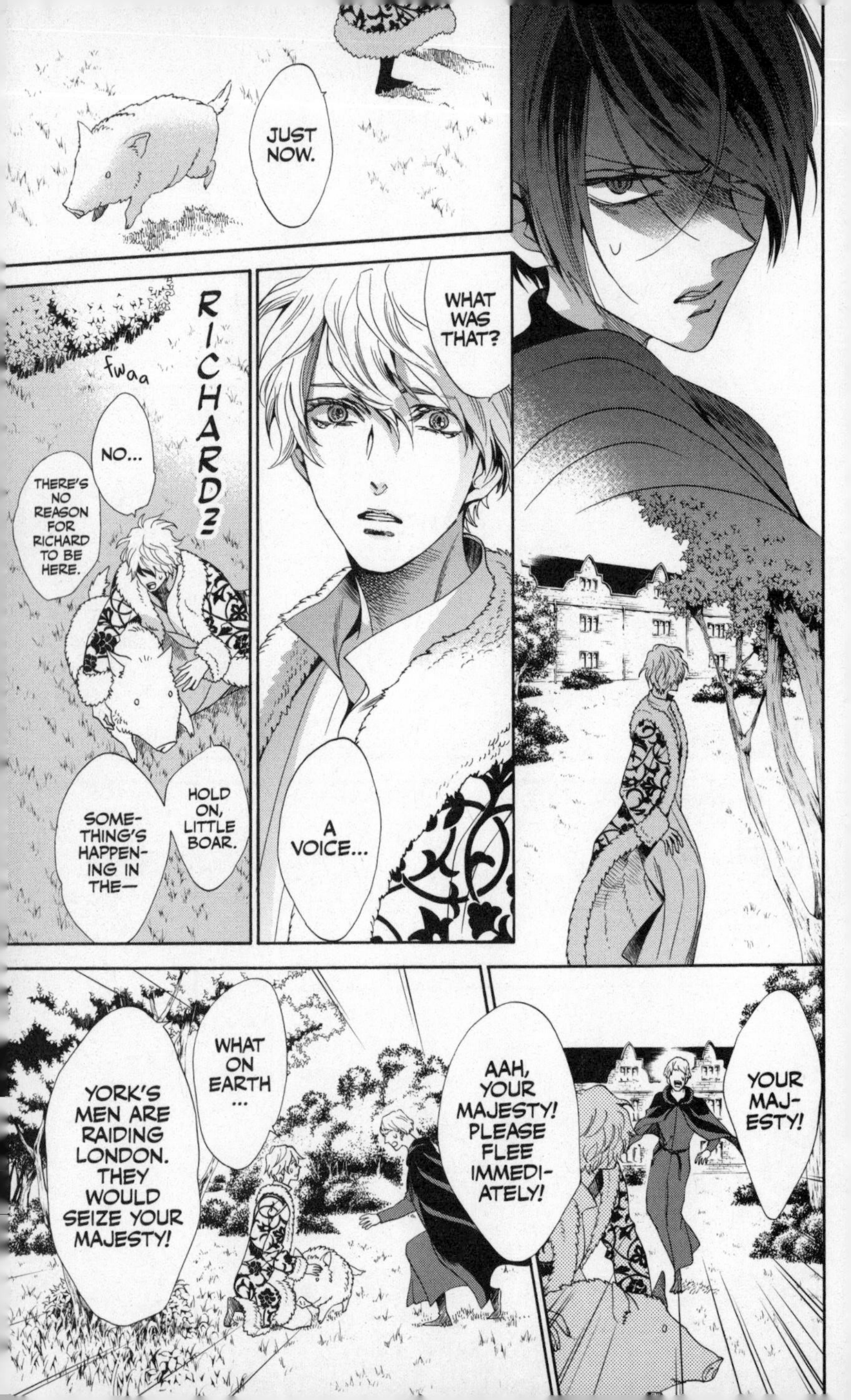
JUST NOW.
WHAT WAS THAT?
A VOICE...
RICHARD?!
fwaa
NO...
THERE'S NO REASON FOR RICHARD TO BE HERE.
HOLD ON, LITTLE BOAR.
SOMETHING'S HAPPENING IN THE—
YOUR MAJESTY!
AAH, YOUR MAJESTY! PLEASE FLEE IMMEDIATELY!
WHAT ON EARTH...
YORK'S MEN ARE RAIDING LONDON. THEY WOULD SEIZE YOUR MAJESTY!

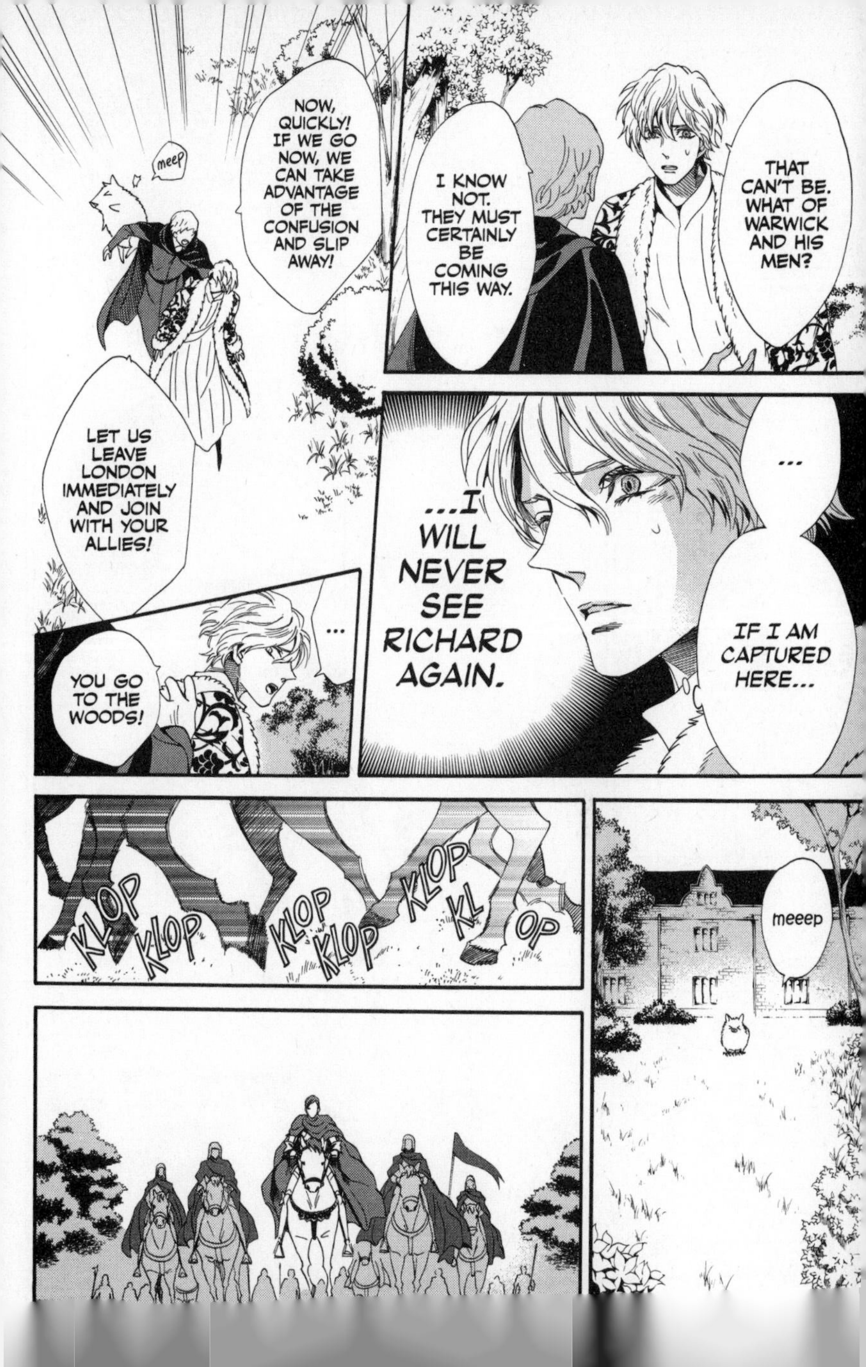
THAT CAN'T BE. WHAT OF WARWICK AND HIS MEN?
I KNOW NOT. THEY MUST CERTAINLY BE COMING THIS WAY.
NOW, QUICKLY! IF WE GO NOW, WE CAN TAKE ADVANTAGE OF THE CONFUSION AND SLIP AWAY!
meep
LET US LEAVE LONDON IMMEDIATELY AND JOIN WITH YOUR ALLIES!
...
IF I AM CAPTURED HERE...
...I WILL NEVER SEE RICHARD AGAIN.
...
YOU GO TO THE WOODS!
meeep
KLOP KLOP KLOP KLOP KLOP KL OP

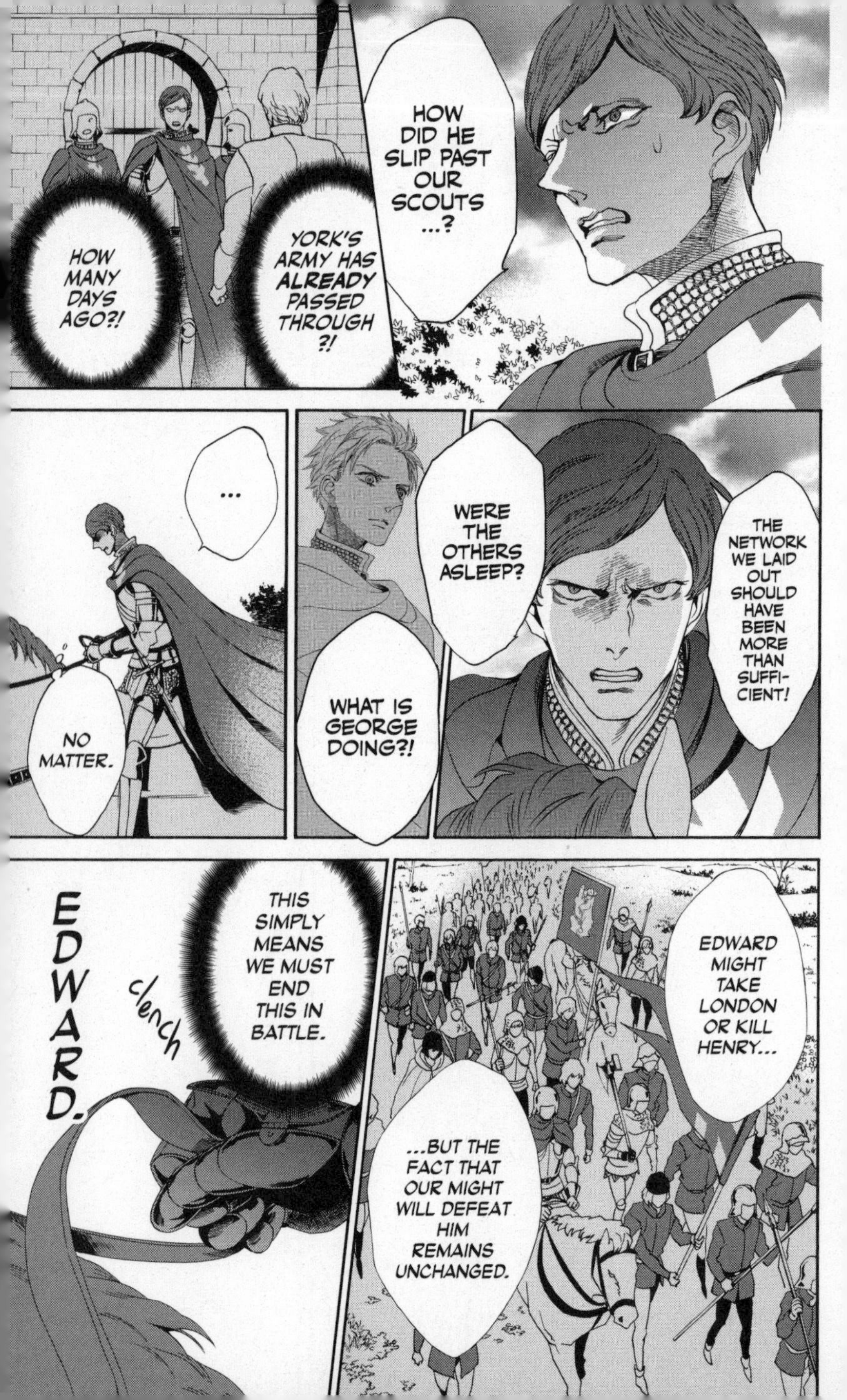
HOW DID HE SLIP PAST OUR SCOUTS ...?
YORK'S ARMY HAS ALREADY PASSED THROUGH ?!
HOW MANY DAYS AGO?!
THE NETWORK WE LAID OUT SHOULD HAVE BEEN MORE THAN SUFFICIENT!
WERE THE OTHERS ASLEEP?
WHAT IS GEORGE DOING?!
...
NO MATTER.
EDWARD MIGHT TAKE LONDON OR KILL HENRY...
...BUT THE FACT THAT OUR MIGHT WILL DEFEAT HIM REMAINS UNCHANGED.
THIS SIMPLY MEANS WE MUST END THIS IN BATTLE.
clench
EDWARD.

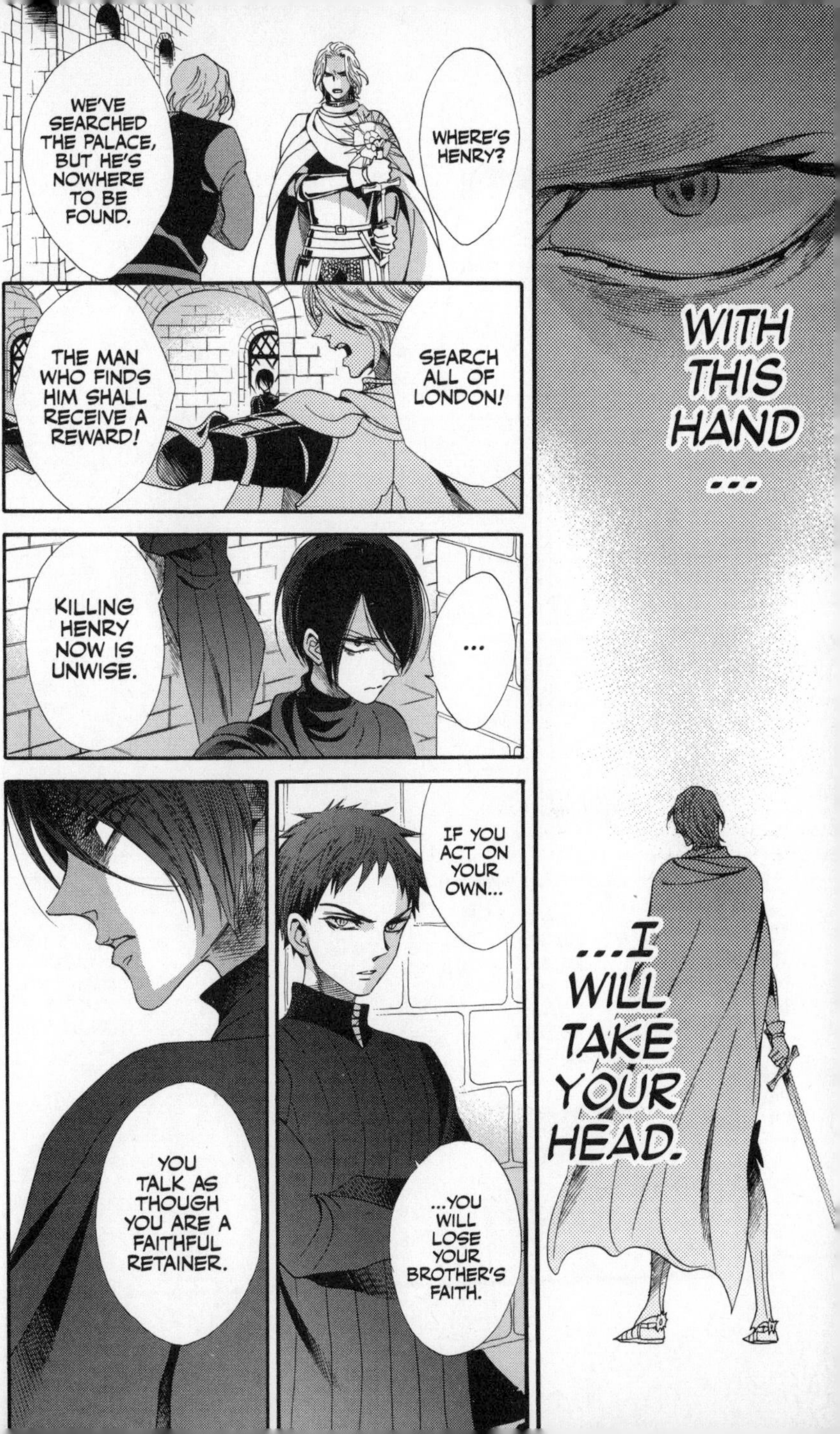
WITH THIS HAND...
...I WILL TAKE YOUR HEAD.
WHERE'S HENRY?
WE'VE SEARCHED THE PALACE, BUT HE'S NOWHERE TO BE FOUND.
SEARCH ALL OF LONDON!
THE MAN WHO FINDS HIM SHALL RECEIVE A REWARD!
...
KILLING HENRY NOW IS UNWISE.
IF YOU ACT ON YOUR OWN...
...YOU WILL LOSE YOUR BROTHER'S FAITH.
YOU TALK AS THOUGH YOU ARE A FAITHFUL RETAINER.

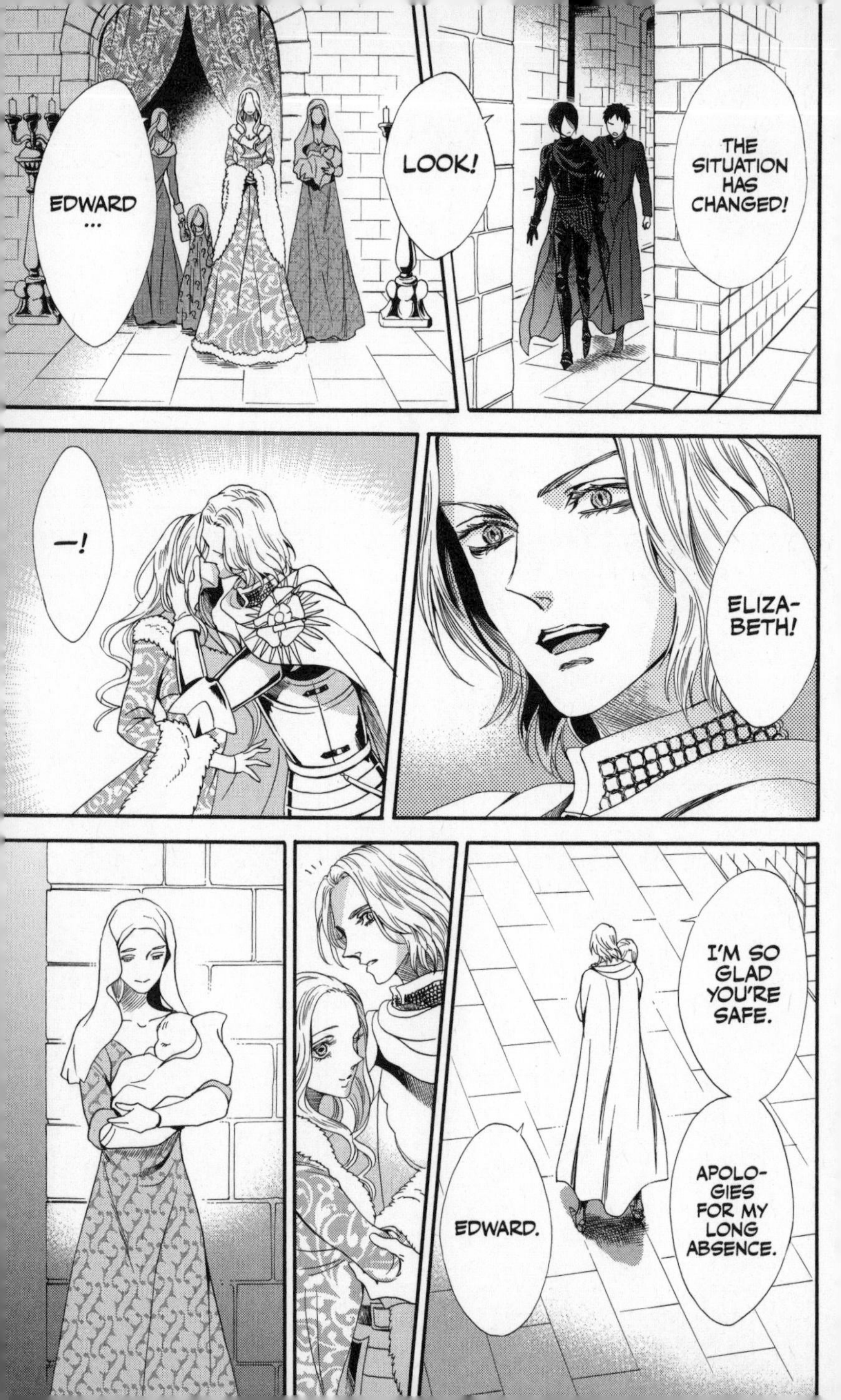
THE SITUATION HAS CHANGED!
LOOK!
EDWARD...
ELIZA-BETH!
—!
I'M SO GLAD YOU'RE SAFE.
APOLOGIES FOR MY LONG ABSENCE.
EDWARD.

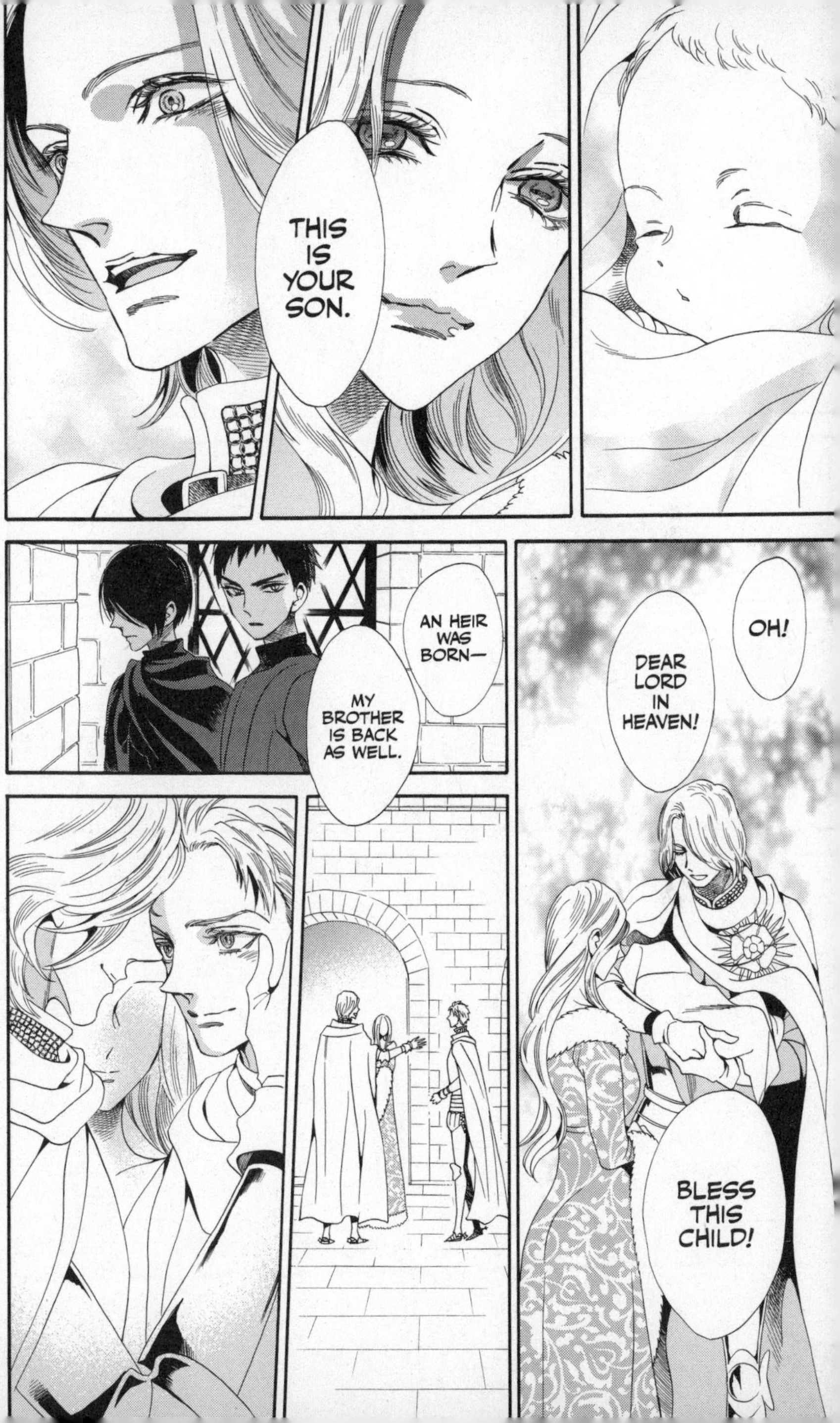
THIS IS YOUR SON.
OH!
DEAR LORD IN HEAVEN!
BLESS THIS CHILD!
AN HEIR WAS BORN—
MY BROTHER IS BACK AS WELL.

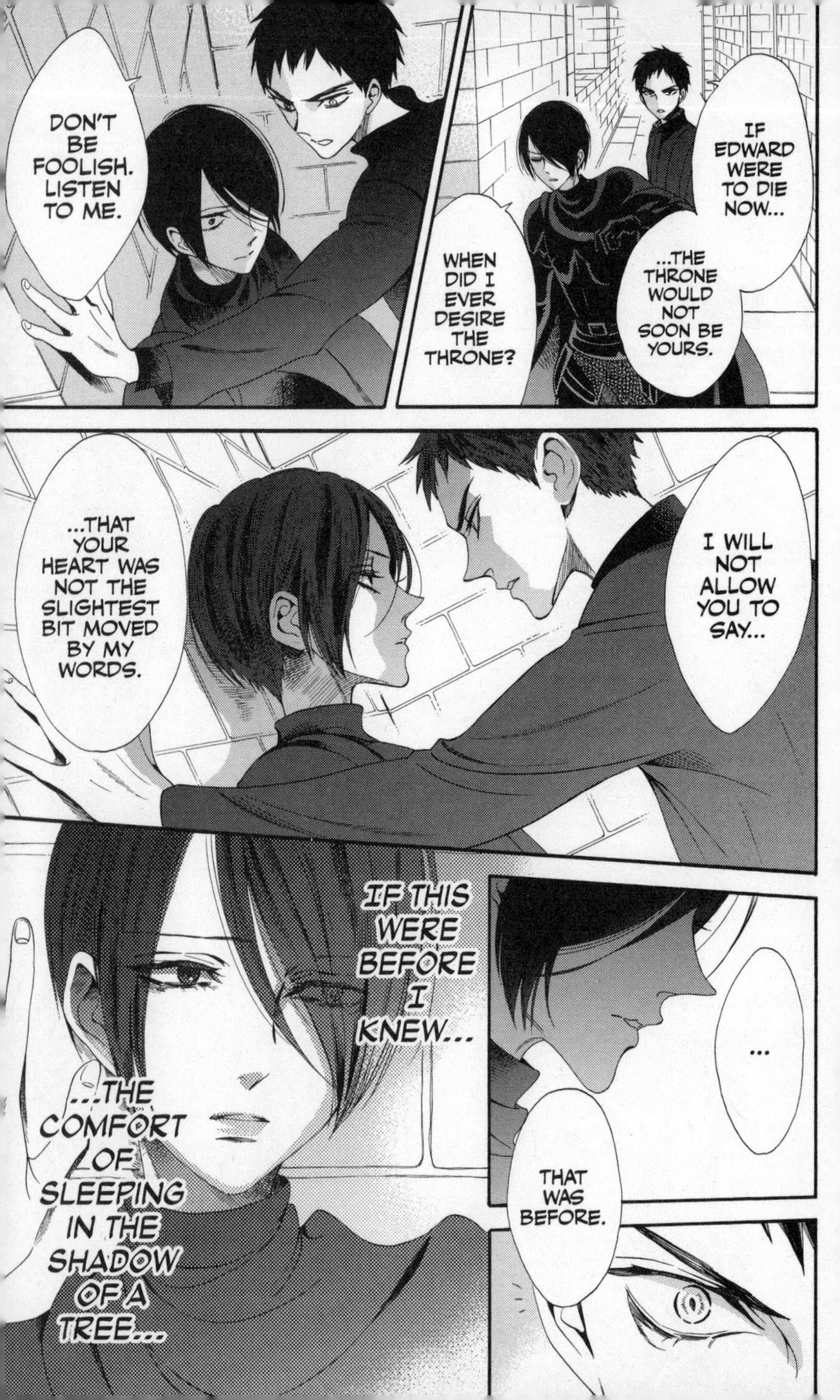
IF EDWARD WERE TO DIE NOW...
...THE THRONE WOULD NOT SOON BE YOURS.
WHEN DID I EVER DESIRE THE THRONE?
DON'T BE FOOLISH. LISTEN TO ME.
I WILL NOT ALLOW YOU TO SAY...
...THAT YOUR HEART WAS NOT THE SLIGHTEST BIT MOVED BY MY WORDS.
...
THAT WAS BEFORE.
IF THIS WERE BEFORE I KNEW...
...THE COMFORT OF SLEEPING IN THE SHADOW OF A TREE...

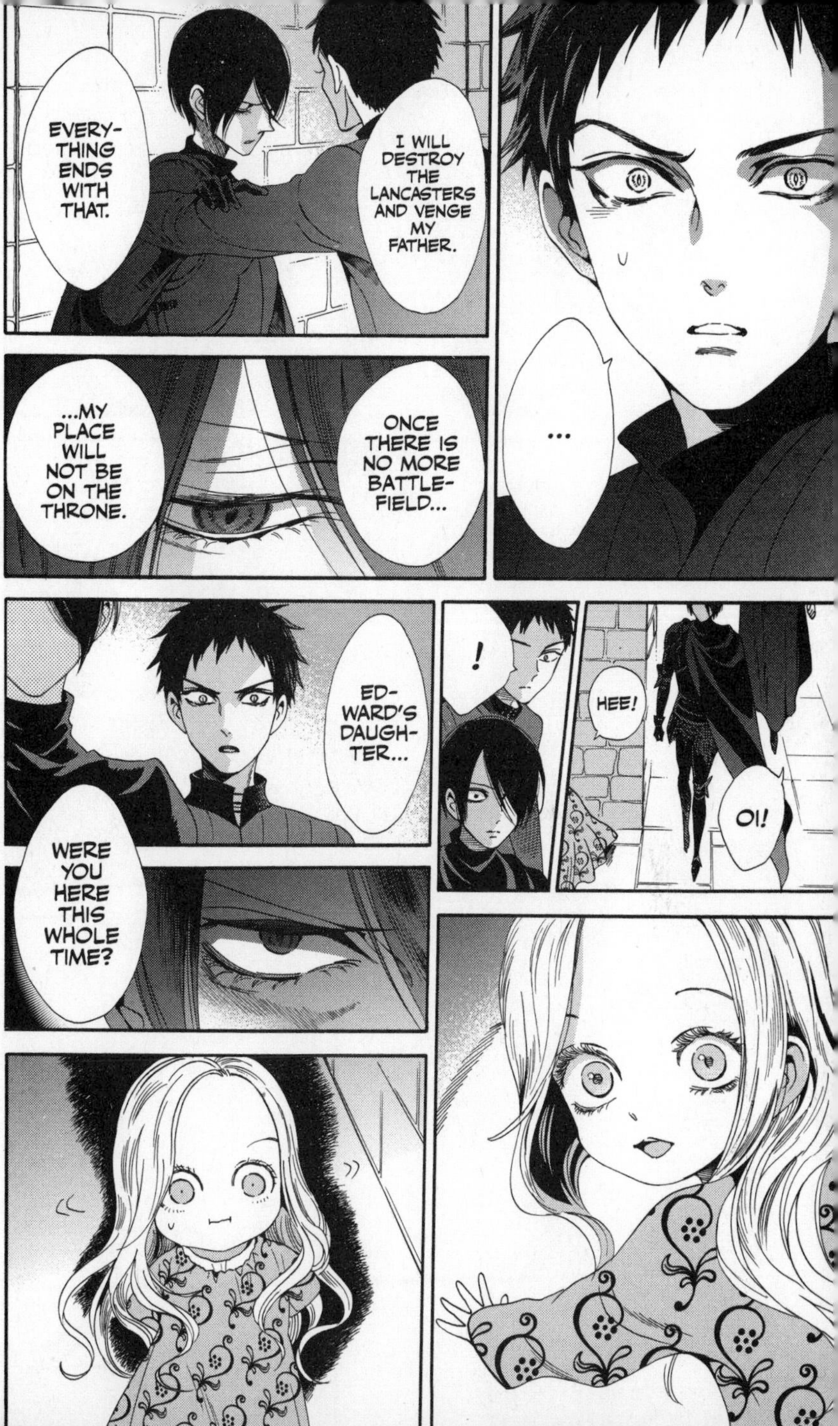
...
I WILL DESTROY THE LANCASTERS AND VENGE MY FATHER.
EVERY-THING ENDS WITH THAT.
ONCE THERE IS NO MORE BATTLE-FIELD...
...MY PLACE WILL NOT BE ON THE THRONE.
HEE!
OI!
!
ED-WARD'S DAUGH-TER...
WERE YOU HERE THIS WHOLE TIME?

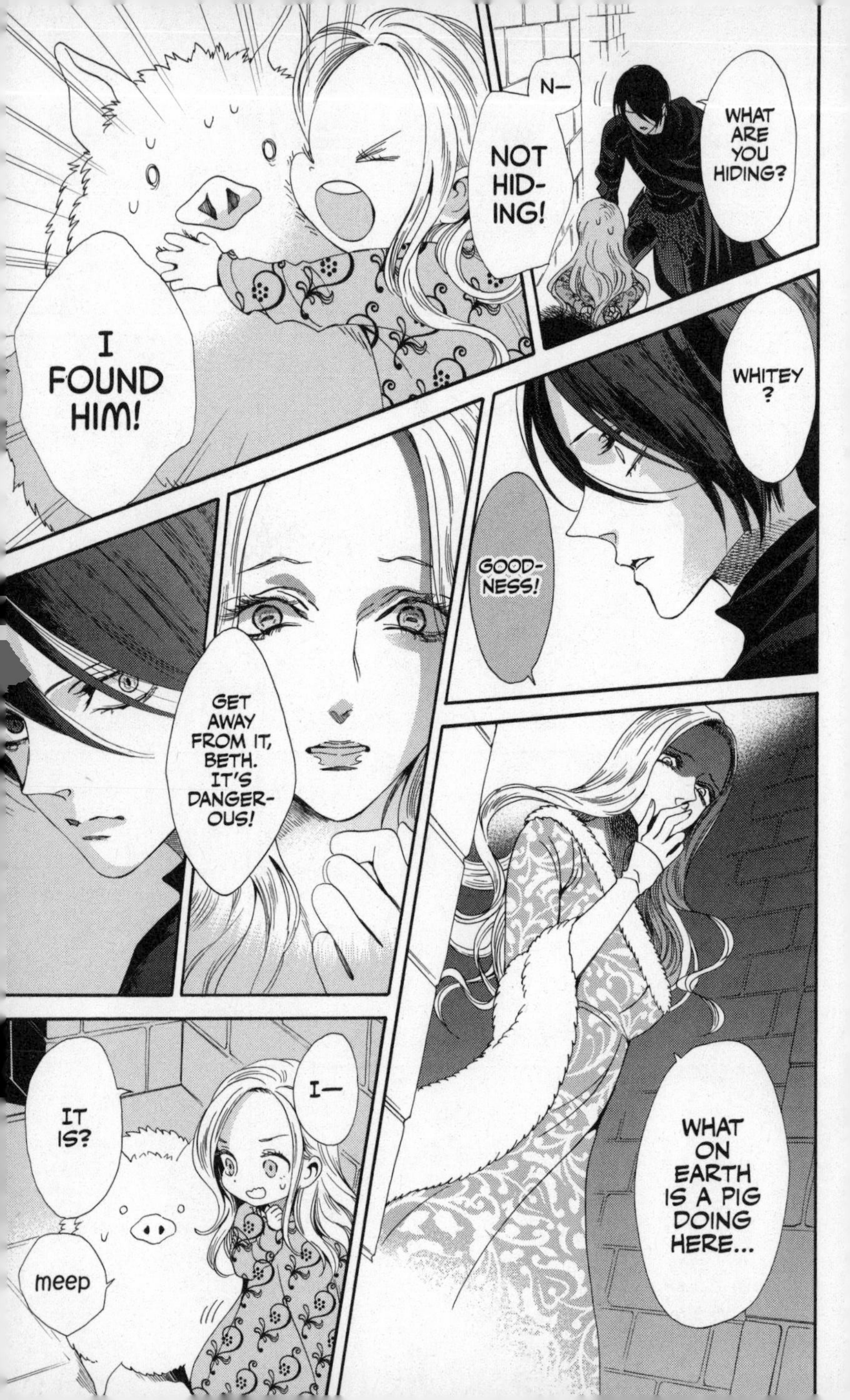
WHAT ARE YOU HIDING?
N—
NOT HID-ING!
I FOUND HIM!
WHITEY?
GOOD-NESS!
GET AWAY FROM IT, BETH. IT'S DANGER-OUS!
WHAT ON EARTH IS A PIG DOING HERE...
I—
IT IS?
meep

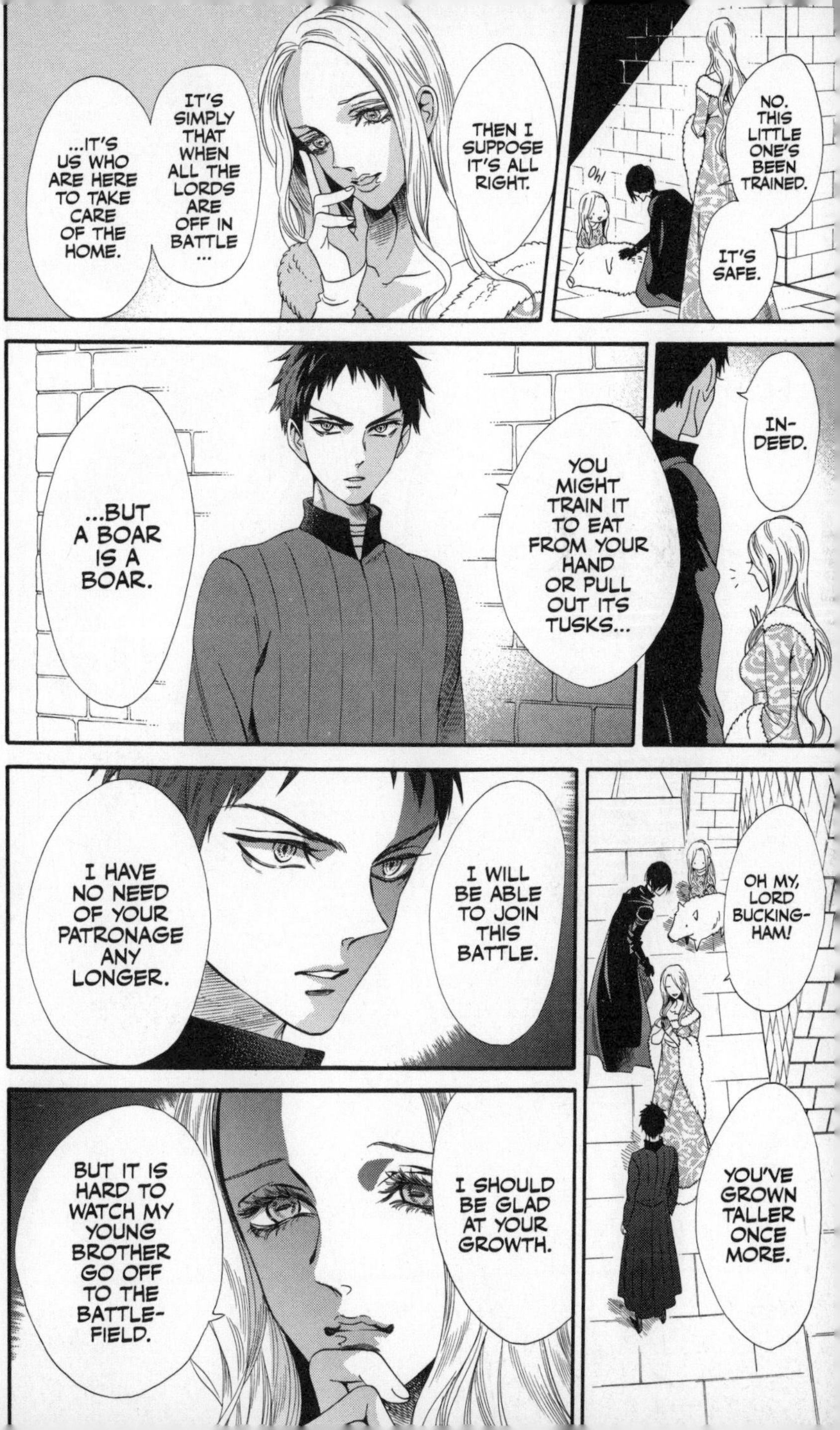
NO. THIS LITTLE ONE'S BEEN TRAINED.
Oh!
IT'S SAFE.
THEN I SUPPOSE IT'S ALL RIGHT.
IT'S SIMPLY THAT WHEN ALL THE LORDS ARE OFF IN BATTLE...
...IT'S US WHO ARE HERE TO TAKE CARE OF THE HOME.
IN-DEED.
YOU MIGHT TRAIN IT TO EAT FROM YOUR HAND OR PULL OUT ITS TUSKS...
...BUT A BOAR IS A BOAR.
OH MY, LORD BUCKING-HAM!
YOU'VE GROWN TALLER ONCE MORE.
I WILL BE ABLE TO JOIN THIS BATTLE.
I HAVE NO NEED OF YOUR PATRONAGE ANY LONGER.
I SHOULD BE GLAD AT YOUR GROWTH.
BUT IT IS HARD TO WATCH MY YOUNG BROTHER GO OFF TO THE BATTLE-FIELD.

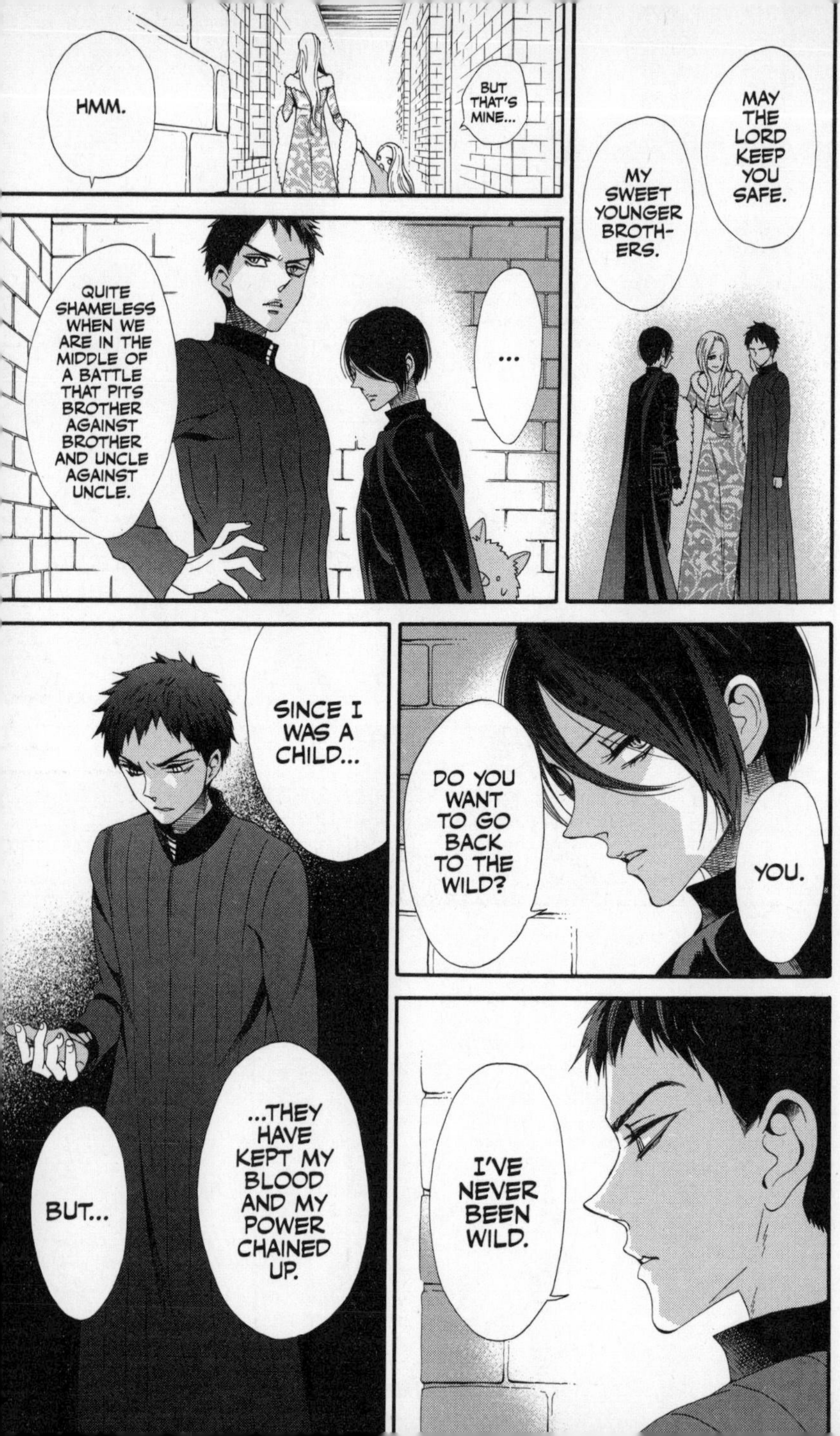
MAY THE LORD KEEP YOU SAFE.
MY SWEET YOUNGER BROTHERS.
BUT THAT'S MINE...
HMM.
...
QUITE SHAMELESS WHEN WE ARE IN THE MIDDLE OF A BATTLE THAT PITS BROTHER AGAINST BROTHER AND UNCLE AGAINST UNCLE.
YOU.
DO YOU WANT TO GO BACK TO THE WILD?
I'VE NEVER BEEN WILD.
SINCE I WAS A CHILD...
...THEY HAVE KEPT MY BLOOD AND MY POWER CHAINED UP.
BUT...

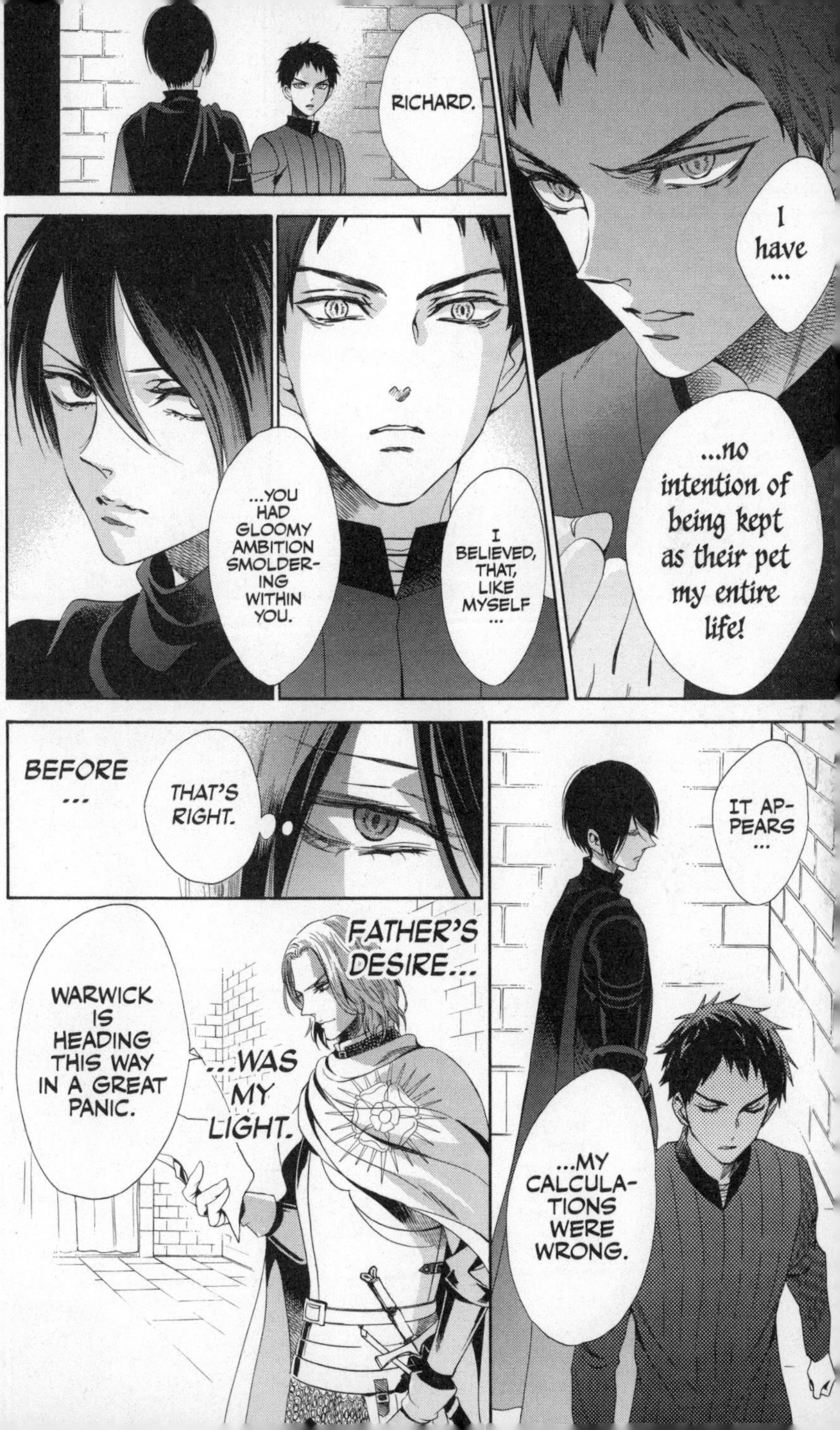
I have...
...no intention of being kept as their pet my entire life!
RICHARD.
I BELIEVED, THAT, LIKE MYSELF...
...YOU HAD GLOOMY AMBITION SMOLDERING WITHIN YOU.
IT APPEARS...
...MY CALCULATIONS WERE WRONG.
THAT'S RIGHT.
BEFORE...
FATHER'S DESIRE...
...WAS MY LIGHT.
WARWICK IS HEADING THIS WAY IN A GREAT PANIC.

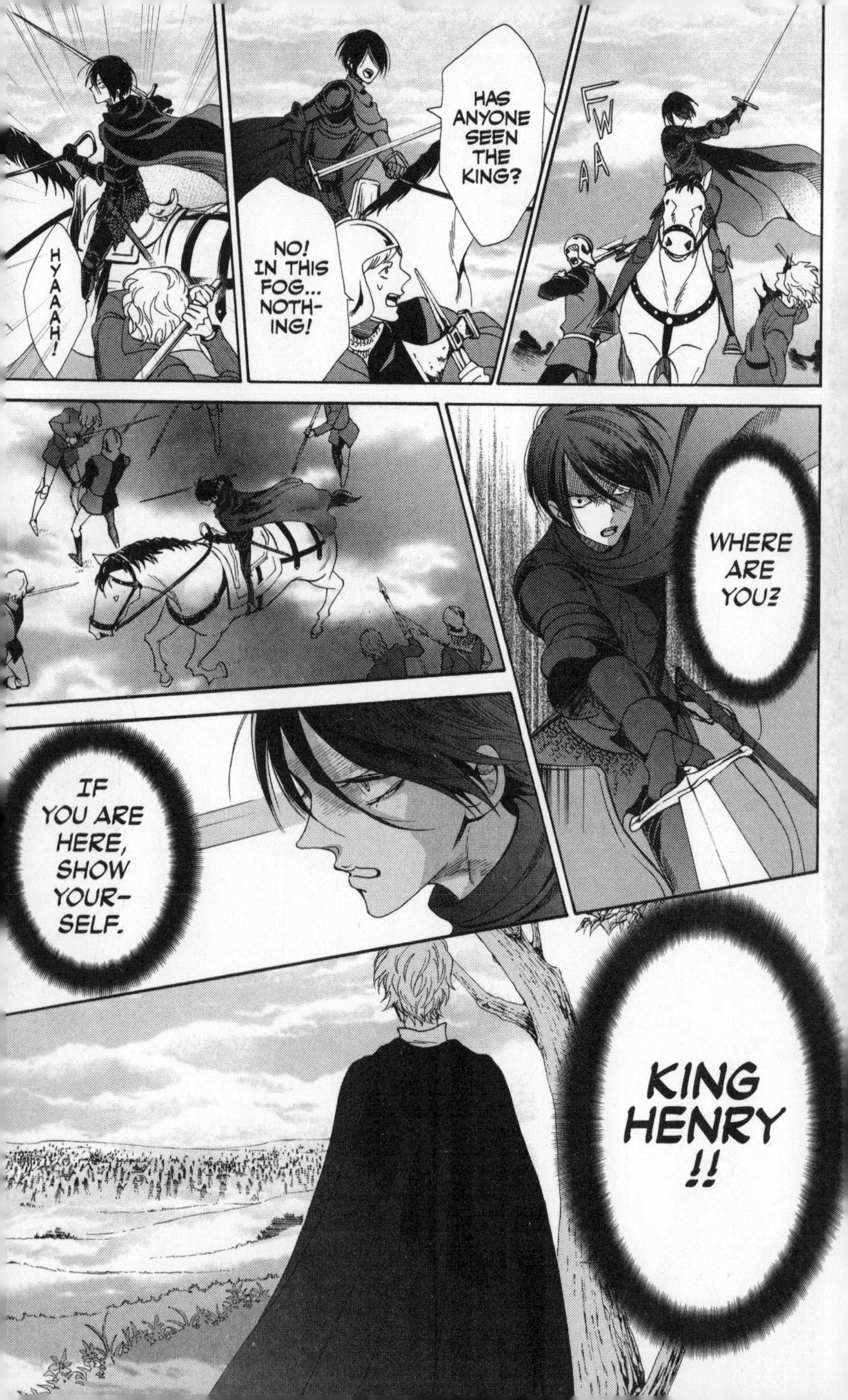
FWAA
HAS ANYONE SEEN THE KING?
NO! IN THIS FOG... NOTHING!
HYAAAAH!
WHERE ARE YOU?
IF YOU ARE HERE, SHOW YOURSELF.
KING HENRY!!

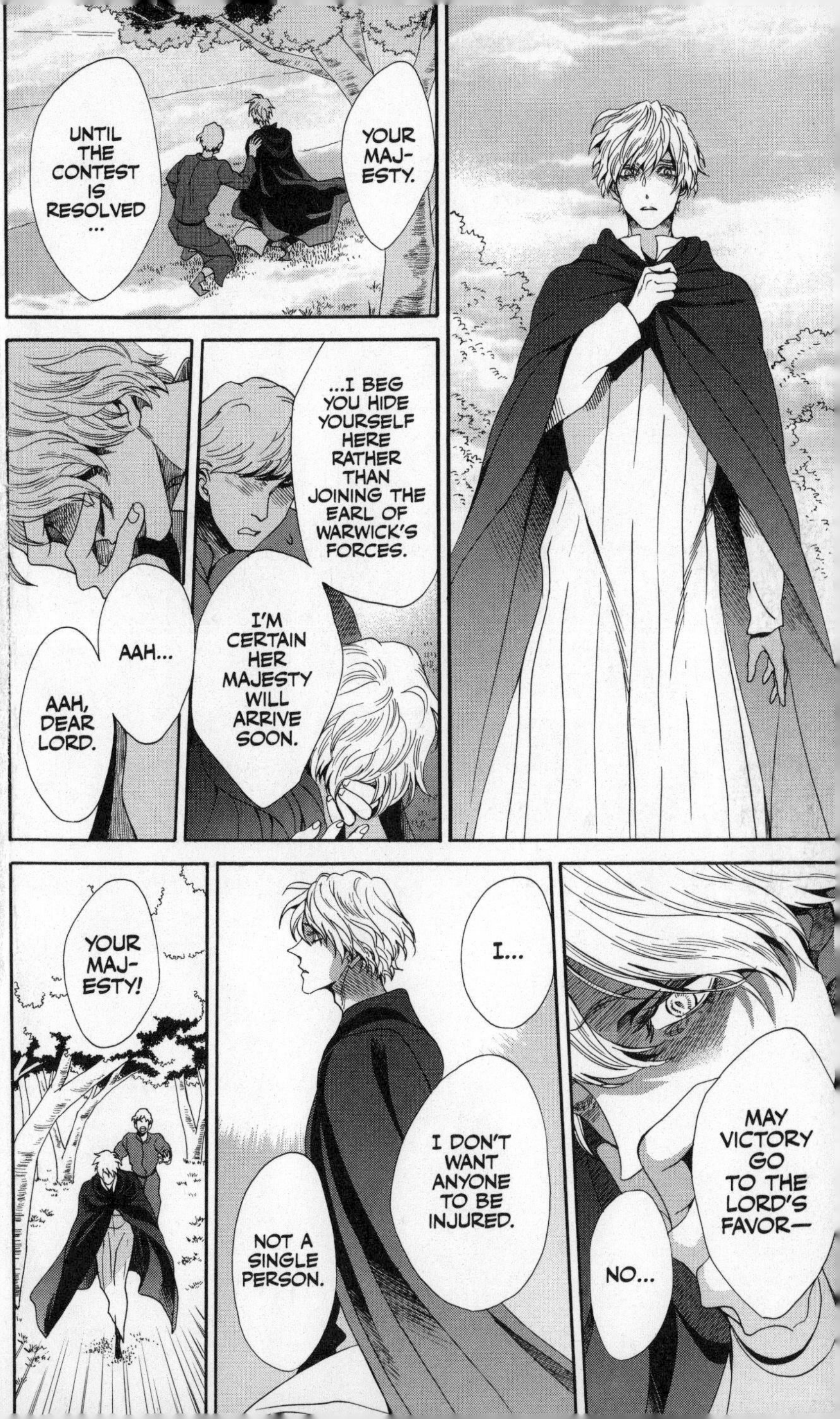
YOUR MAJESTY.
UNTIL THE CONTEST IS RESOLVED...
...I BEG YOU HIDE YOURSELF HERE RATHER THAN JOINING THE EARL OF WARWICK'S FORCES.
I'M CERTAIN HER MAJESTY WILL ARRIVE SOON.
AAH...
AAH, DEAR LORD.
MAY VICTORY GO TO THE LORD'S FAVOR—
NO...
I...
I DON'T WANT ANYONE TO BE INJURED.
NOT A SINGLE PERSON.
YOUR MAJESTY!

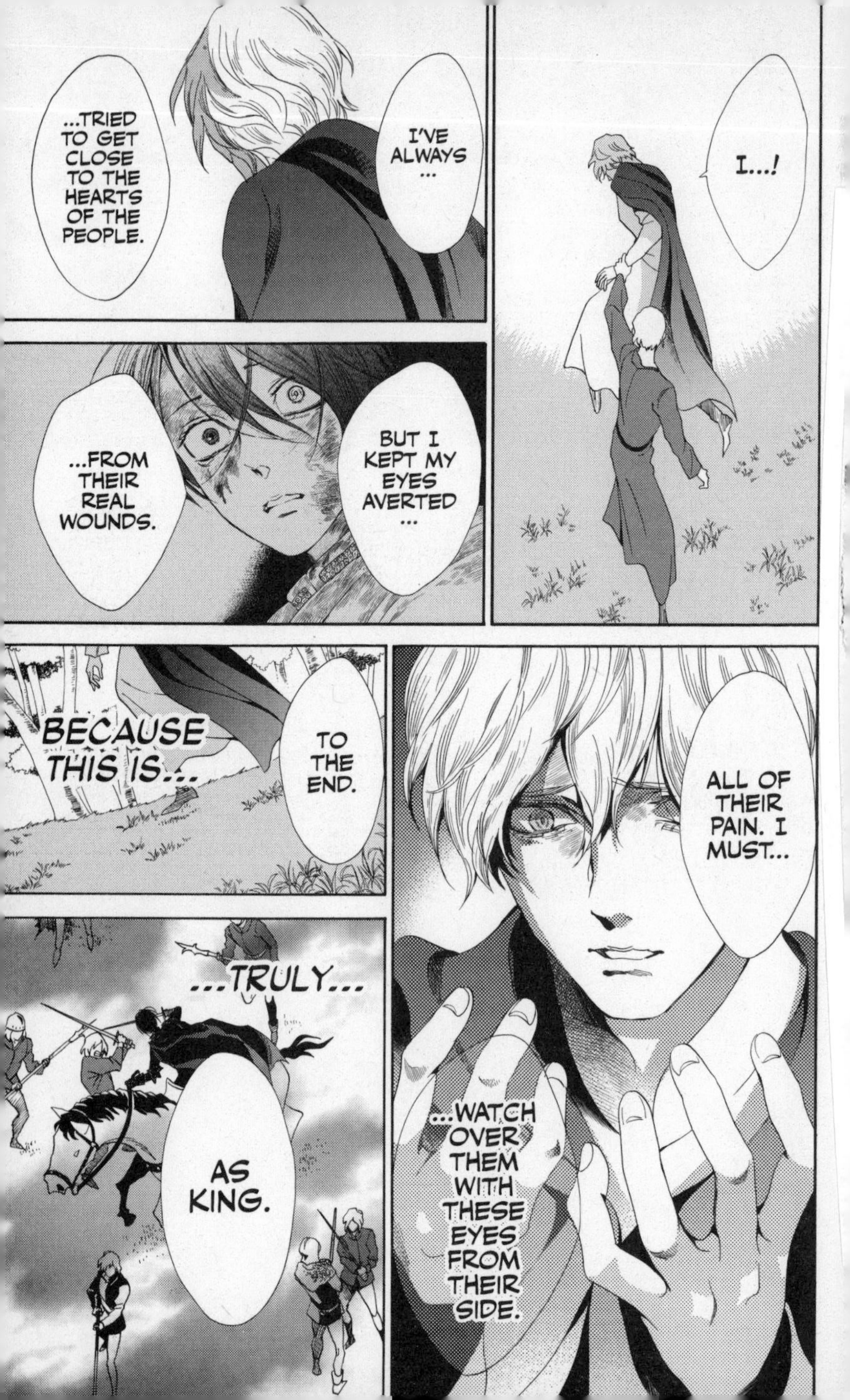
I...!
I'VE ALWAYS...
...TRIED TO GET CLOSE TO THE HEARTS OF THE PEOPLE.
BUT I KEPT MY EYES AVERTED...
...FROM THEIR REAL WOUNDS.
ALL OF THEIR PAIN. I MUST...
...WATCH OVER THEM WITH THESE EYES FROM THEIR SIDE.
TO THE END.
BECAUSE THIS IS...
...TRULY...
AS KING.

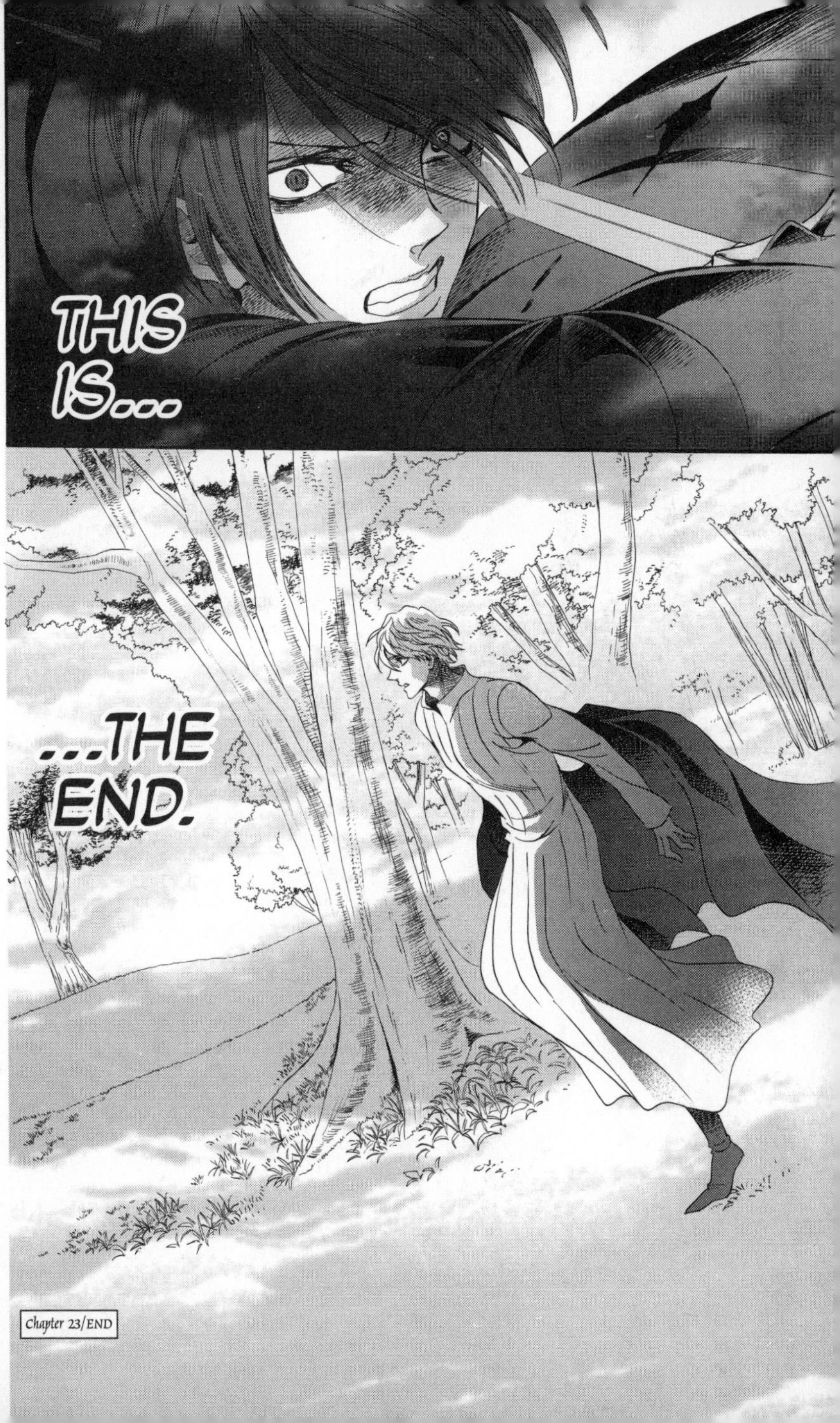
THIS IS...
...THE END.
Chapter 23/END

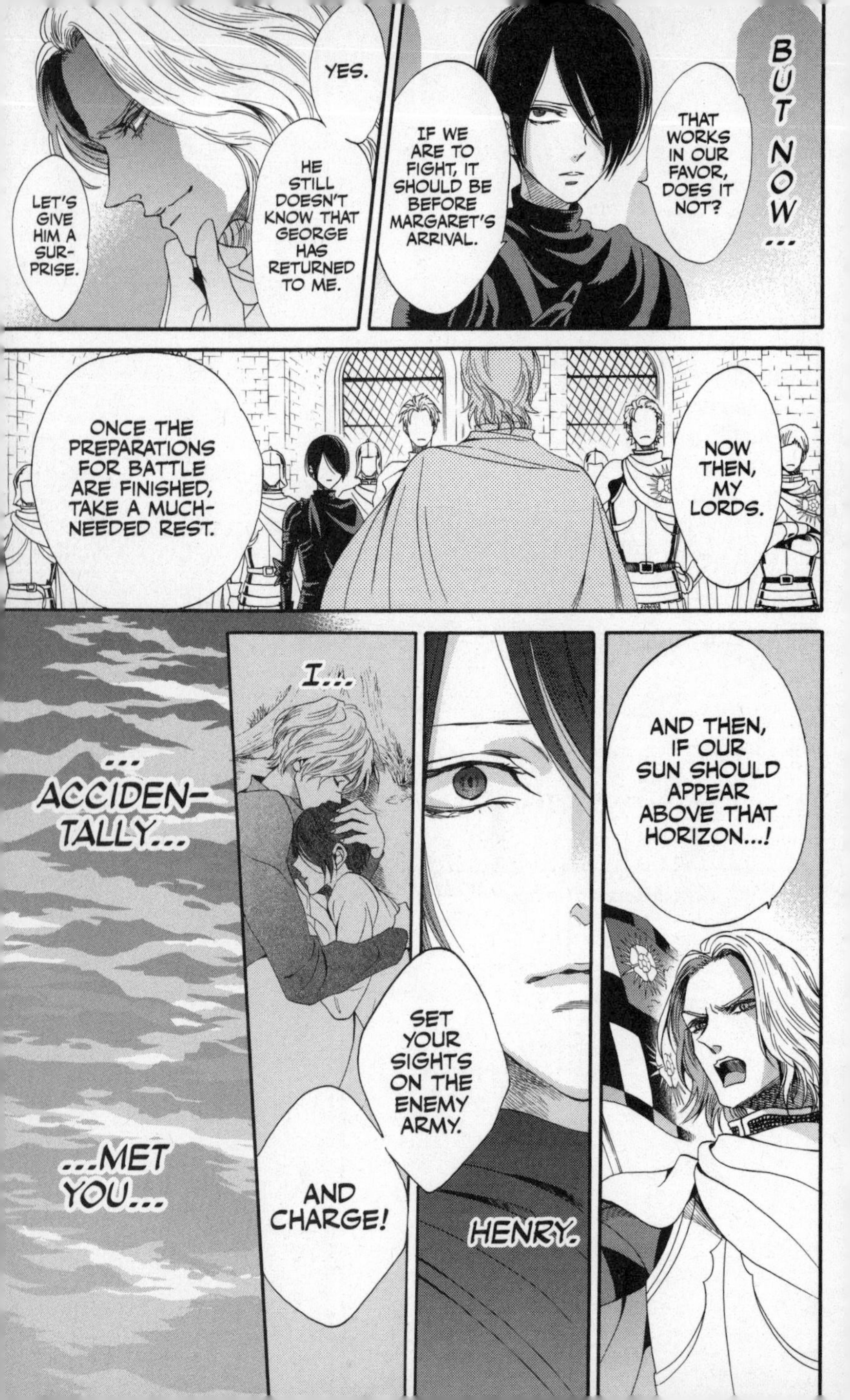
BUT NOW...
THAT WORKS IN OUR FAVOR, DOES IT NOT?
IF WE ARE TO FIGHT, IT SHOULD BE BEFORE MARGARET'S ARRIVAL.
YES.
HE STILL DOESN'T KNOW THAT GEORGE HAS RETURNED TO ME.
LET'S GIVE HIM A SUR-PRISE.
NOW THEN, MY LORDS.
ONCE THE PREPARATIONS FOR BATTLE ARE FINISHED, TAKE A MUCH-NEEDED REST.
AND THEN, IF OUR SUN SHOULD APPEAR ABOVE THAT HORIZON...!
SET YOUR SIGHTS ON THE ENEMY ARMY.
AND CHARGE!
HENRY.
I...
...ACCIDEN-TALLY...
...MET YOU...

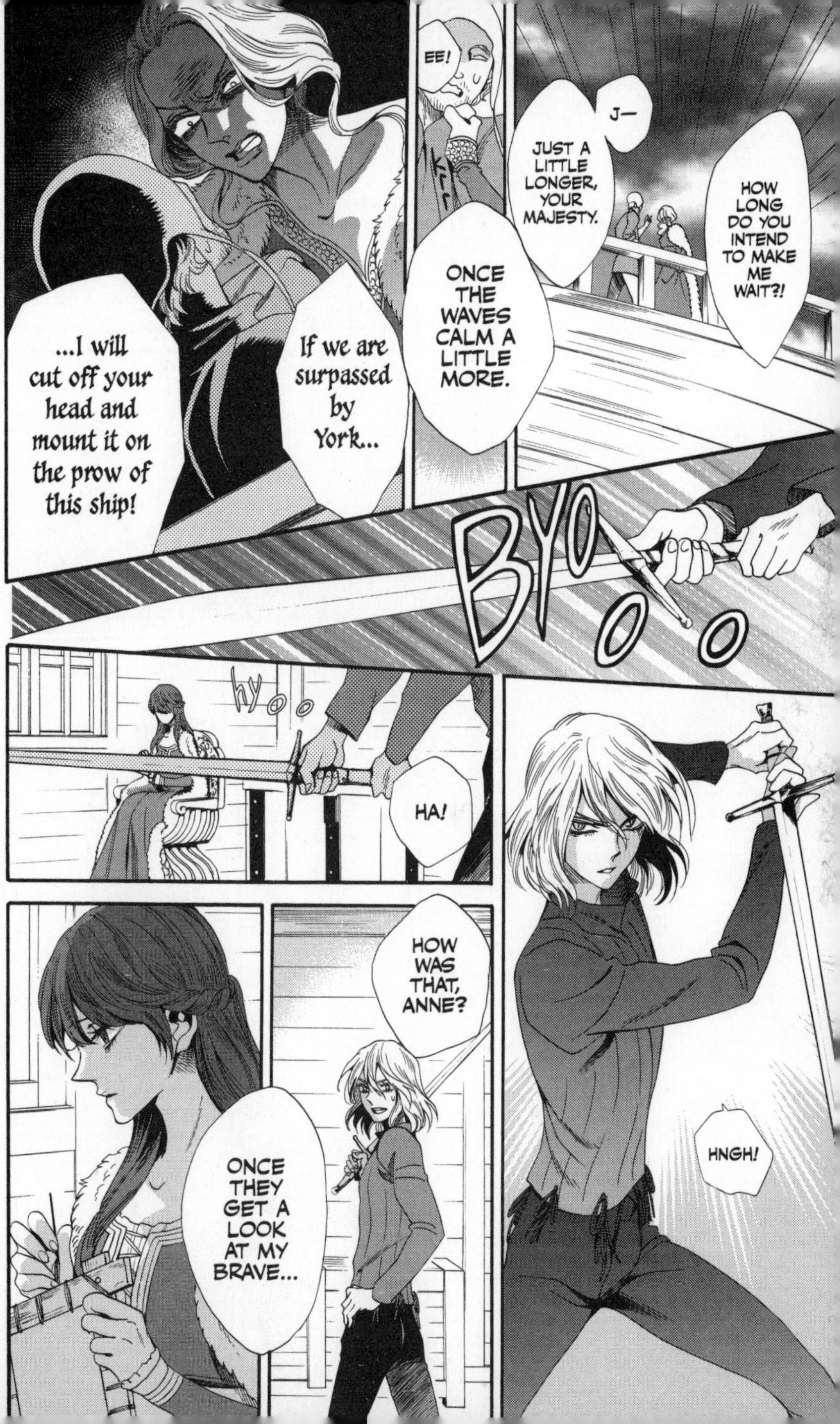
HOW LONG DO YOU INTEND TO MAKE ME WAIT?!
J—
JUST A LITTLE LONGER, YOUR MAJESTY.
ONCE THE WAVES CALM A LITTLE MORE.
EE!
If we are surpassed by York...
...I will cut off your head and mount it on the prow of this ship!
BYOOOO
HNGH!
hyoo
HA!
HOW WAS THAT, ANNE?
ONCE THEY GET A LOOK AT MY BRAVE...

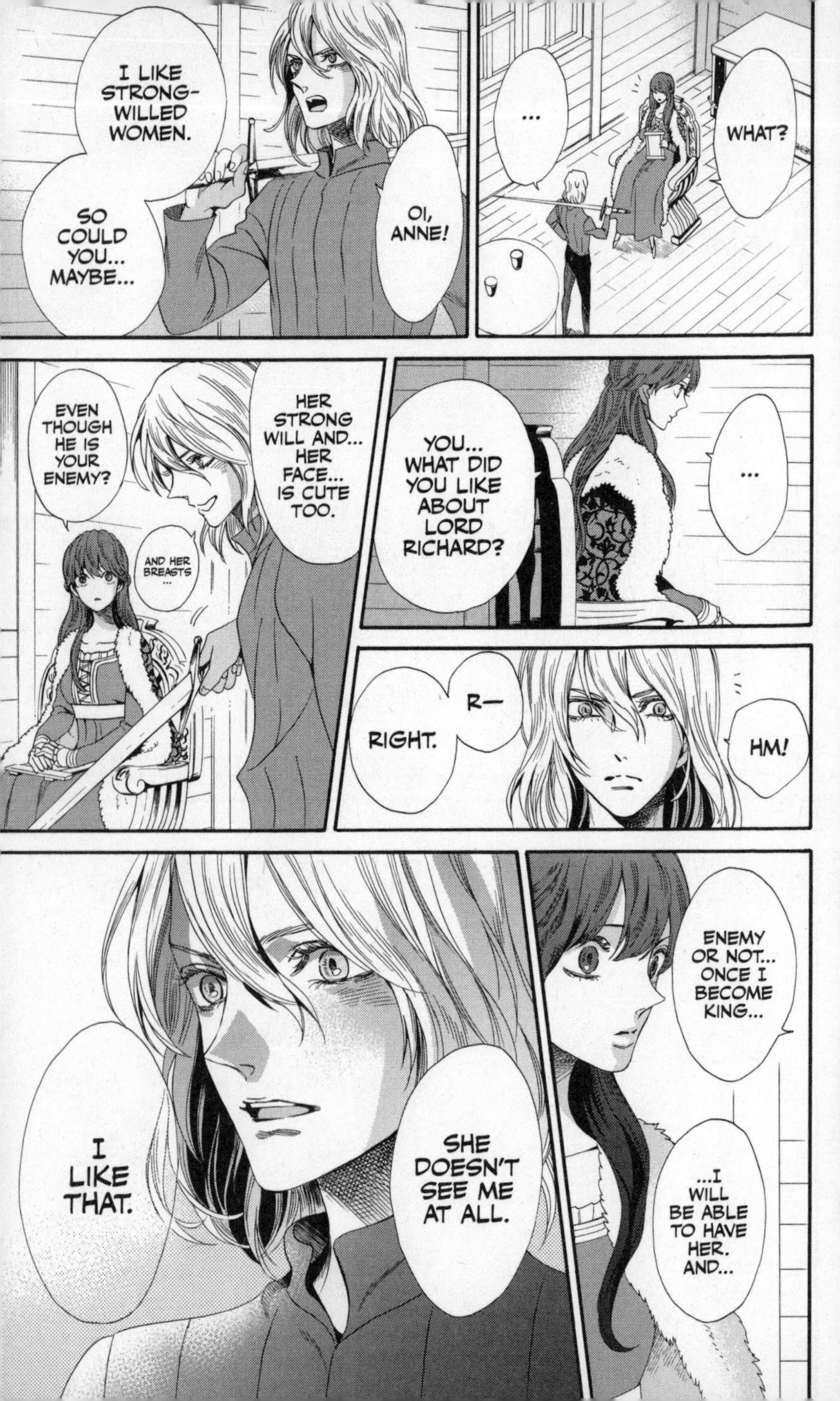
WHAT?
...
OI, ANNE!
I LIKE STRONG-WILLED WOMEN.
SO COULD YOU... MAYBE...
...
YOU... WHAT DID YOU LIKE ABOUT LORD RICHARD?
HM!
R—
RIGHT.
HER STRONG WILL AND... HER FACE... IS CUTE TOO.
AND HER BREASTS ...
EVEN THOUGH HE IS YOUR ENEMY?
ENEMY OR NOT... ONCE I BECOME KING...
...I WILL BE ABLE TO HAVE HER. AND...
SHE DOESN'T SEE ME AT ALL.
I LIKE THAT.

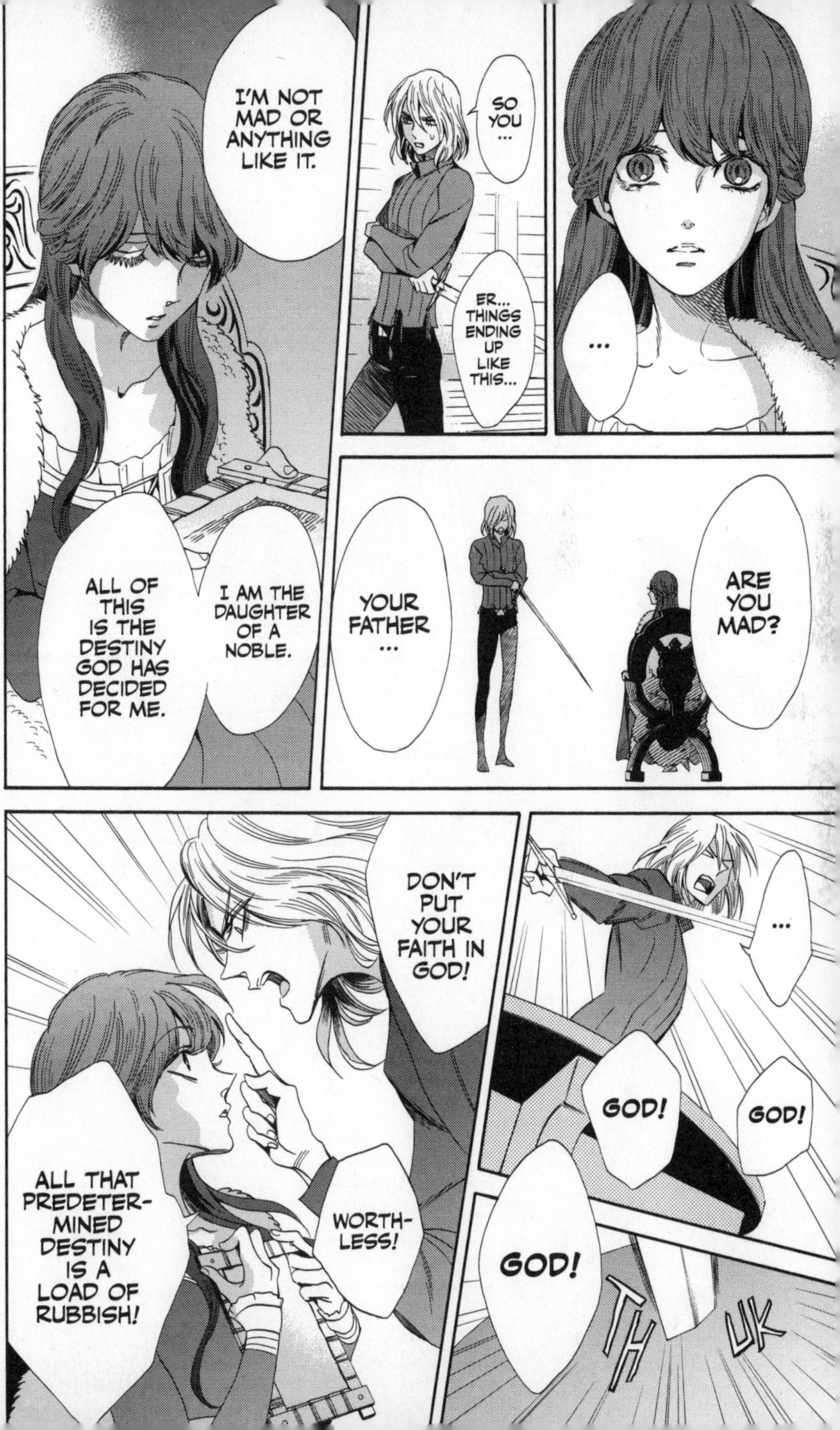
...
SO YOU ...
ER... THINGS ENDING UP LIKE THIS...
ARE YOU MAD?
YOUR FATHER ...
I'M NOT MAD OR ANYTHING LIKE IT.
I AM THE DAUGHTER OF A NOBLE.
ALL OF THIS IS THE DESTINY GOD HAS DECIDED FOR ME.
...
GOD!
GOD!
GOD!
THUK
DON'T PUT YOUR FAITH IN GOD!
WORTH-LESS!
ALL THAT PREDETER-MINED DESTINY IS A LOAD OF RUBBISH!

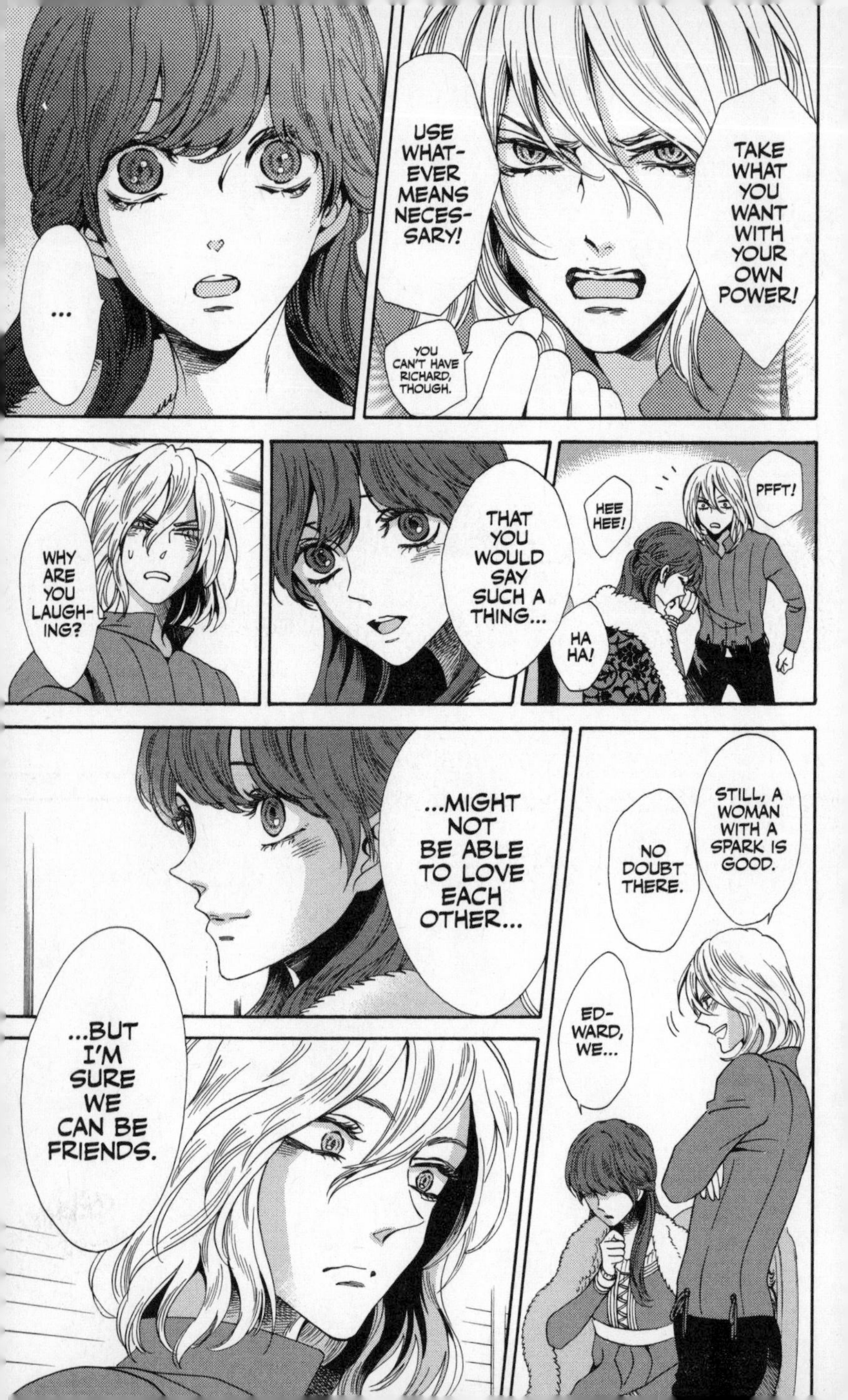
TAKE WHAT YOU WANT WITH YOUR OWN POWER!
USE WHAT-EVER MEANS NECES-SARY!
YOU CAN'T HAVE RICHARD, THOUGH.
...
PFFT!
HEE HEE!
HA HA!
THAT YOU WOULD SAY SUCH A THING...
WHY ARE YOU LAUGH-ING?
STILL, A WOMAN WITH A SPARK IS GOOD.
NO DOUBT THERE.
ED-WARD, WE...
...MIGHT NOT BE ABLE TO LOVE EACH OTHER...
...BUT I'M SURE WE CAN BE FRIENDS.

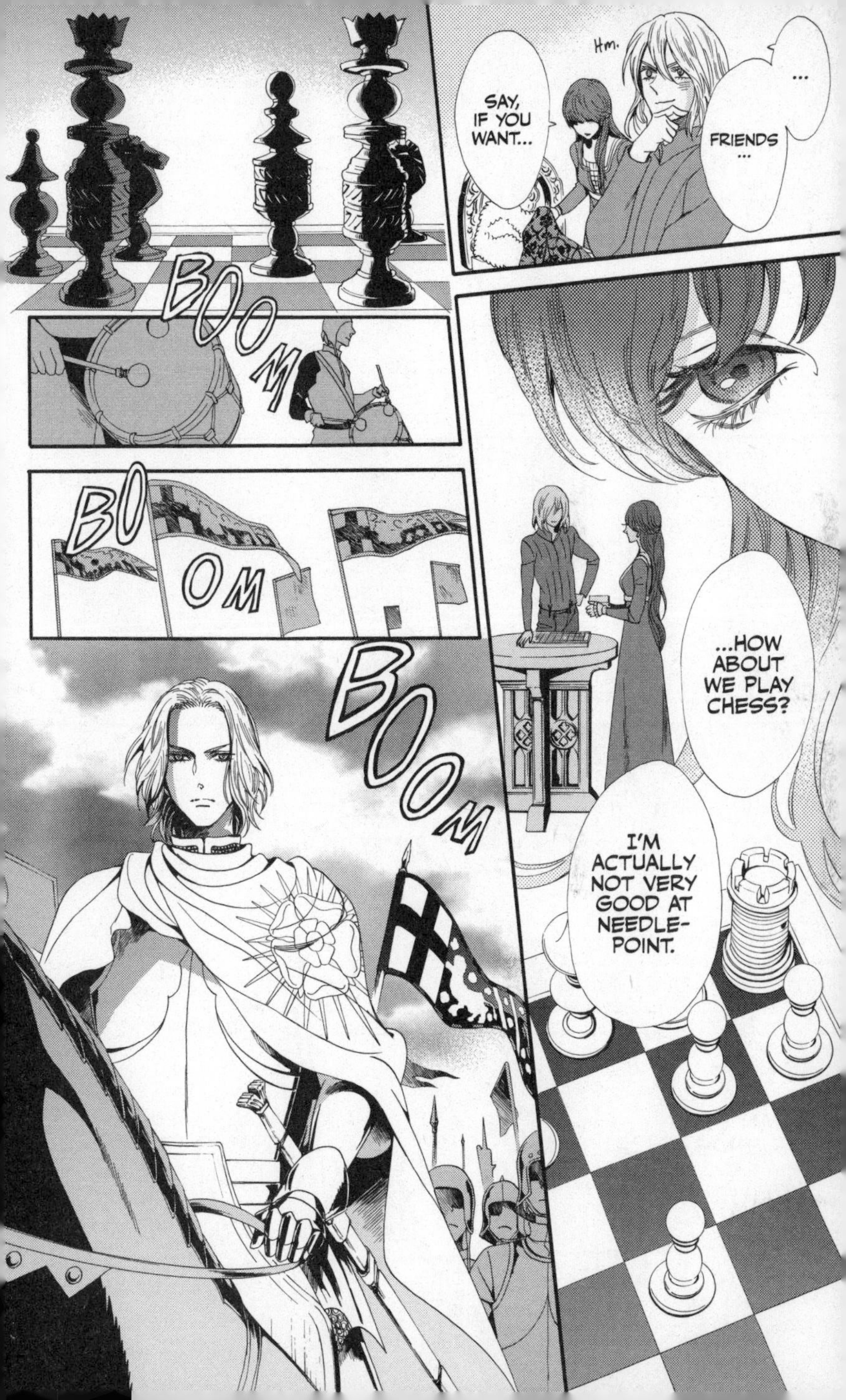
...
Hm.
FRIENDS ...
SAY, IF YOU WANT...
BOOM
...HOW ABOUT WE PLAY CHESS?
I'M ACTUALLY NOT VERY GOOD AT NEEDLE-POINT.
BO OM
BOOM

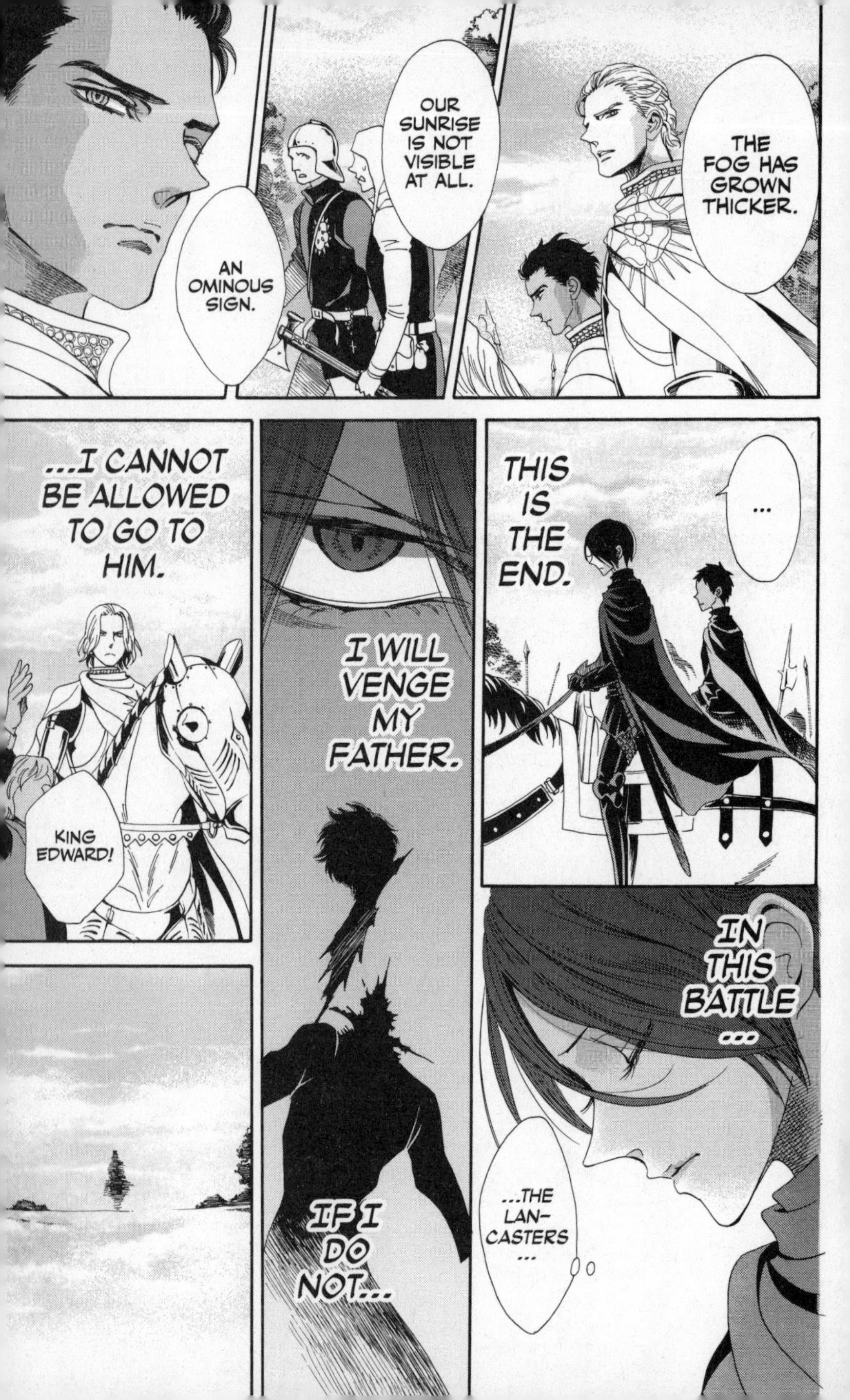
THE FOG HAS GROWN THICKER.
OUR SUNRISE IS NOT VISIBLE AT ALL.
AN OMINOUS SIGN.
...
THIS IS THE END.
IN THIS BATTLE...
...THE LANCASTERS...
I WILL VENGE MY FATHER.
IF I DO NOT...
...I CANNOT BE ALLOWED TO GO TO HIM.
KING EDWARD!

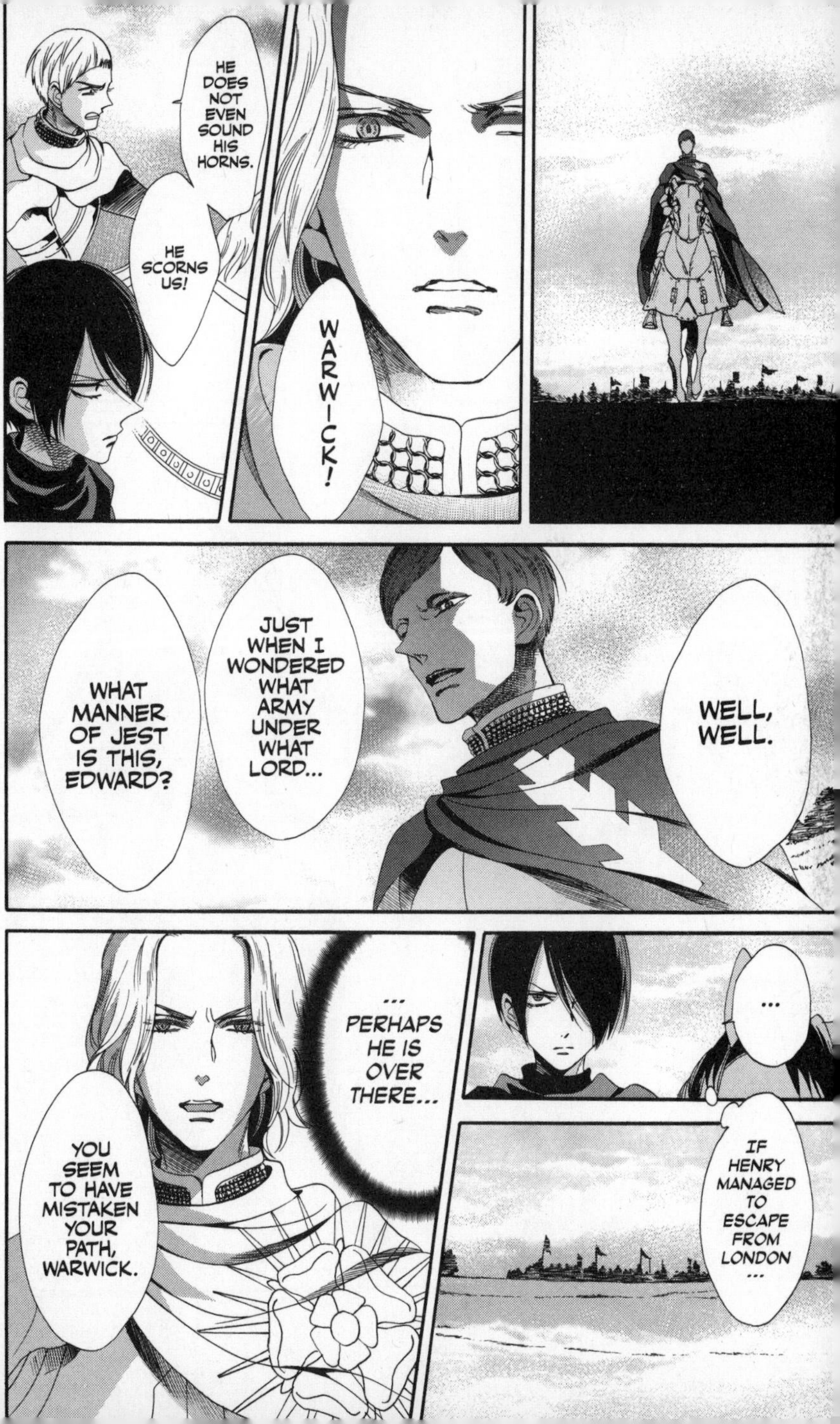
WARWICK!
HE DOES NOT EVEN SOUND HIS HORNS.
HE SCORNS US!
WELL, WELL.
JUST WHEN I WONDERED WHAT ARMY UNDER WHAT LORD...
WHAT MANNER OF JEST IS THIS, EDWARD?
...
IF HENRY MANAGED TO ESCAPE FROM LONDON ...
... PERHAPS HE IS OVER THERE...
YOU SEEM TO HAVE MISTAKEN YOUR PATH, WARWICK.

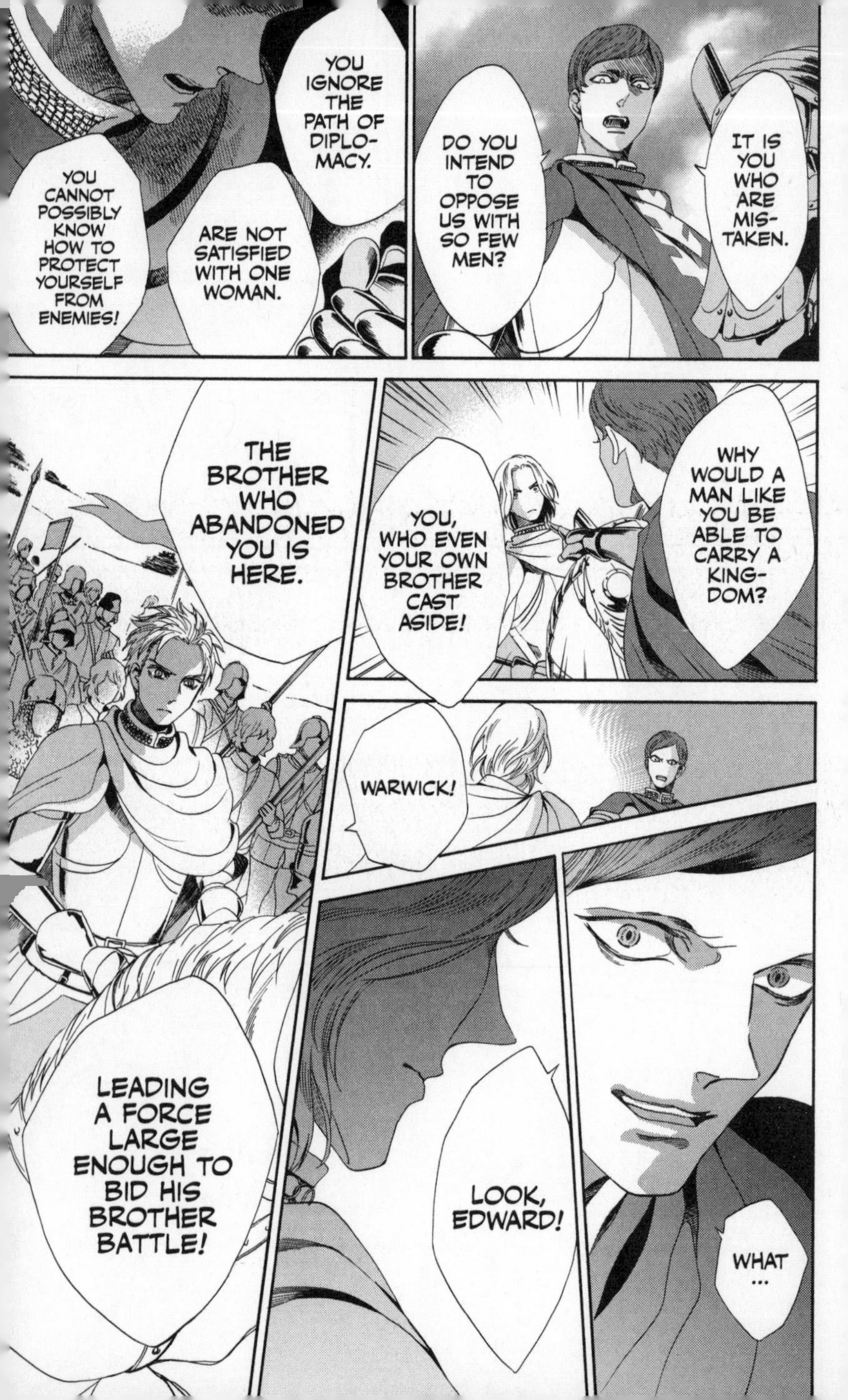
DO YOU INTEND TO OPPOSE US WITH SO FEW MEN?
IT IS YOU WHO ARE MISTAKEN.
YOU IGNORE THE PATH OF DIPLOMACY.
ARE NOT SATISFIED WITH ONE WOMAN.
YOU CANNOT POSSIBLY KNOW HOW TO PROTECT YOURSELF FROM ENEMIES!
WHY WOULD A MAN LIKE YOU BE ABLE TO CARRY A KINGDOM?
YOU, WHO EVEN YOUR OWN BROTHER CAST ASIDE!
WARWICK!
WHAT...
LOOK, EDWARD!
THE BROTHER WHO ABANDONED YOU IS HERE.
LEADING A FORCE LARGE ENOUGH TO BID HIS BROTHER BATTLE!

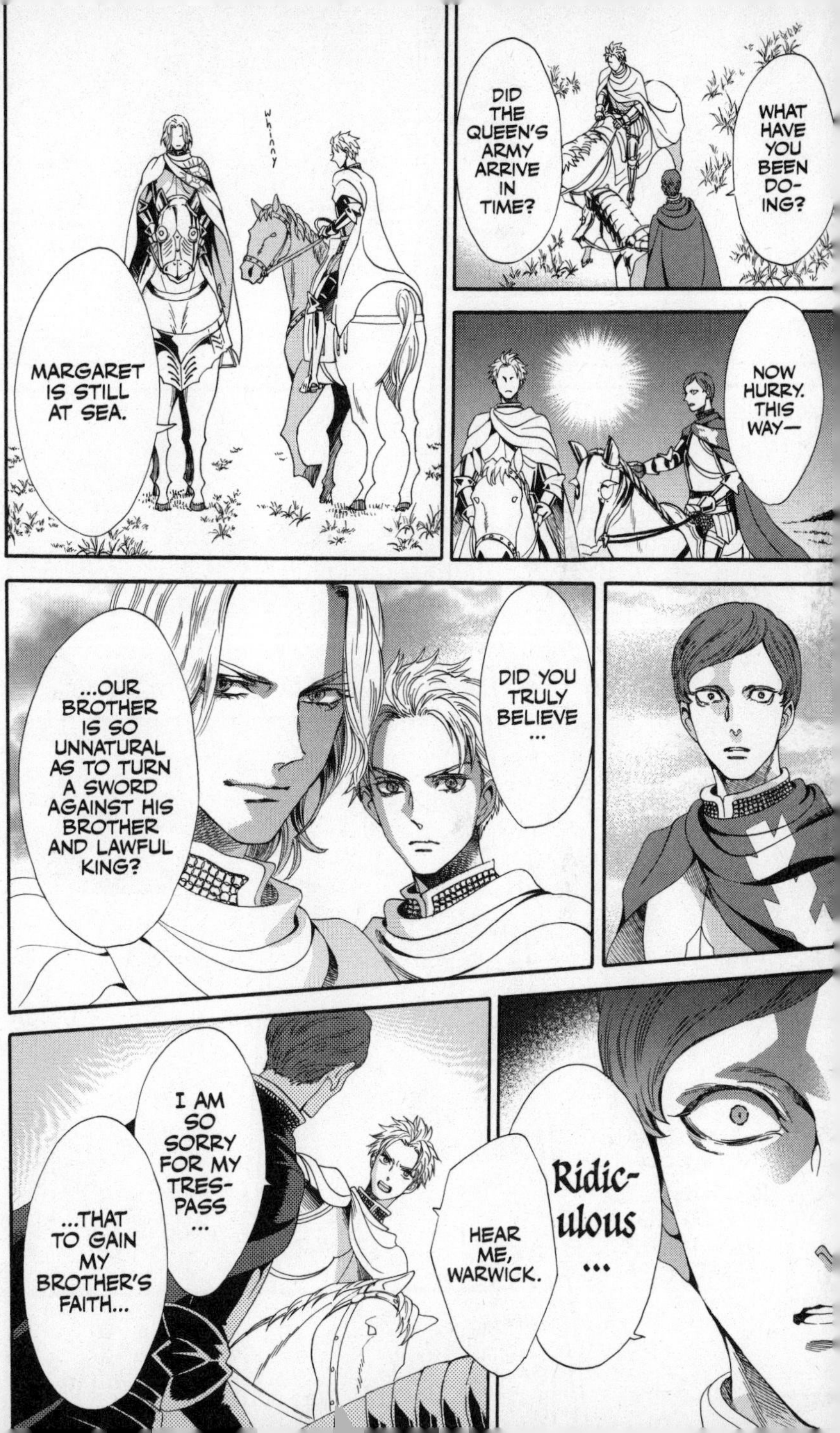
WHAT HAVE YOU BEEN DO-ING?
DID THE QUEEN'S ARMY ARRIVE IN TIME?
NOW HURRY. THIS WAY—
whinny
MARGARET IS STILL AT SEA.
DID YOU TRULY BELIEVE...
...OUR BROTHER IS SO UNNATURAL AS TO TURN A SWORD AGAINST HIS BROTHER AND LAWFUL KING?
Ridic-ulous...
HEAR ME, WARWICK.
I AM SO SORRY FOR MY TRES-PASS...
...THAT TO GAIN MY BROTHER'S FAITH...

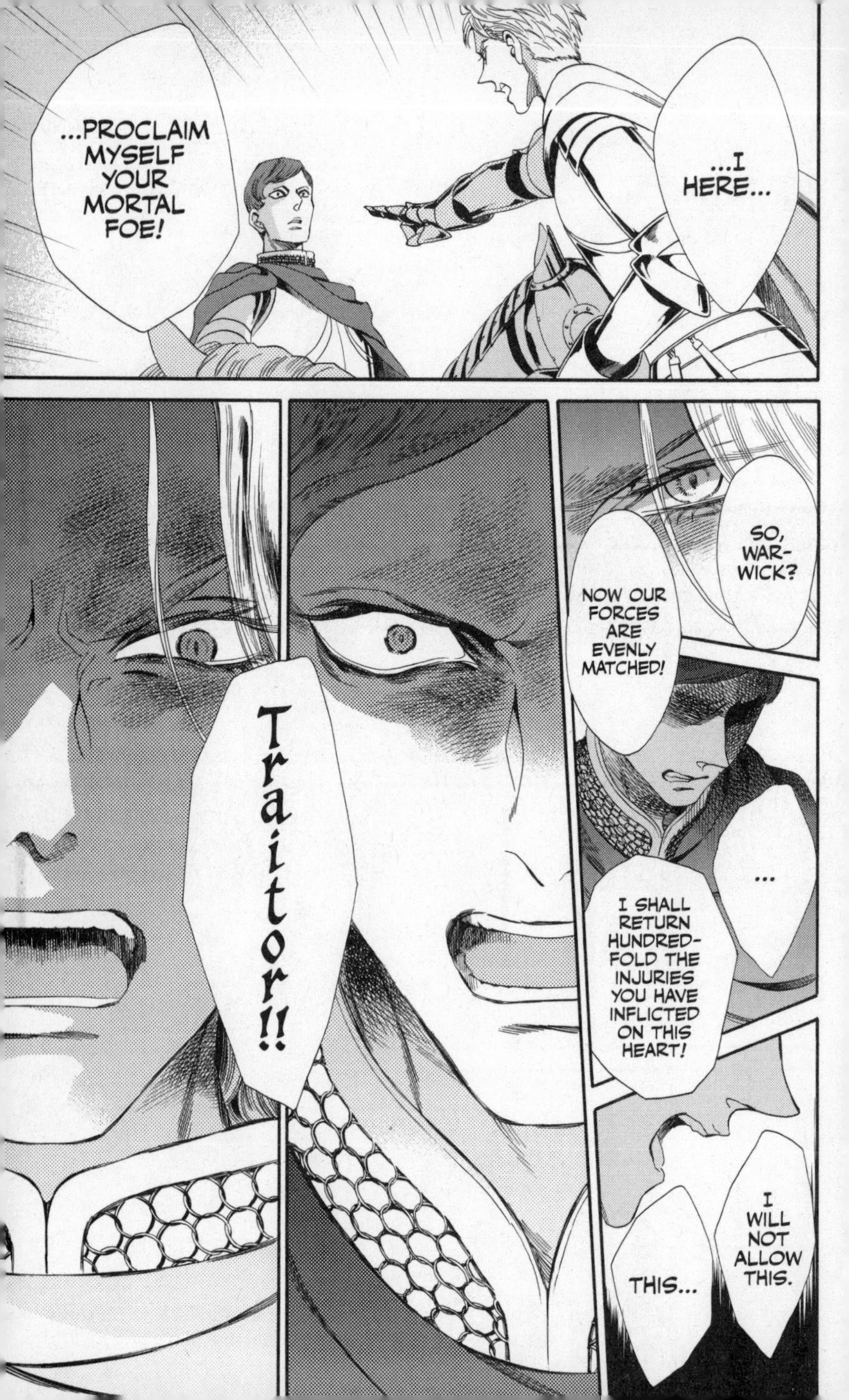
...I HERE...
...PROCLAIM MYSELF YOUR MORTAL FOE!
SO, WAR-WICK?
NOW OUR FORCES ARE EVENLY MATCHED!
...
I SHALL RETURN HUNDRED-FOLD THE INJURIES YOU HAVE INFLICTED ON THIS HEART!
I WILL NOT ALLOW THIS.
THIS...
Traitor!!

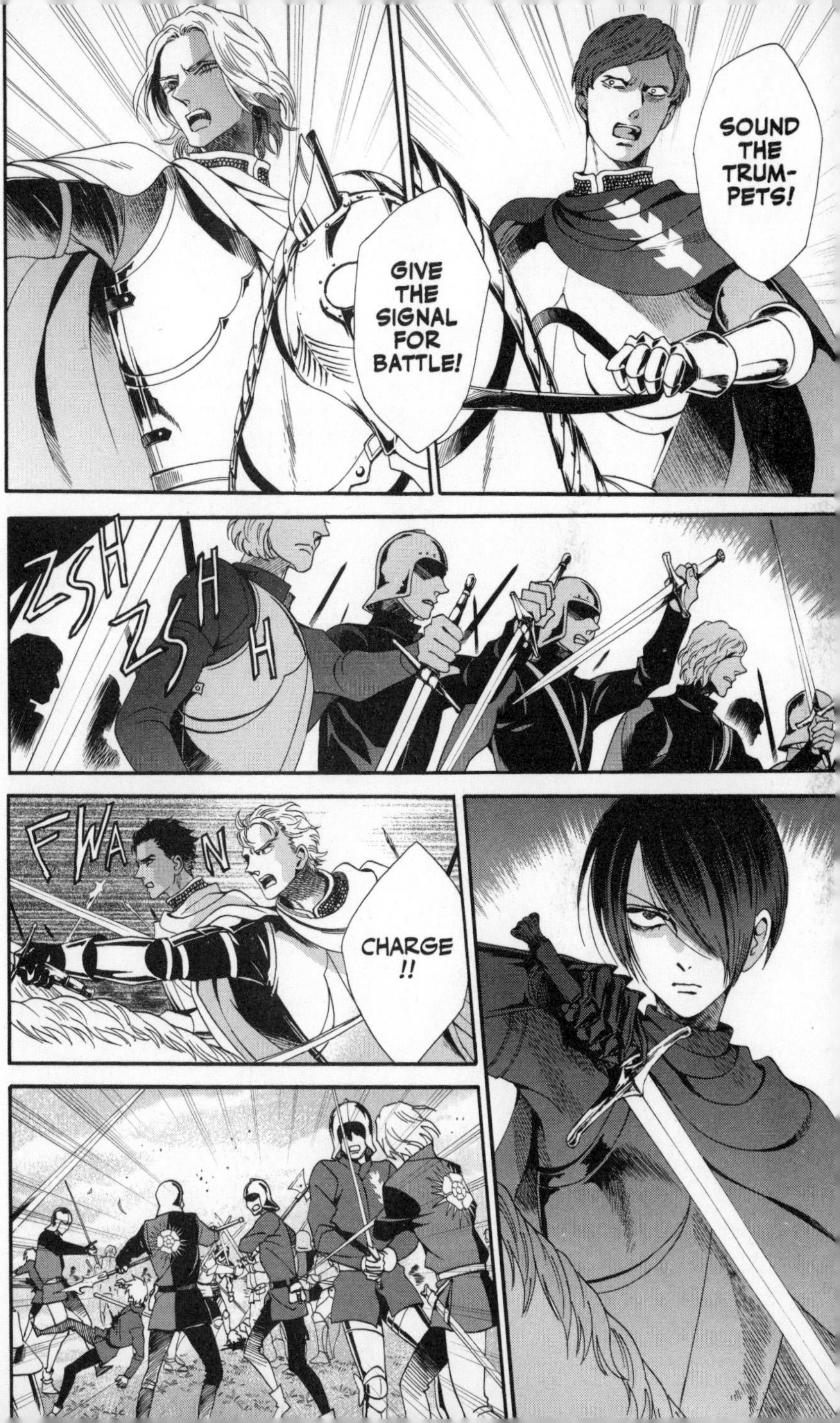
SOUND THE TRUM-PETS!
GIVE THE SIGNAL FOR BATTLE!
ZSH
ZSH
FWAN
CHARGE!!

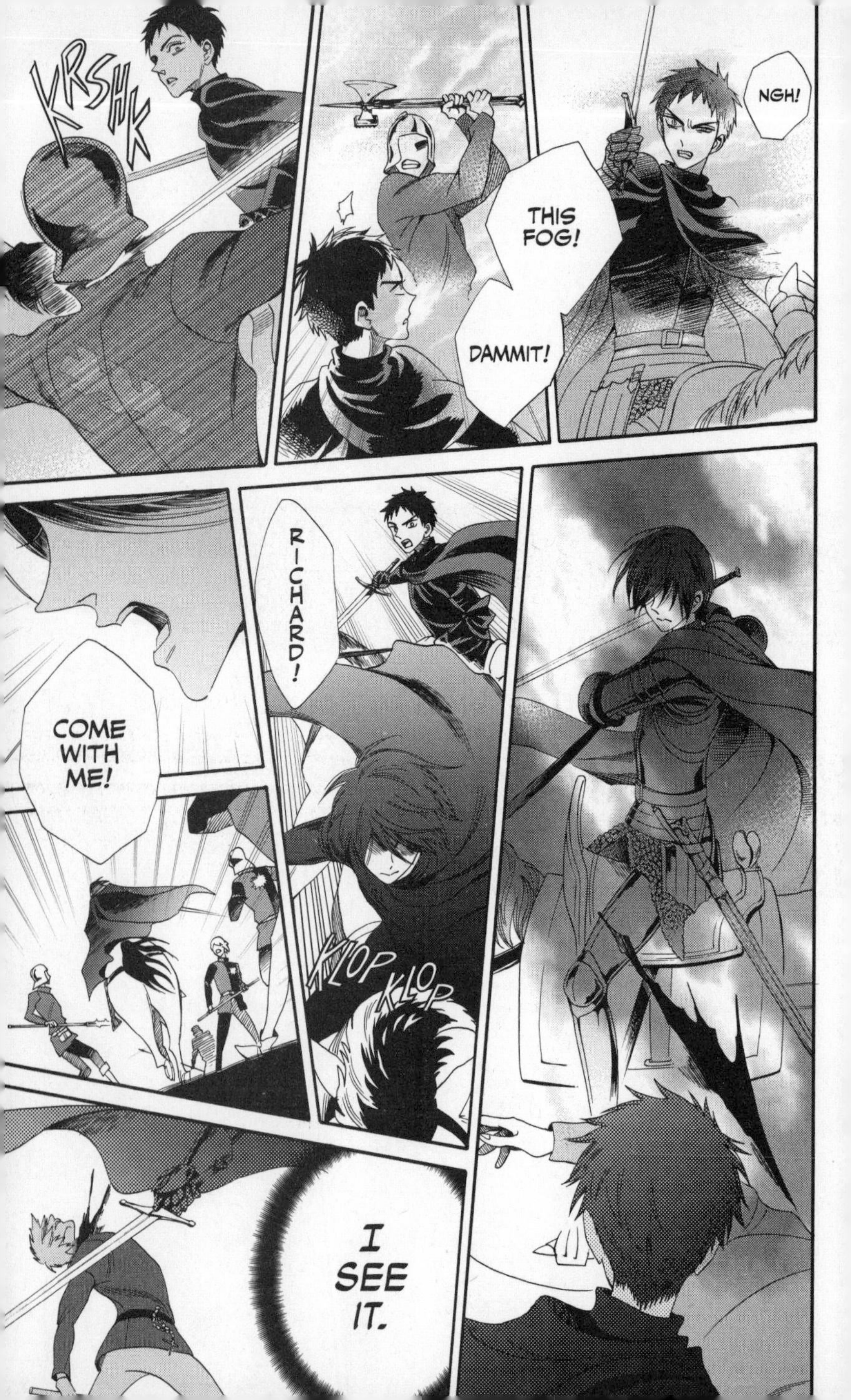
NGH!
THIS FOG!
DAMMIT!
KRSHK
RICHARD!
KLOP KLOP
COME WITH ME!
I SEE IT.

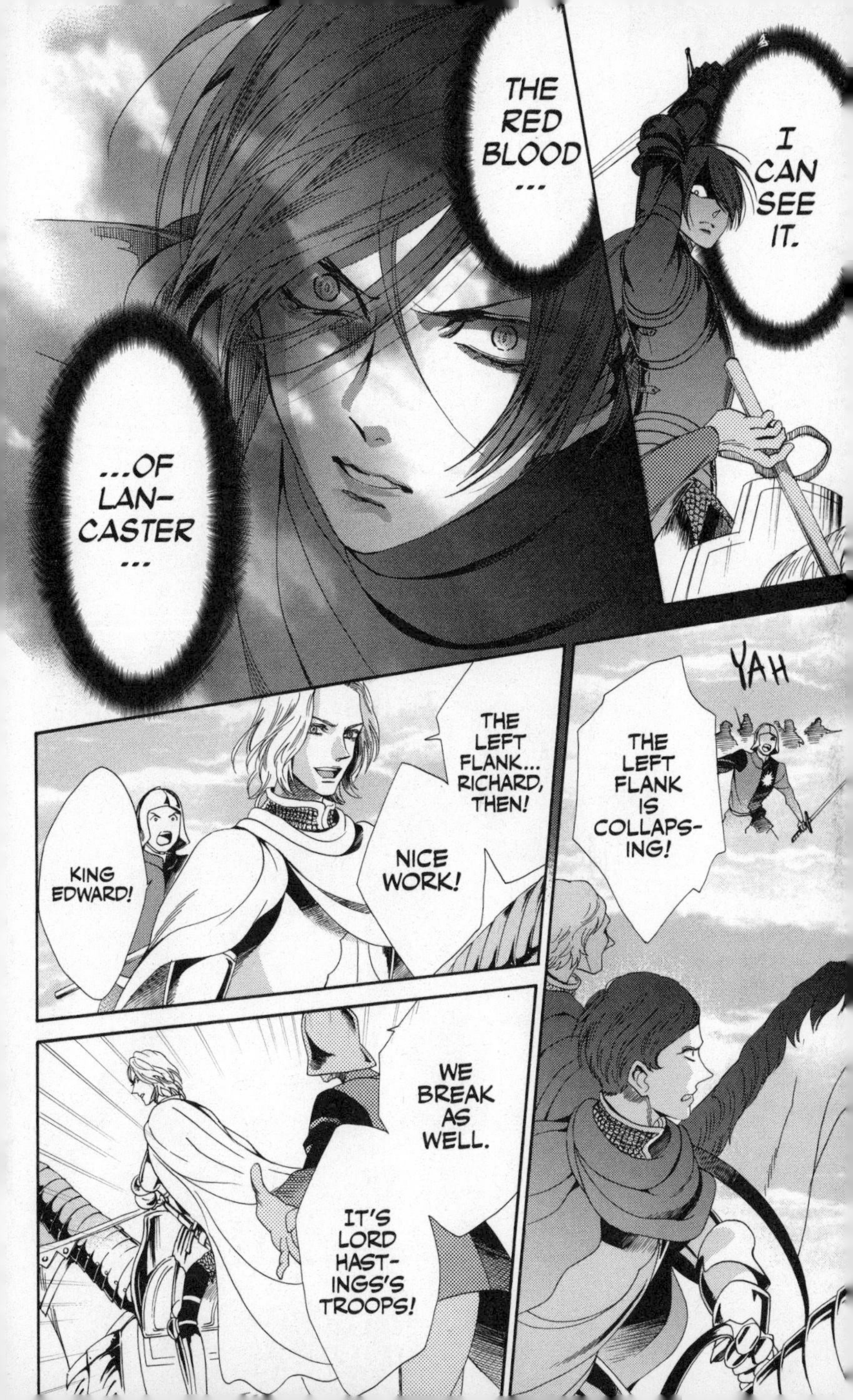
I CAN SEE IT.
THE RED BLOOD...
...OF LANCASTER...
YAH
THE LEFT FLANK IS COLLAPSING!
IT'S LORD HASTINGS'S TROOPS!
THE LEFT FLANK... RICHARD, THEN!
NICE WORK!
KING EDWARD!
WE BREAK AS WELL.

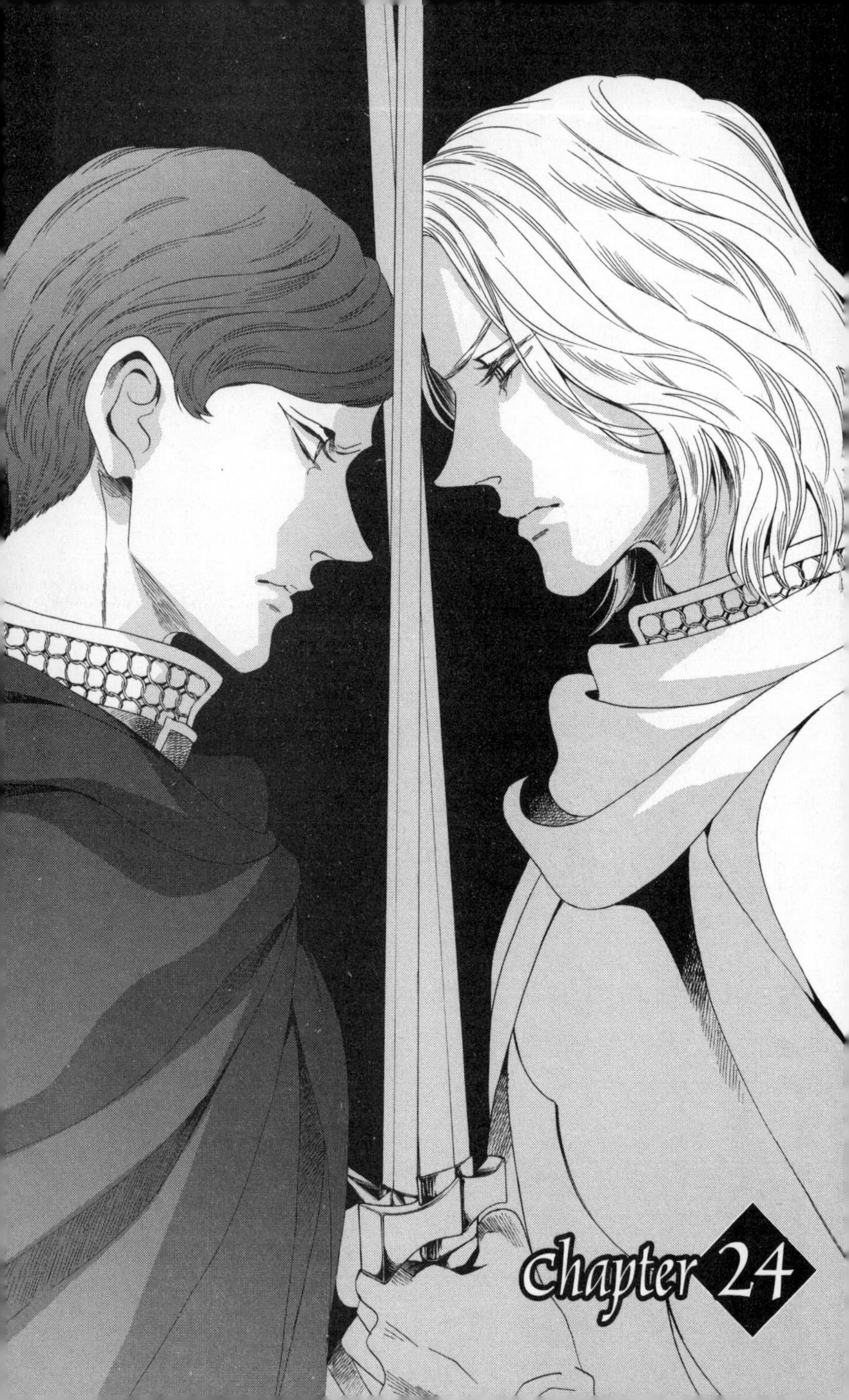
Chapter 24

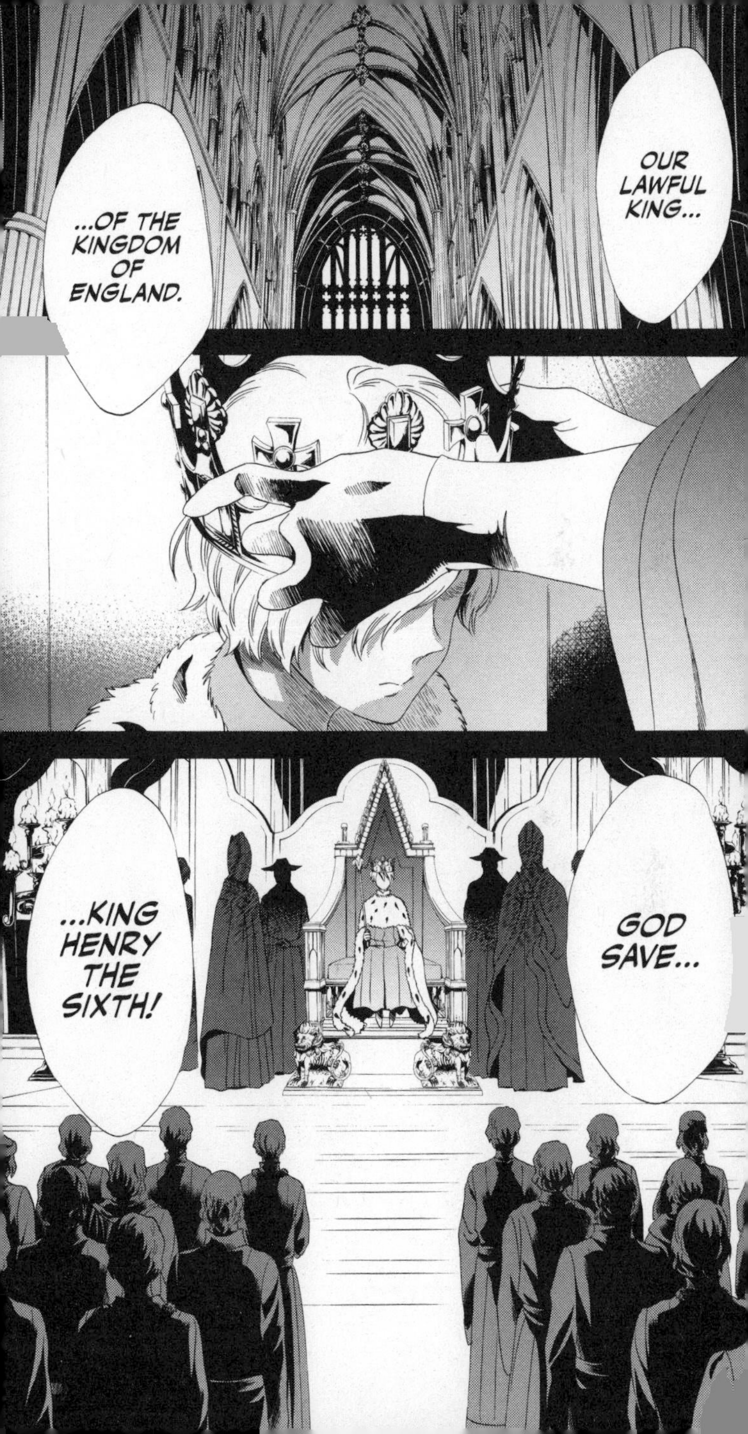
OUR LAWFUL KING...
...OF THE KINGDOM OF ENGLAND.
GOD SAVE...
...KING HENRY THE SIXTH!

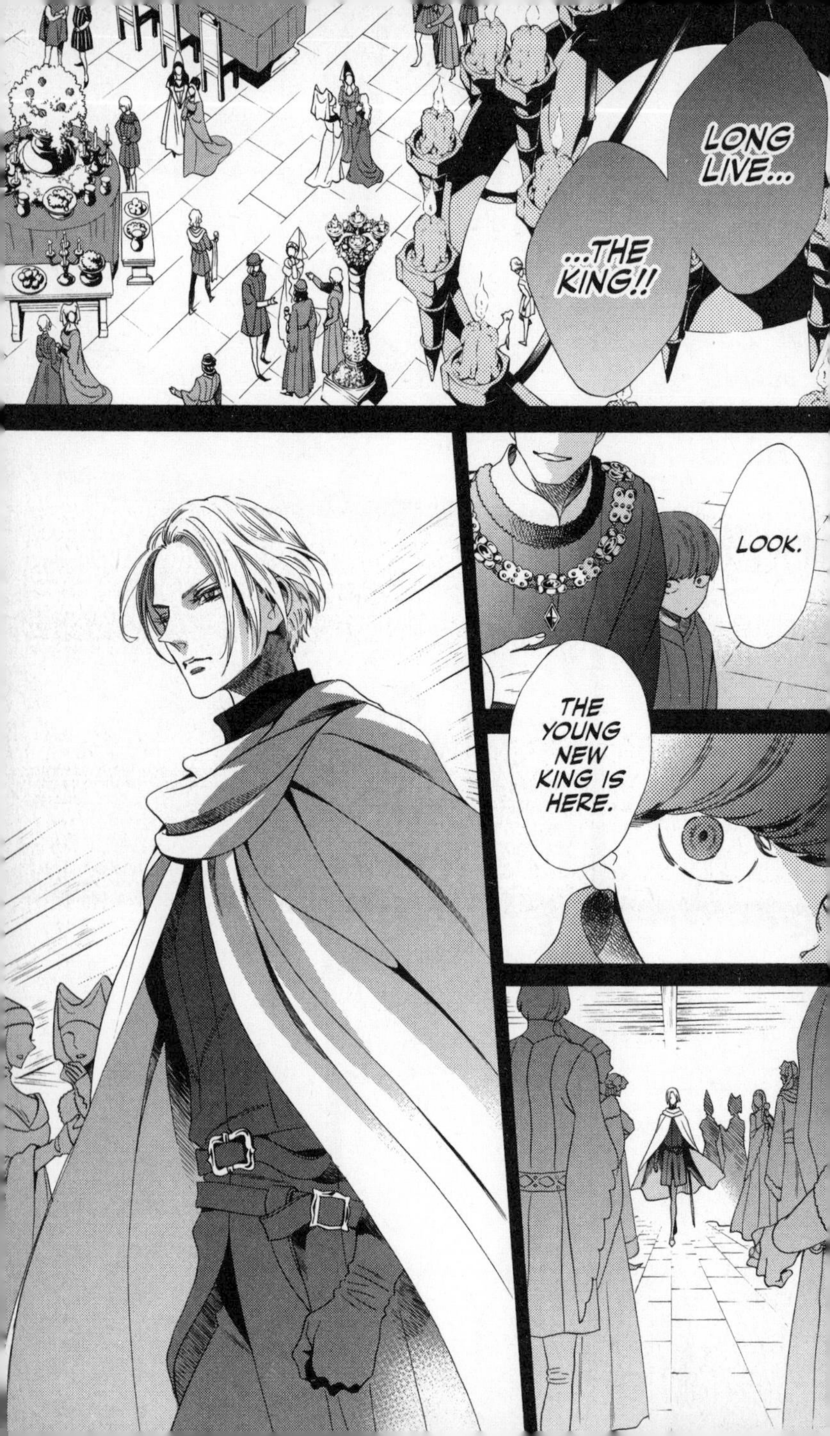
LONG LIVE...
...THE KING!!
LOOK.
THE YOUNG NEW KING IS HERE.

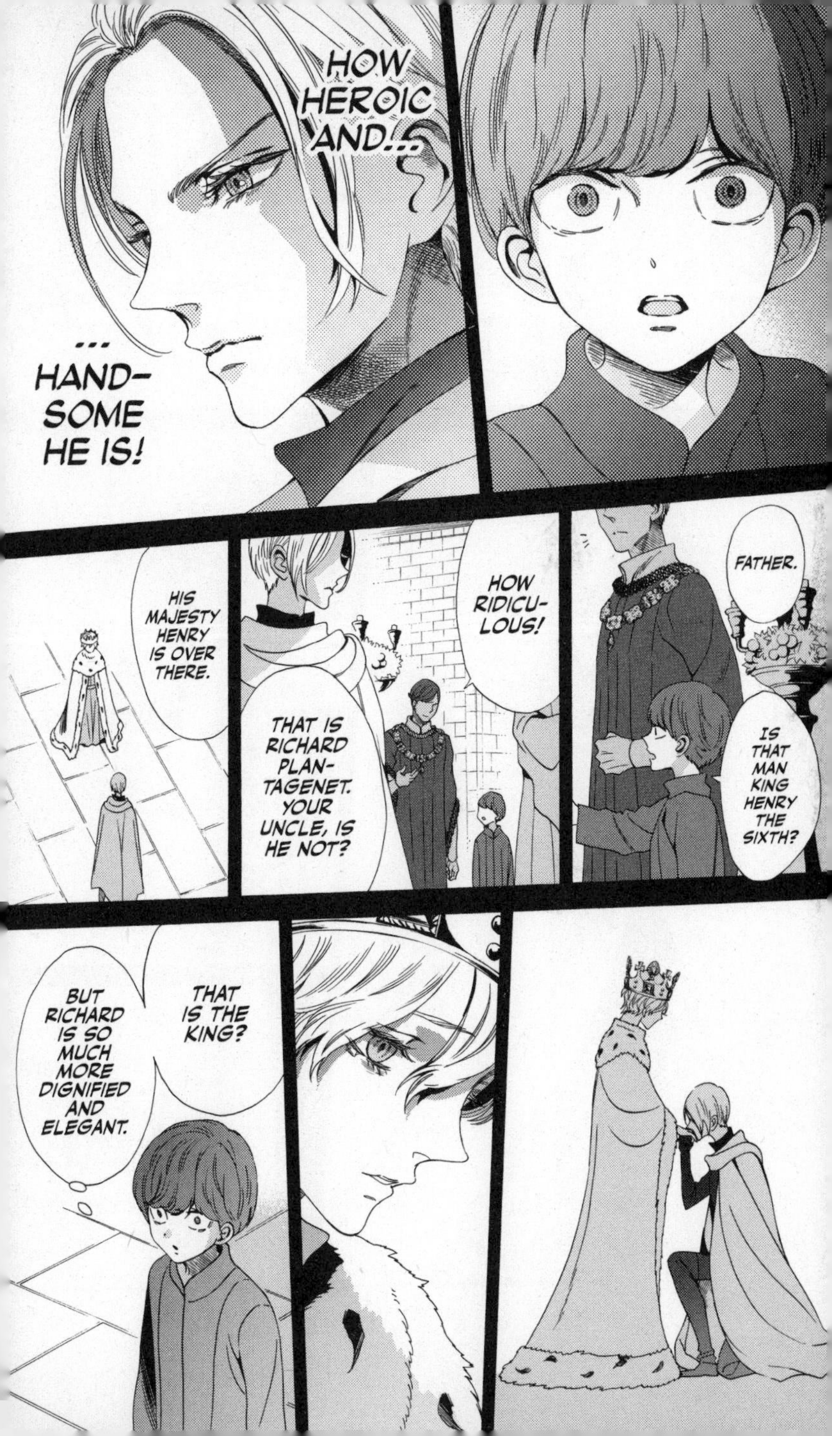
HOW HEROIC AND...
... HAND-SOME HE IS!
FATHER.
IS THAT MAN KING HENRY THE SIXTH?
HOW RIDICU-LOUS!
THAT IS RICHARD PLAN-TAGENET. YOUR UNCLE, IS HE NOT?
HIS MAJESTY HENRY IS OVER THERE.
THAT IS THE KING?
BUT RICHARD IS SO MUCH MORE DIGNIFIED AND ELEGANT.

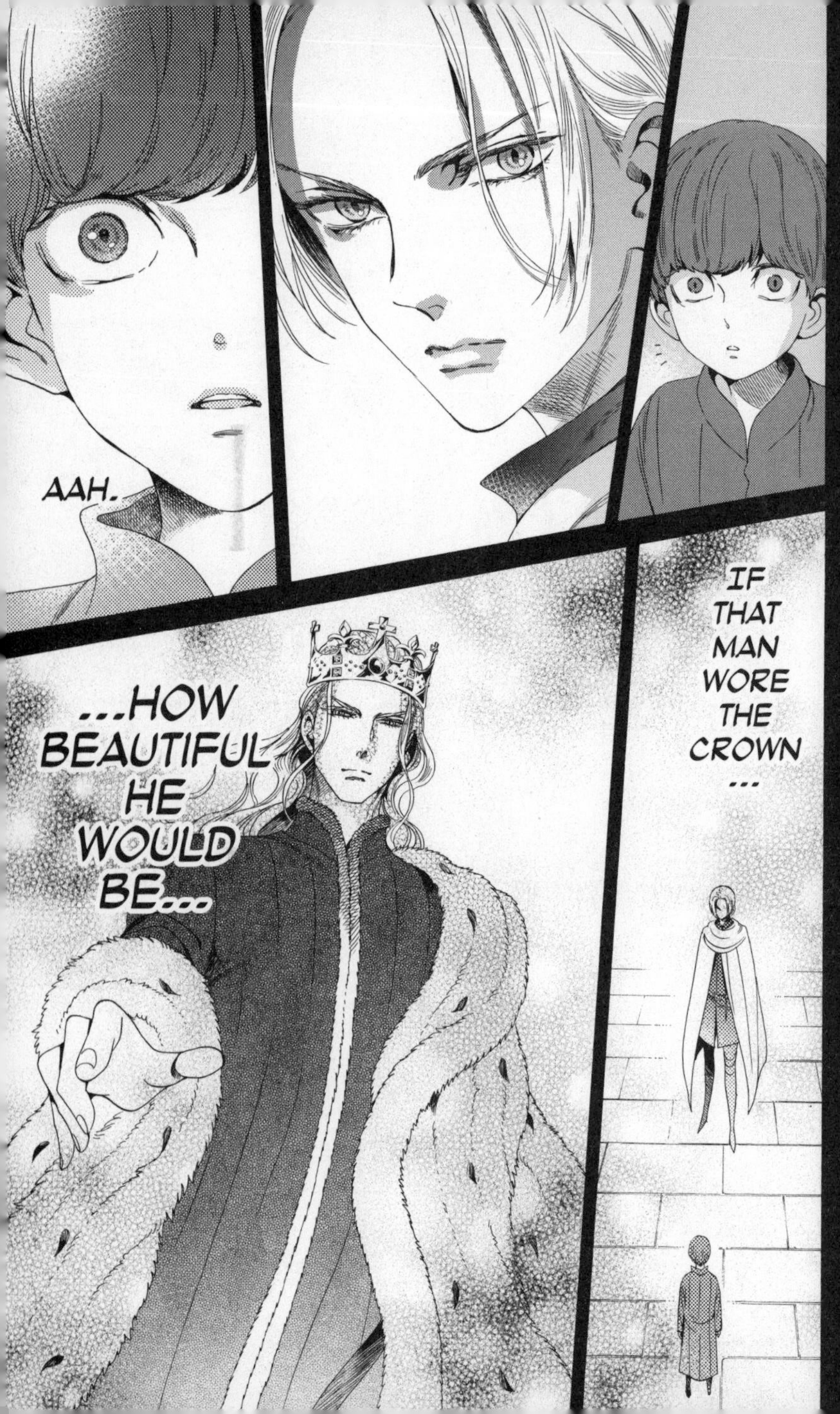
AAH.
IF THAT MAN WORE THE CROWN...
...HOW BEAUTIFUL HE WOULD BE...

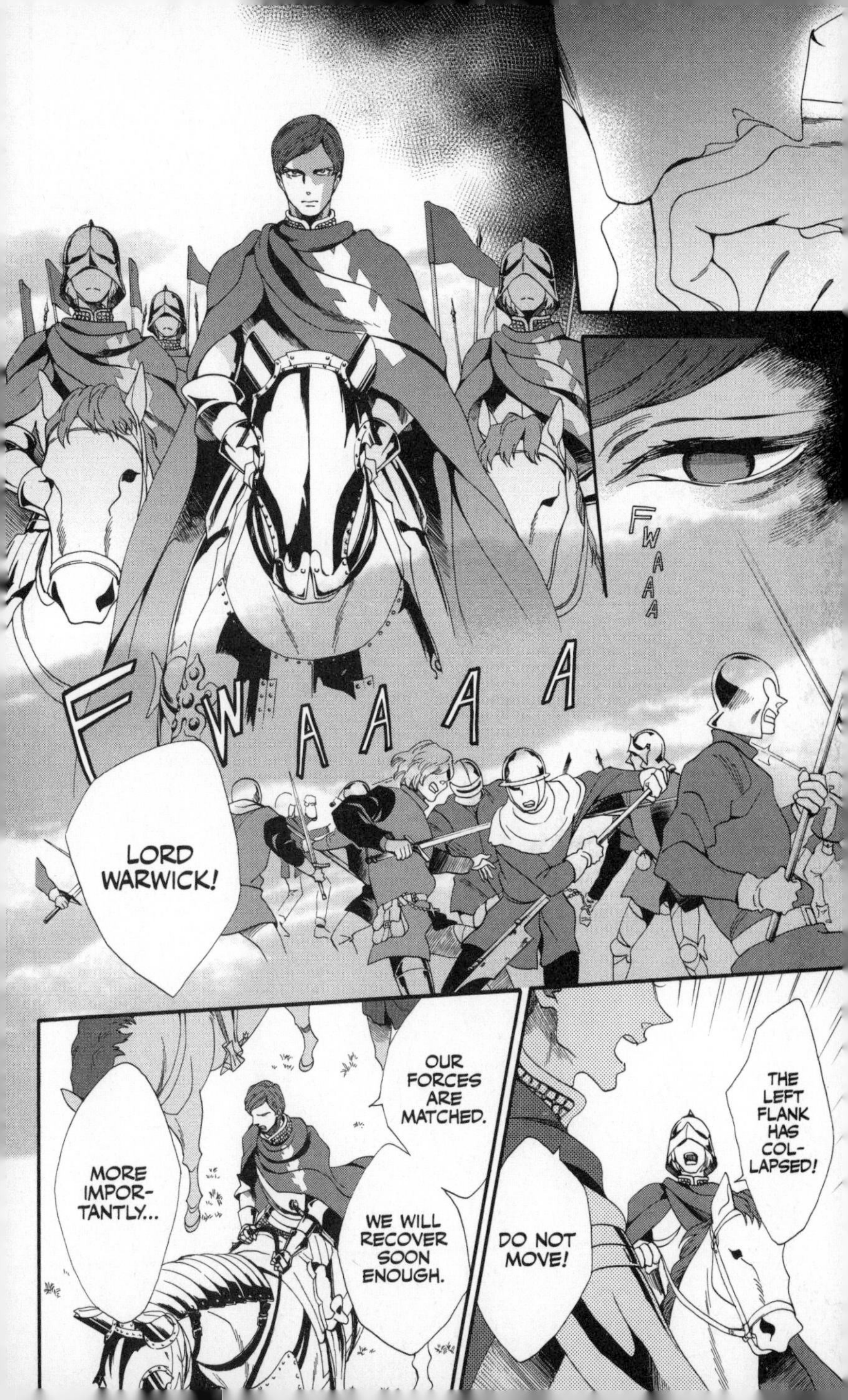
FWAAA
FWAAAA
LORD WARWICK!
THE LEFT FLANK HAS COL-LAPSED!
DO NOT MOVE!
OUR FORCES ARE MATCHED.
WE WILL RECOVER SOON ENOUGH.
MORE IMPOR-TANTLY...

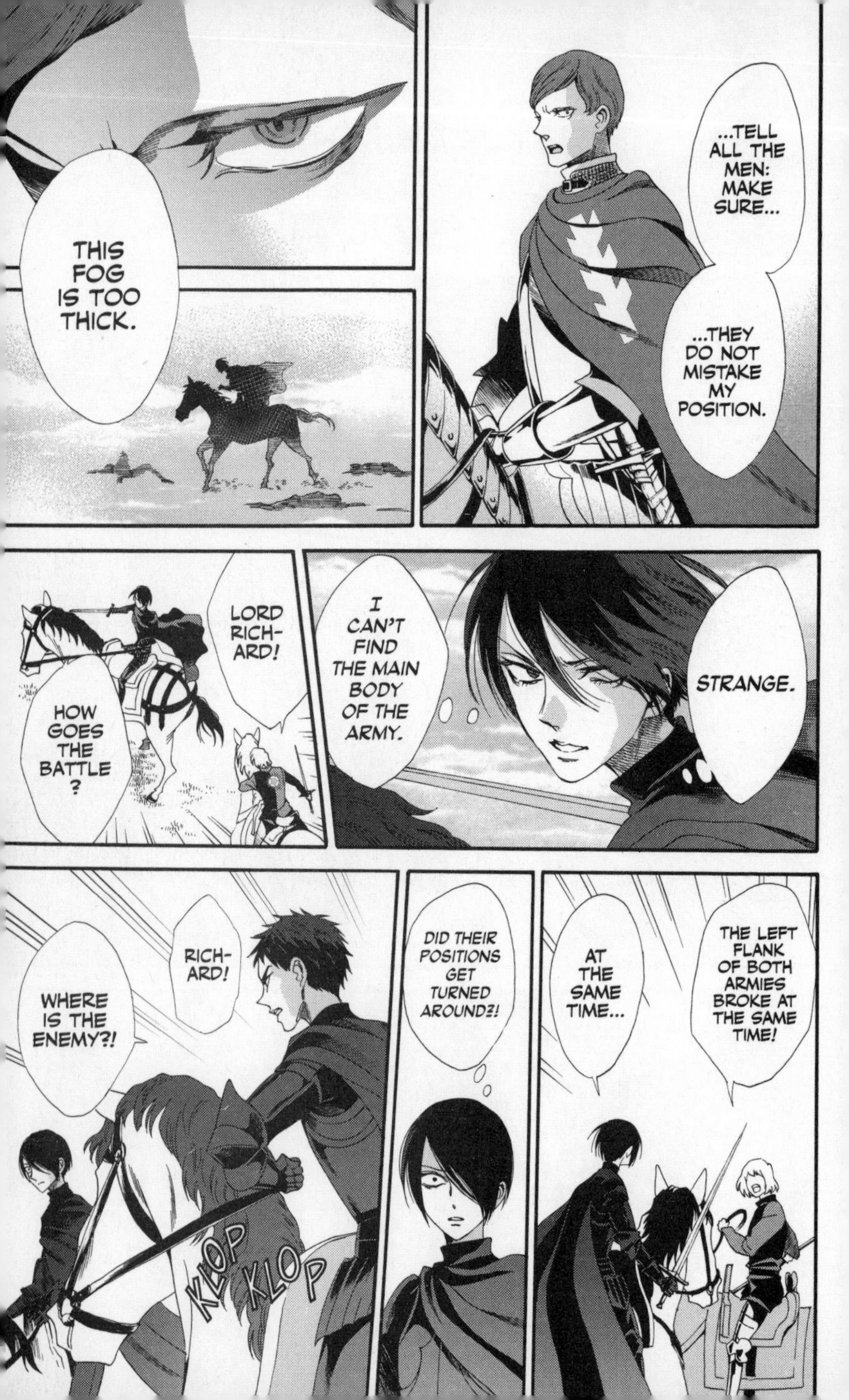
...TELL ALL THE MEN: MAKE SURE...
...THEY DO NOT MISTAKE MY POSITION.
THIS FOG IS TOO THICK.
STRANGE.
I CAN'T FIND THE MAIN BODY OF THE ARMY.
LORD RICHARD!
HOW GOES THE BATTLE?
THE LEFT FLANK OF BOTH ARMIES BROKE AT THE SAME TIME!
AT THE SAME TIME...
DID THEIR POSITIONS GET TURNED AROUND?!
RICHARD!
WHERE IS THE ENEMY?!
KLOP KLOP

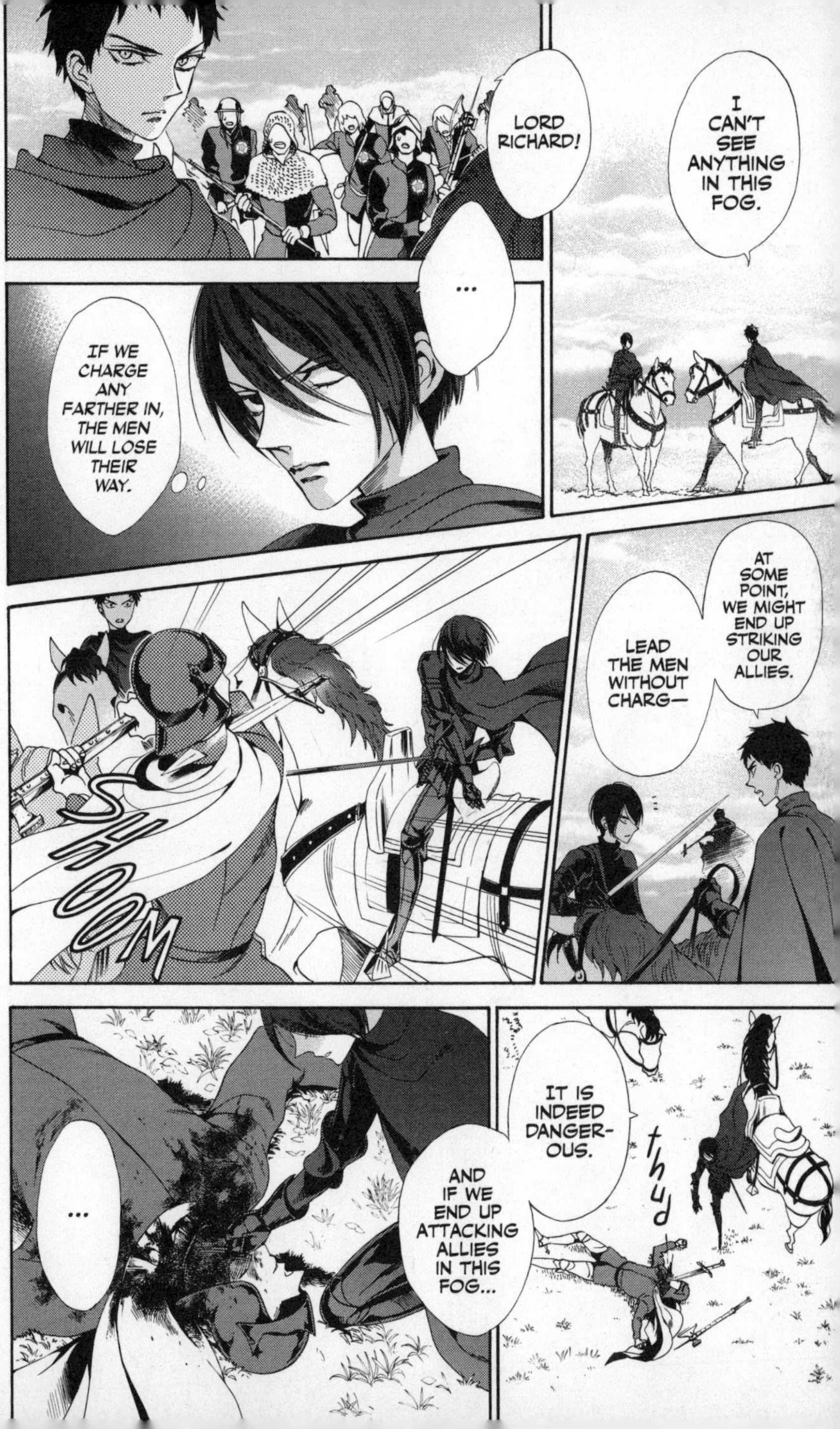
I CAN'T SEE ANYTHING IN THIS FOG.
LORD RICHARD!
...
IF WE CHARGE ANY FARTHER IN, THE MEN WILL LOSE THEIR WAY.
AT SOME POINT, WE MIGHT END UP STRIKING OUR ALLIES.
LEAD THE MEN WITHOUT CHARG—
SHOOOM
IT IS INDEED DANGER-OUS.
thud
AND IF WE END UP ATTACKING ALLIES IN THIS FOG...
...

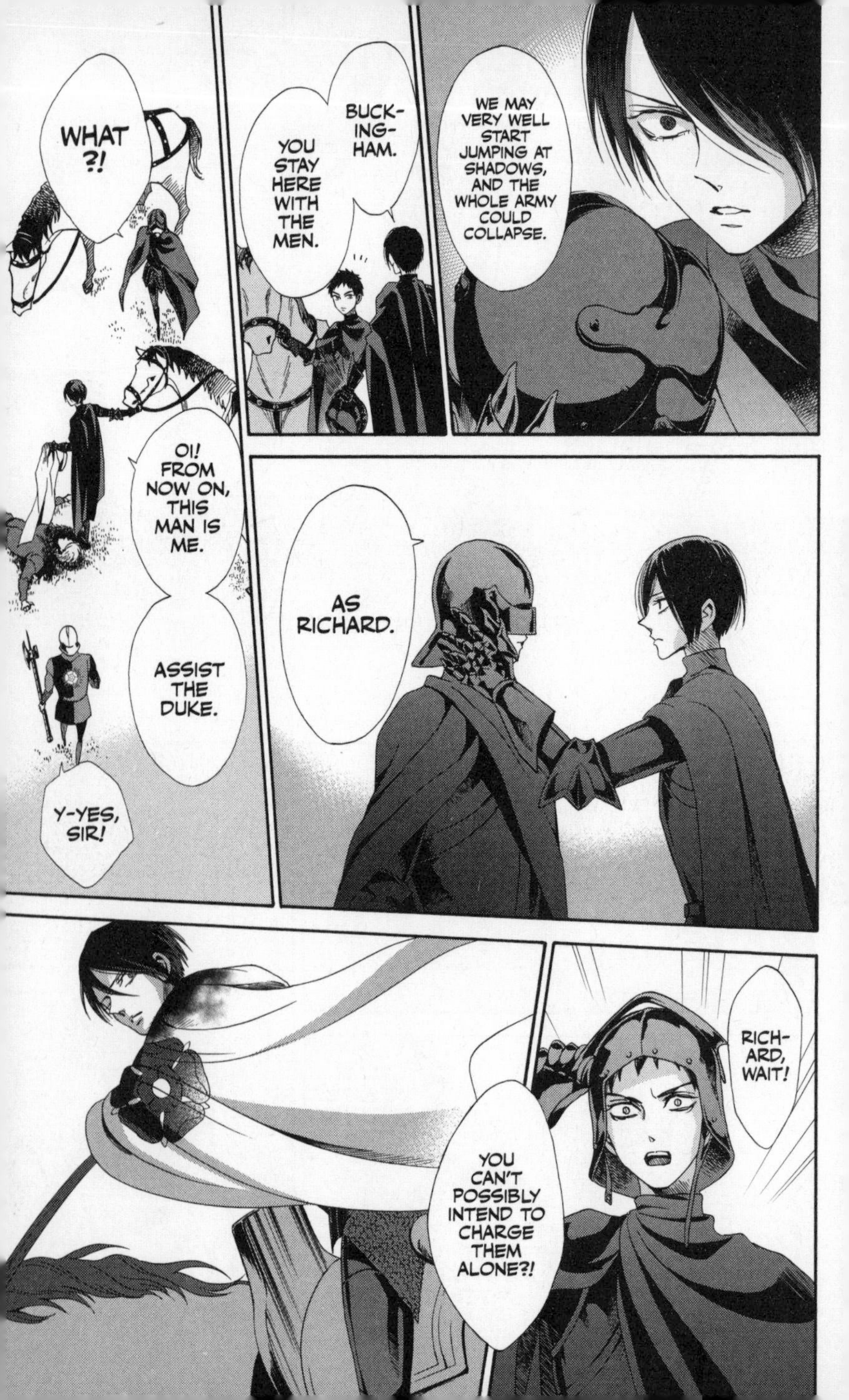
WE MAY VERY WELL START JUMPING AT SHADOWS, AND THE WHOLE ARMY COULD COLLAPSE.
BUCKINGHAM.
YOU STAY HERE WITH THE MEN.
AS RICHARD.
WHAT?!
OI! FROM NOW ON, THIS MAN IS ME.
ASSIST THE DUKE.
Y-YES, SIR!
RICHARD, WAIT!
YOU CAN'T POSSIBLY INTEND TO CHARGE THEM ALONE?!

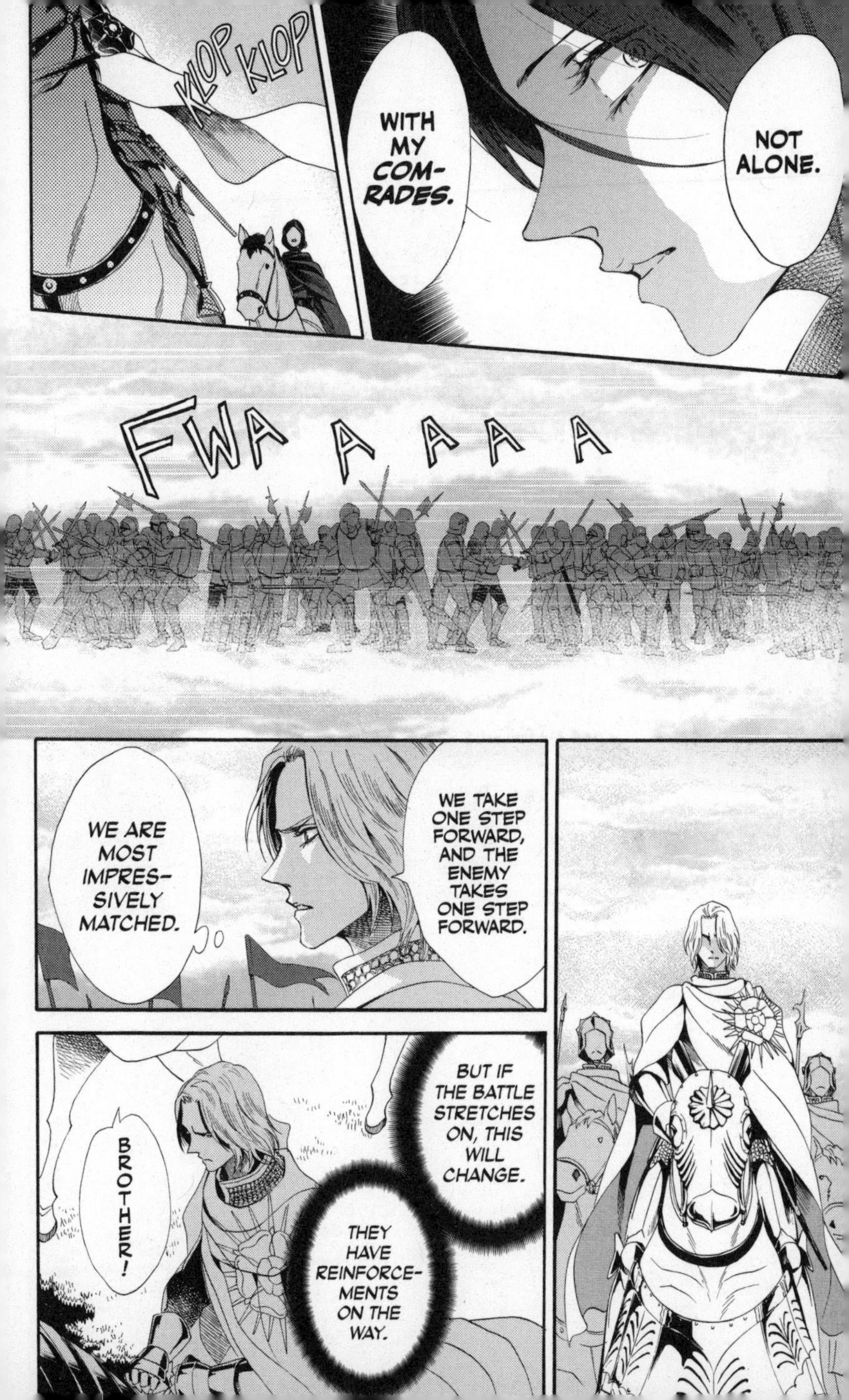
NOT ALONE.
WITH MY COMRADES.
KLOP KLOP
FWAAAAA
WE TAKE ONE STEP FORWARD, AND THE ENEMY TAKES ONE STEP FORWARD.
WE ARE MOST IMPRESSIVELY MATCHED.
BUT IF THE BATTLE STRETCHES ON, THIS WILL CHANGE.
THEY HAVE REINFORCEMENTS ON THE WAY.
BROTHER!

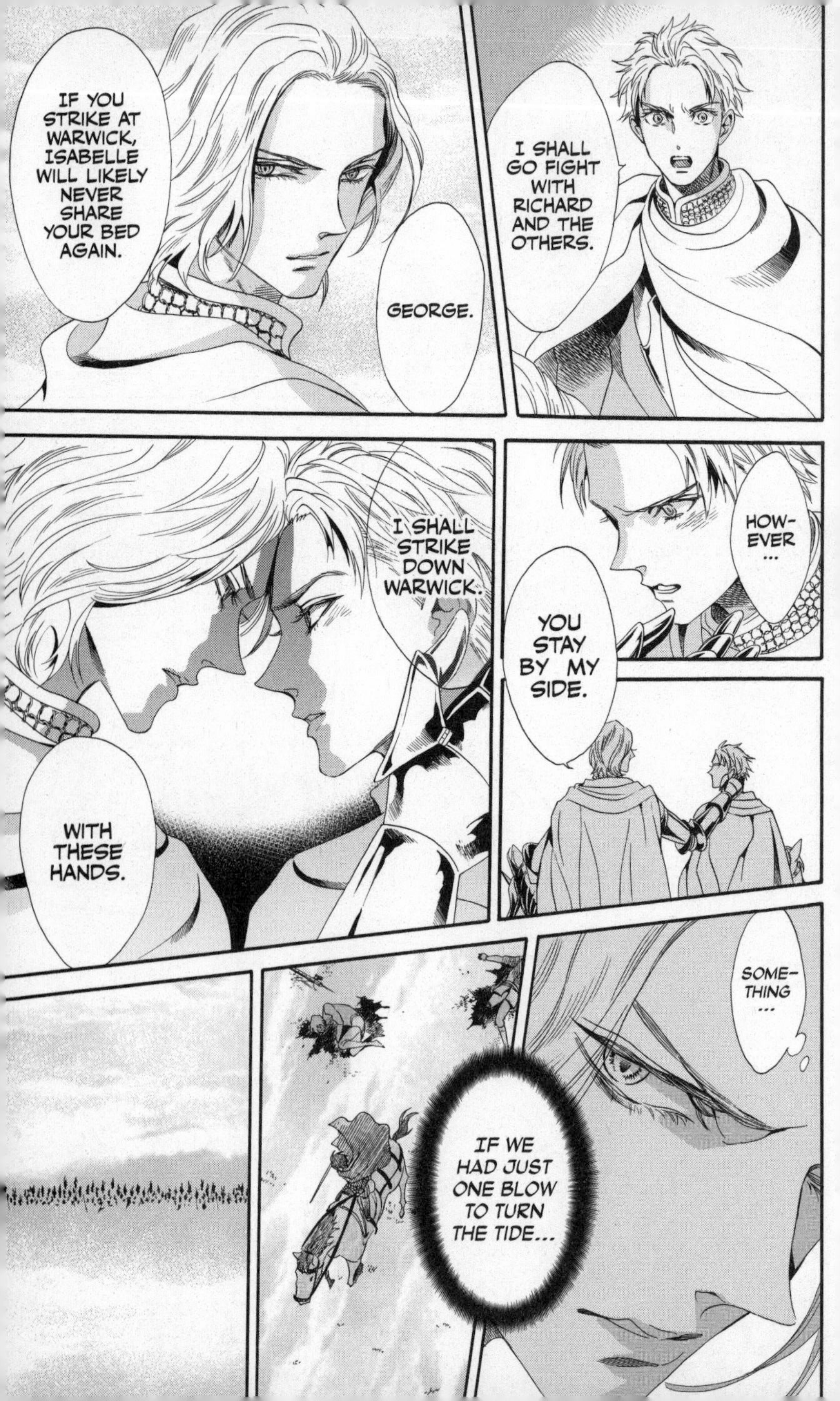
I SHALL GO FIGHT WITH RICHARD AND THE OTHERS.
GEORGE.
IF YOU STRIKE AT WARWICK, ISABELLE WILL LIKELY NEVER SHARE YOUR BED AGAIN.
HOW-EVER...
YOU STAY BY MY SIDE.
I SHALL STRIKE DOWN WARWICK.
WITH THESE HANDS.
SOME-THING...
IF WE HAD JUST ONE BLOW TO TURN THE TIDE...

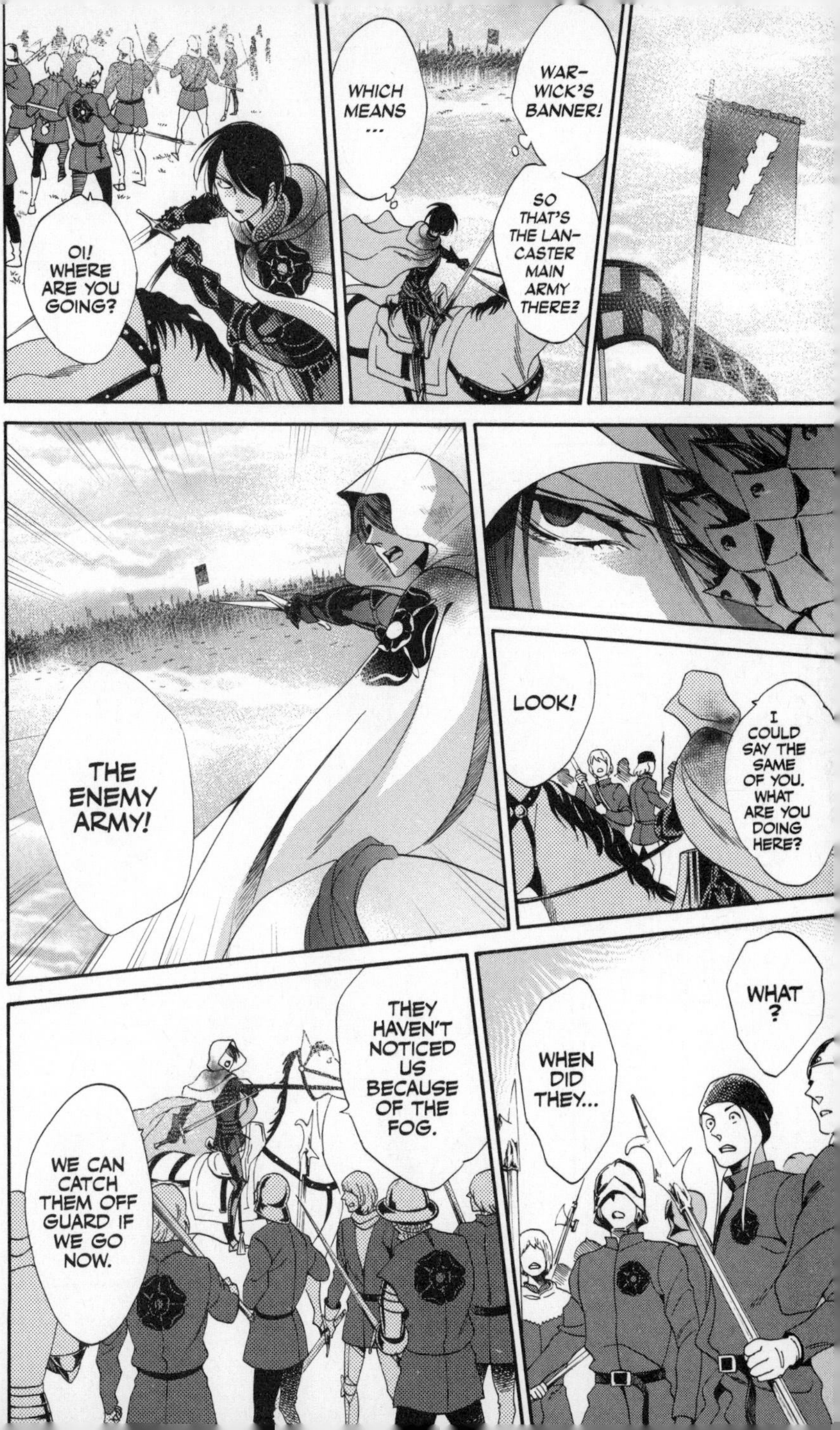

WAR-WICK'S BANNER!
SO THAT'S THE LAN-CASTER MAIN ARMY THERE?
WHICH MEANS ...
OI! WHERE ARE YOU GOING?
I COULD SAY THE SAME OF YOU. WHAT ARE YOU DOING HERE?
LOOK!
THE ENEMY ARMY!
WHAT?
WHEN DID THEY...
THEY HAVEN'T NOTICED US BECAUSE OF THE FOG.
WE CAN CATCH THEM OFF GUARD IF WE GO NOW.

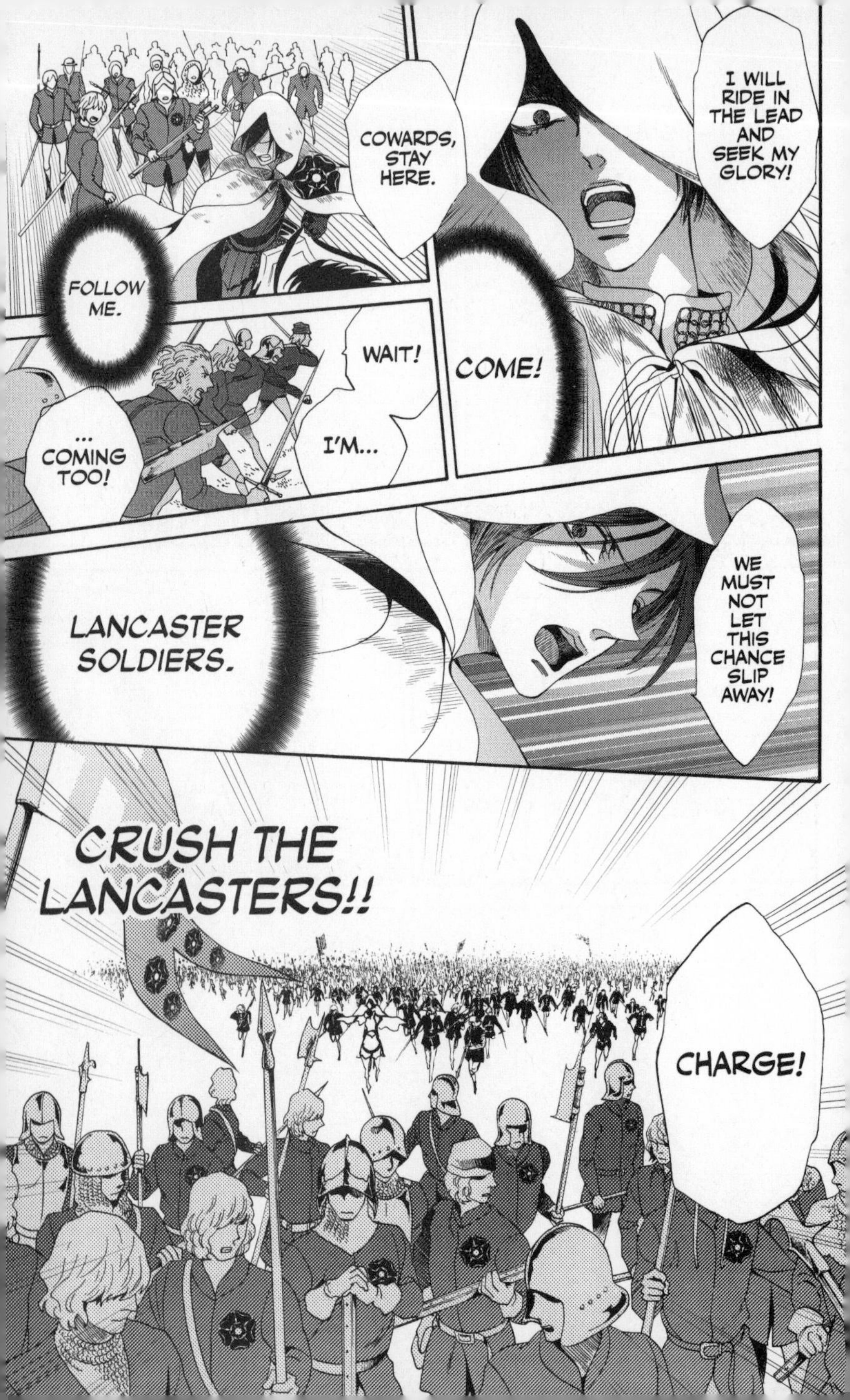
I WILL RIDE IN THE LEAD AND SEEK MY GLORY!
COME!
COWARDS, STAY HERE.
FOLLOW ME.
WAIT!
I'M...
... COMING TOO!
WE MUST NOT LET THIS CHANCE SLIP AWAY!
LANCASTER SOLDIERS.
CRUSH THE LANCASTERS!!
CHARGE!

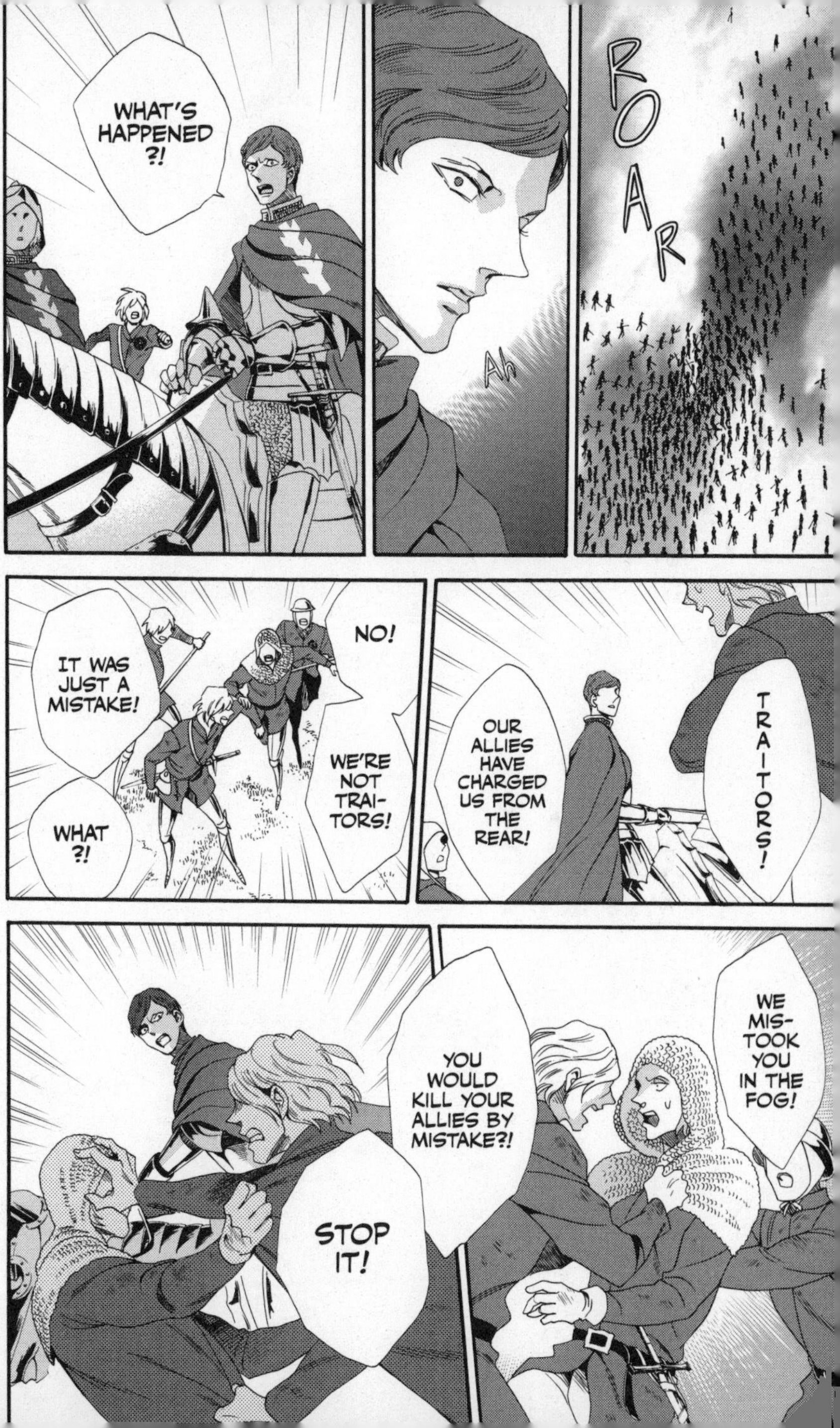
ROAR
Ah
WHAT'S HAPPENED ?!
TRAITORS!
OUR ALLIES HAVE CHARGED US FROM THE REAR!
NO!
WE'RE NOT TRAI-TORS!
IT WAS JUST A MISTAKE!
WHAT ?!
WE MIS-TOOK YOU IN THE FOG!
YOU WOULD KILL YOUR ALLIES BY MISTAKE?!
STOP IT!

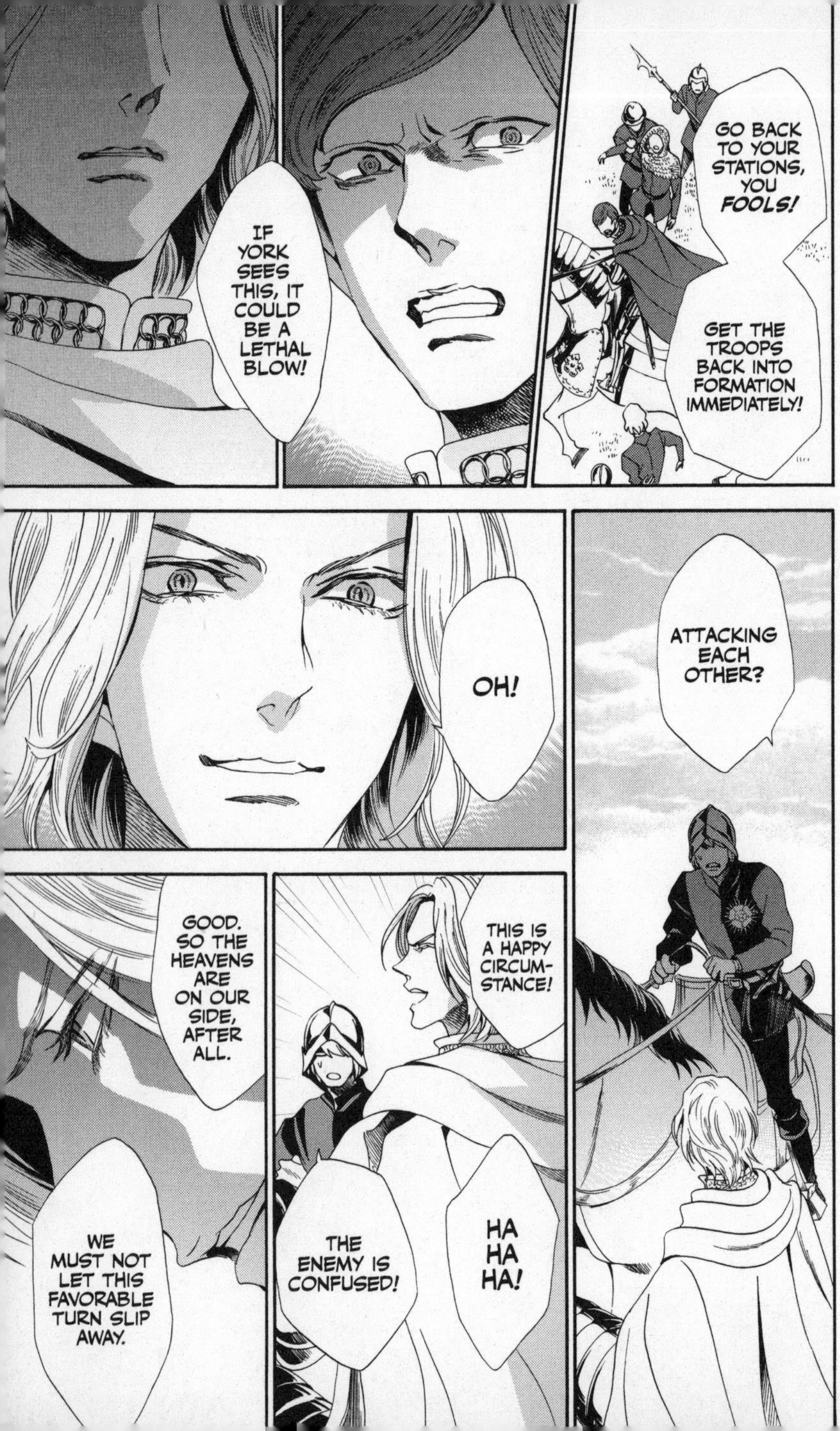
GO BACK TO YOUR STATIONS, YOU *FOOLS!*
GET THE TROOPS BACK INTO FORMATION IMMEDIATELY!
IF YORK SEES THIS, IT COULD BE A LETHAL BLOW!
ATTACKING EACH OTHER?
OH!
THIS IS A HAPPY CIRCUMSTANCE!
HA HA HA!
THE ENEMY IS CONFUSED!
GOOD. SO THE HEAVENS ARE ON OUR SIDE, AFTER ALL.
WE MUST NOT LET THIS FAVORABLE TURN SLIP AWAY.

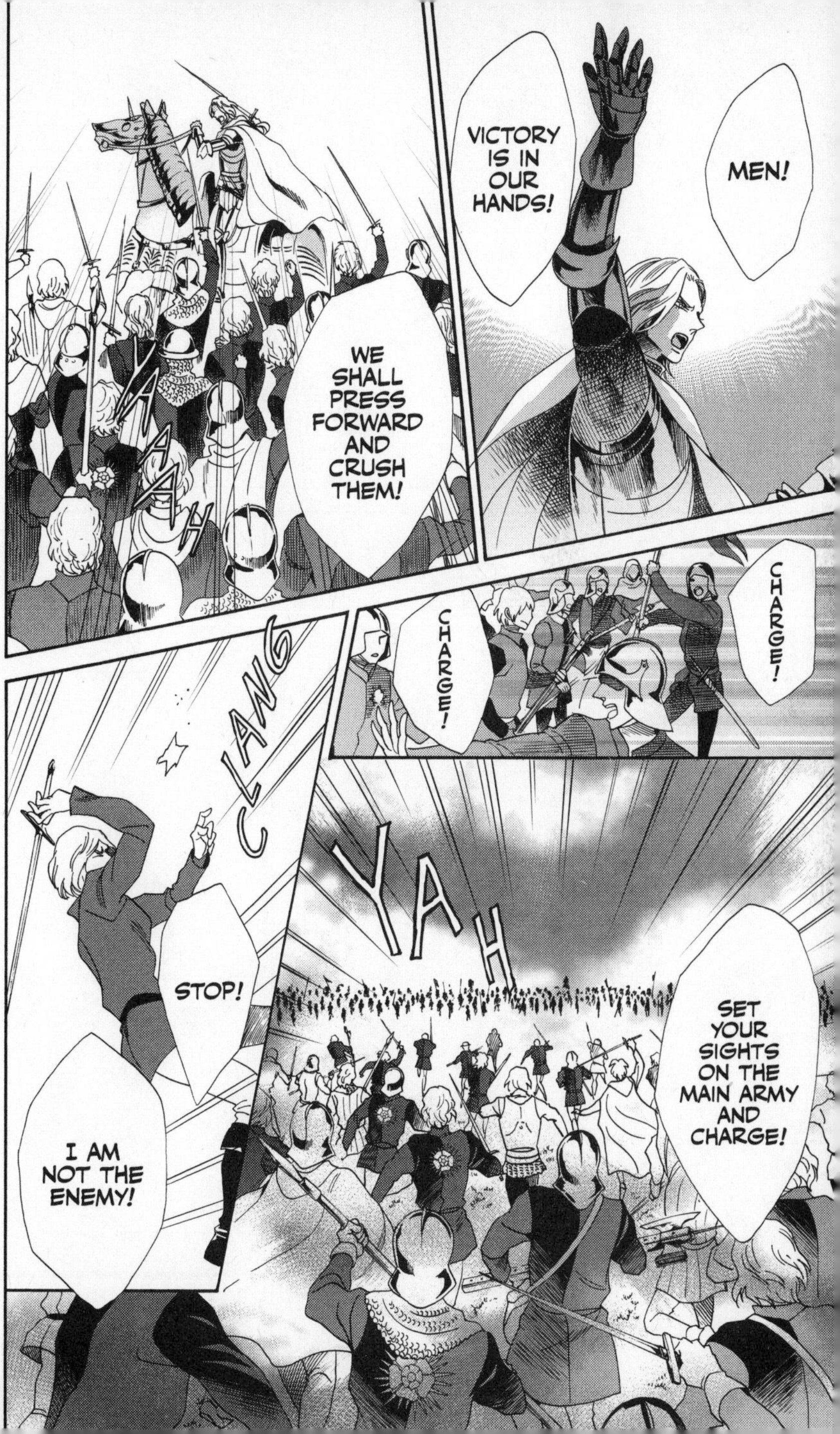
MEN!
VICTORY IS IN OUR HANDS!
WE SHALL PRESS FORWARD AND CRUSH THEM!
YAAH
CHARGE!
CHARGE!
YAH
SET YOUR SIGHTS ON THE MAIN ARMY AND CHARGE!
CLANG
STOP!
I AM NOT THE ENEMY!

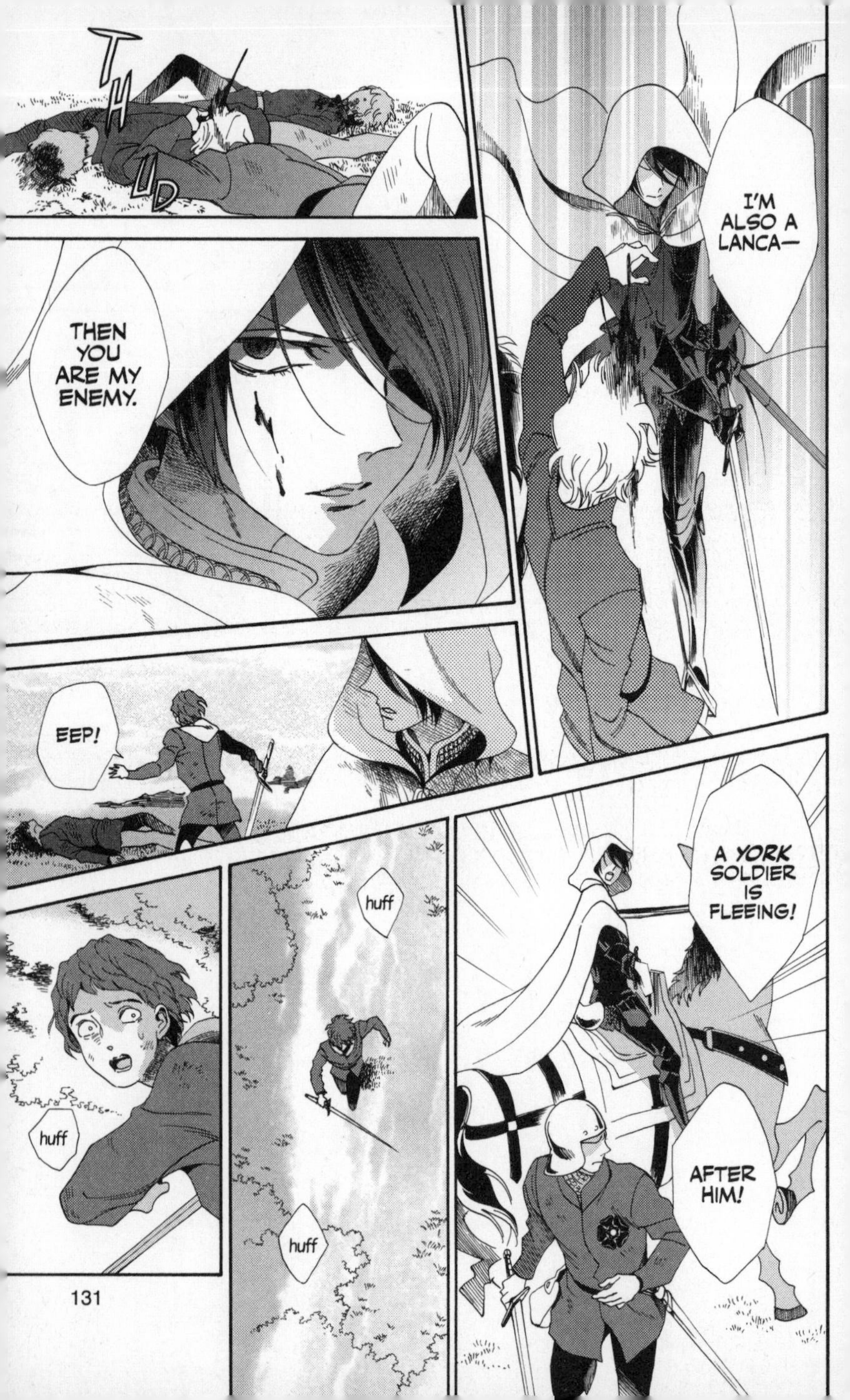
I'M ALSO A LANCA—
THUD
THEN YOU ARE MY ENEMY.
EEP!
A YORK SOLDIER IS FLEEING!
AFTER HIM!
huff
huff
huff

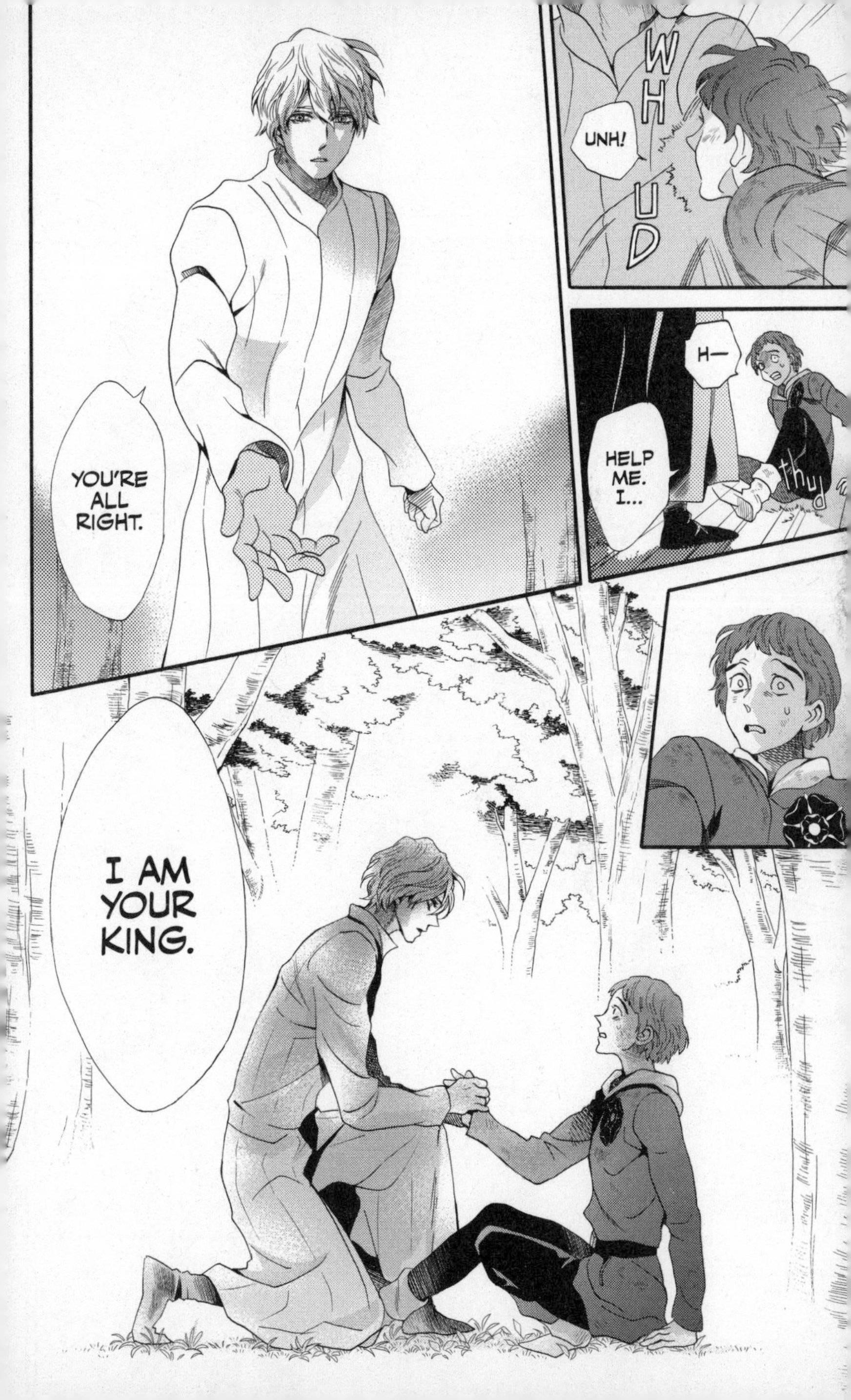
WHUD
UNH!
H—
HELP ME. I...
thud
YOU'RE ALL RIGHT.
I AM YOUR KING.

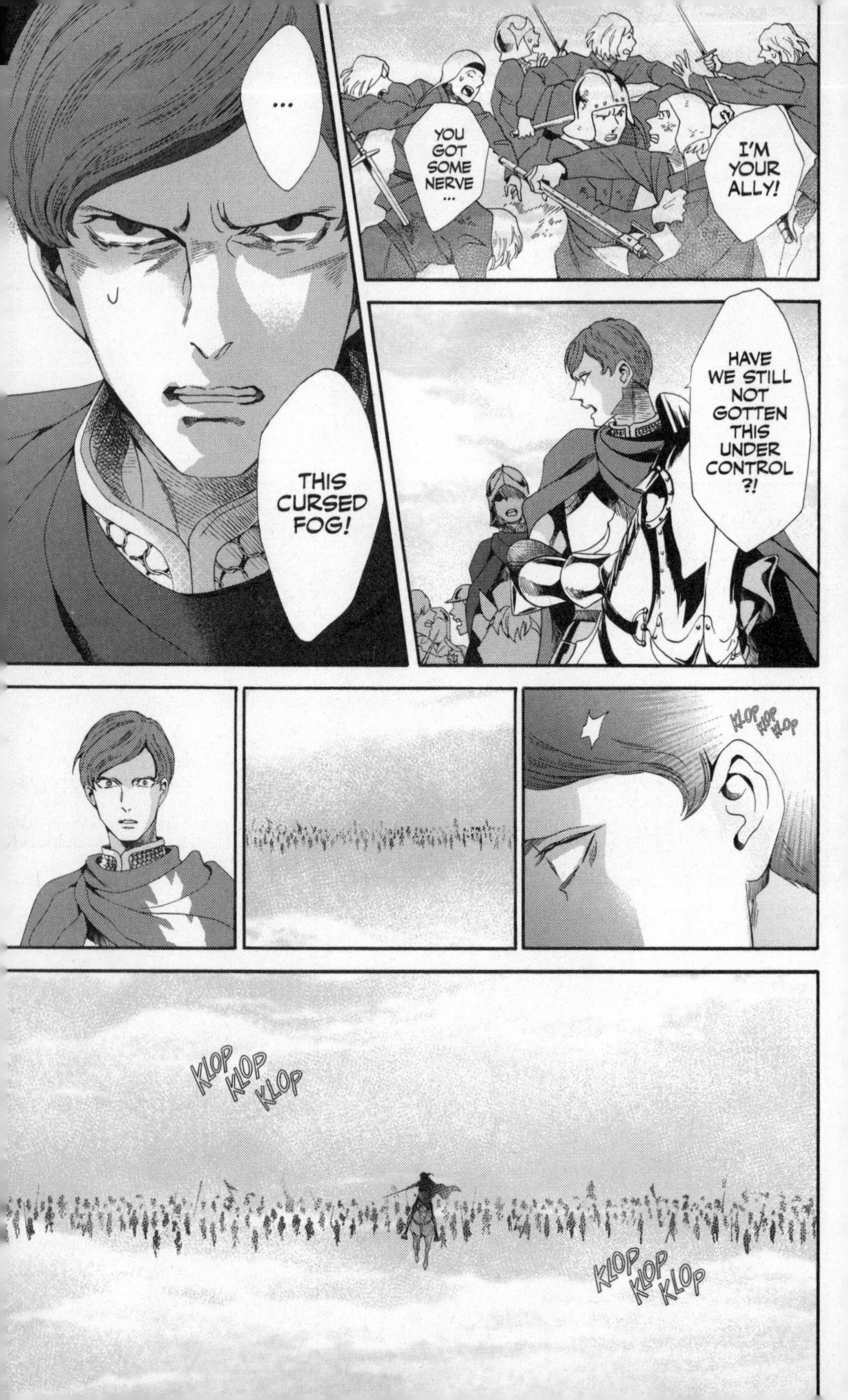
I'M YOUR ALLY!
YOU GOT SOME NERVE...
HAVE WE STILL NOT GOTTEN THIS UNDER CONTROL?!
...
THIS CURSED FOG!
KLOP KLOP KLOP
KLOP KLOP KLOP
KLOP KLOP KLOP

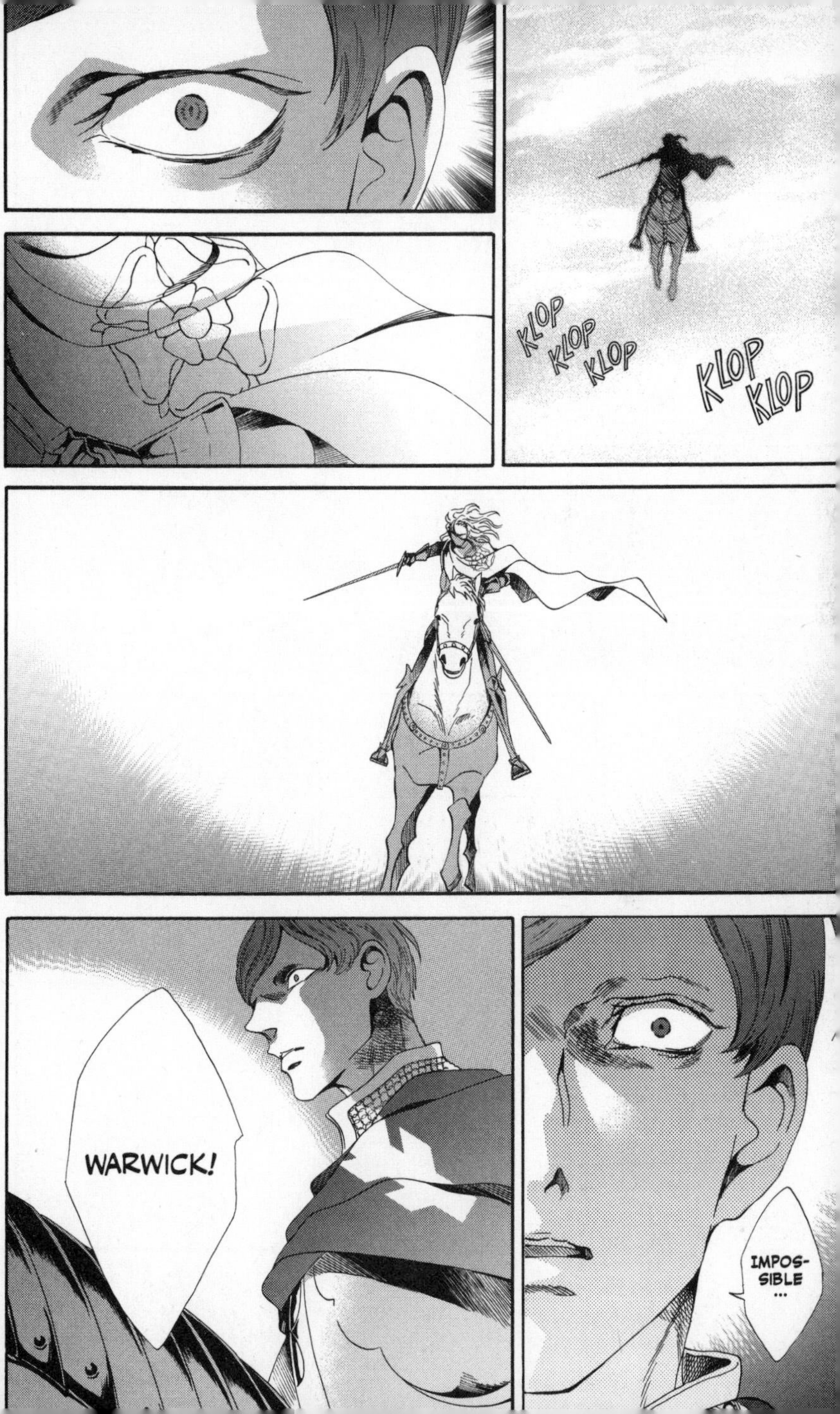
KLOP KLOP KLOP
KLOP KLOP
IMPOS-SIBLE ...
WARWICK!

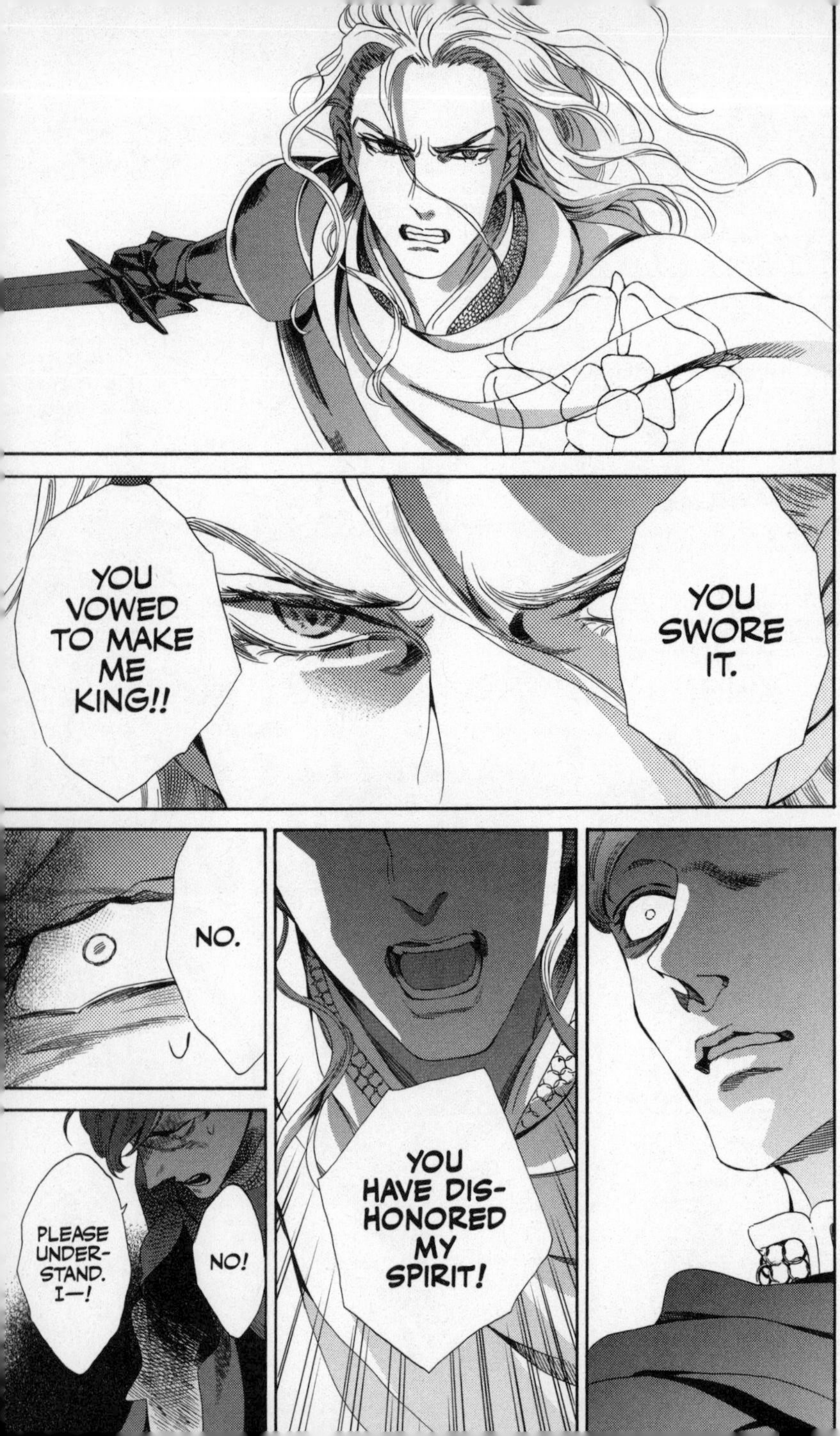
YOU SWORE IT.
YOU VOWED TO MAKE ME KING!!
YOU HAVE DIS-HONORED MY SPIRIT!
NO.
NO!
PLEASE UNDER-STAND. I—!

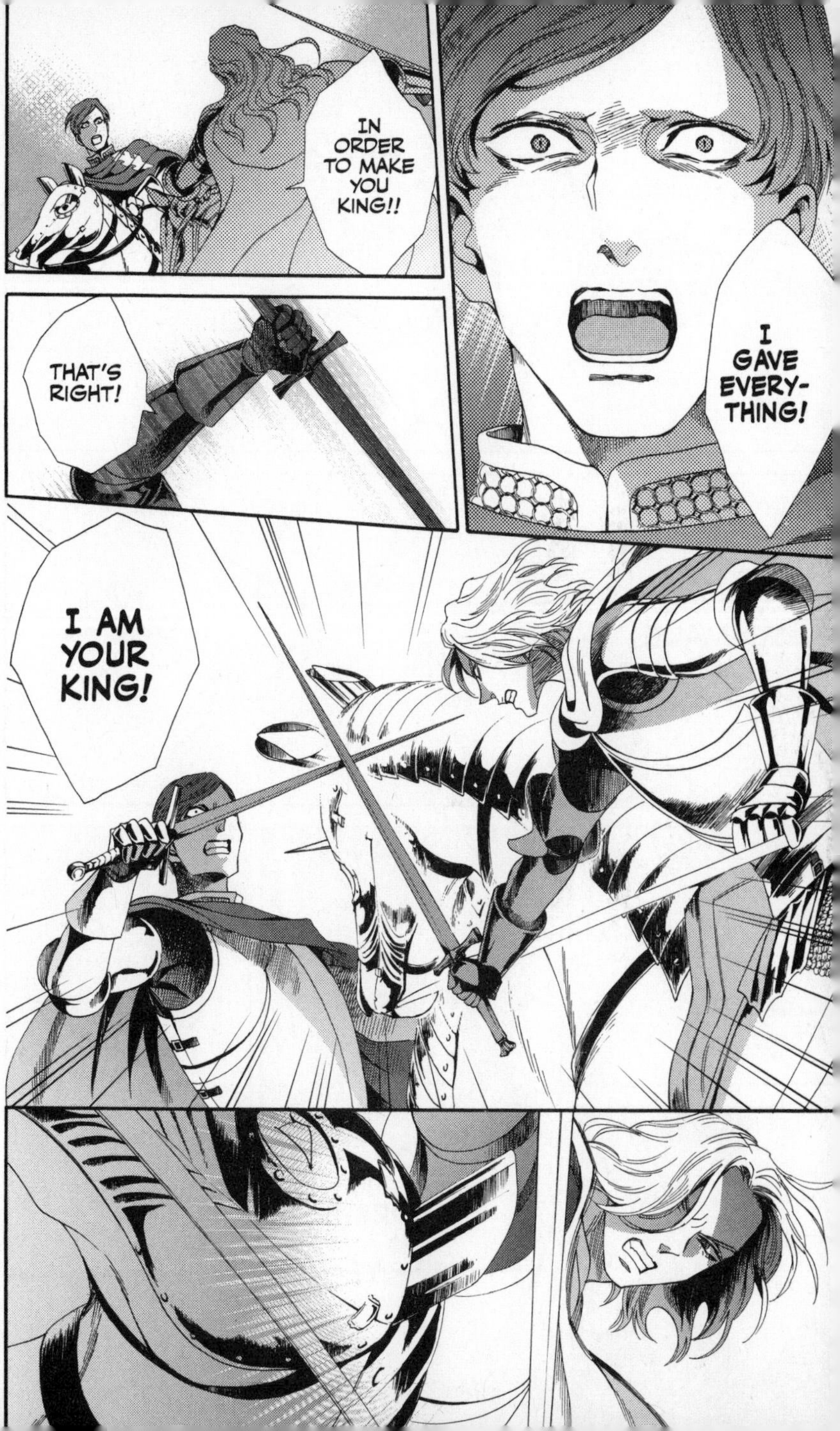
I GAVE EVERY-THING!
IN ORDER TO MAKE YOU KING!!
THAT'S RIGHT!
I AM YOUR KING!

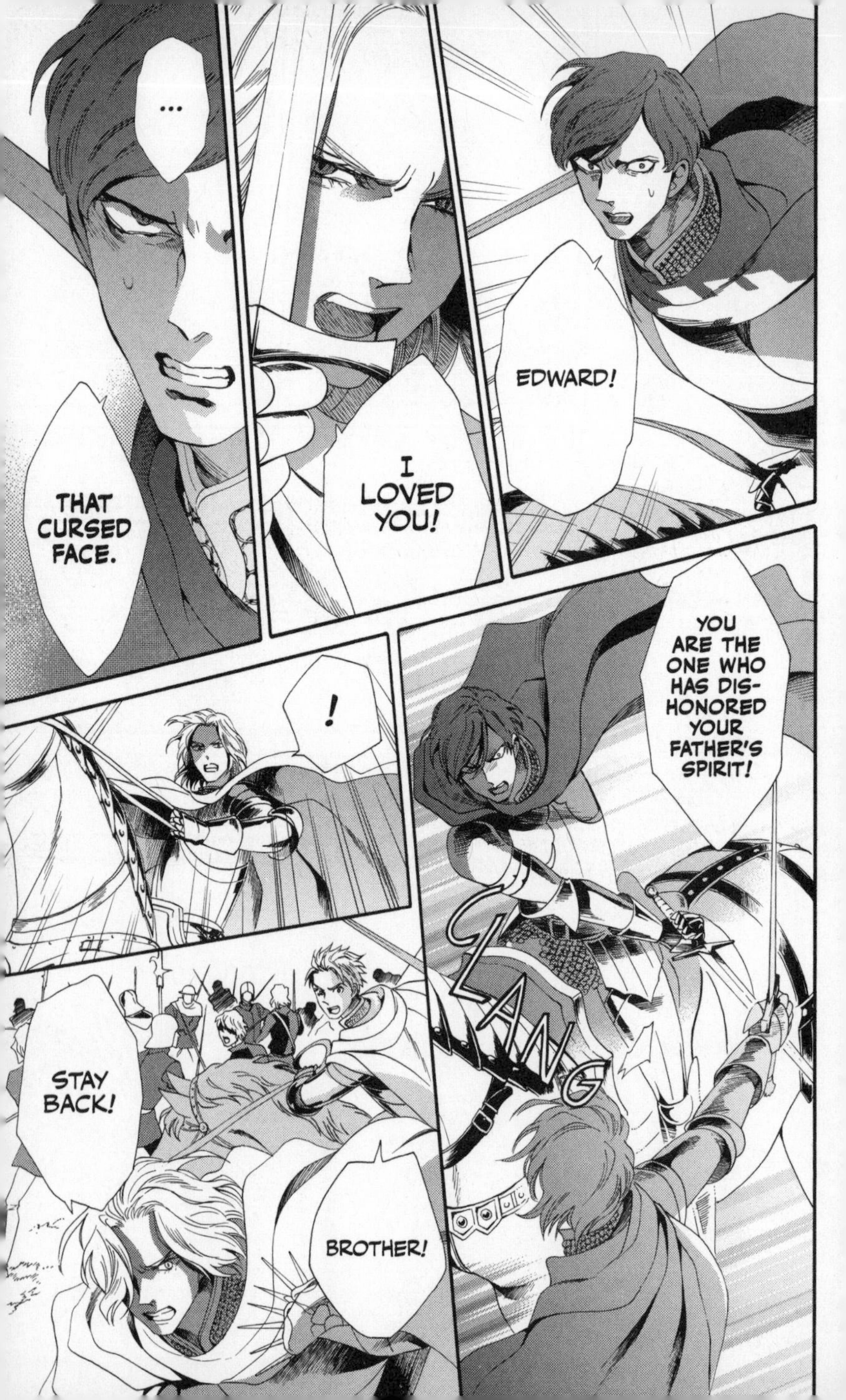
EDWARD!
I LOVED YOU!
...
THAT CURSED FACE.
YOU ARE THE ONE WHO HAS DIS-HONORED YOUR FATHER'S SPIRIT!
CLANG
!
STAY BACK!
BROTHER!

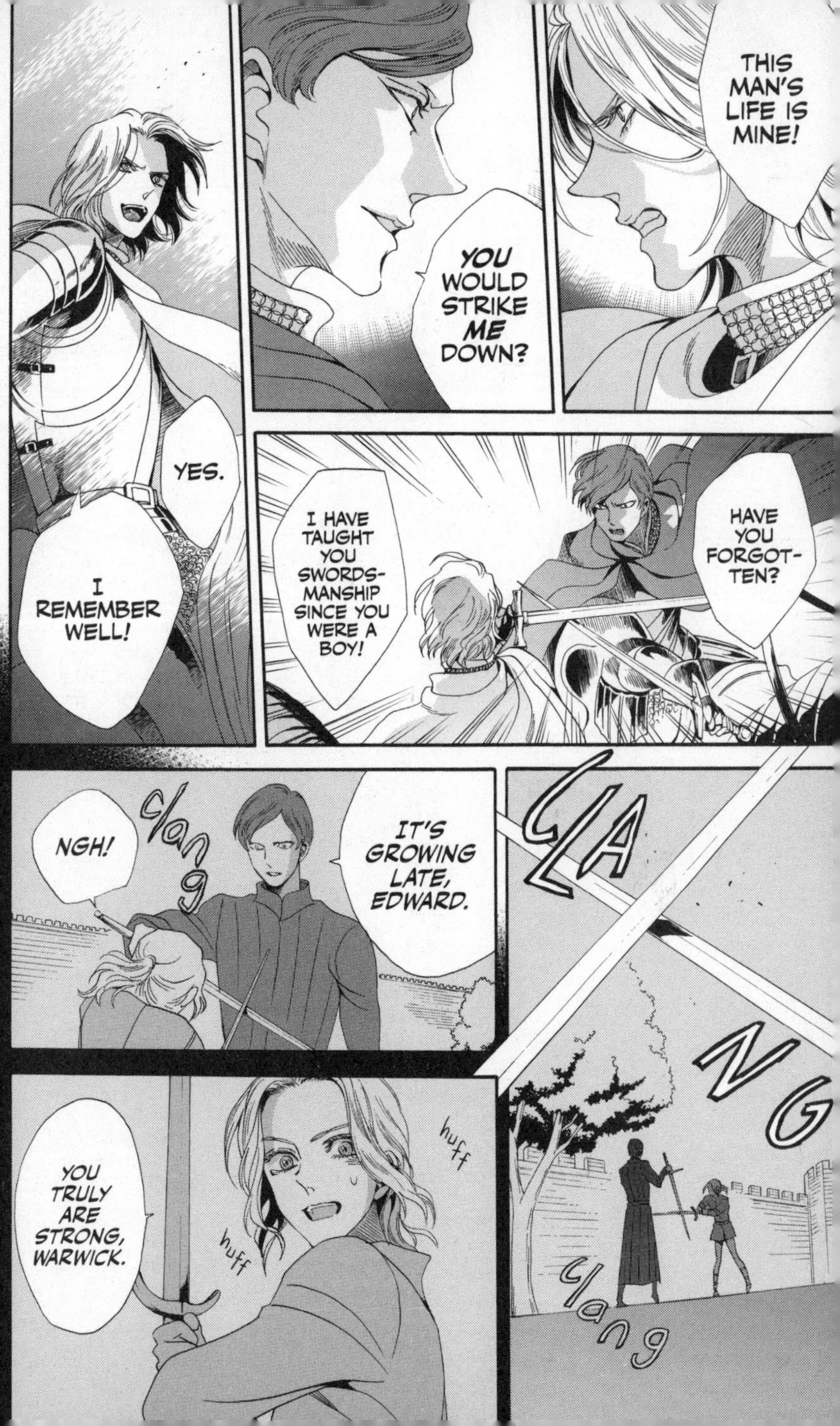
THIS MAN'S LIFE IS MINE!
YOU WOULD STRIKE ME DOWN?
HAVE YOU FORGOT-TEN?
I HAVE TAUGHT YOU SWORDS-MANSHIP SINCE YOU WERE A BOY!
YES.
I REMEMBER WELL!
CLANG
clang
IT'S GROWING LATE, EDWARD.
NGH!
clang
huff
YOU TRULY ARE STRONG, WARWICK.
huff

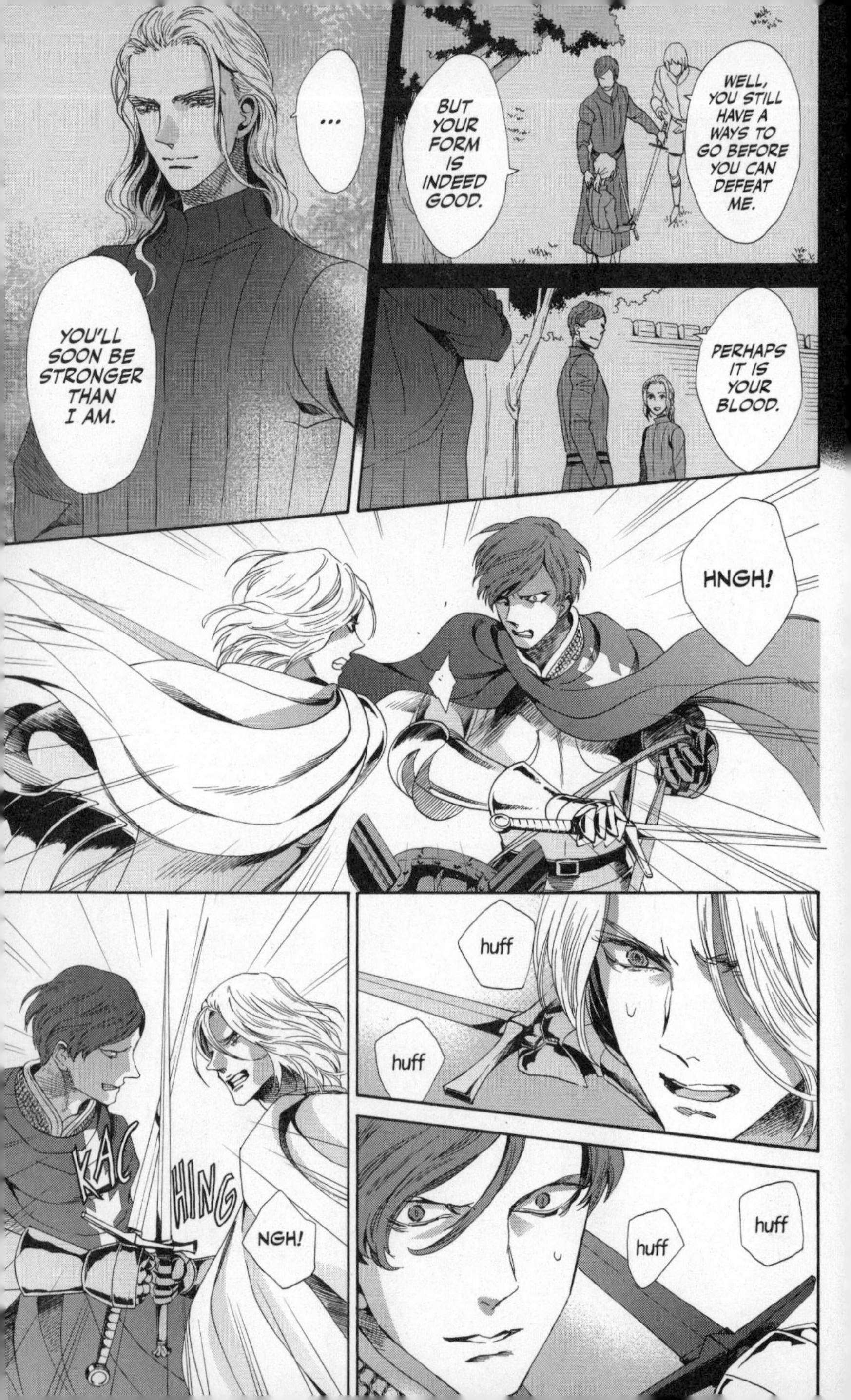
WELL, YOU STILL HAVE A WAYS TO GO BEFORE YOU CAN DEFEAT ME.
BUT YOUR FORM IS INDEED GOOD.
PERHAPS IT IS YOUR BLOOD.
...
YOU'LL SOON BE STRONGER THAN I AM.
HNGH!
huff
huff
huff
huff
KACHING
NGH!

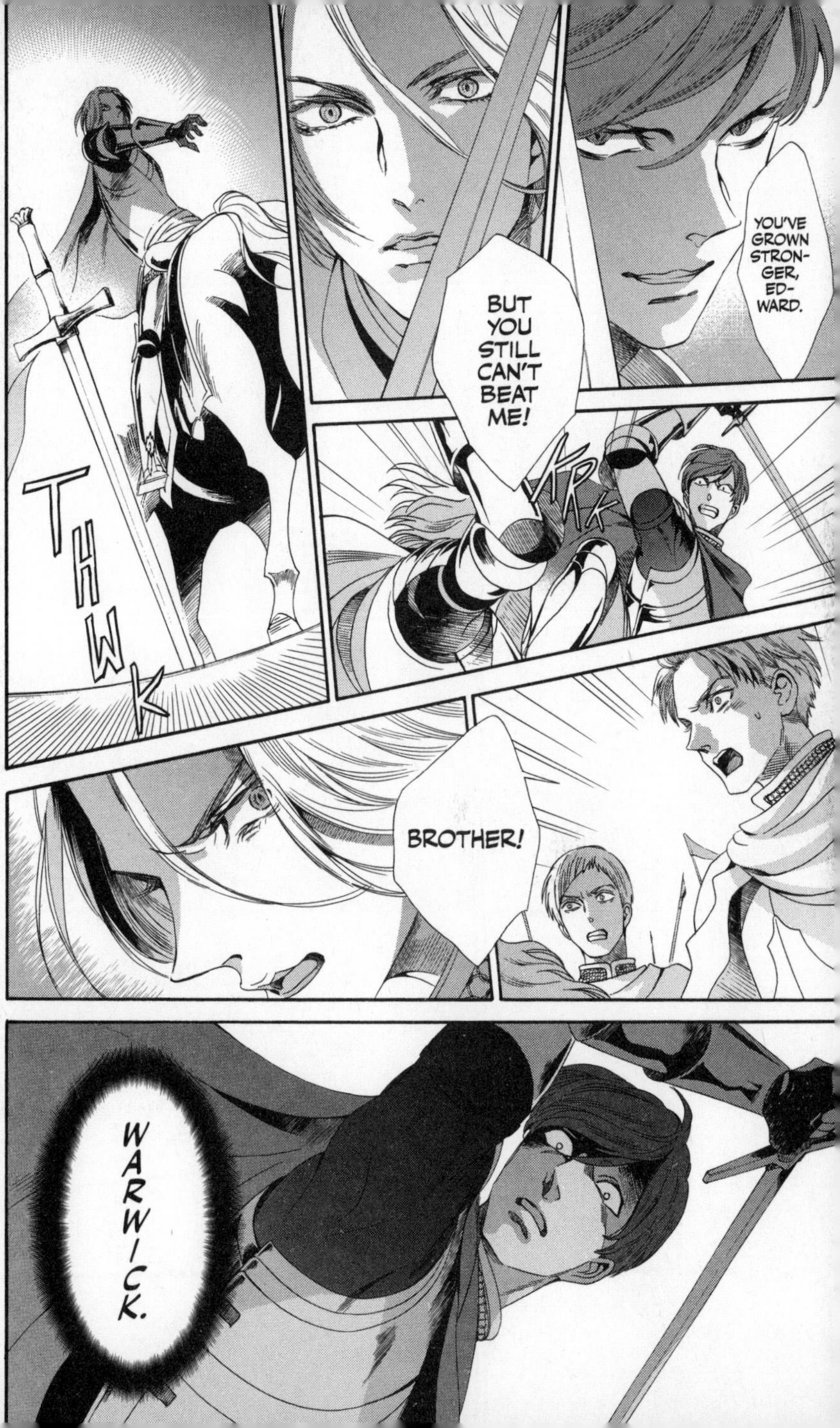
YOU'VE GROWN STRONGER, ED-WARD.
BUT YOU STILL CAN'T BEAT ME!
KRK
THWK
BROTHER!
WARWICK.

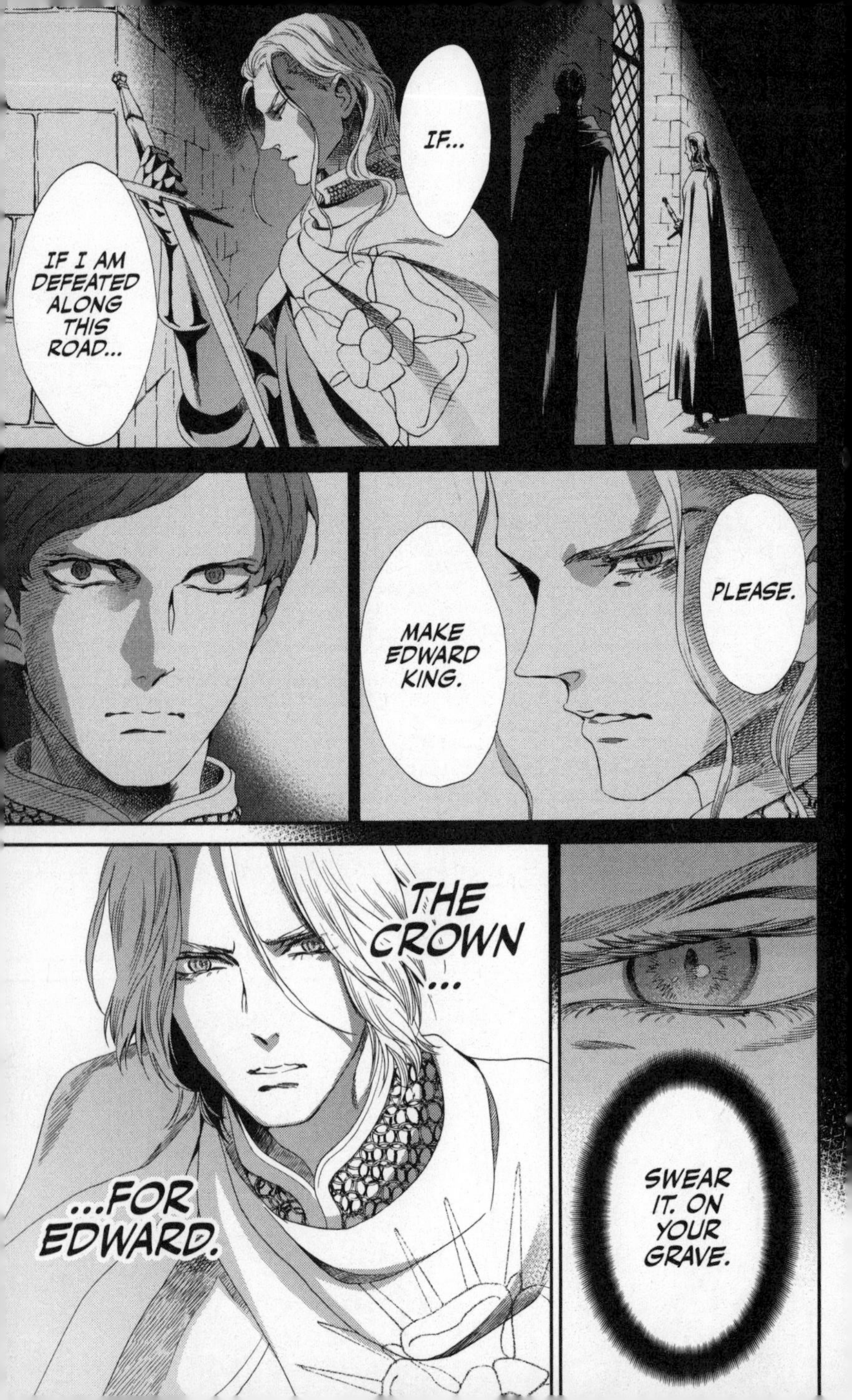
IF...
IF I AM DEFEATED ALONG THIS ROAD...
PLEASE.
MAKE EDWARD KING.
SWEAR IT. ON YOUR GRAVE.
THE CROWN...
...FOR EDWARD.

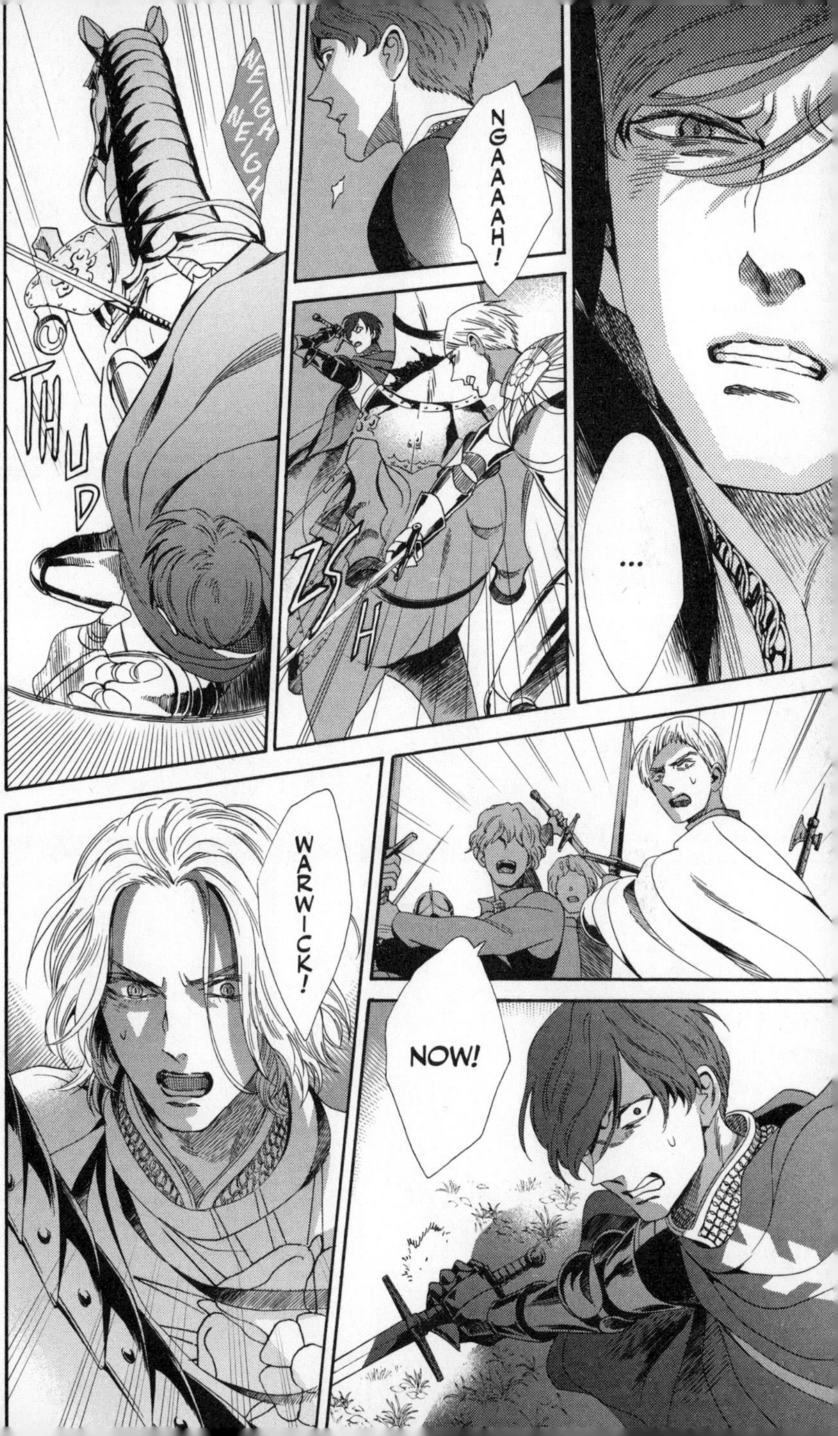
...
NGAAAAH!
ZSH
NEIGH NEIGH
THUD
NOW!
WARWICK!

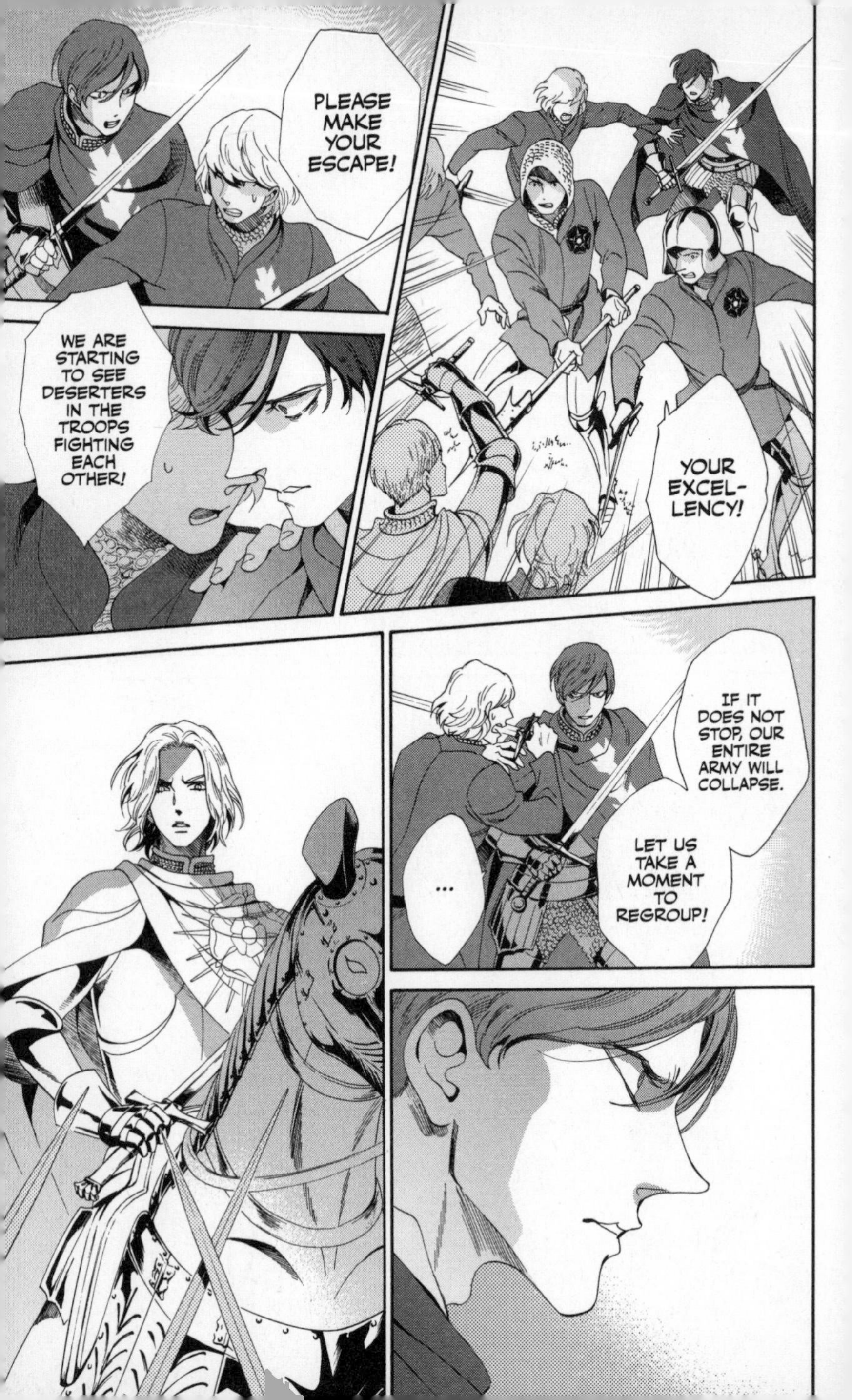
YOUR EXCEL-LENCY!
PLEASE MAKE YOUR ESCAPE!
WE ARE STARTING TO SEE DESERTERS IN THE TROOPS FIGHTING EACH OTHER!
IF IT DOES NOT STOP, OUR ENTIRE ARMY WILL COLLAPSE.
LET US TAKE A MOMENT TO REGROUP!
...

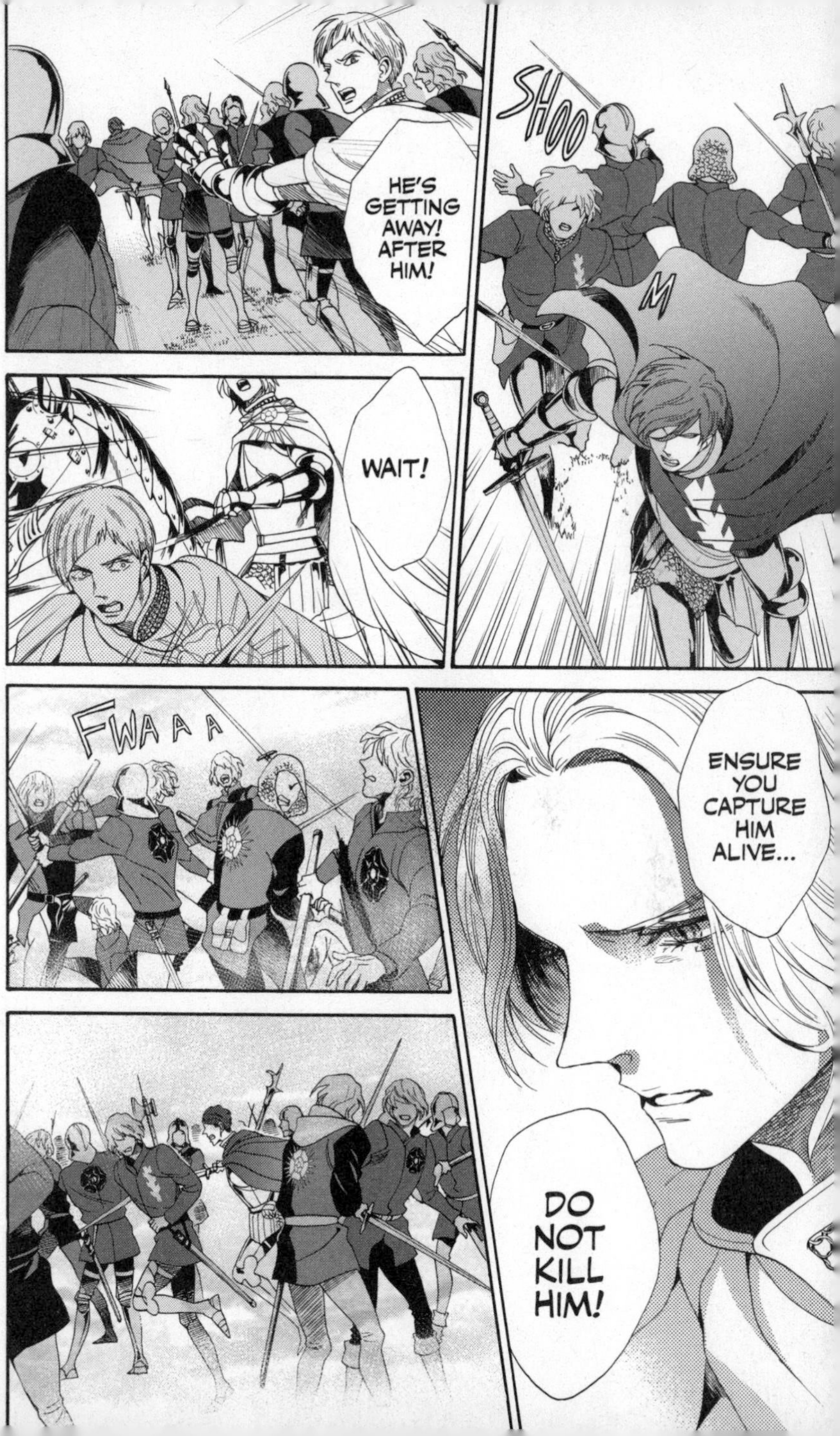
SHOOM
HE'S GETTING AWAY! AFTER HIM!
WAIT!
ENSURE YOU CAPTURE HIM ALIVE...
DO NOT KILL HIM!
FWAAA

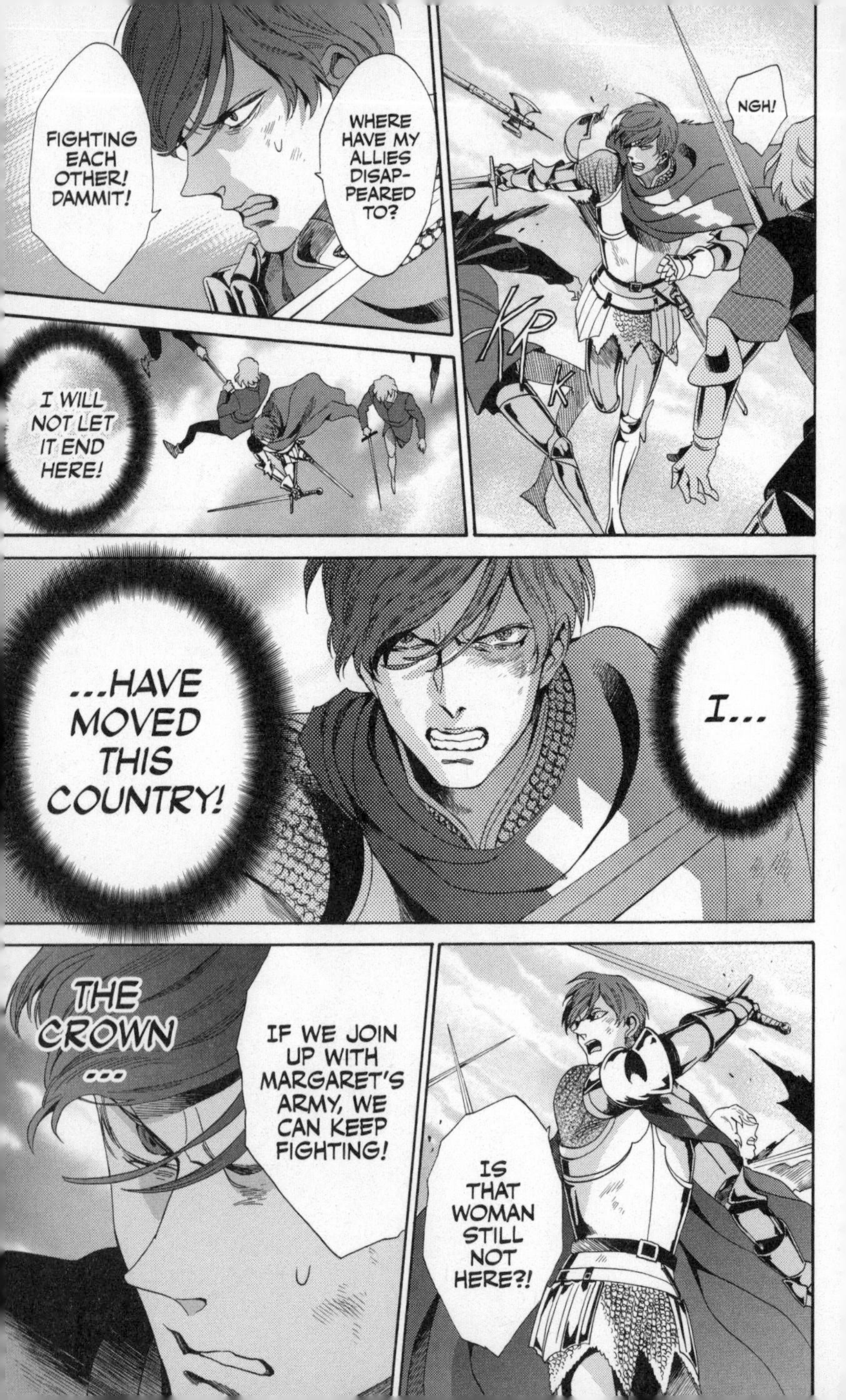
NGH!
KRK
WHERE HAVE MY ALLIES DISAPPEARED TO?
FIGHTING EACH OTHER! DAMMIT!
I WILL NOT LET IT END HERE!
I...
...HAVE MOVED THIS COUNTRY!
IS THAT WOMAN STILL NOT HERE?!
IF WE JOIN UP WITH MARGARET'S ARMY, WE CAN KEEP FIGHTING!
THE CROWN ...

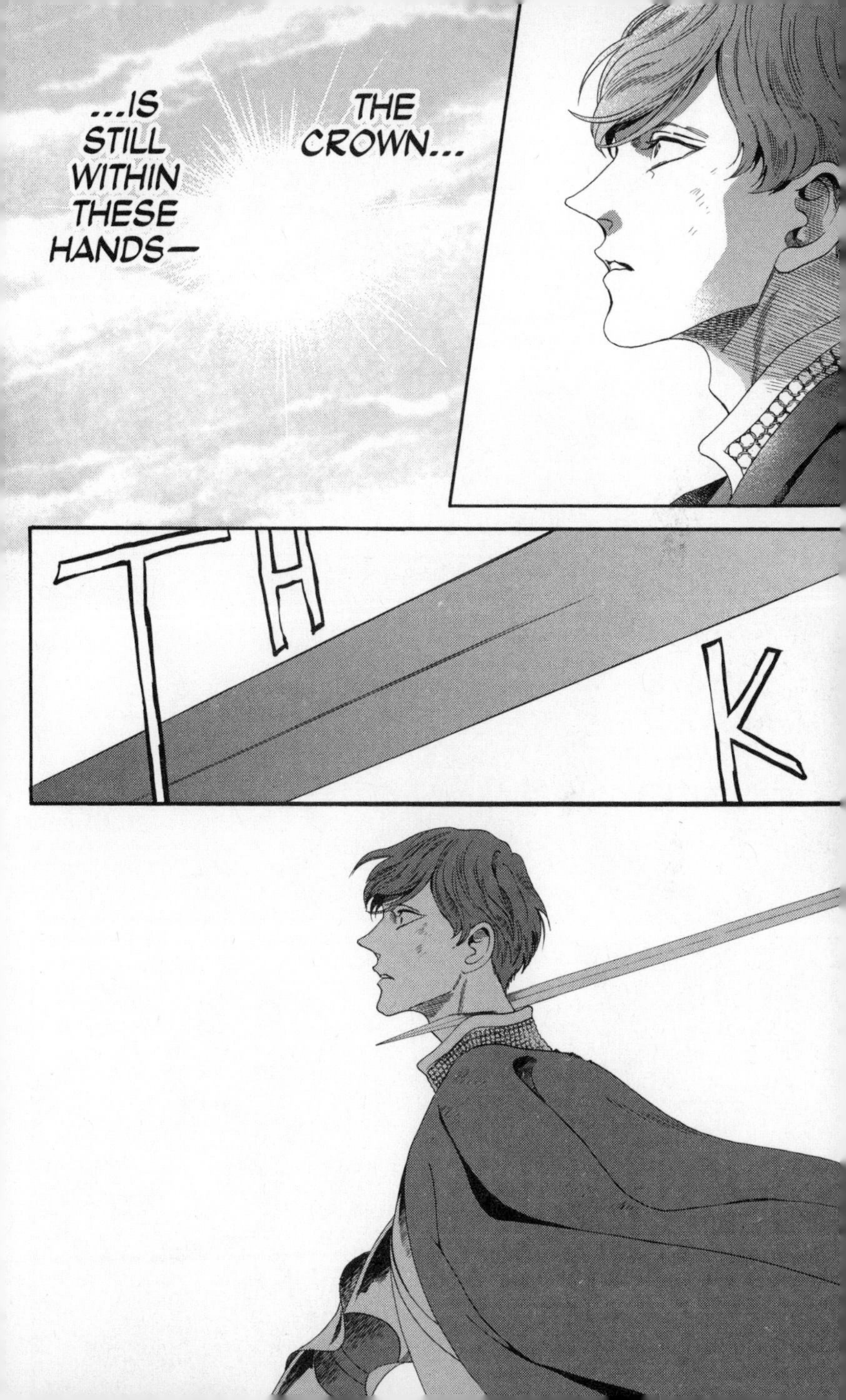
THE CROWN...
...IS STILL WITHIN THESE HANDS—
THK

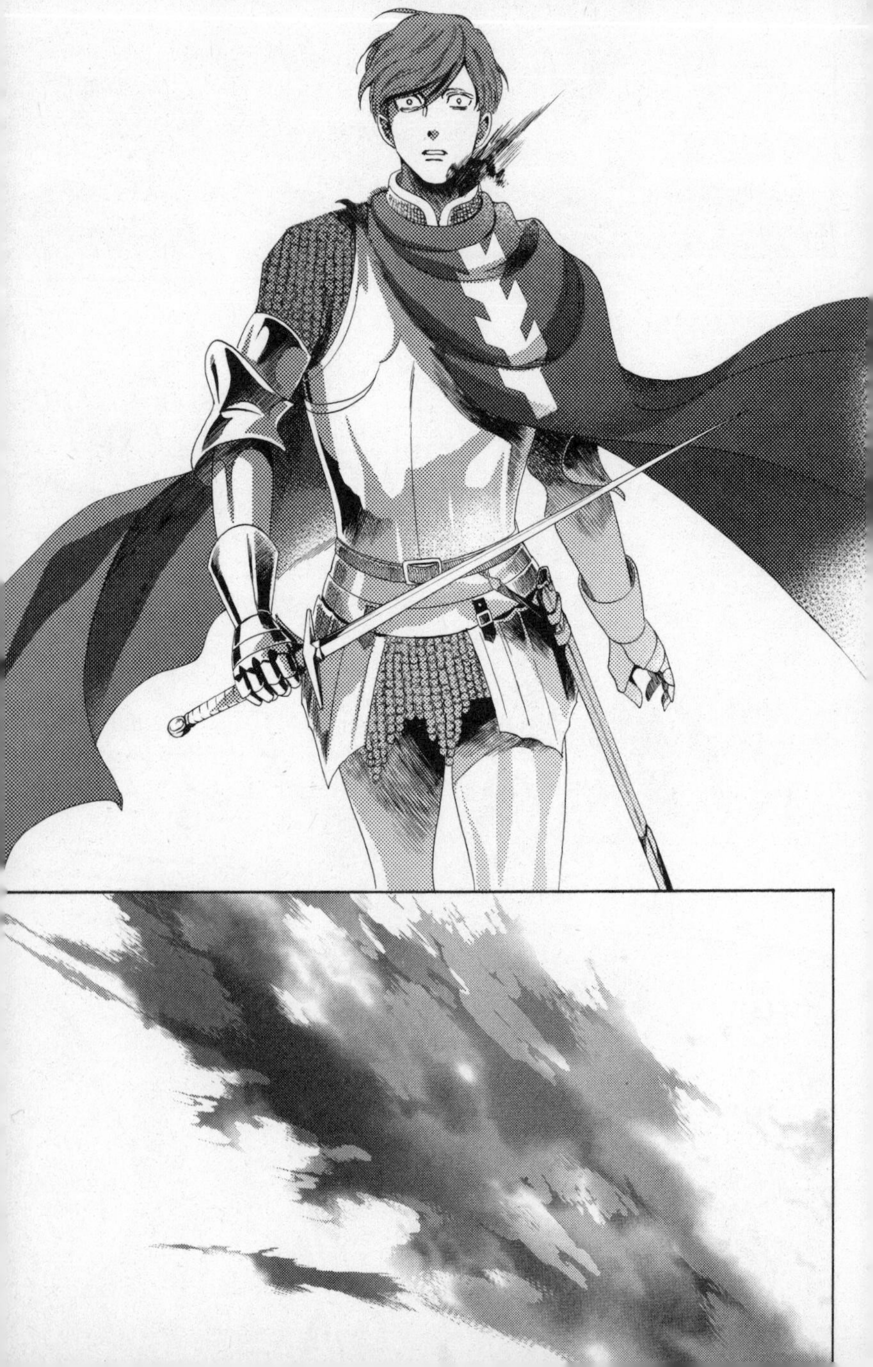

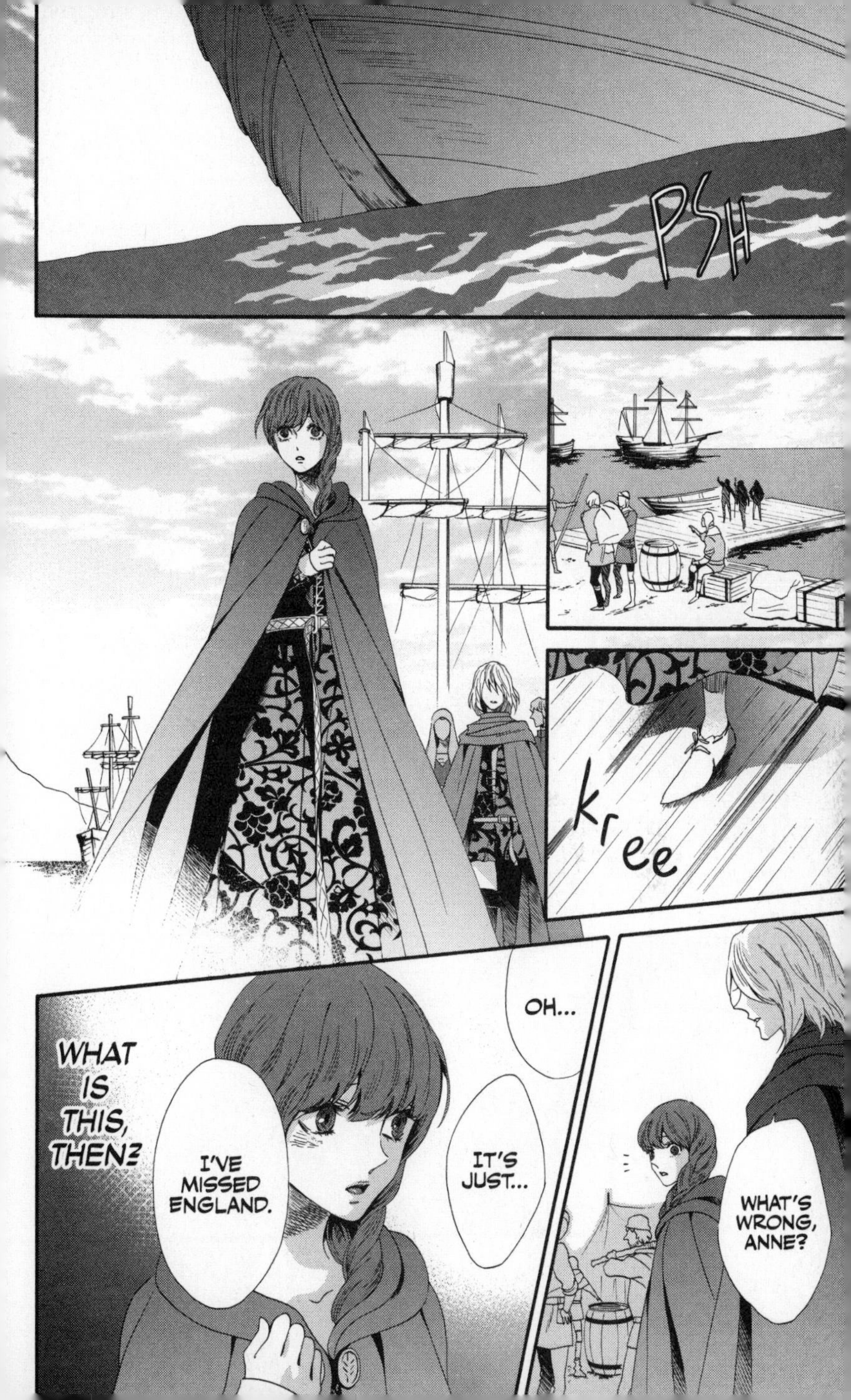
PSH
kree
WHAT'S WRONG, ANNE?
OH...
IT'S JUST...
I'VE MISSED ENGLAND.
WHAT IS THIS, THEN?

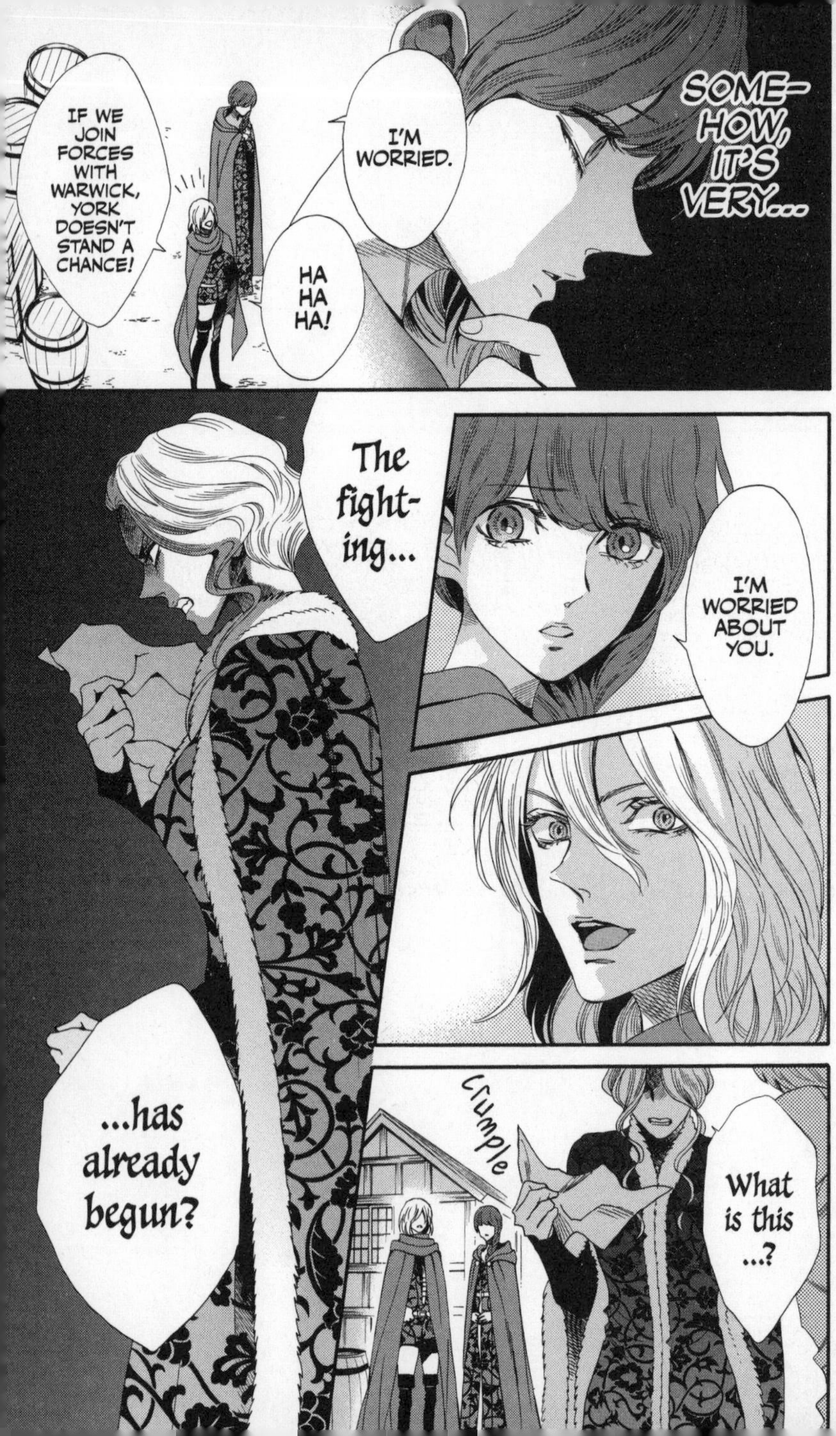
SOME-HOW, IT'S VERY...
I'M WORRIED.
HA HA HA!
IF WE JOIN FORCES WITH WARWICK, YORK DOESN'T STAND A CHANCE!
I'M WORRIED ABOUT YOU.
What is this ...?
Crumple
The fight-ing...
...has already begun?

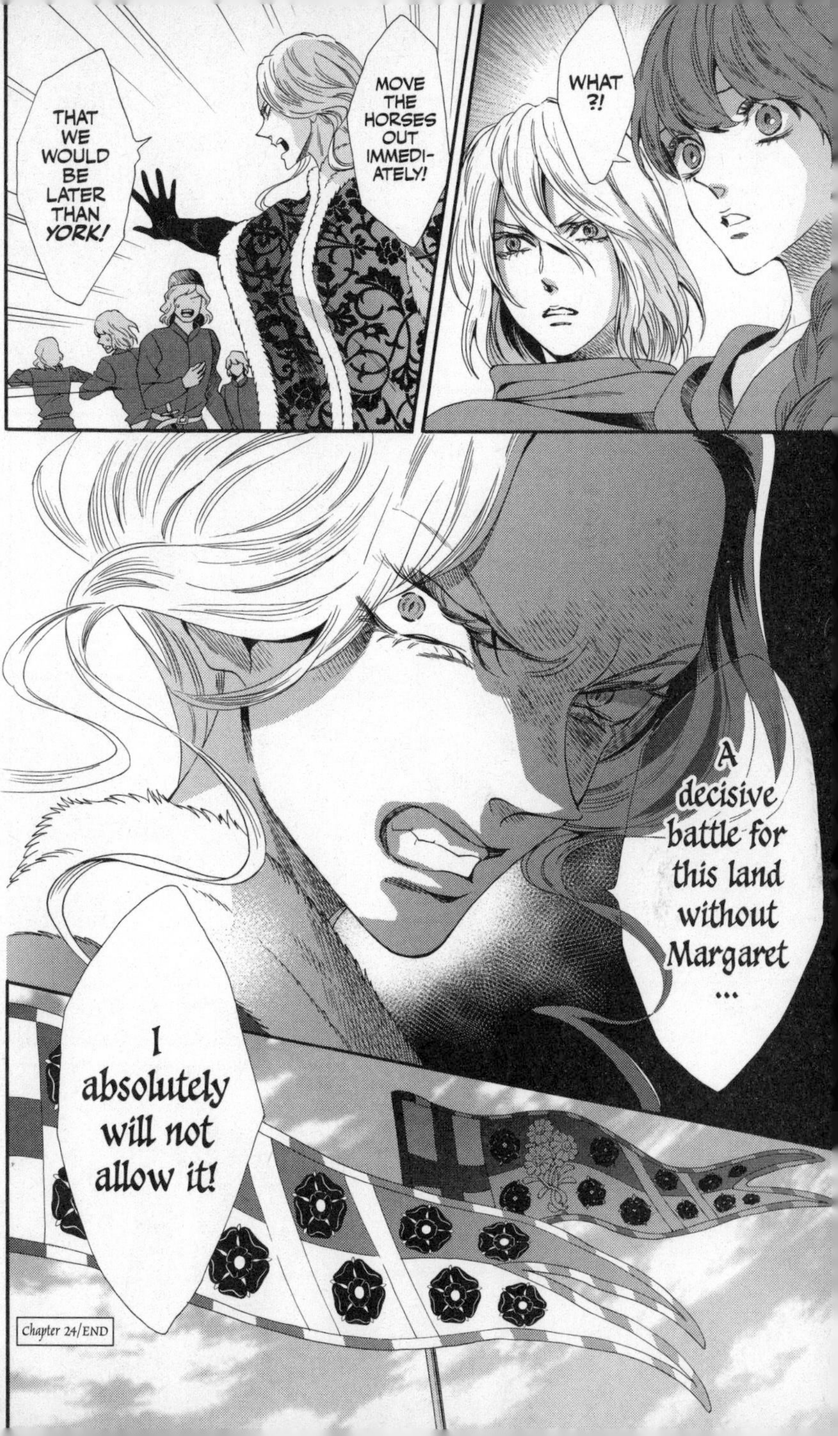
WHAT?!
MOVE THE HORSES OUT IMMEDIATELY!
THAT WE WOULD BE LATER THAN YORK!
A decisive battle for this land without Margaret...
I absolutely will not allow it!
Chapter 24/END

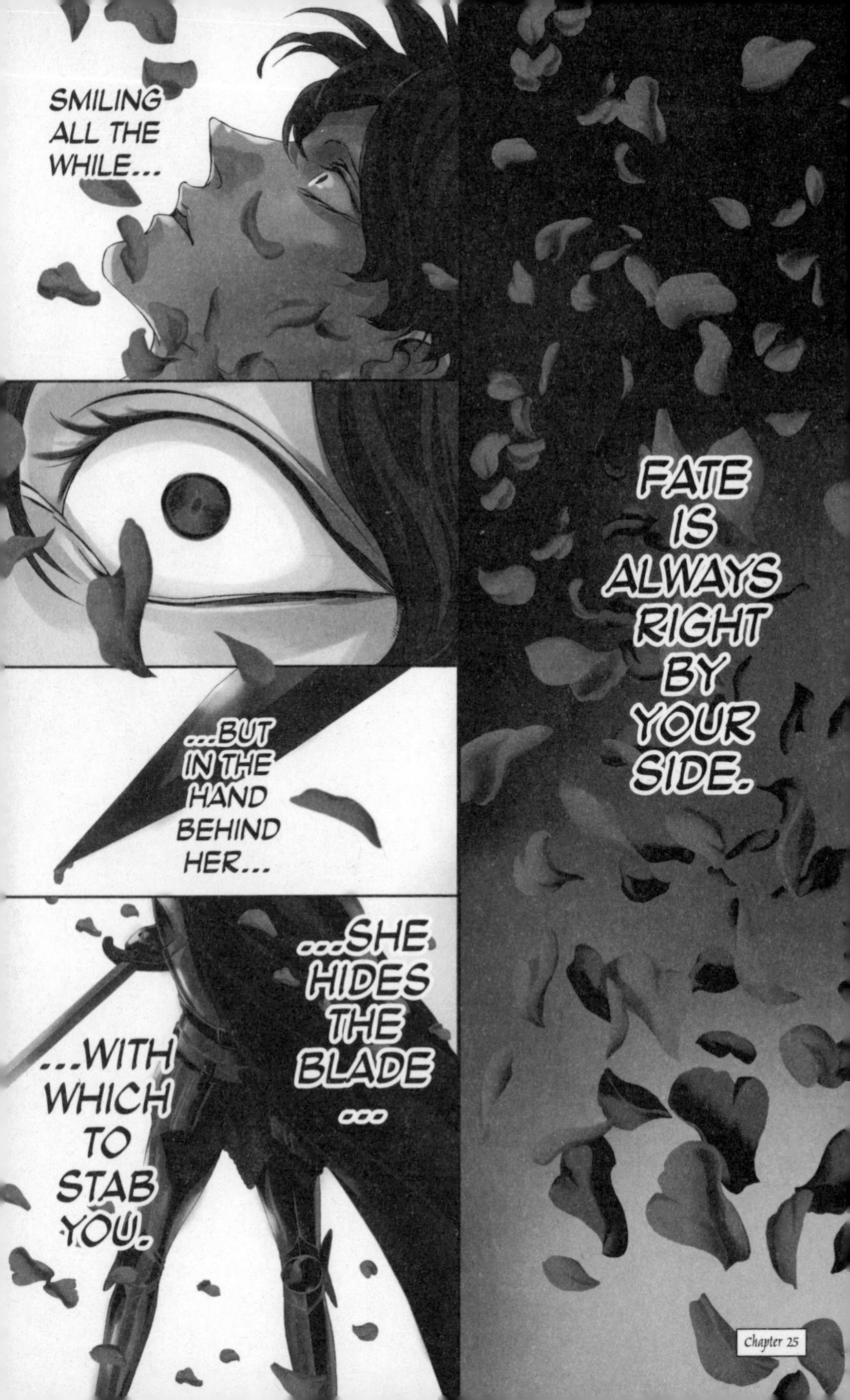
FATE IS ALWAYS RIGHT BY YOUR SIDE.
Chapter 25
SMILING ALL THE WHILE...
...BUT IN THE HAND BEHIND HER...
...SHE HIDES THE BLADE...
...WITH WHICH TO STAB YOU.

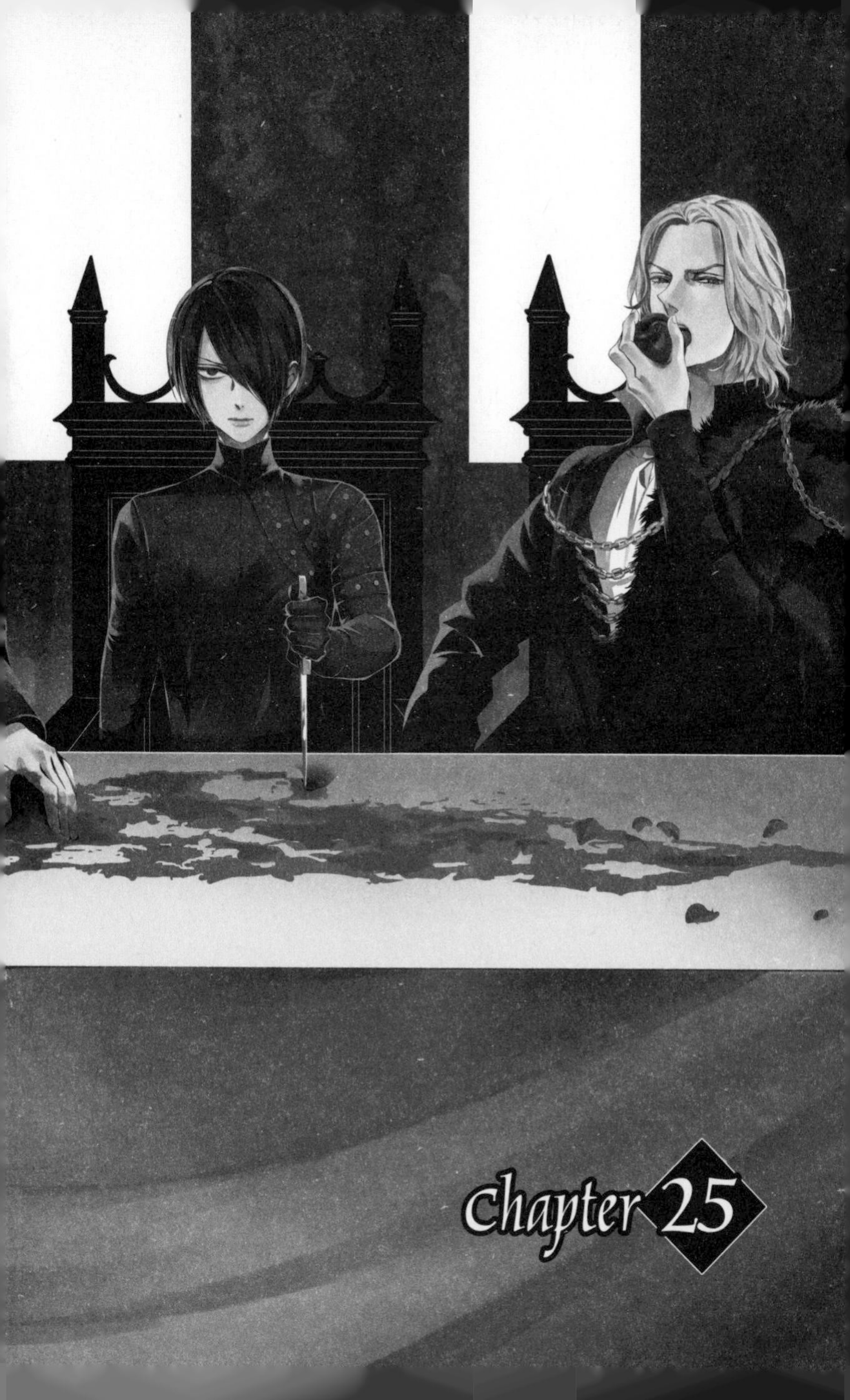
chapter 25

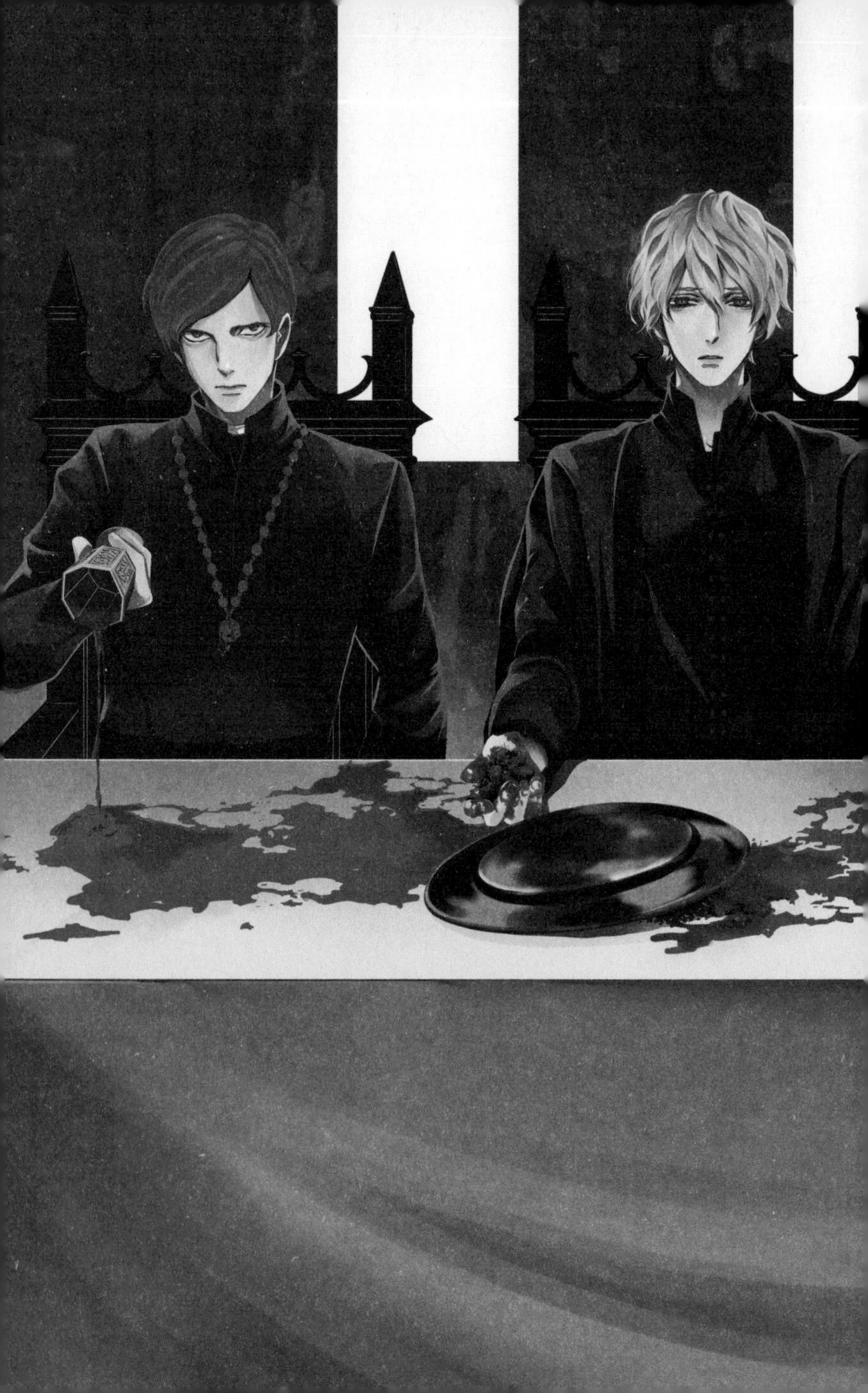

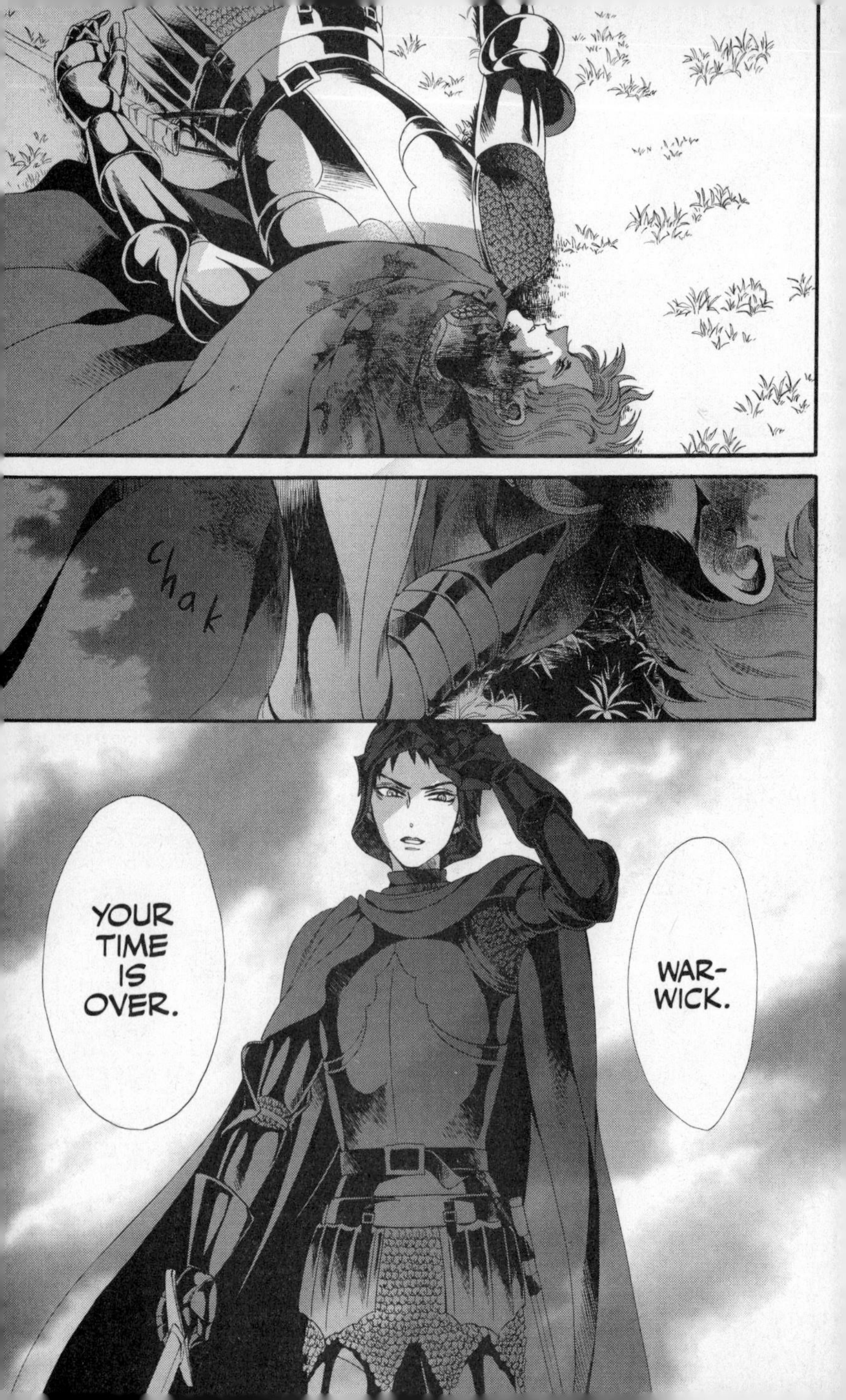
chak
WAR-WICK.
YOUR TIME IS OVER.

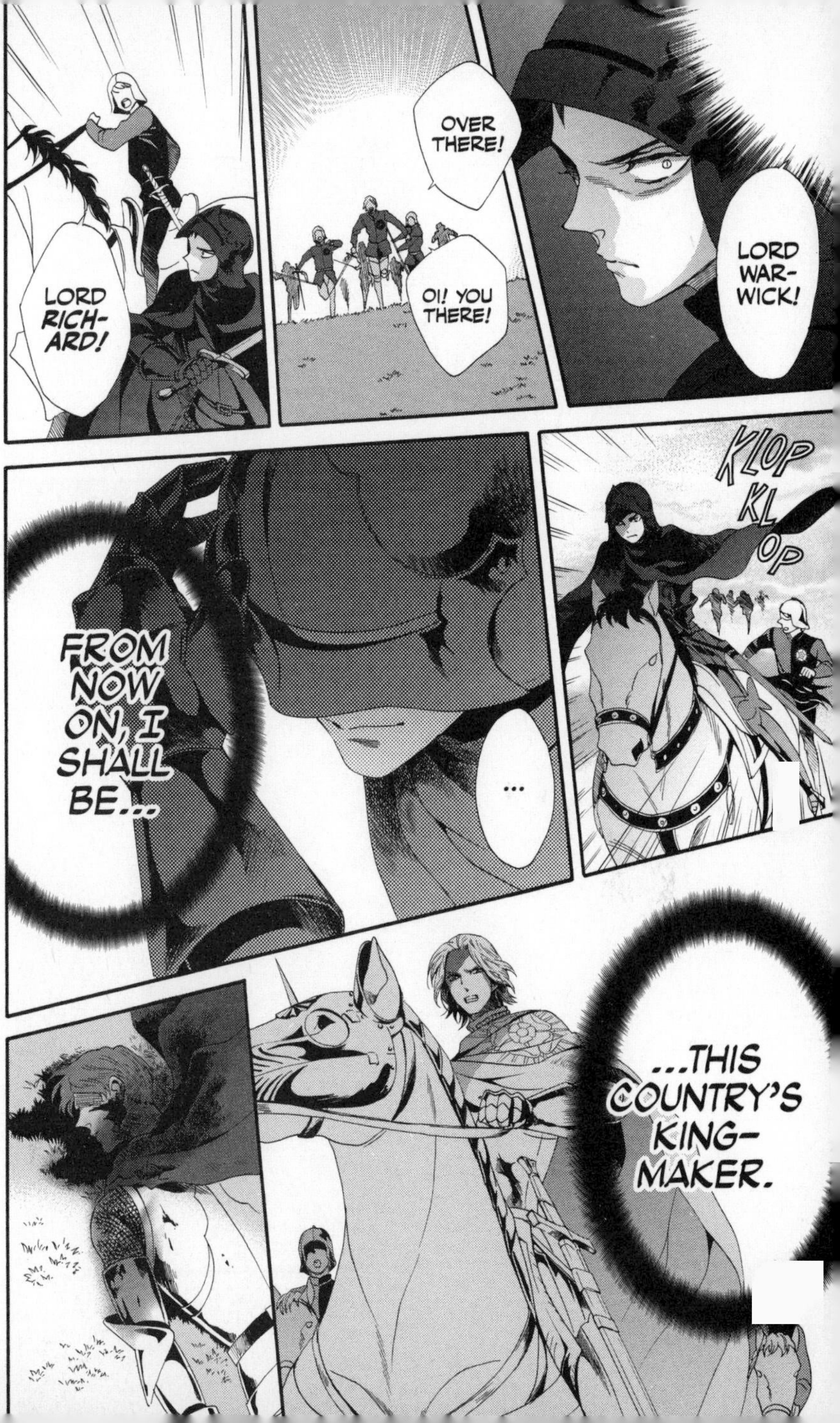
LORD WAR-WICK!
OVER THERE!
OI! YOU THERE!
LORD RICH-ARD!
KLOP KLOP
...
FROM NOW ON, I SHALL BE...
...THIS COUNTRY'S KING-MAKER.

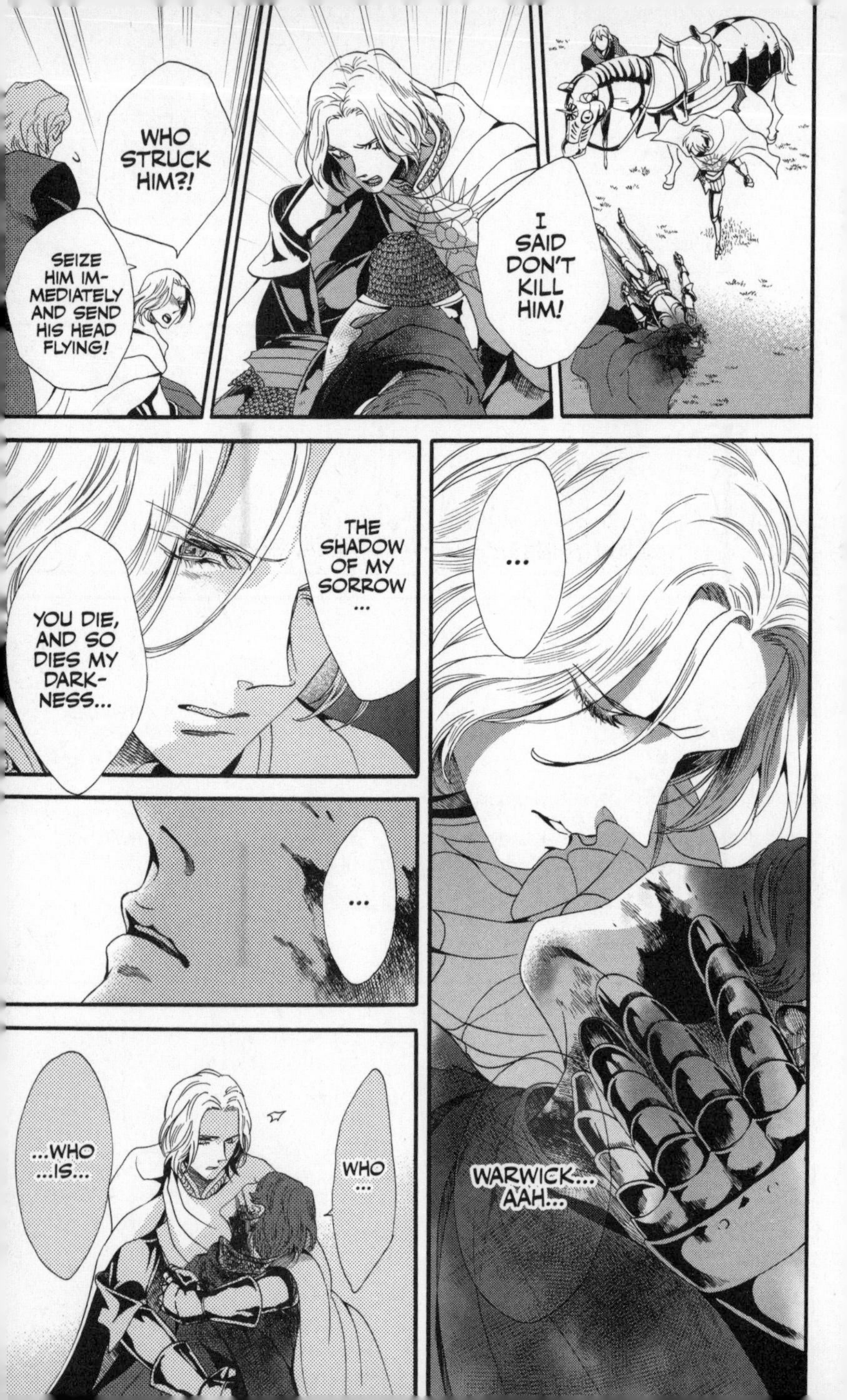
I SAID DON'T KILL HIM!
WHO STRUCK HIM?!
SEIZE HIM IMMEDIATELY AND SEND HIS HEAD FLYING!
...
WARWICK... AAH...
THE SHADOW OF MY SORROW...
YOU DIE, AND SO DIES MY DARKNESS...
...
WHO ...
...WHO ...IS...

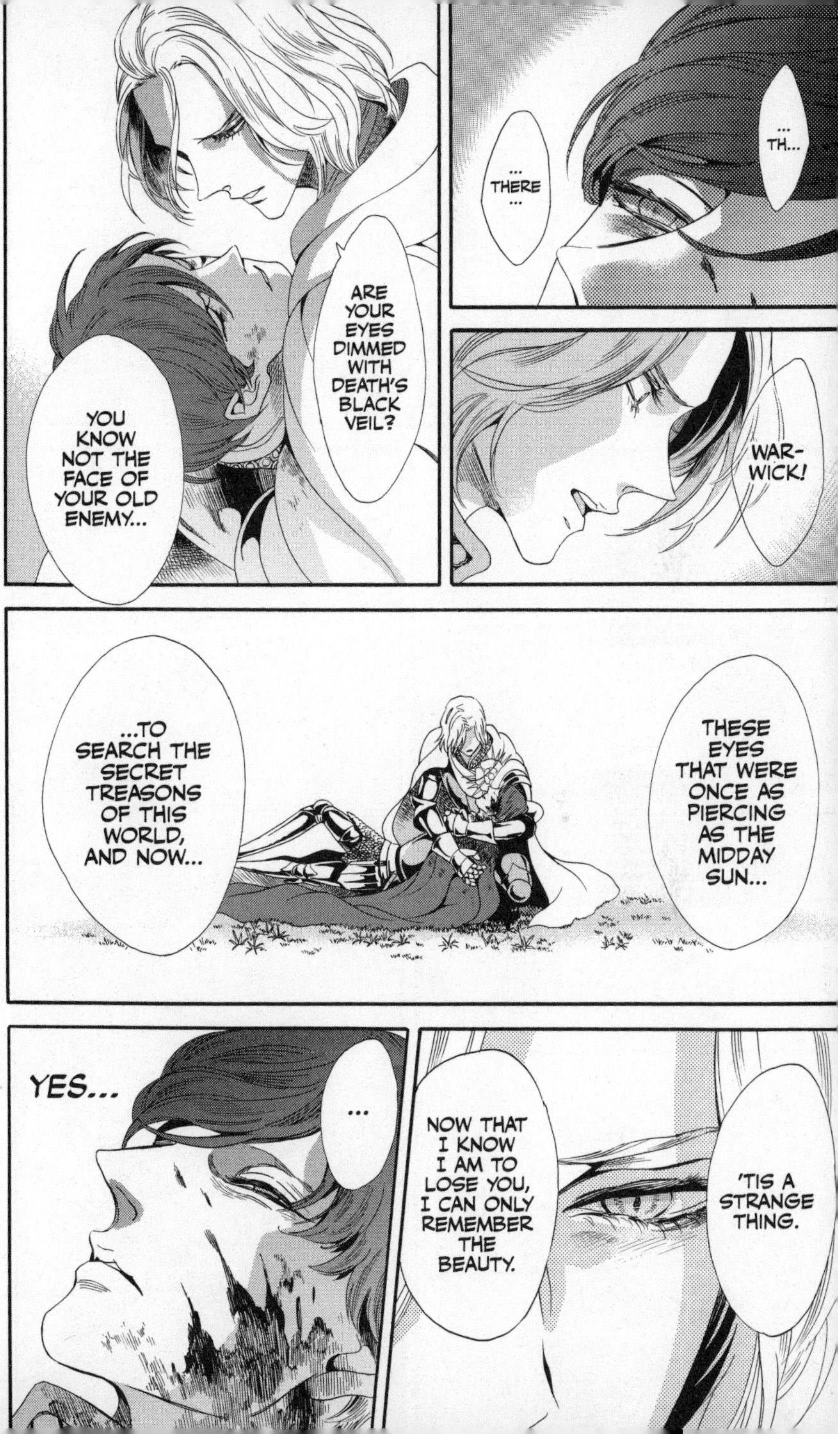
... TH...
... THERE ...
WAR- WICK!
ARE YOUR EYES DIMMED WITH DEATH'S BLACK VEIL?
YOU KNOW NOT THE FACE OF YOUR OLD ENEMY...
THESE EYES THAT WERE ONCE AS PIERCING AS THE MIDDAY SUN...
...TO SEARCH THE SECRET TREASONS OF THIS WORLD, AND NOW...
'TIS A STRANGE THING.
NOW THAT I KNOW I AM TO LOSE YOU, I CAN ONLY REMEMBER THE BEAUTY.
...
YES...

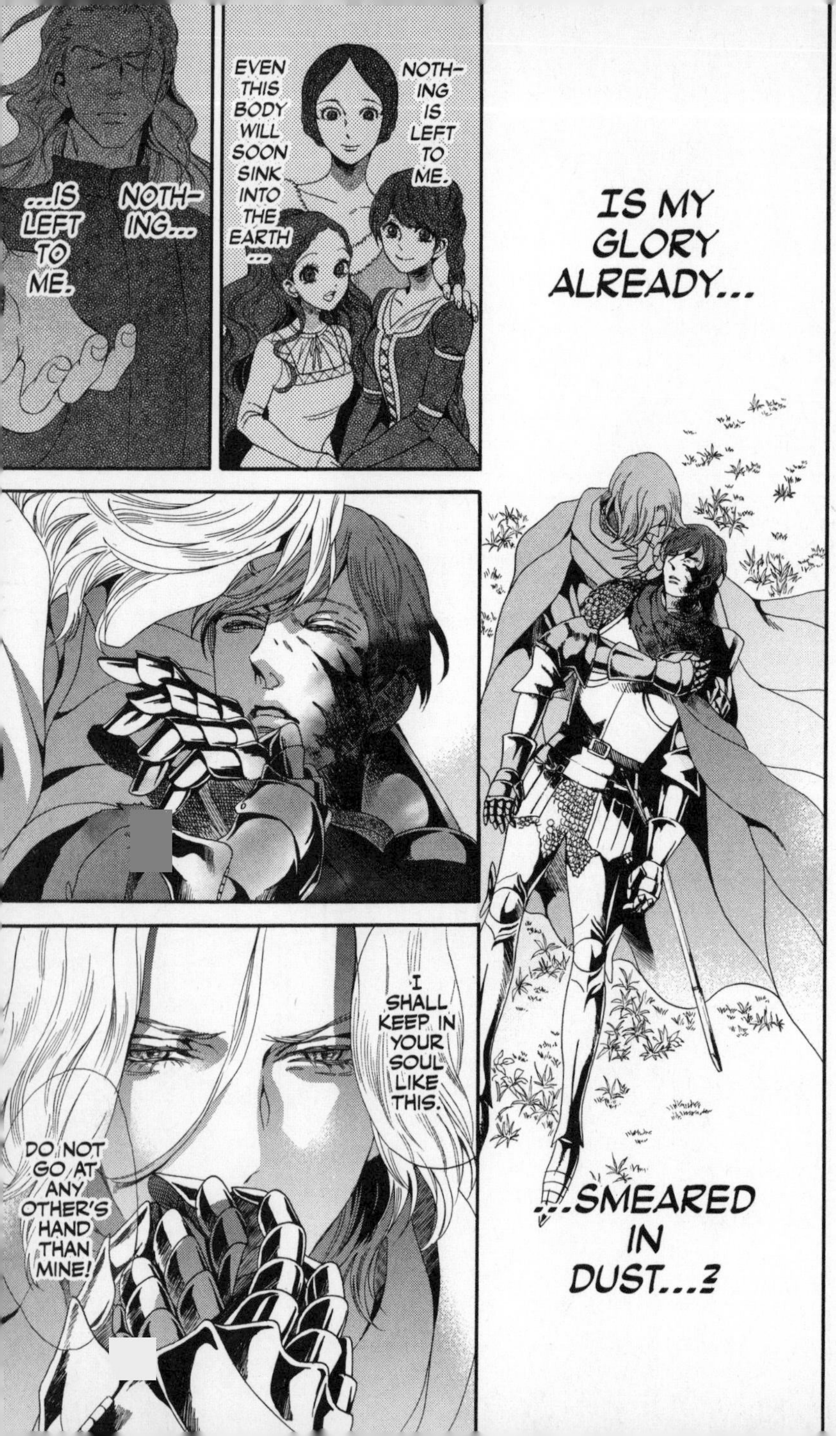
IS MY GLORY ALREADY...
...SMEARED IN DUST...?
NOTH-ING IS LEFT TO ME.
EVEN THIS BODY WILL SOON SINK INTO THE EARTH...
NOTH-ING...
...IS LEFT TO ME.
I SHALL KEEP IN YOUR SOUL LIKE THIS.
DO NOT GO AT ANY OTHER'S HAND THAN MINE!

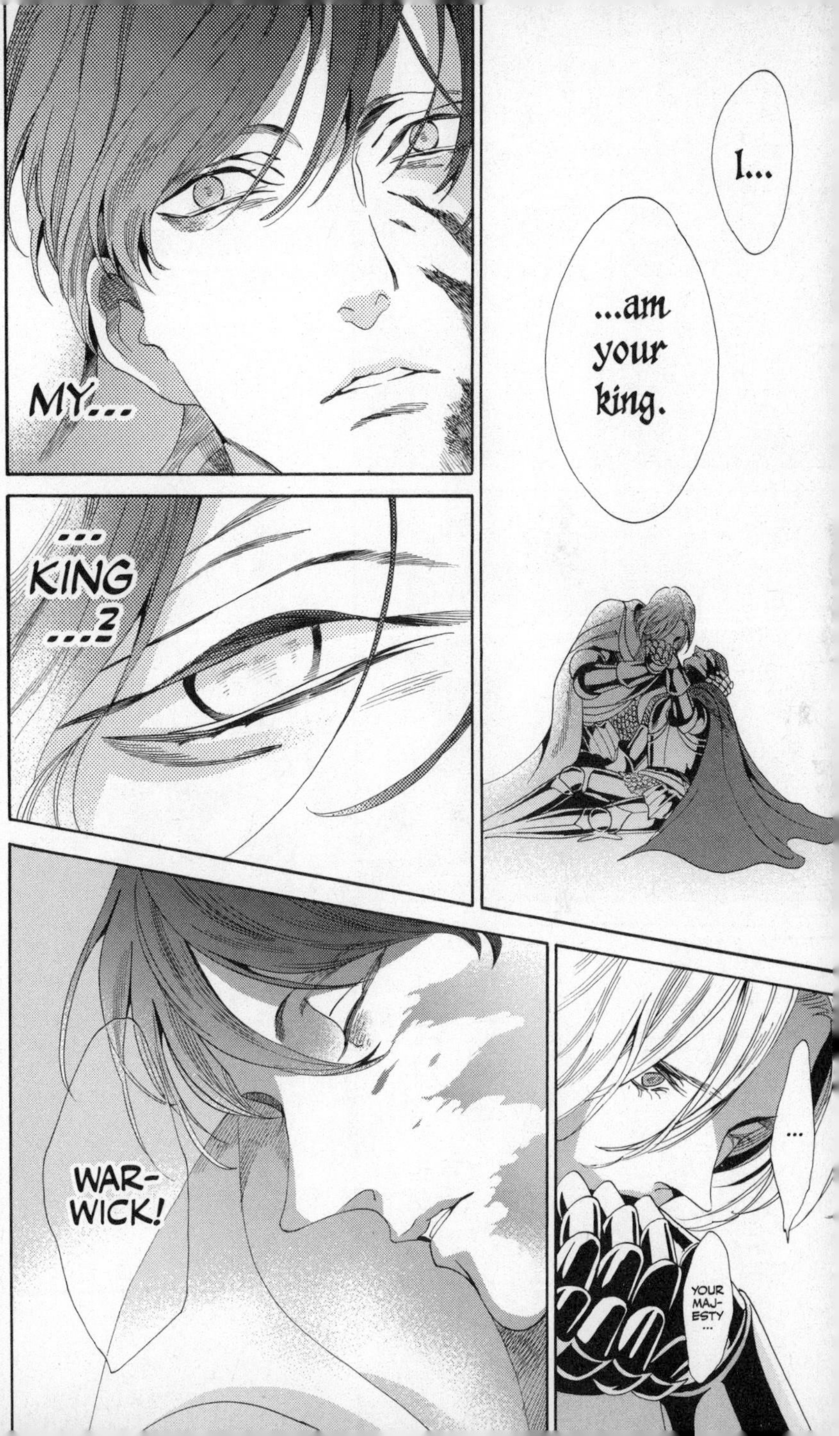

I...
...am your king.
MY...
...KING...?
...
YOUR MAJESTY...
WAR-WICK!

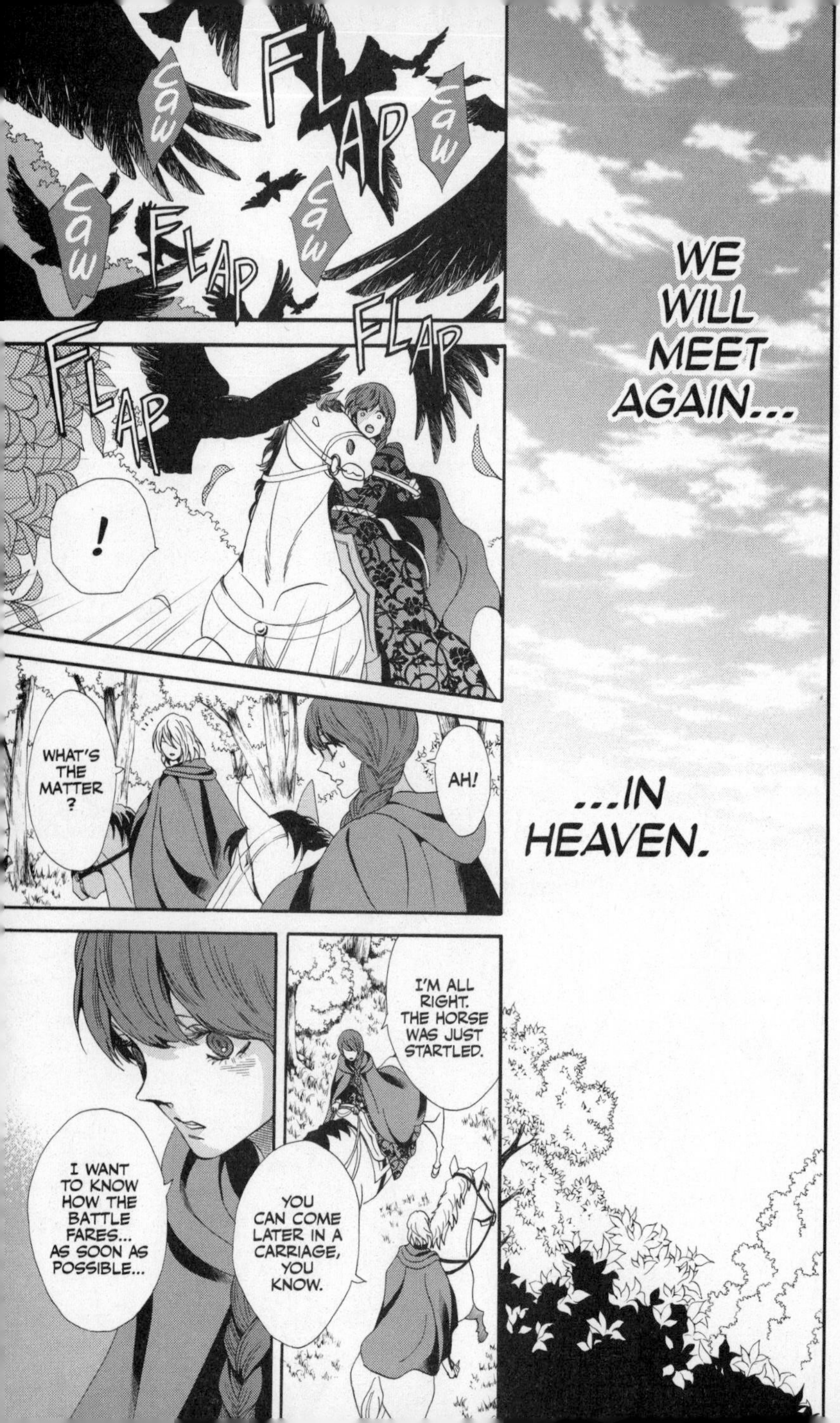
WE WILL MEET AGAIN...
...IN HEAVEN.
FLAP
caw
caw
caw
FLAP
caw
FLAP
FLAP
FLAP
!
AH!
WHAT'S THE MATTER?
I'M ALL RIGHT. THE HORSE WAS JUST STARTLED.
YOU CAN COME LATER IN A CARRIAGE, YOU KNOW.
I WANT TO KNOW HOW THE BATTLE FARES... AS SOON AS POSSIBLE...

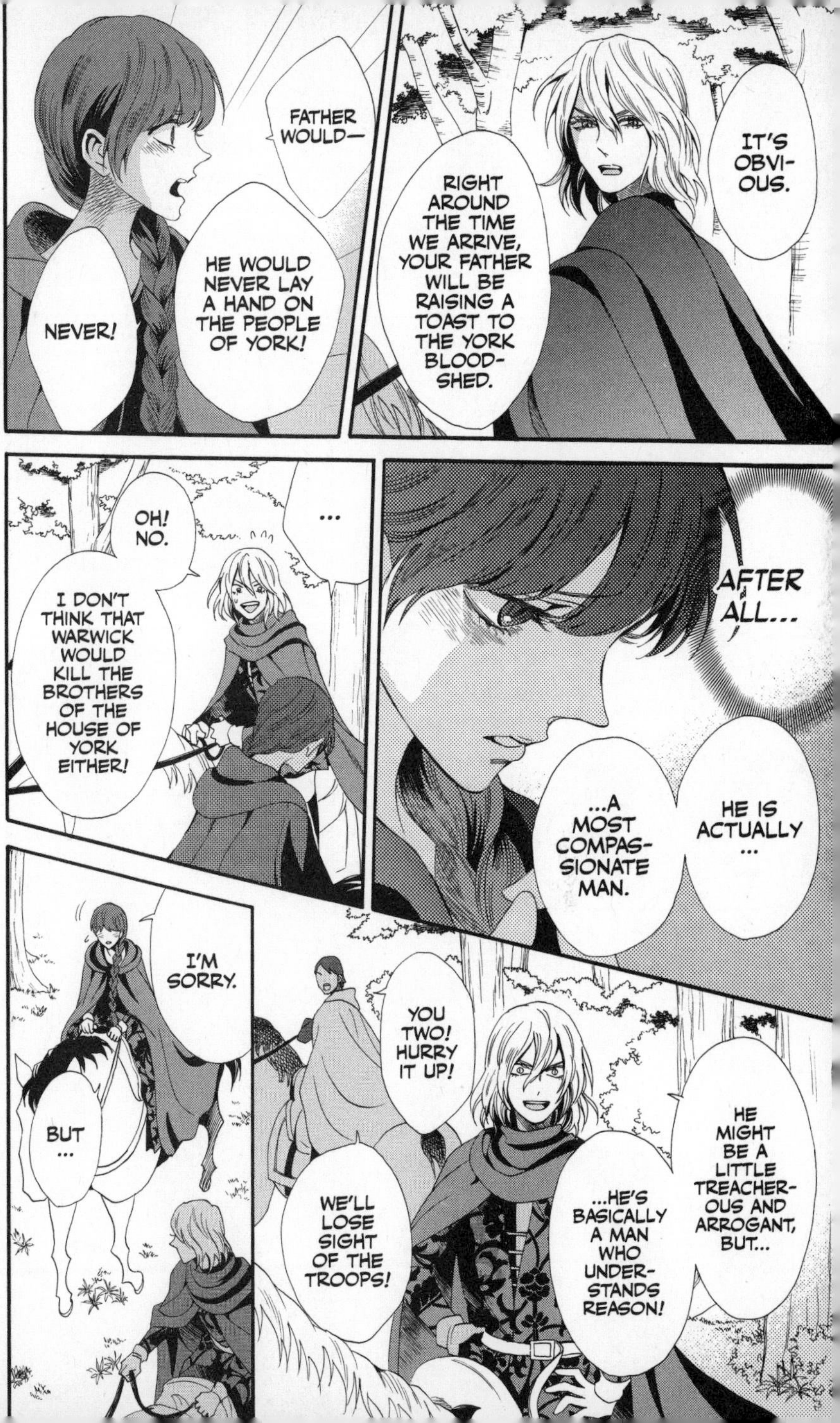
IT'S OBVIOUS.
RIGHT AROUND THE TIME WE ARRIVE, YOUR FATHER WILL BE RAISING A TOAST TO THE YORK BLOODSHED.
FATHER WOULD—
HE WOULD NEVER LAY A HAND ON THE PEOPLE OF YORK!
NEVER!
AFTER ALL...
HE IS ACTUALLY ...
...A MOST COMPASSIONATE MAN.
...
OH! NO.
I DON'T THINK THAT WARWICK WOULD KILL THE BROTHERS OF THE HOUSE OF YORK EITHER!
HE MIGHT BE A LITTLE TREACHEROUS AND ARROGANT, BUT...
...HE'S BASICALLY A MAN WHO UNDERSTANDS REASON!
YOU TWO! HURRY IT UP!
WE'LL LOSE SIGHT OF THE TROOPS!
I'M SORRY.
BUT ...

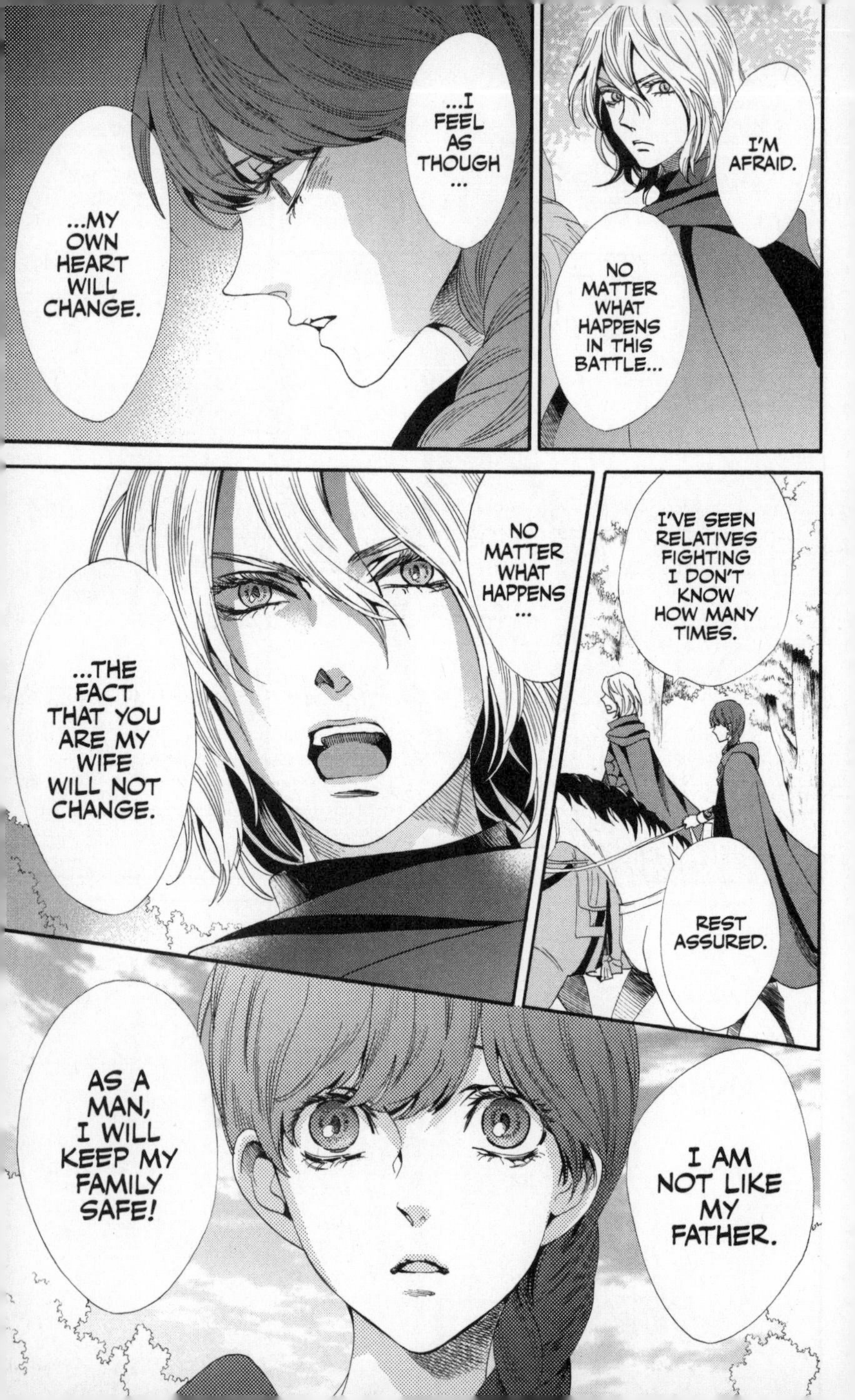
I'M AFRAID.
NO MATTER WHAT HAPPENS IN THIS BATTLE...
...I FEEL AS THOUGH...
...MY OWN HEART WILL CHANGE.
I'VE SEEN RELATIVES FIGHTING I DON'T KNOW HOW MANY TIMES.
REST ASSURED.
NO MATTER WHAT HAPPENS...
...THE FACT THAT YOU ARE MY WIFE WILL NOT CHANGE.
I AM NOT LIKE MY FATHER.
AS A MAN, I WILL KEEP MY FAMILY SAFE!

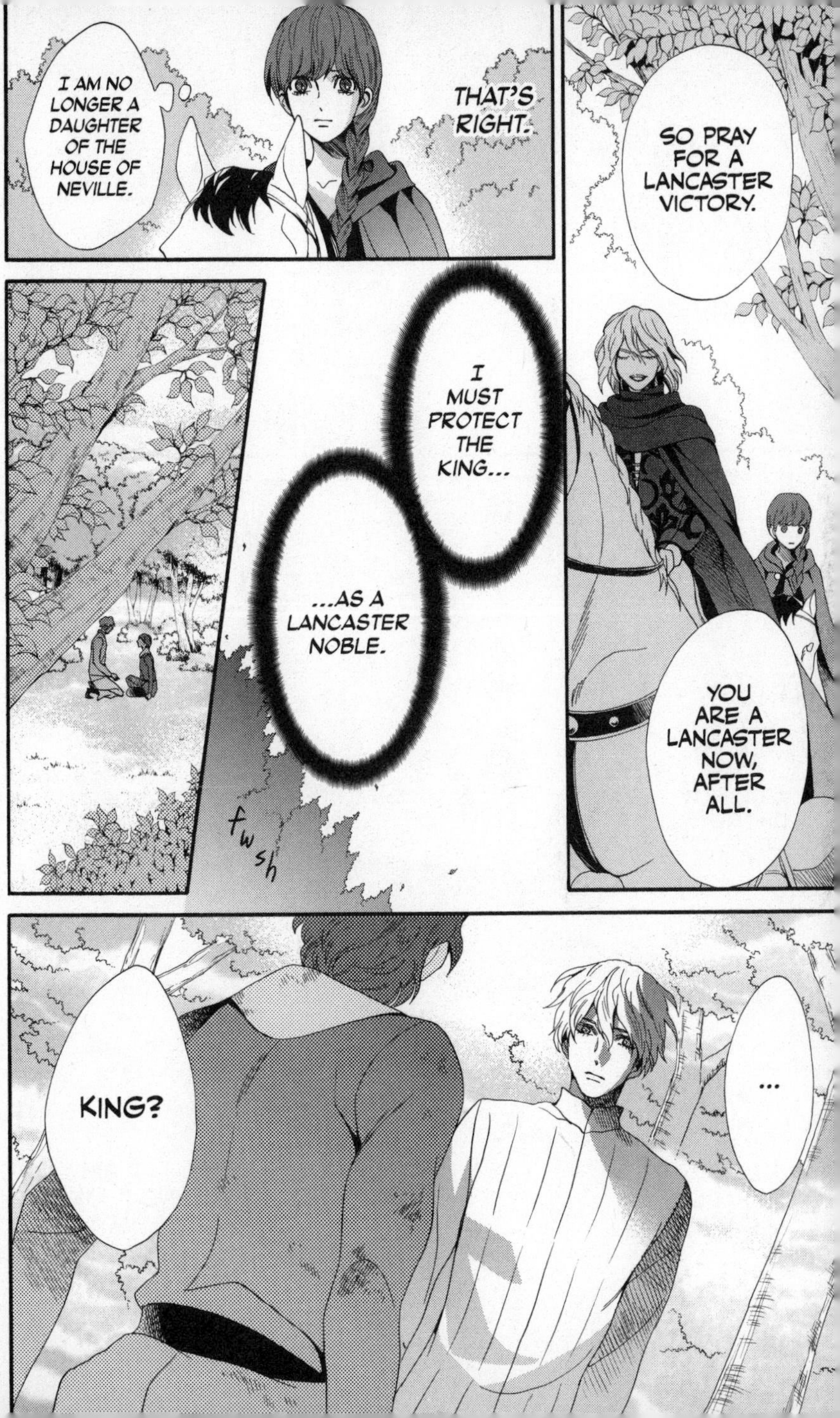
SO PRAY FOR A LANCASTER VICTORY.
YOU ARE A LANCASTER NOW, AFTER ALL.
THAT'S RIGHT.
I AM NO LONGER A DAUGHTER OF THE HOUSE OF NEVILLE.
I MUST PROTECT THE KING...
...AS A LANCASTER NOBLE.
fwsh
...
KING?

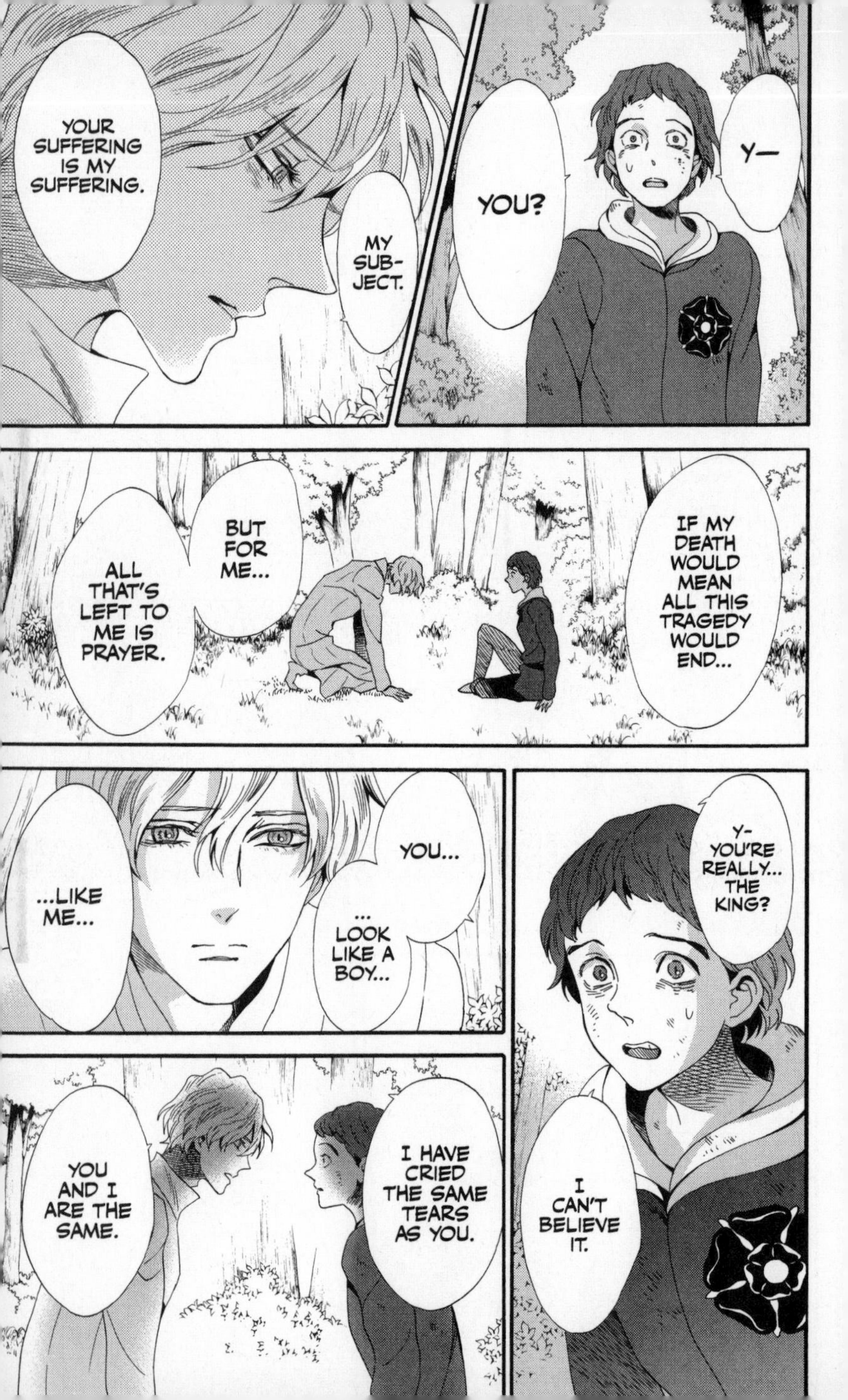
Y—
YOU?
MY SUB-JECT.
YOUR SUFFERING IS MY SUFFERING.
IF MY DEATH WOULD MEAN ALL THIS TRAGEDY WOULD END...
BUT FOR ME...
ALL THAT'S LEFT TO ME IS PRAYER.
Y-YOU'RE REALLY... THE KING?
I CAN'T BELIEVE IT.
YOU...
...LOOK LIKE A BOY...
...LIKE ME...
I HAVE CRIED THE SAME TEARS AS YOU.
YOU AND I ARE THE SAME.

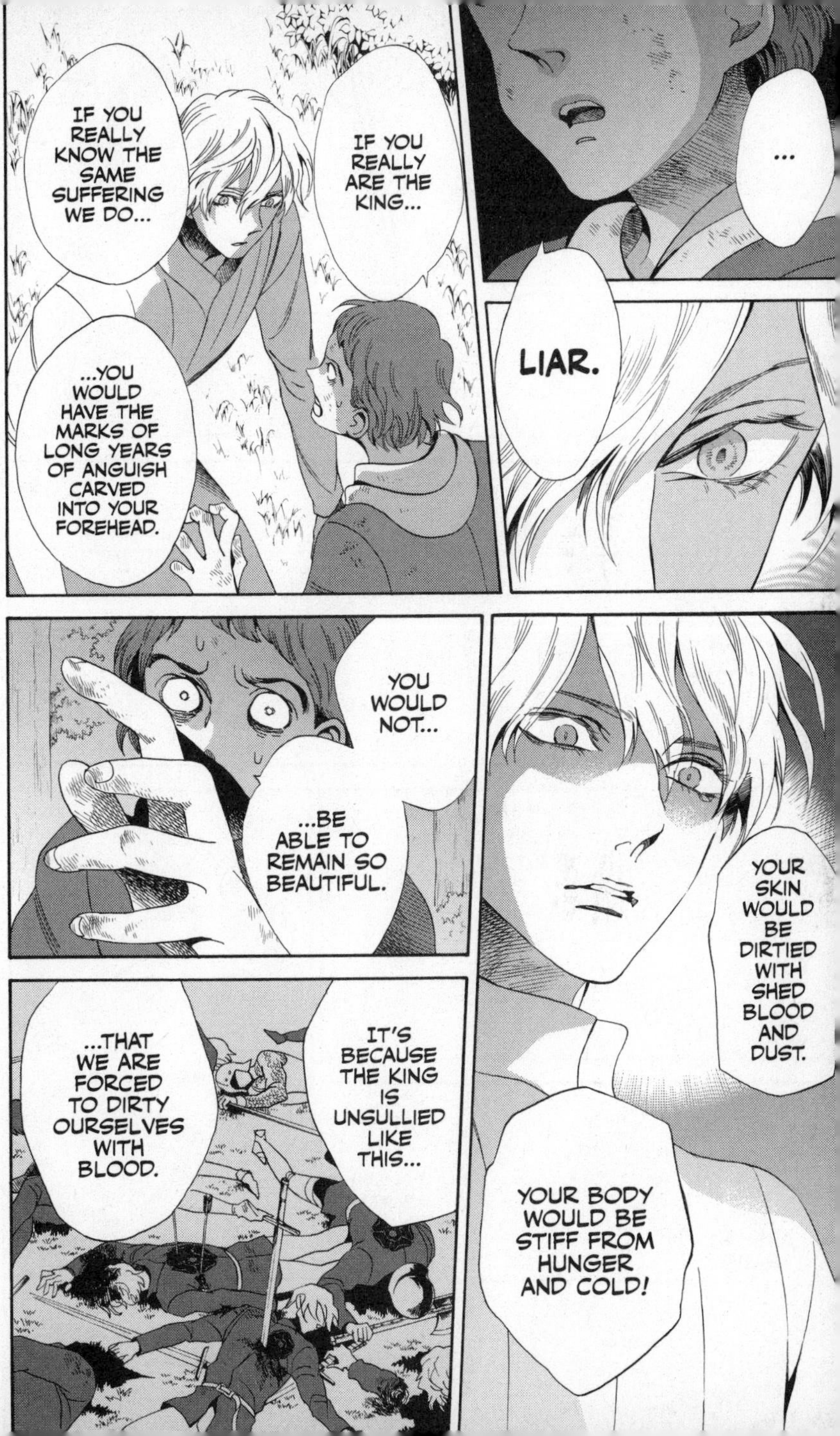
...
LIAR.
IF YOU REALLY ARE THE KING...
IF YOU REALLY KNOW THE SAME SUFFERING WE DO...
...YOU WOULD HAVE THE MARKS OF LONG YEARS OF ANGUISH CARVED INTO YOUR FOREHEAD.
YOUR SKIN WOULD BE DIRTIED WITH SHED BLOOD AND DUST.
YOUR BODY WOULD BE STIFF FROM HUNGER AND COLD!
YOU WOULD NOT...
...BE ABLE TO REMAIN SO BEAUTIFUL.
IT'S BECAUSE THE KING IS UNSULLIED LIKE THIS...
...THAT WE ARE FORCED TO DIRTY OURSELVES WITH BLOOD.

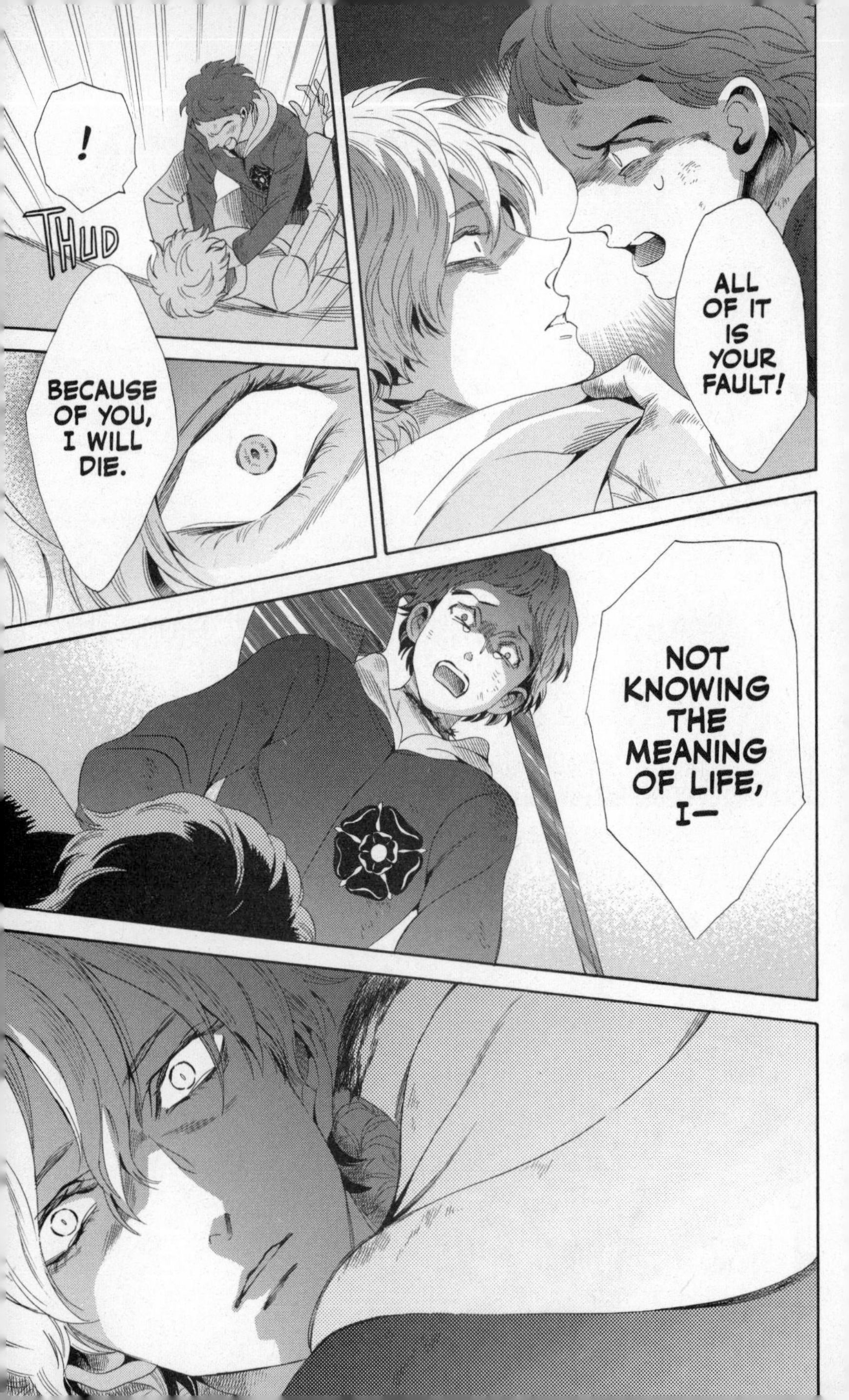
ALL OF IT IS YOUR FAULT!
!
THUD
BECAUSE OF YOU, I WILL DIE.
NOT KNOWING THE MEANING OF LIFE, I—

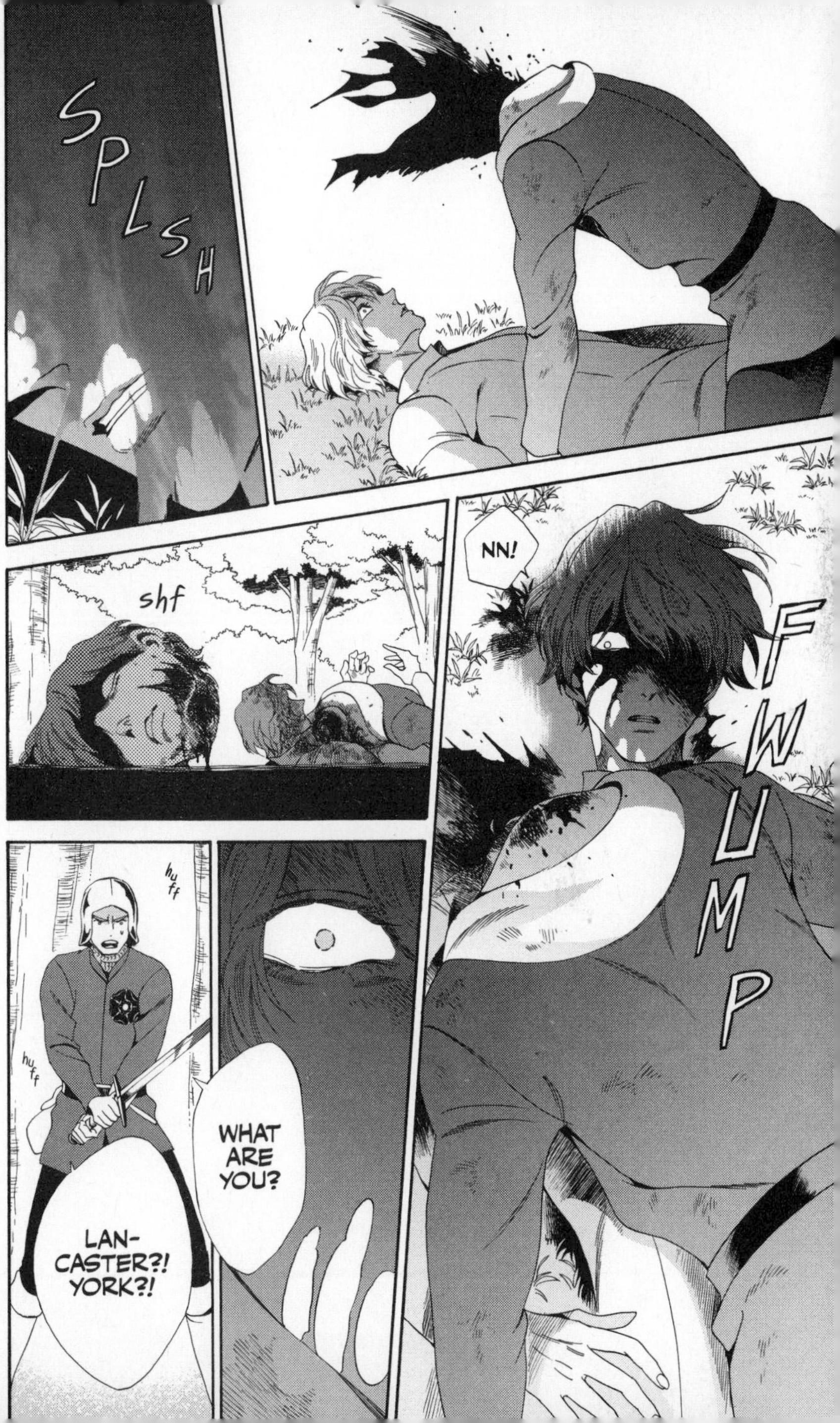
SPLSH
NN!
FWUMP
shf
WHAT ARE YOU?
huff
huff
LAN-CASTER?! YORK?!

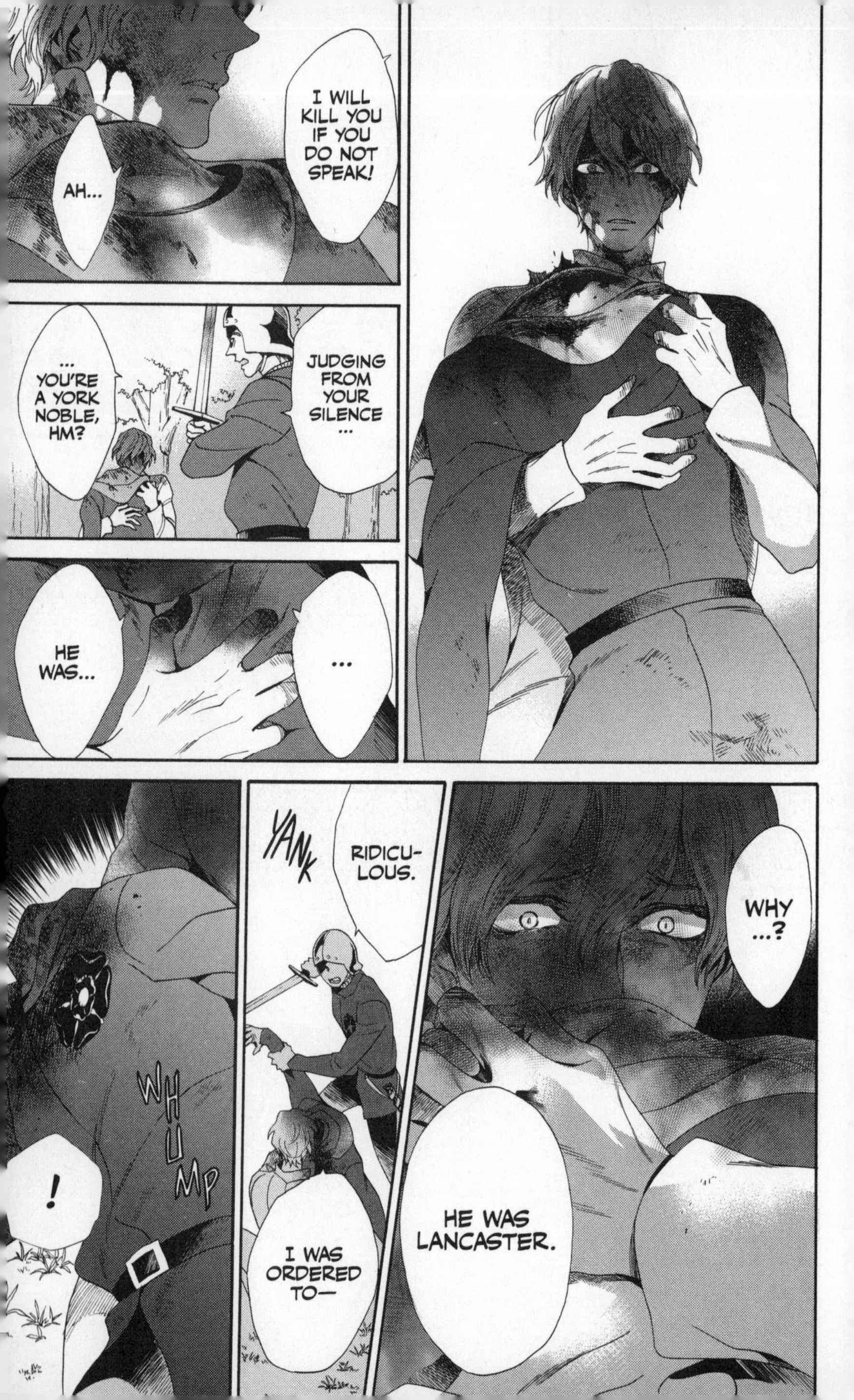
I WILL KILL YOU IF YOU DO NOT SPEAK!
AH...
JUDGING FROM YOUR SILENCE...
...YOU'RE A YORK NOBLE, HM?
...
HE WAS...
WHY...?
HE WAS LANCASTER.
YANK
RIDICULOUS.
I WAS ORDERED TO—
WHUMP
!

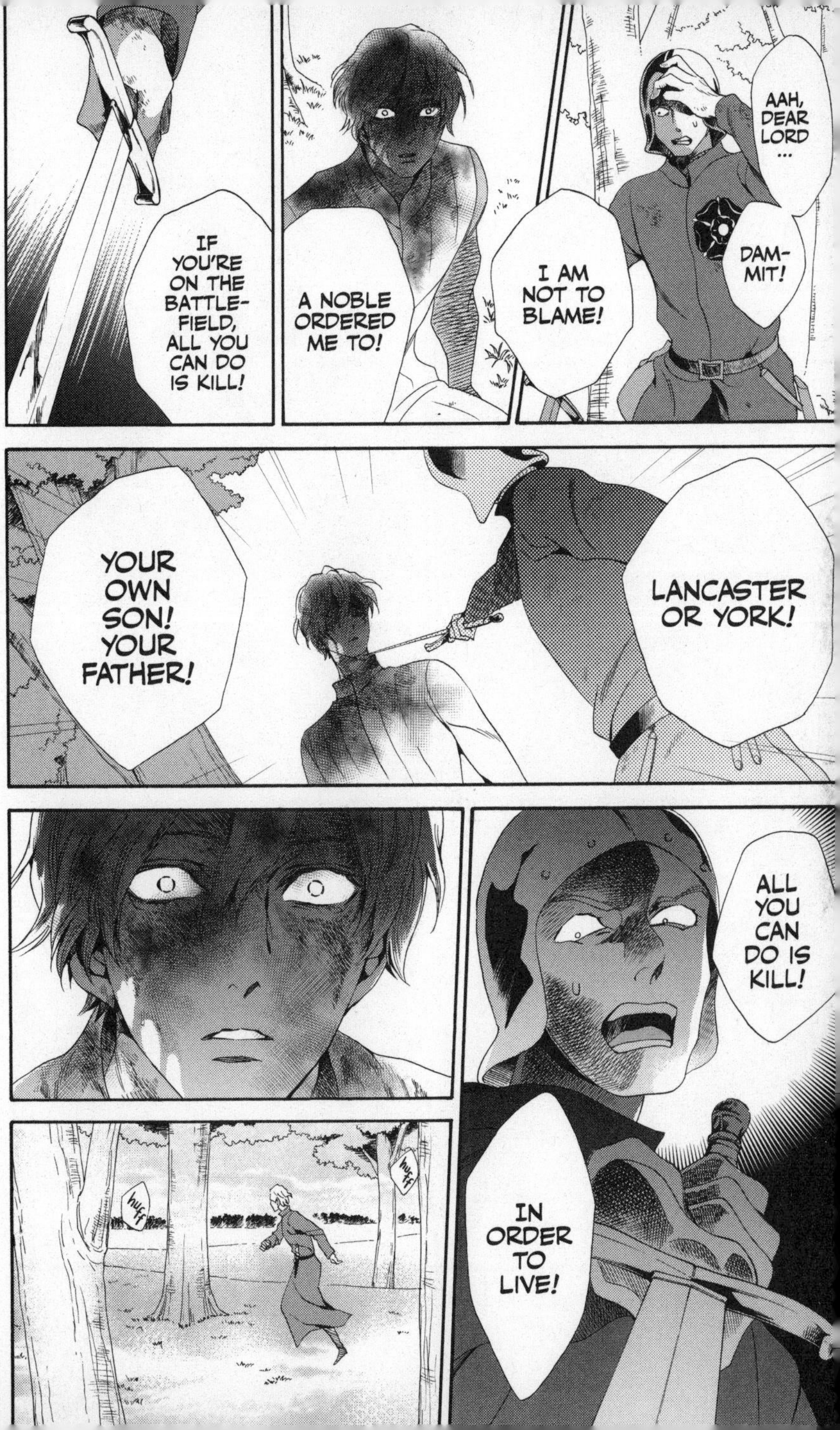
AAH, DEAR LORD...
DAM-MIT!
I AM NOT TO BLAME!
A NOBLE ORDERED ME TO!
IF YOU'RE ON THE BATTLE-FIELD, ALL YOU CAN DO IS KILL!
LANCASTER OR YORK!
YOUR OWN SON! YOUR FATHER!
ALL YOU CAN DO IS KILL!
IN ORDER TO LIVE!
huff
huff

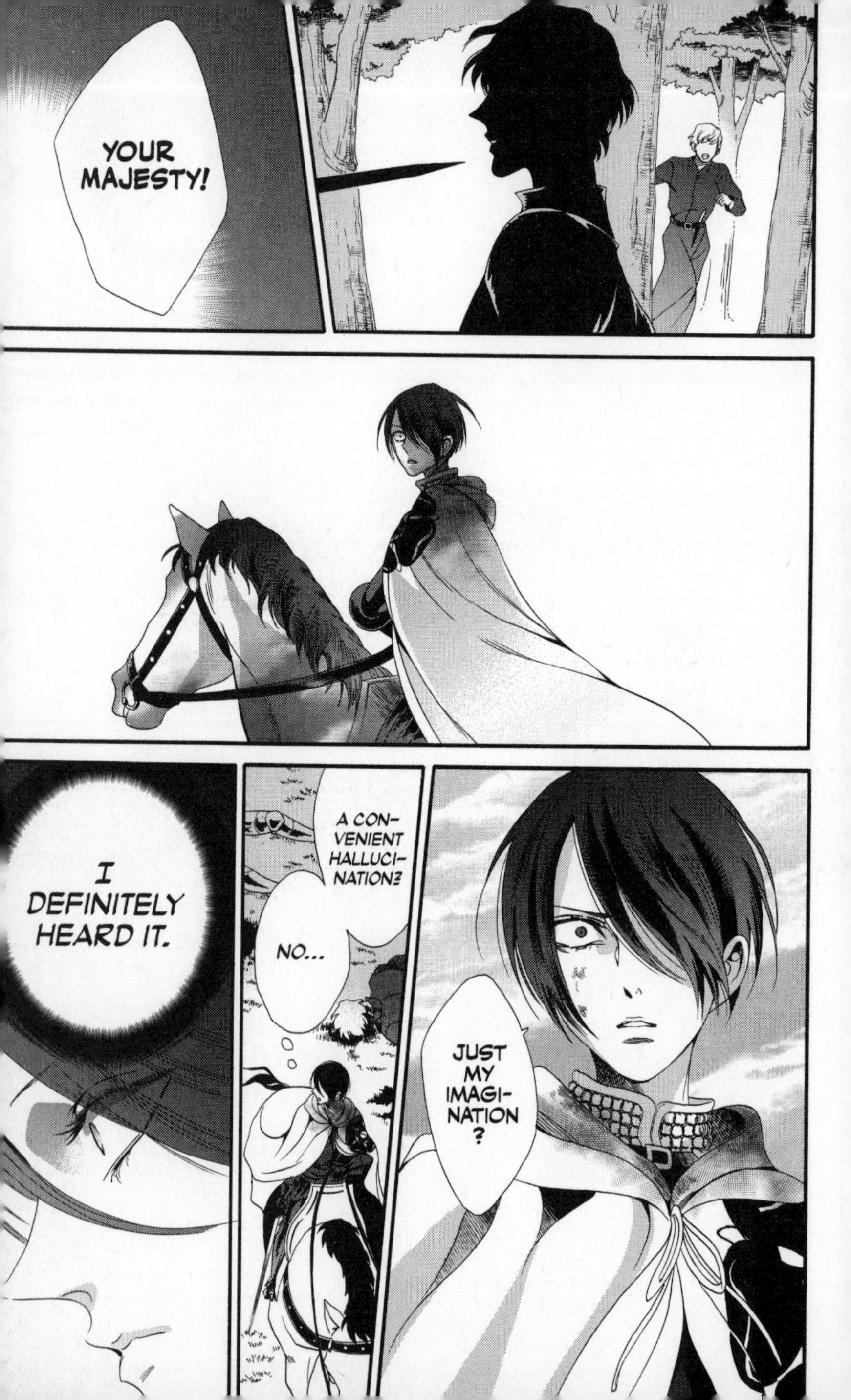
YOUR MAJESTY!
JUST MY IMAGINATION?
A CON-VENIENT HALLUCI-NATION?
NO...
I DEFINITELY HEARD IT.

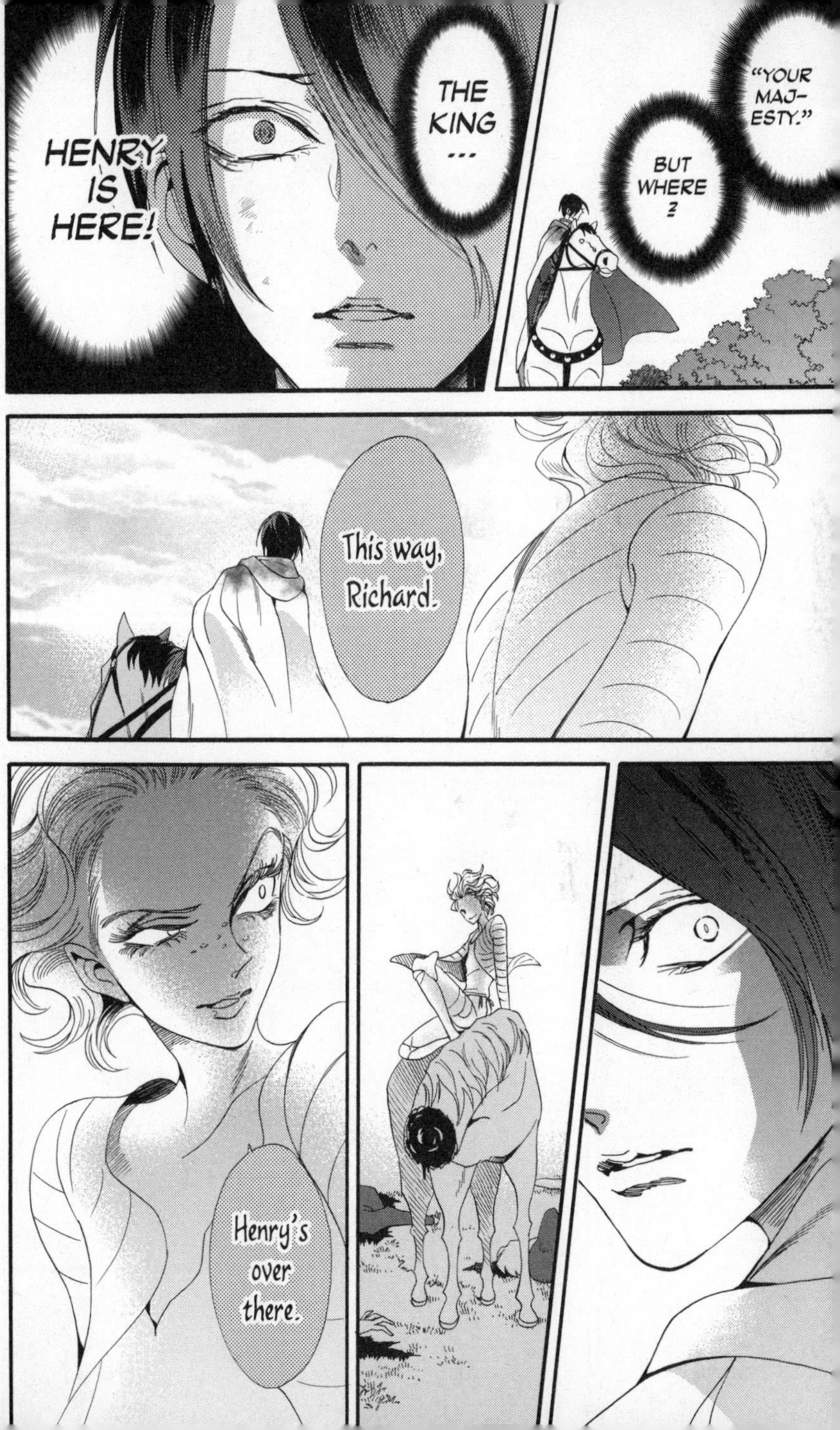
"YOUR MAJ-ESTY."
BUT WHERE?
THE KING...
HENRY IS HERE!
This way, Richard.
Henry's over there.

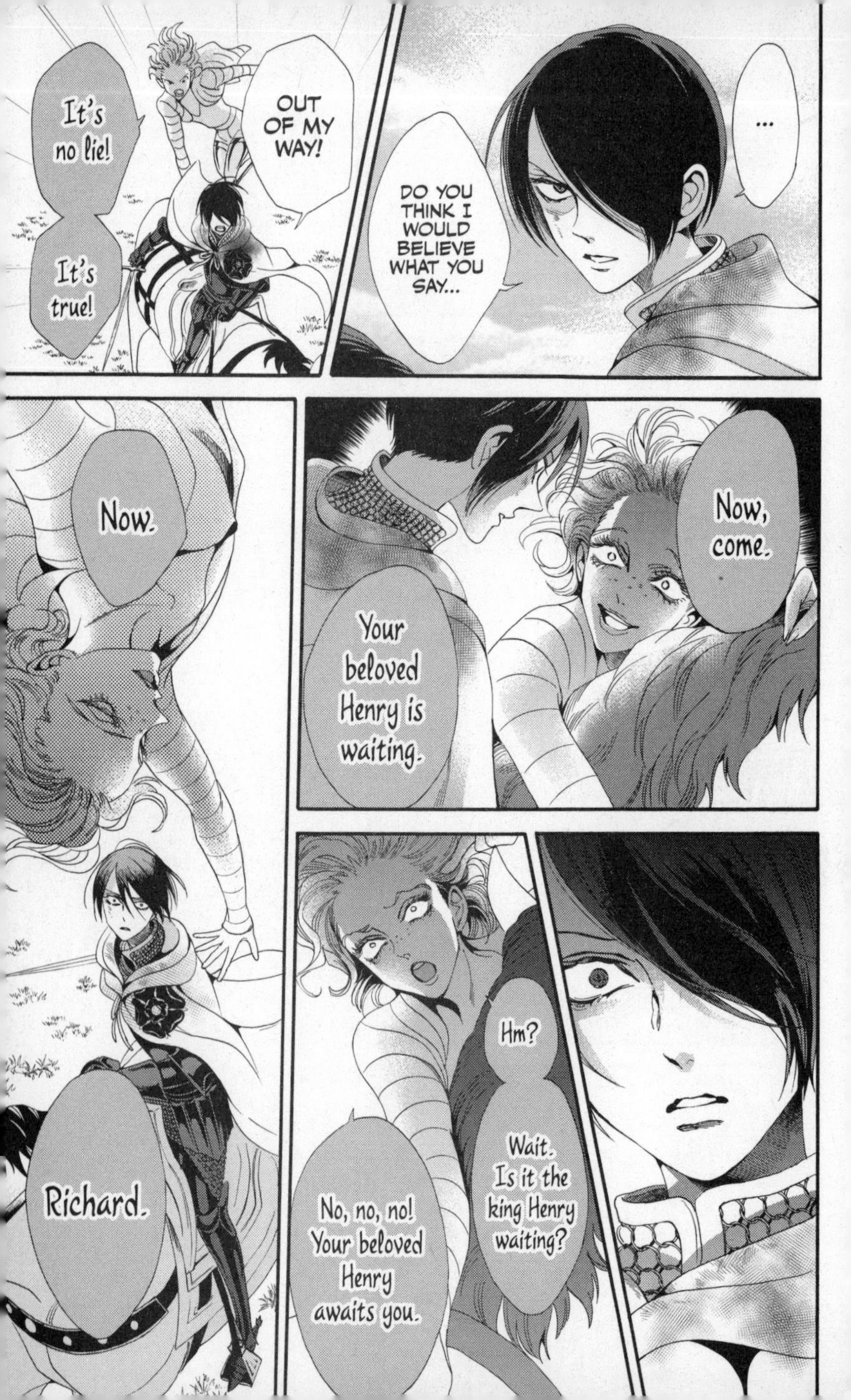
...
DO YOU THINK I WOULD BELIEVE WHAT YOU SAY...
OUT OF MY WAY!
It's no lie!
It's true!
Now, come.
Your beloved Henry is waiting.
Hm?
Wait. Is it the king Henry waiting?
No, no, no! Your beloved Henry awaits you.
Now.
Richard.

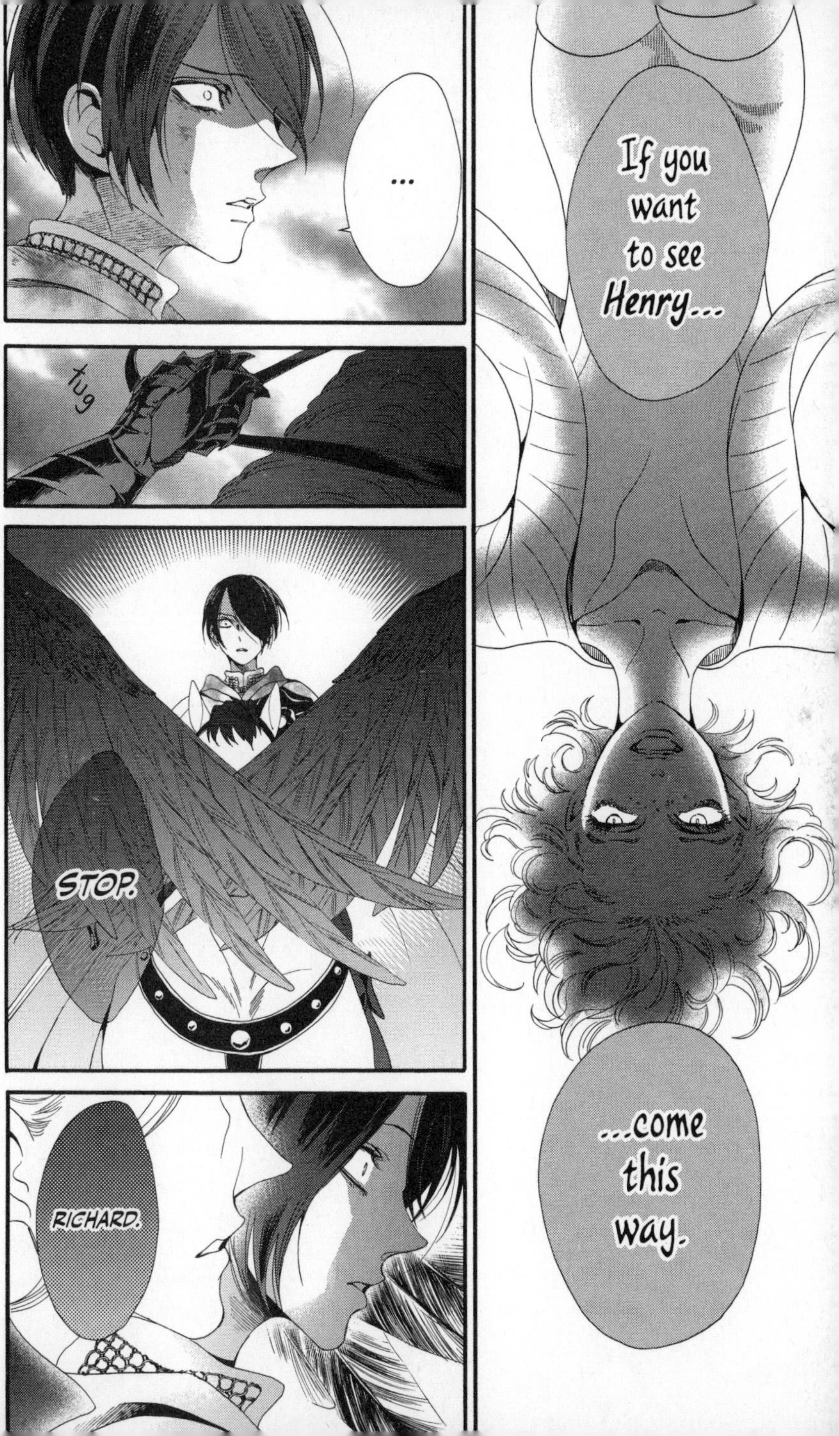
If you want to see Henry...
...come this way.
...
tug
STOP.
RICHARD.

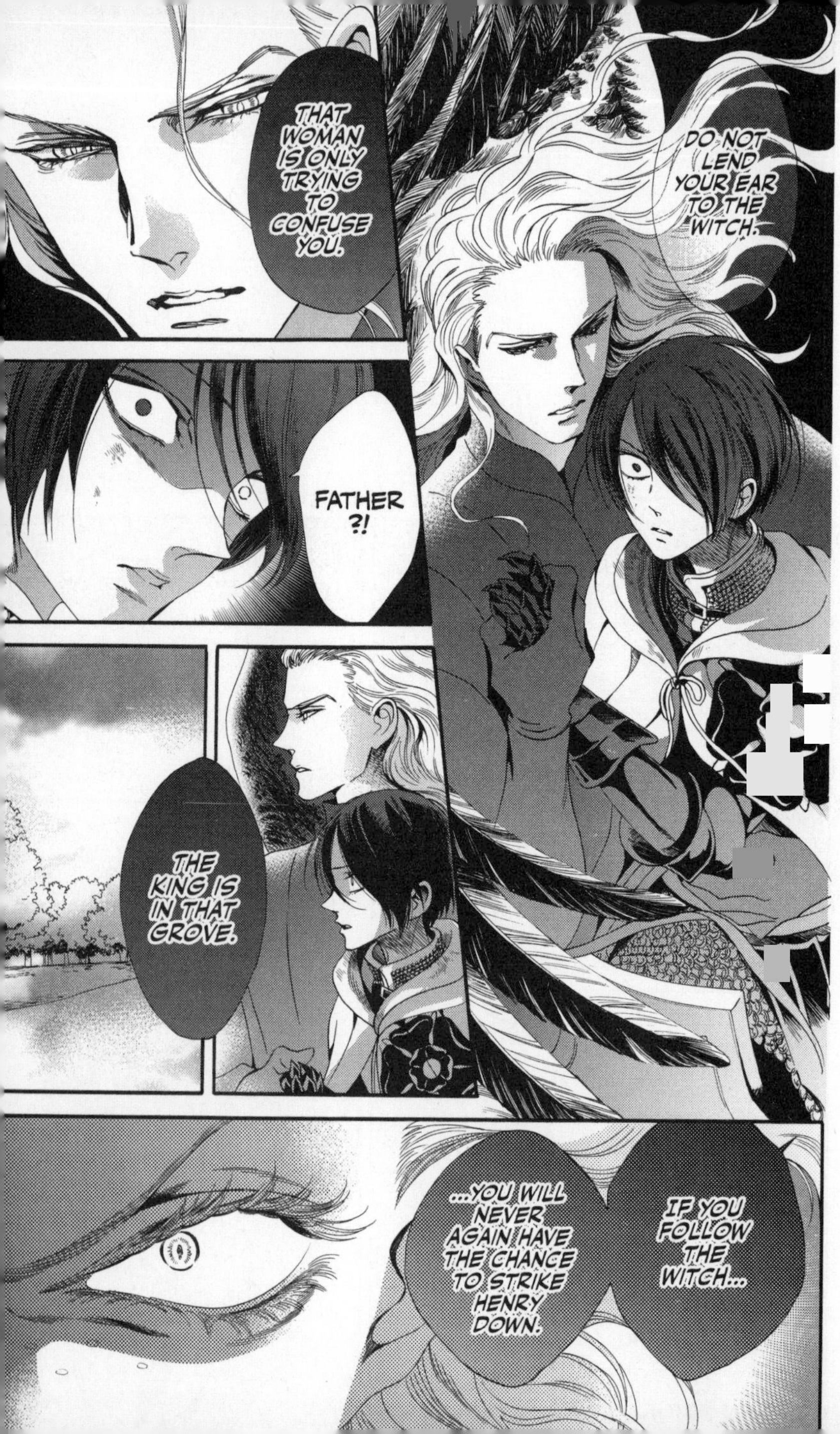
DO NOT LEND YOUR EAR TO THE WITCH.
THAT WOMAN IS ONLY TRYING TO CONFUSE YOU.
FATHER?!
THE KING IS IN THAT GROVE.
IF YOU FOLLOW THE WITCH...
...YOU WILL NEVER AGAIN HAVE THE CHANCE TO STRIKE HENRY DOWN.

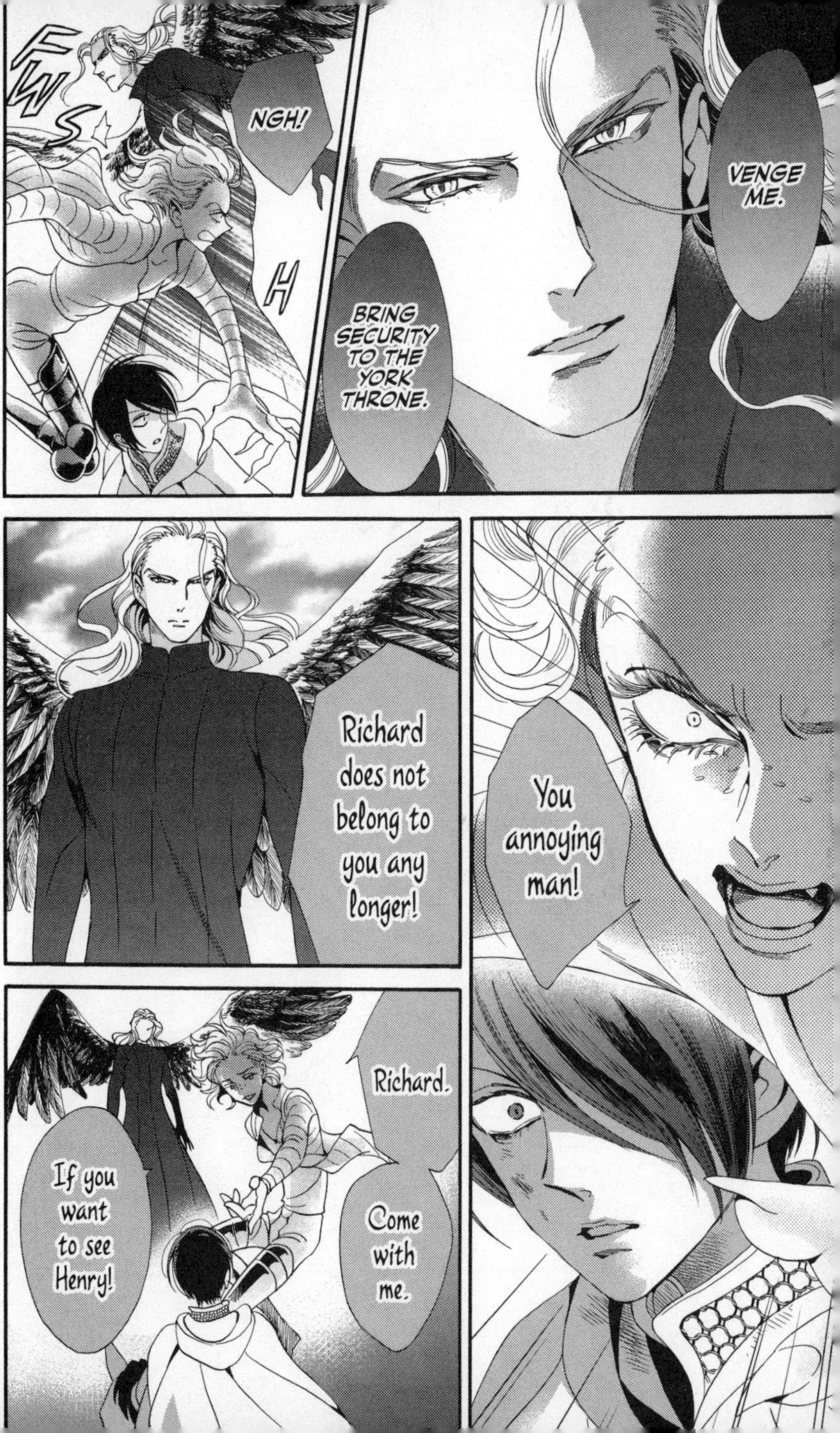
VENGE ME.
BRING SECURITY TO THE YORK THRONE.
NGH!
FWSH
You annoying man!
Richard does not belong to you any longer!
Richard.
Come with me.
If you want to see Henry!

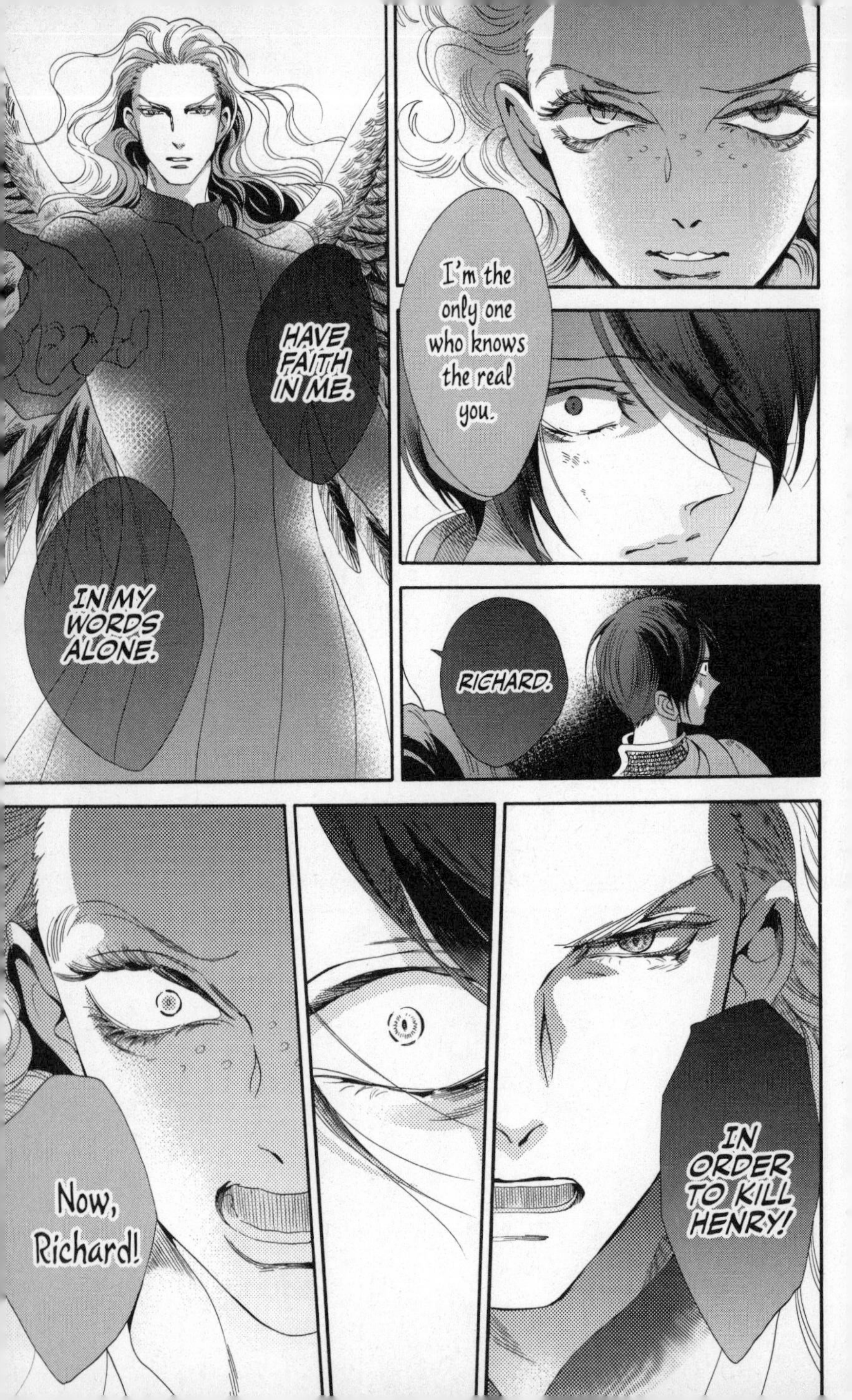
I'm the only one who knows the real you.
RICHARD.
HAVE FAITH IN ME.
IN MY WORDS ALONE.
IN ORDER TO KILL HENRY!
Now, Richard!

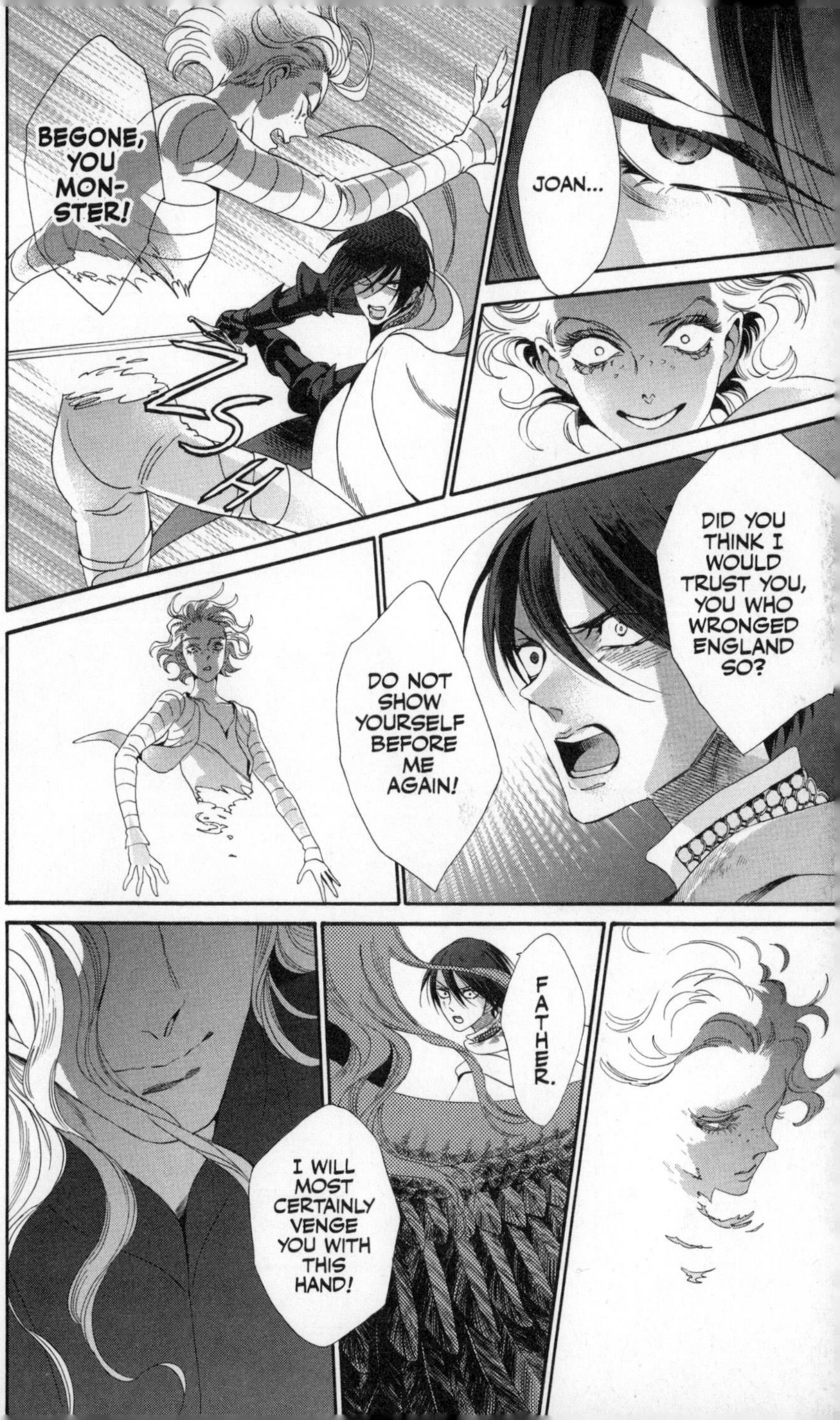
JOAN...
BEGONE, YOU MONSTER!
ZSH
DID YOU THINK I WOULD TRUST YOU, YOU WHO WRONGED ENGLAND SO?
DO NOT SHOW YOURSELF BEFORE ME AGAIN!
FATHER.
I WILL MOST CERTAINLY VENGE YOU WITH THIS HAND!

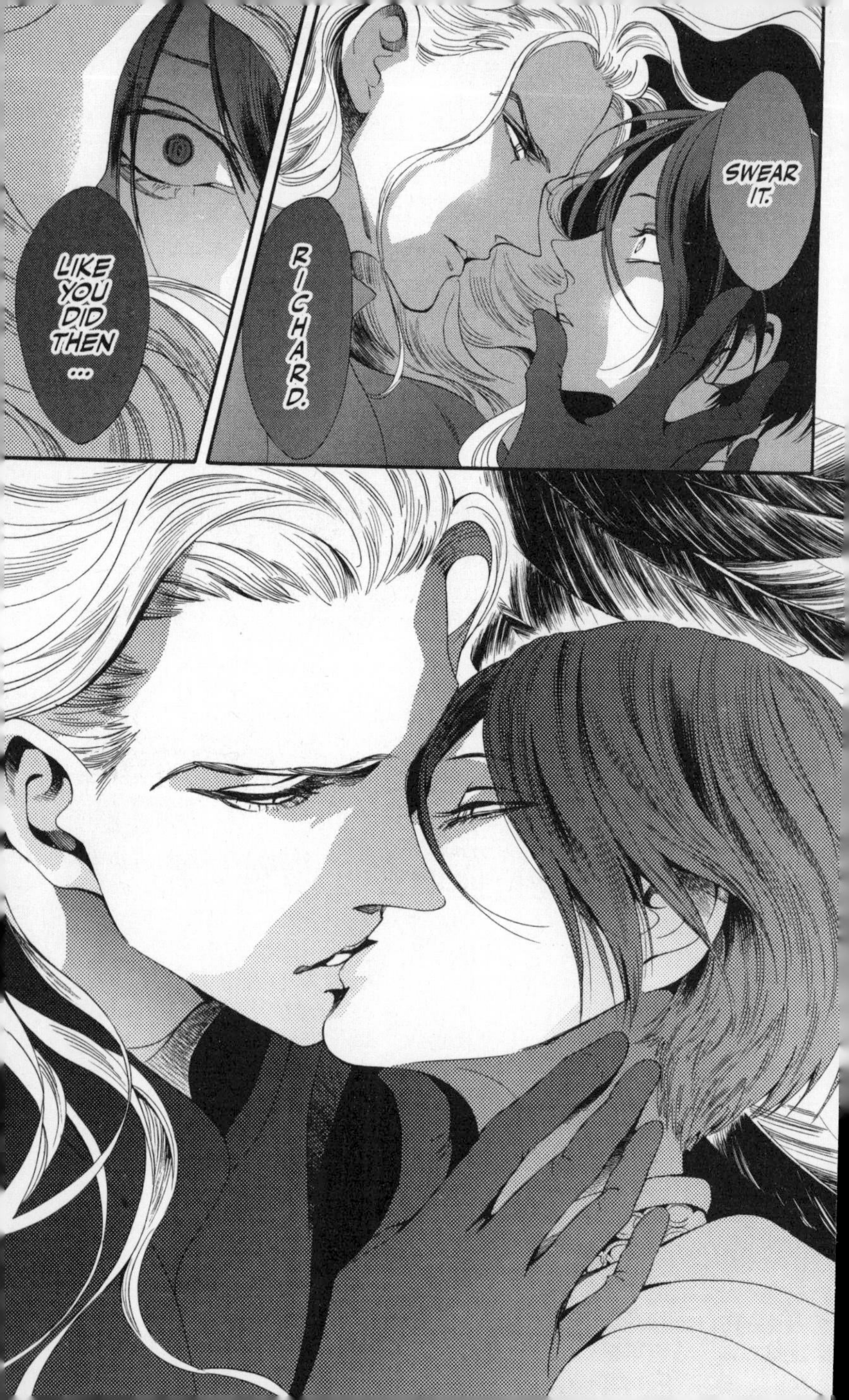
SWEAR IT.
RICHARD.
LIKE YOU DID THEN ...

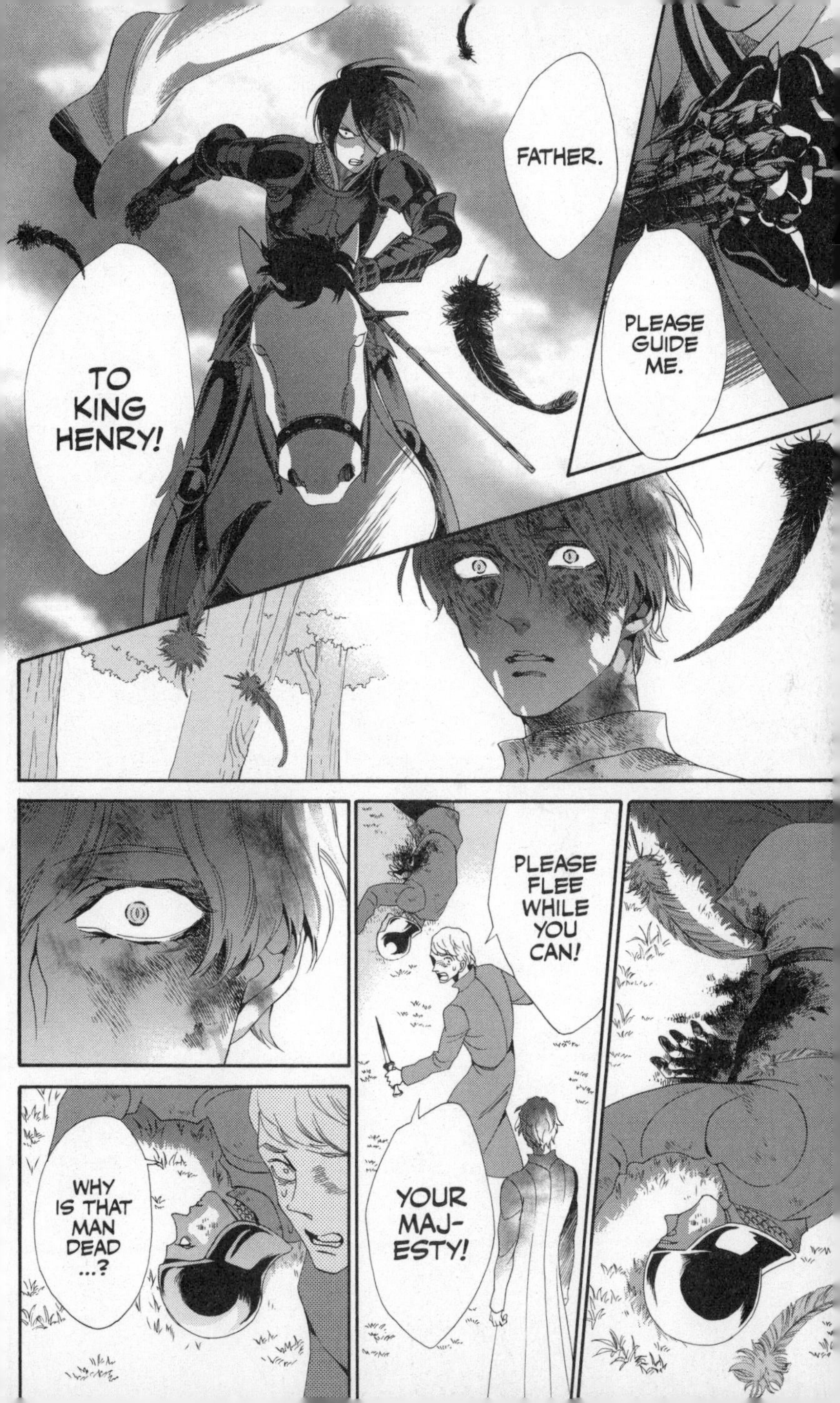
FATHER.
PLEASE GUIDE ME.
TO KING HENRY!
PLEASE FLEE WHILE YOU CAN!
YOUR MAJ-ESTY!
WHY IS THAT MAN DEAD ...?

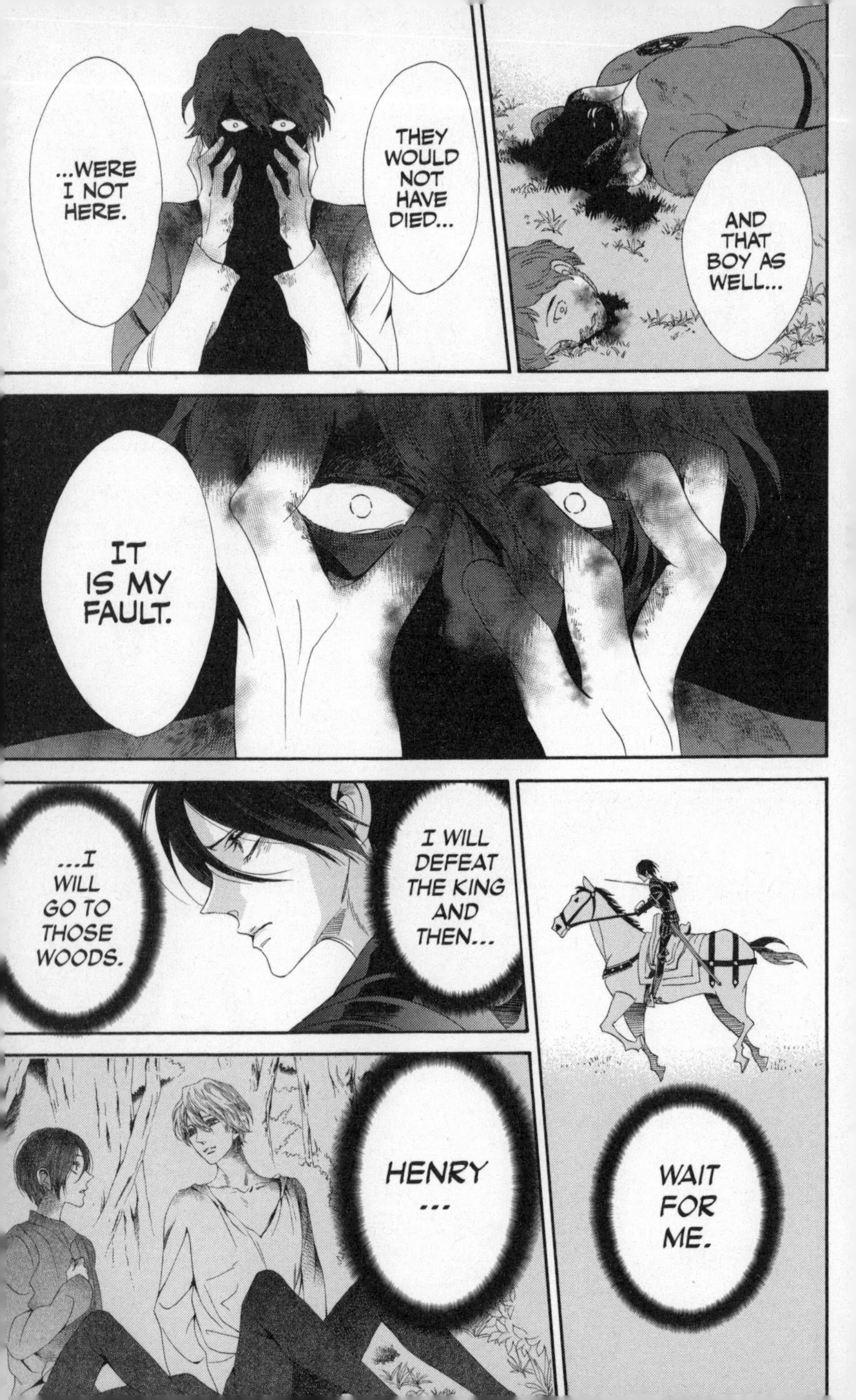
AND THAT BOY AS WELL...
THEY WOULD NOT HAVE DIED...
...WERE I NOT HERE.
IT IS MY FAULT.
WAIT FOR ME.
I WILL DEFEAT THE KING AND THEN...
...I WILL GO TO THOSE WOODS.
HENRY...

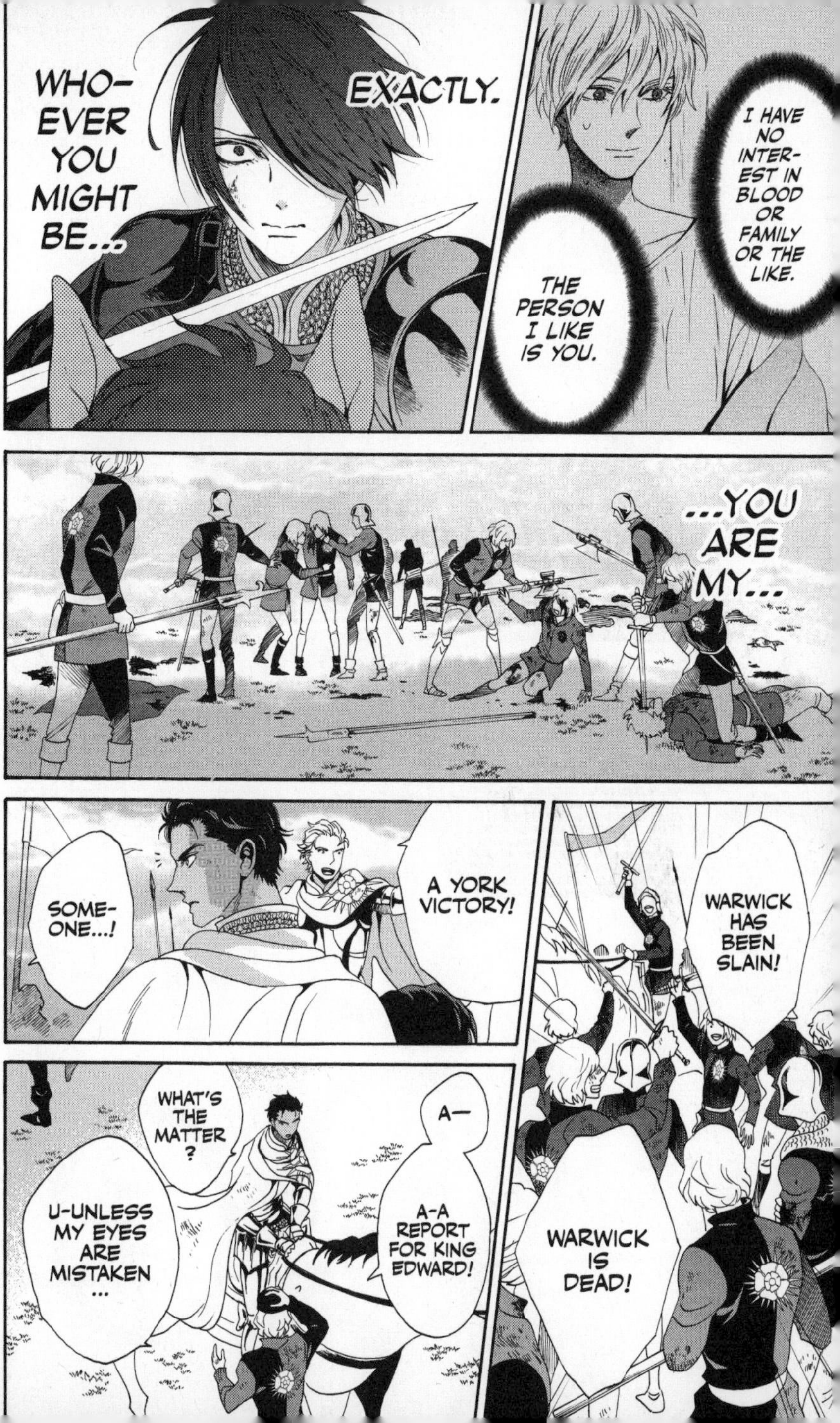

I HAVE NO INTER-EST IN BLOOD OR FAMILY OR THE LIKE.
THE PERSON I LIKE IS YOU.
EXACTLY.
WHO-EVER YOU MIGHT BE...
...YOU ARE MY...
WARWICK HAS BEEN SLAIN!
WARWICK IS DEAD!
A YORK VICTORY!
SOME-ONE...!
A—
WHAT'S THE MATTER?
A-A REPORT FOR KING EDWARD!
U-UNLESS MY EYES ARE MISTAKEN...

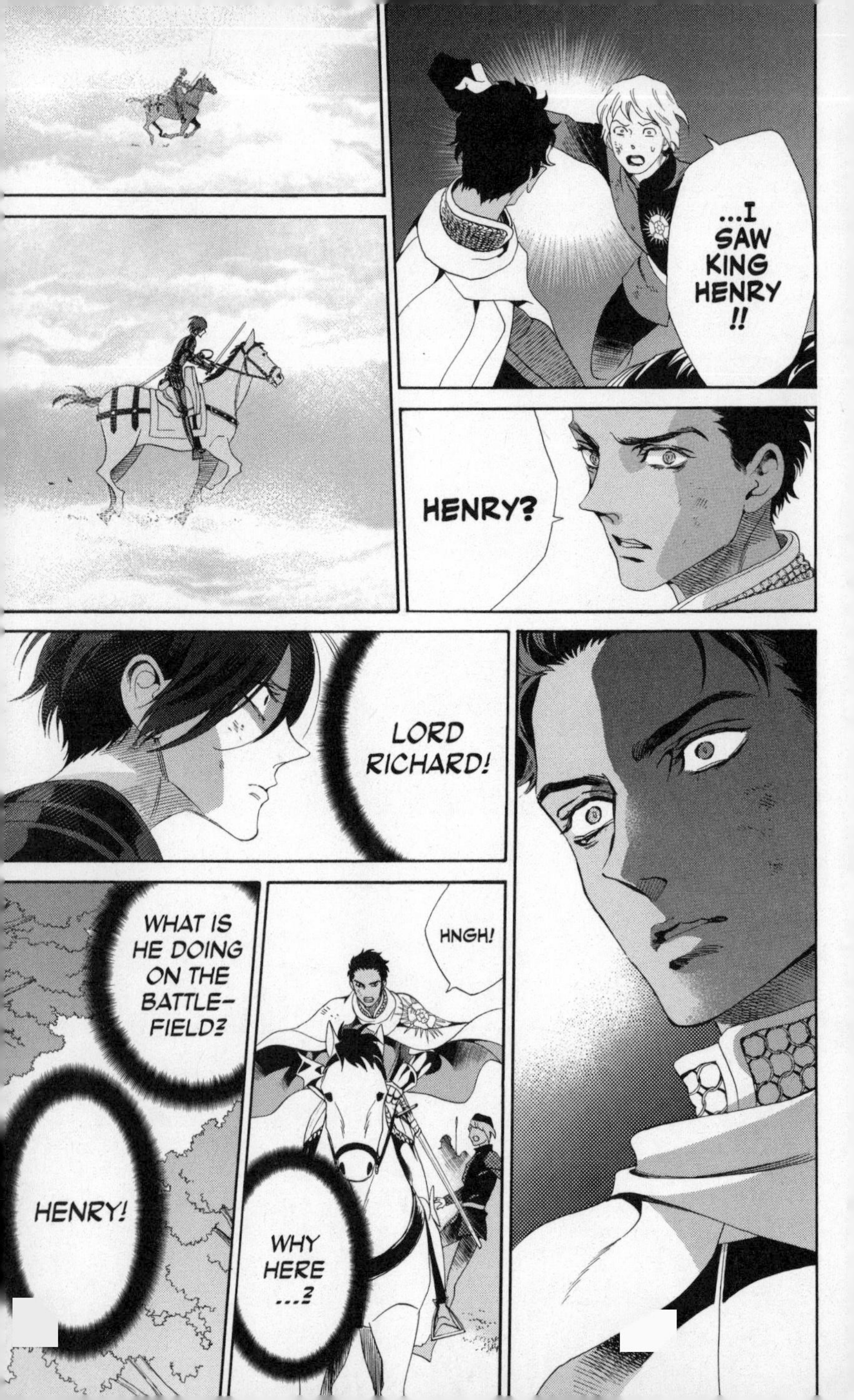
...I SAW KING HENRY!!
HENRY?
LORD RICHARD!
HNGH!
WHY HERE ...?
WHAT IS HE DOING ON THE BATTLE-FIELD?
HENRY!

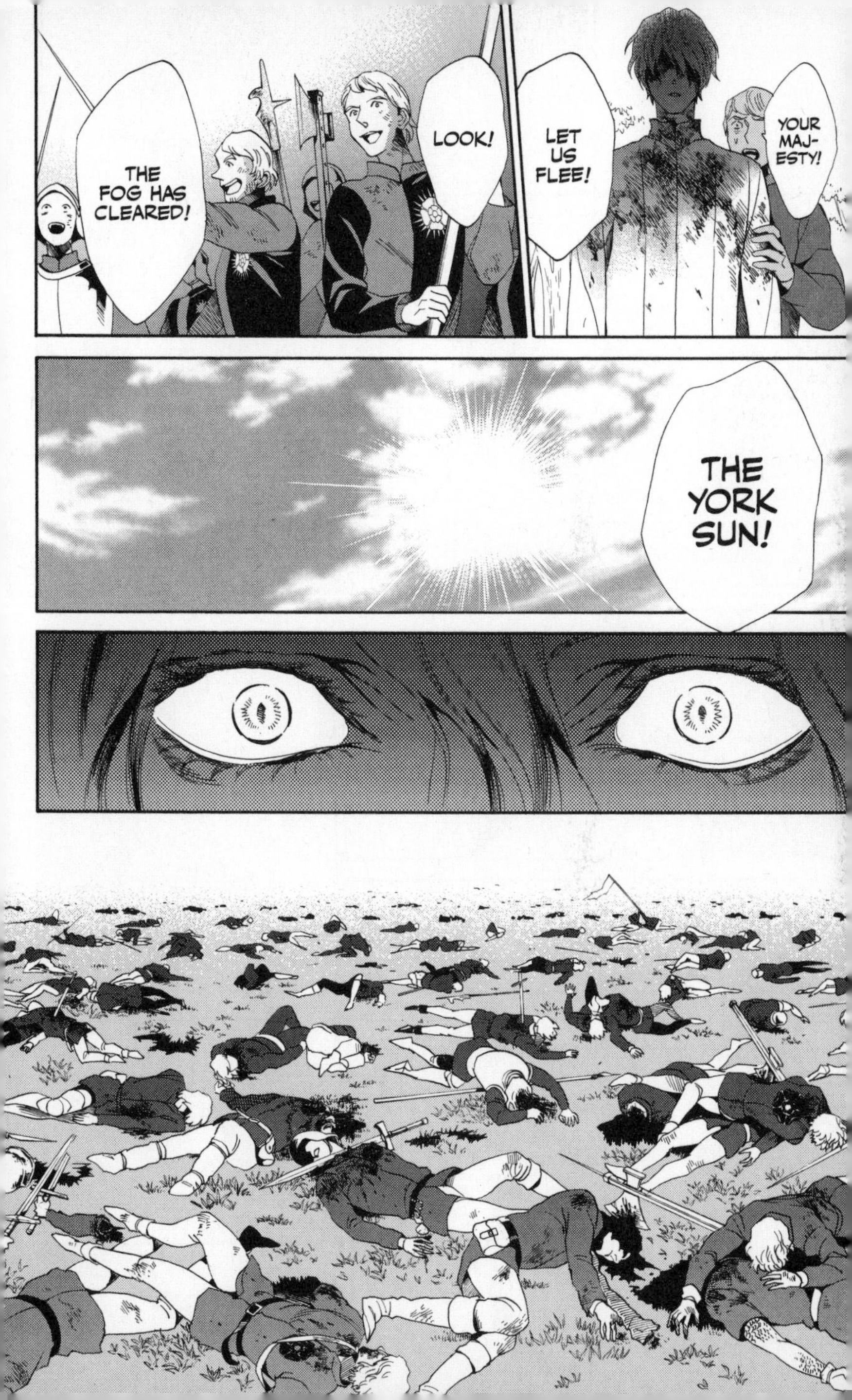
YOUR MAJ-ESTY!
LET US FLEE!
LOOK!
THE FOG HAS CLEARED!
THE YORK SUN!

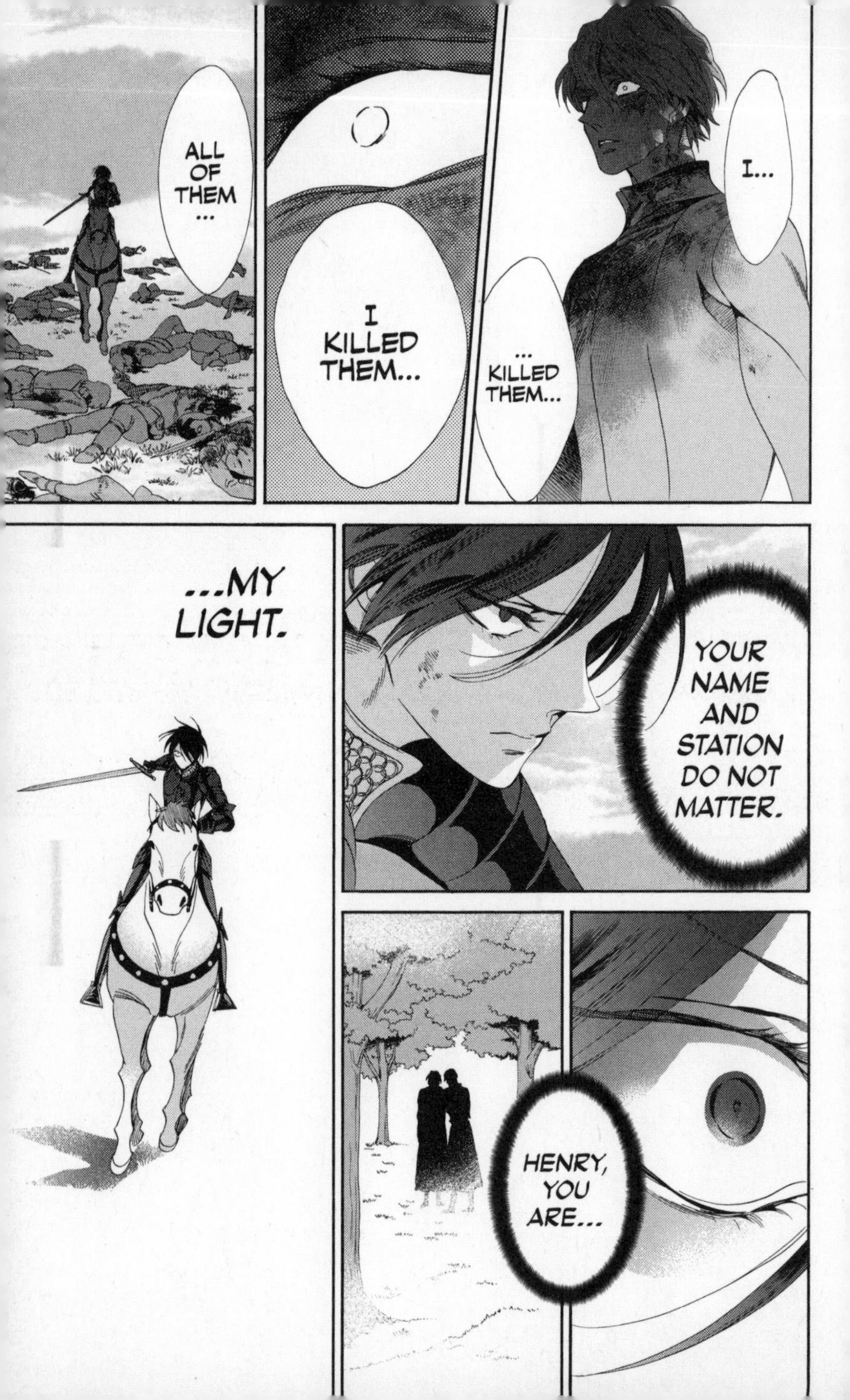
I...
...KILLED THEM...
I KILLED THEM...
ALL OF THEM ...
YOUR NAME AND STATION DO NOT MATTER.
HENRY, YOU ARE...
...MY LIGHT.

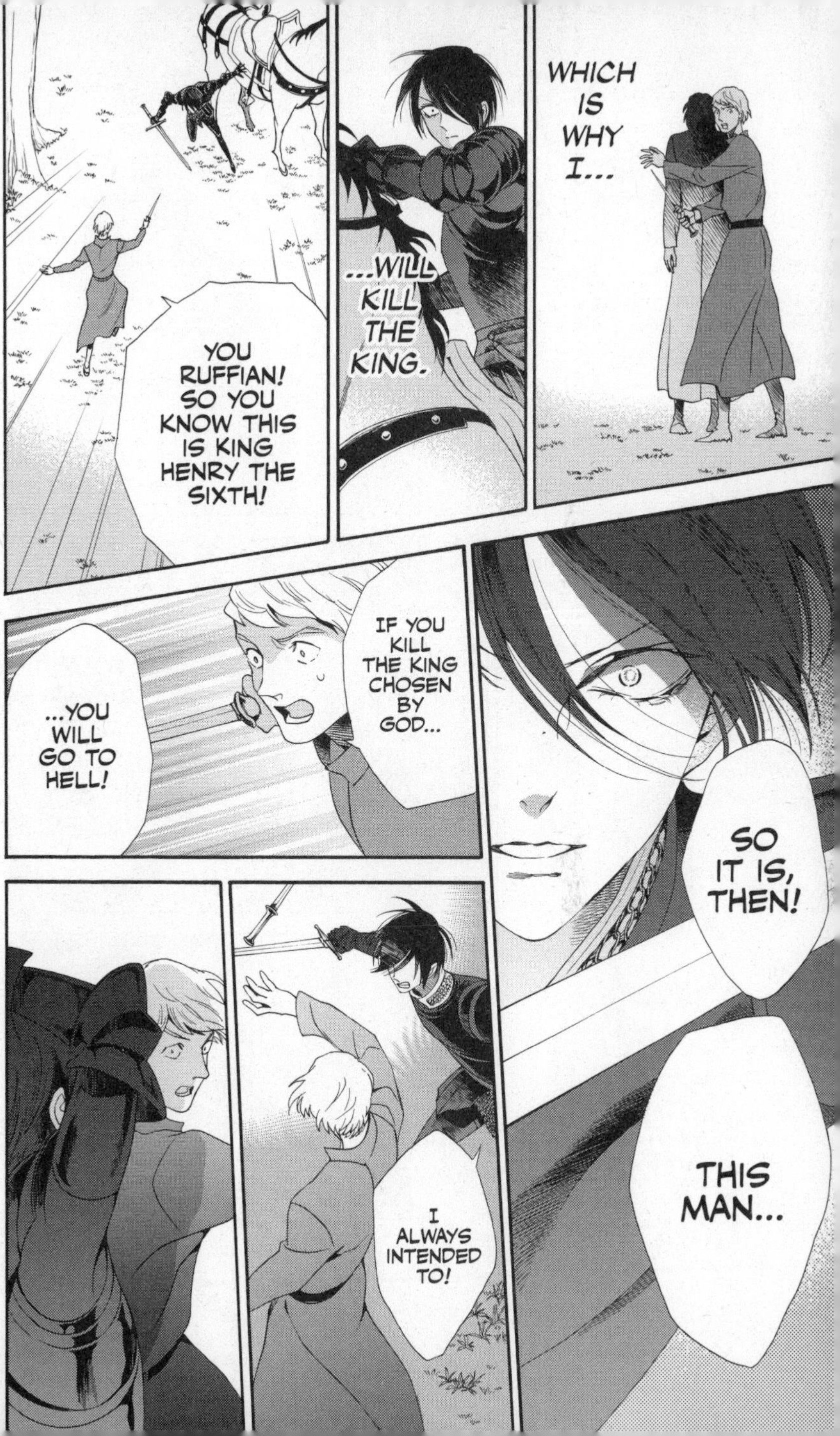
WHICH IS WHY I...
...WILL KILL THE KING.
YOU RUFFIAN! SO YOU KNOW THIS IS KING HENRY THE SIXTH!
SO IT IS, THEN!
THIS MAN...
IF YOU KILL THE KING CHOSEN BY GOD...
...YOU WILL GO TO HELL!
I ALWAYS INTENDED TO!

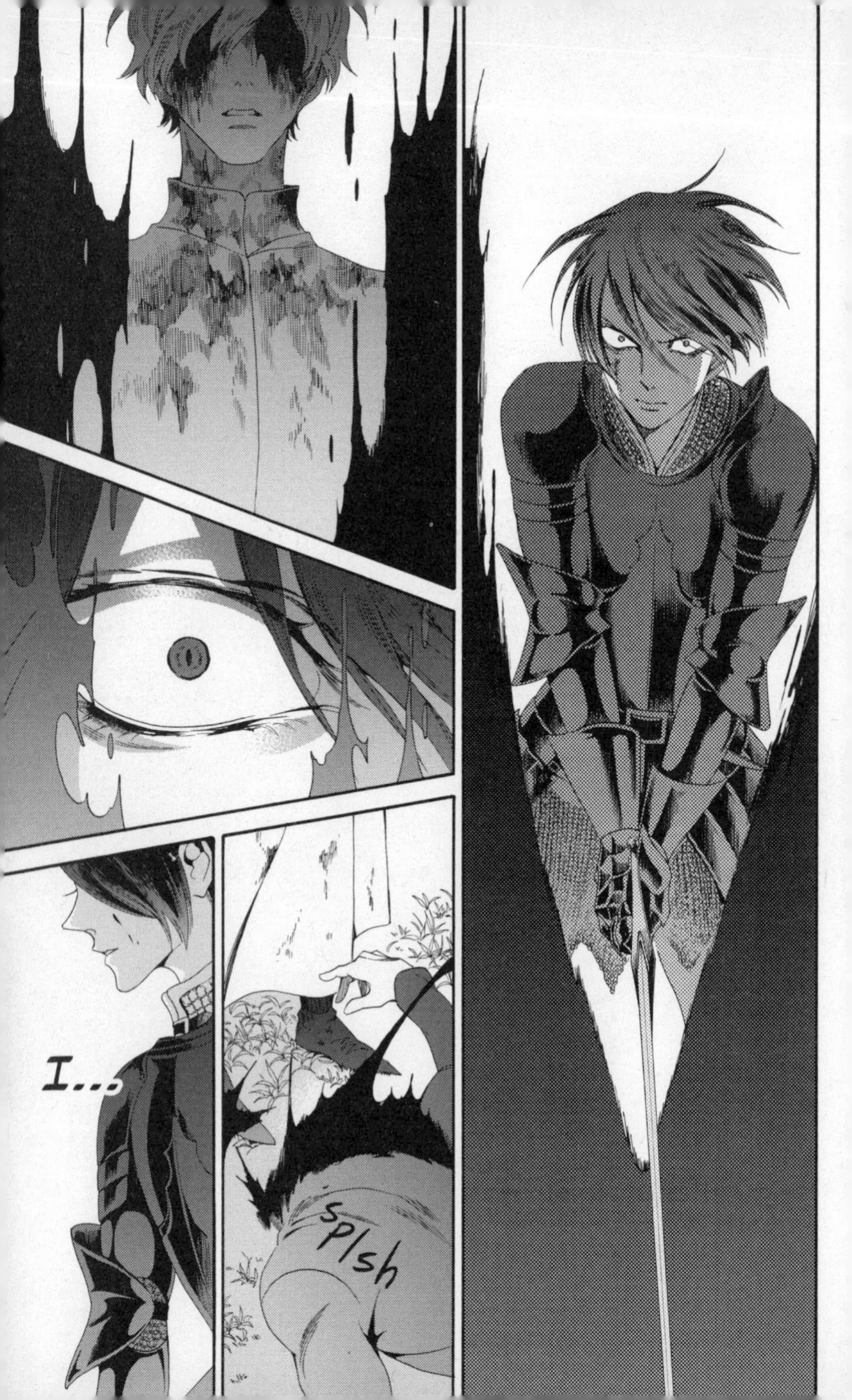
I...
splsh

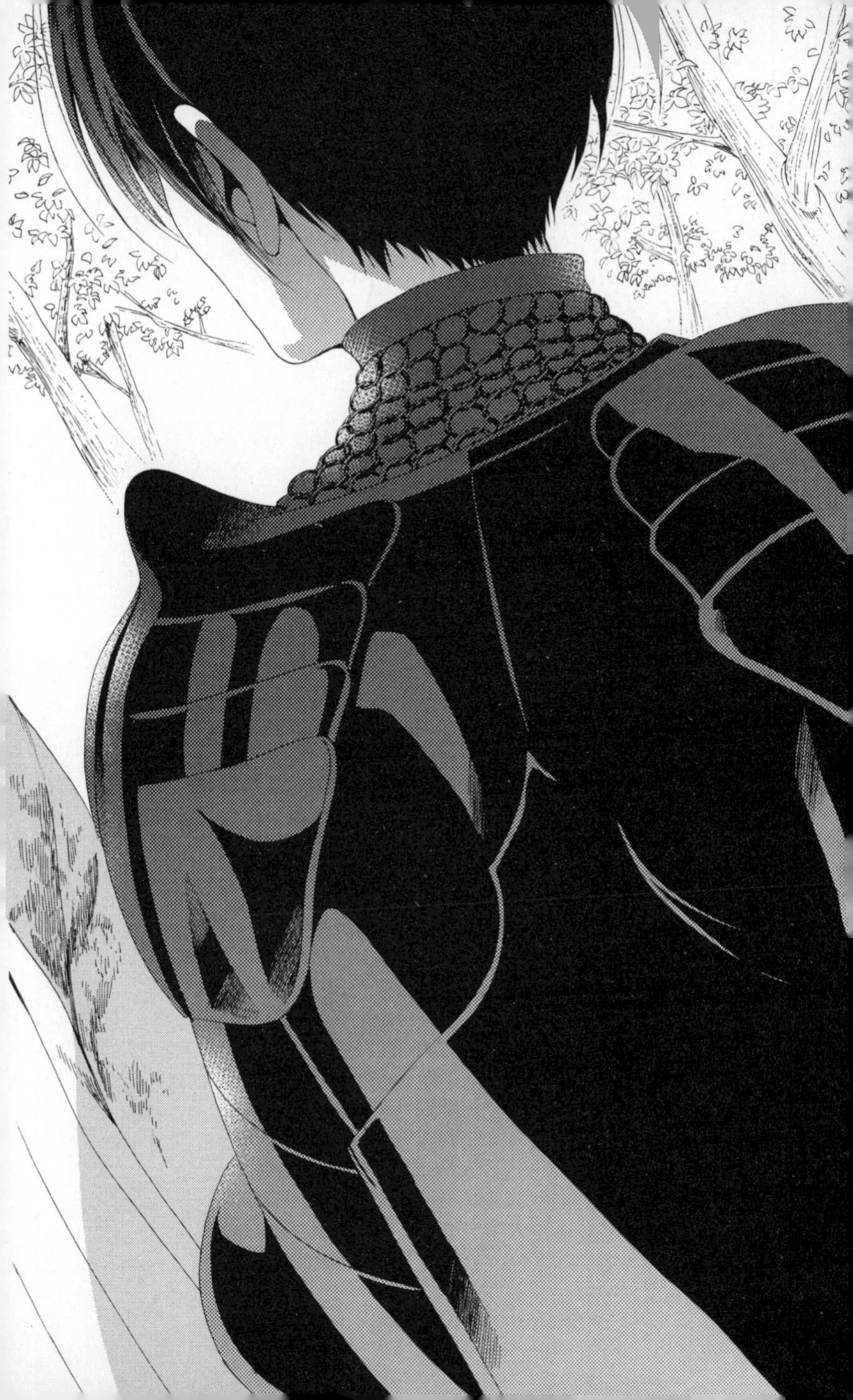

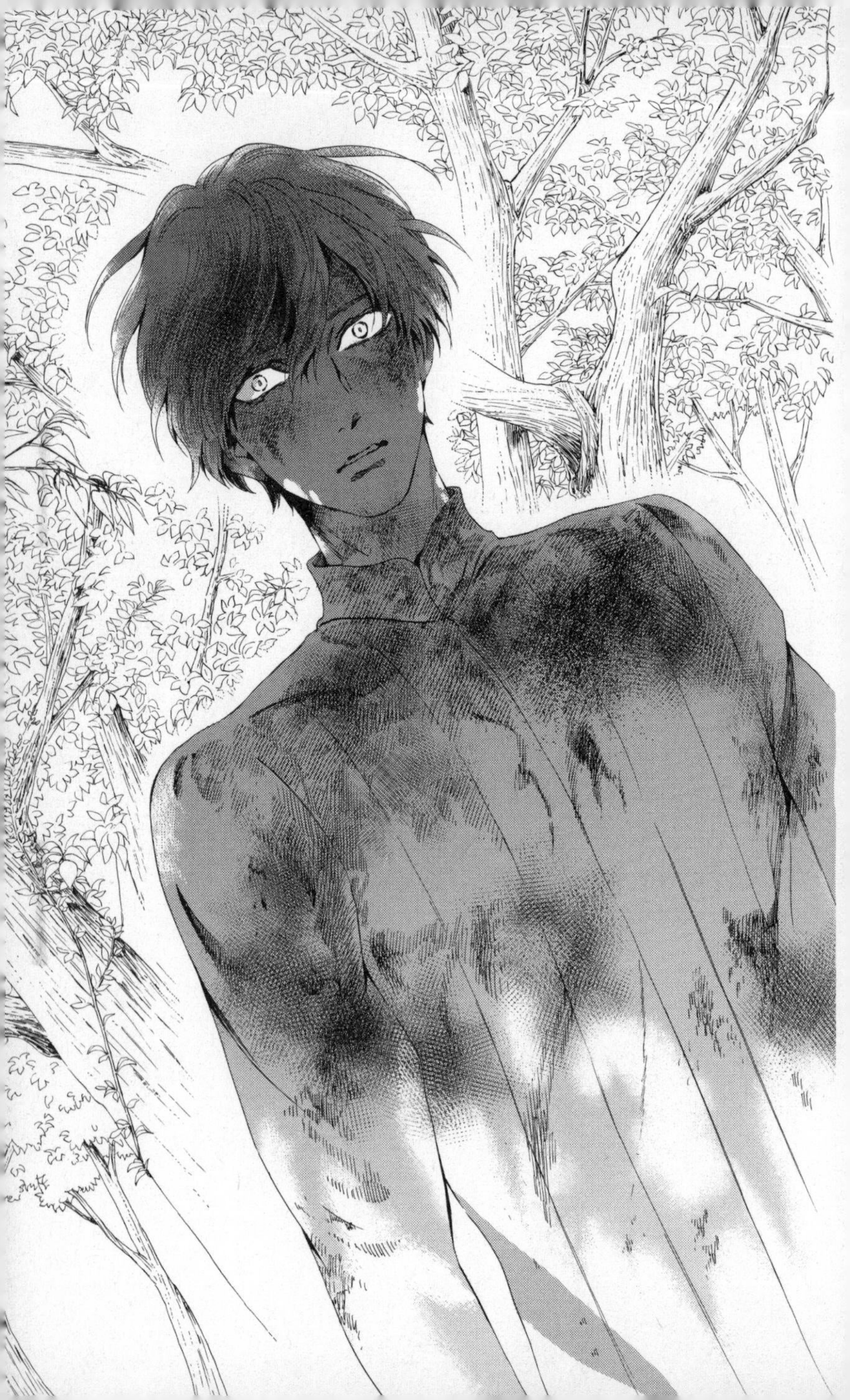

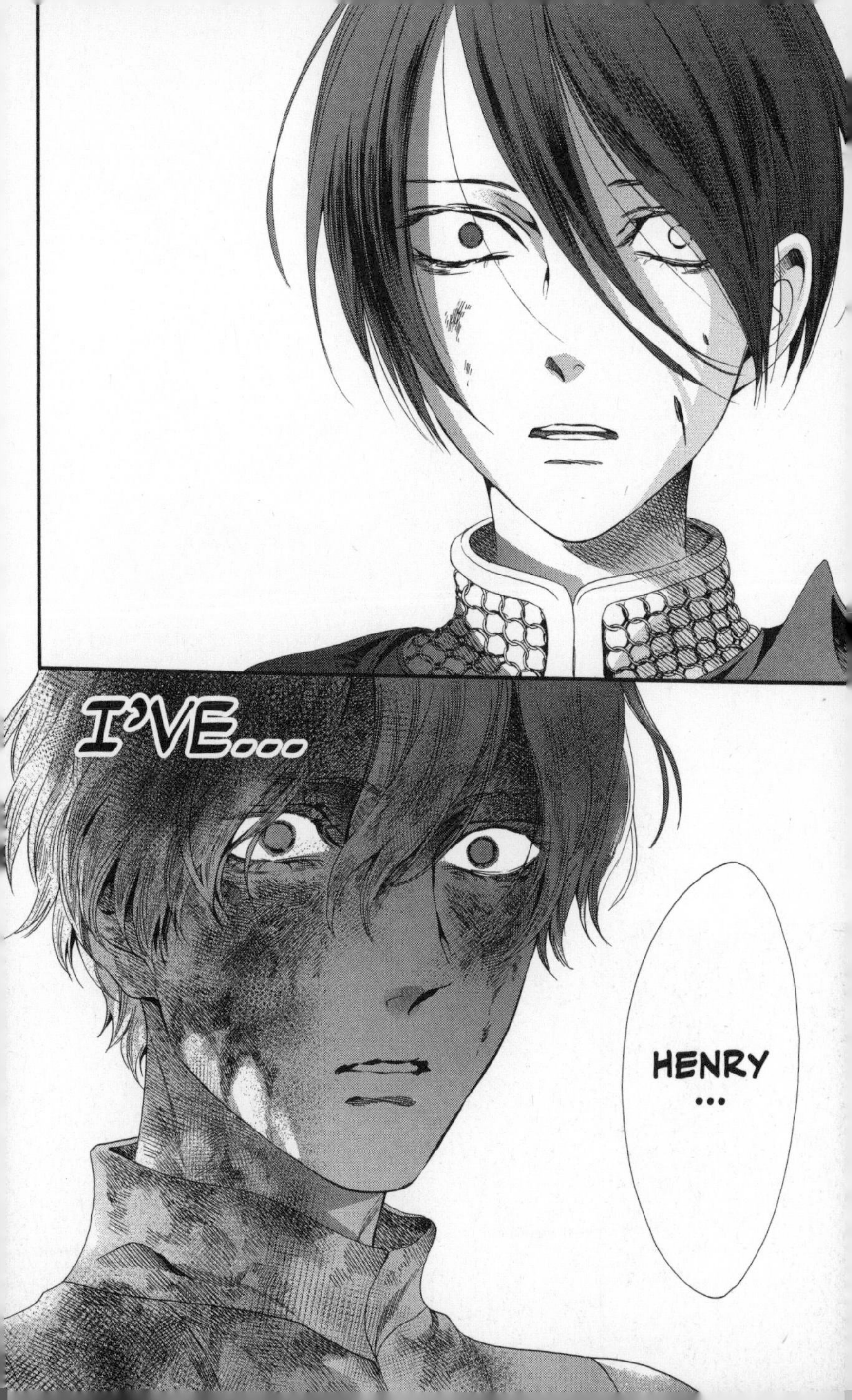
I'VE...
HENRY ...

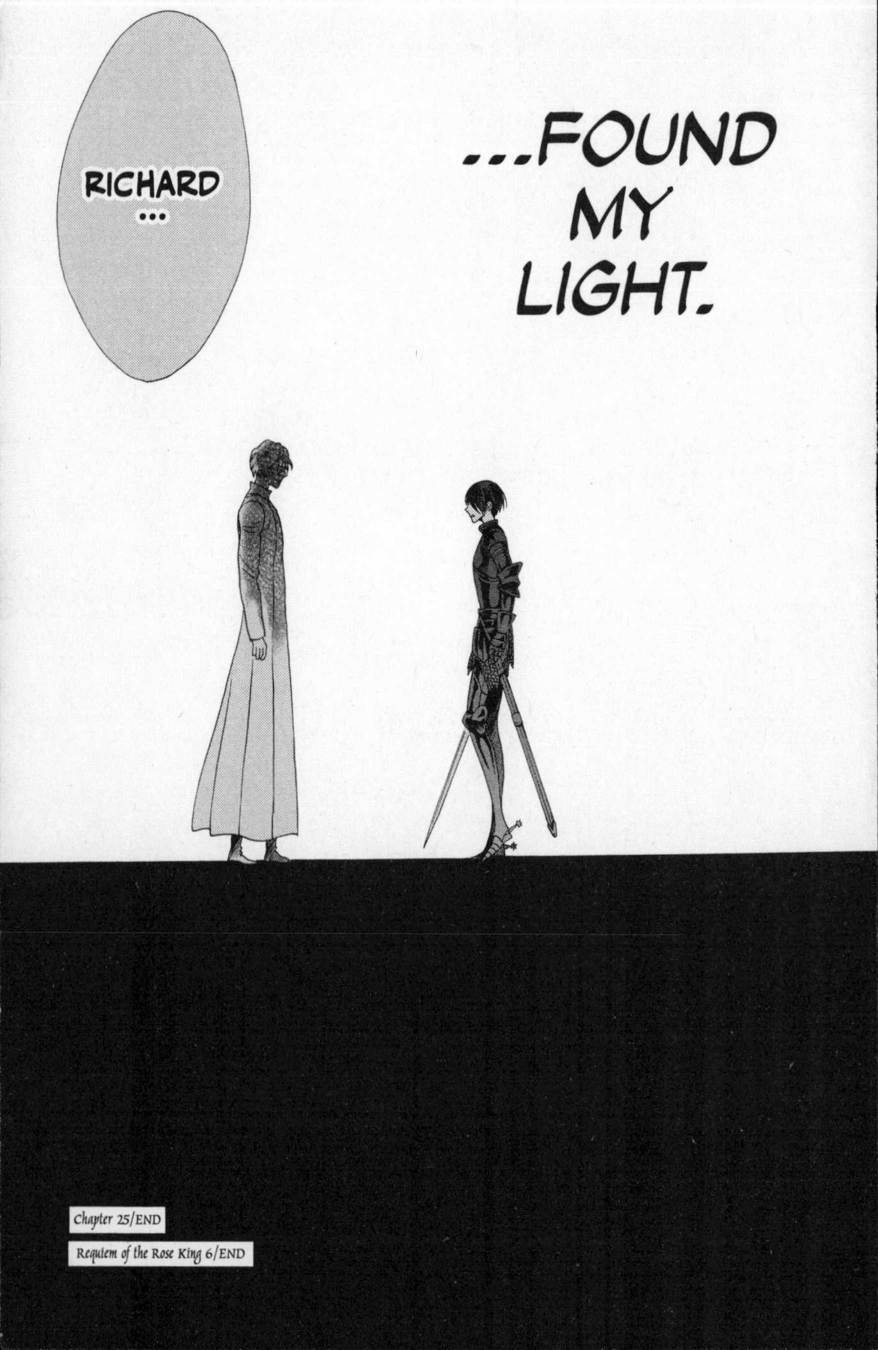
...FOUND MY LIGHT.
RICHARD ...

Chapter 25/END

Requiem of the Rose King 6/END

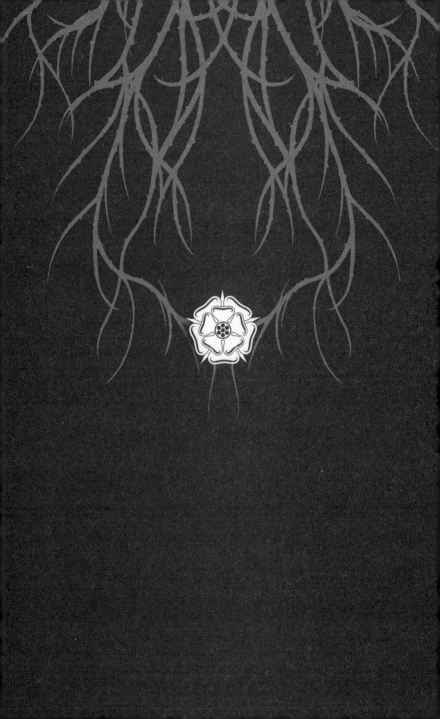

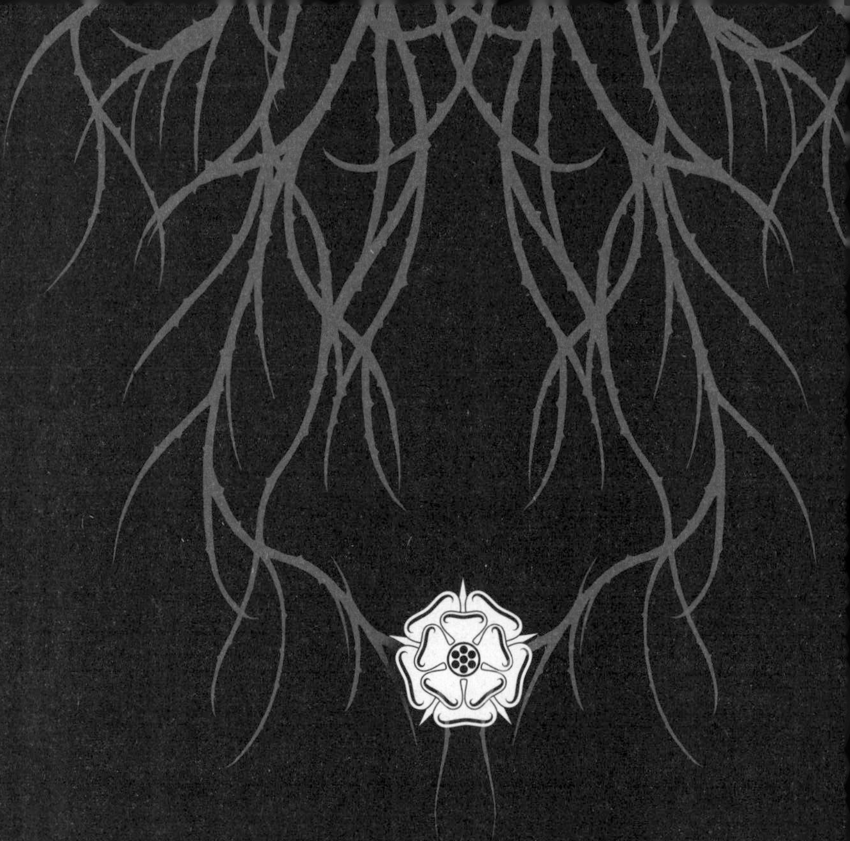

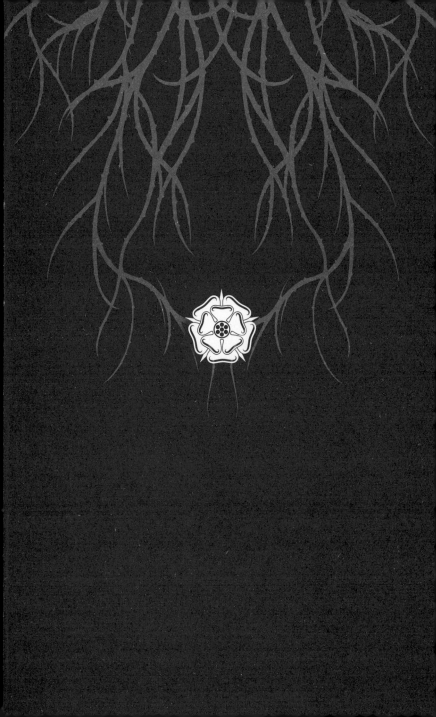

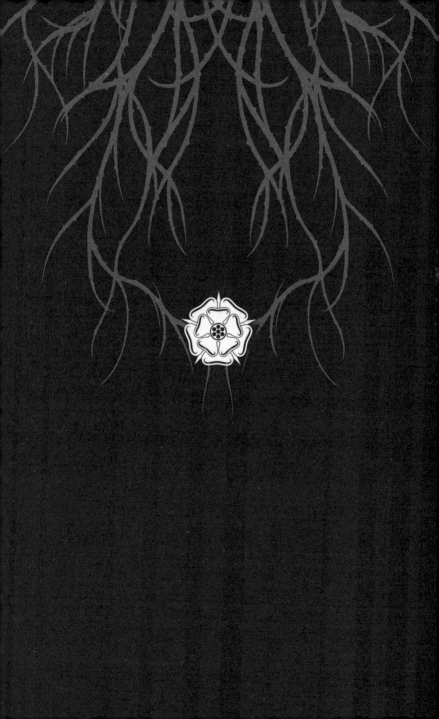

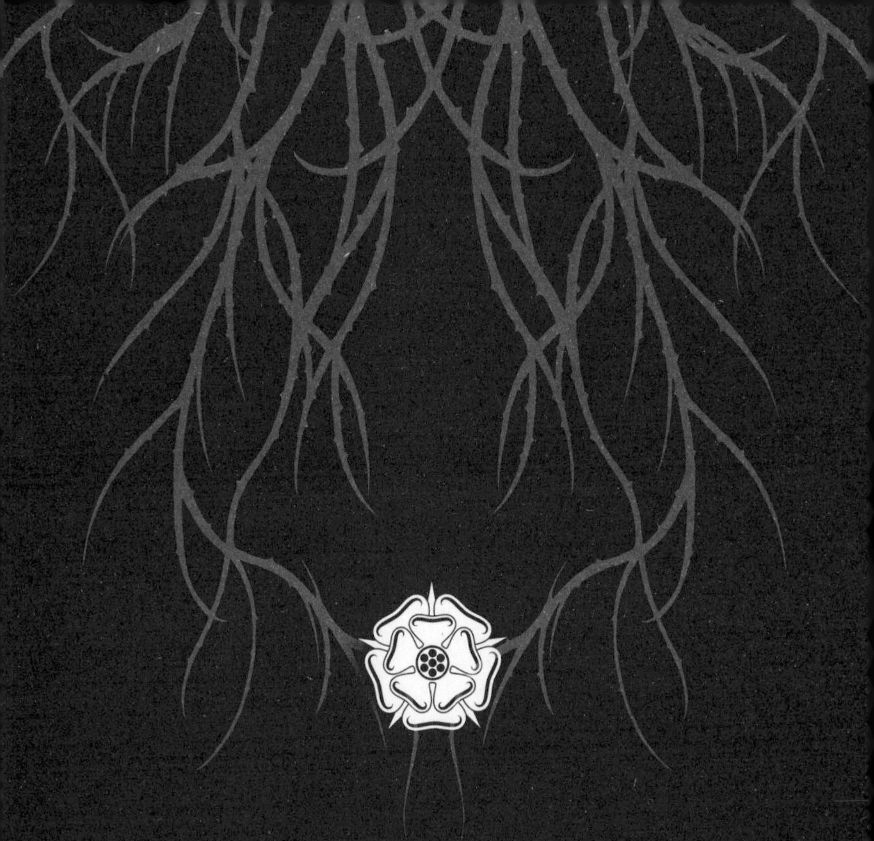

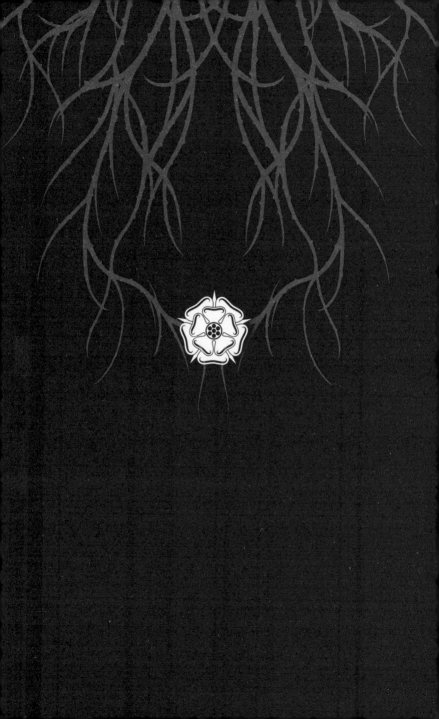

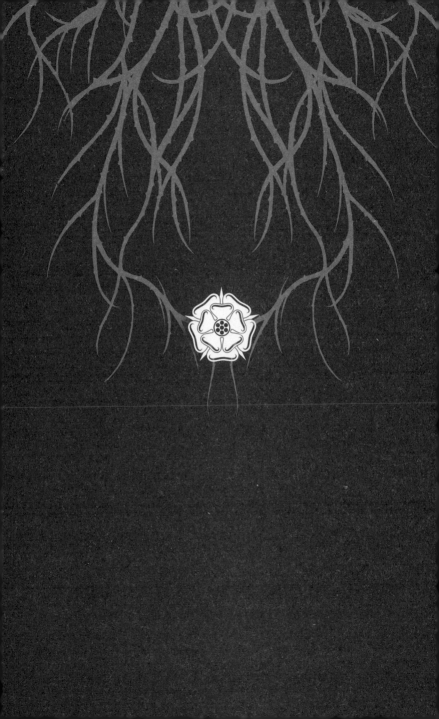